THE NEXT CHRISTENDOM

THE NEXT
CHRISTENDOM

The Coming of Global Christianity

Third Edition

PHILIP JENKINS

OXFORD
UNIVERSITY PRESS

OXFORD
UNIVERSITY PRESS

Oxford University Press, Inc., publishes works that further
Oxford University's objective of excellence
in research, scholarship, and education.

Oxford   New York
Auckland   Cape Town   Dar es Salaam   Hong Kong   Karachi
Kuala Lumpur   Madrid   Melbourne   Mexico City   Nairobi
New Delhi   Shanghai   Taipei   Toronto

With offices in
Argentina   Austria   Brazil   Chile   Czech Republic   France   Greece
Guatemala   Hungary   Italy   Japan   Poland   Portugal   Singapore
South Korea   Switzerland   Thailand   Turkey   Ukraine   Vietnam

Published by Oxford University Press, Inc.
198 Madison Avenue, New York, New York 10016

www.oup.com

Oxford is a registered trademark of Oxford University Press

Library of Congress Cataloging-in-Publication Data
Jenkins, Philip, 1952–
The next christendom : the coming of global
Christianity / Philip Jenkins.—3rd ed.
    p.   cm.
Includes bibliographical references and index.
ISBN 978-0-19-976746-5
1. Christianity—Forecasting.   2. Church membership.   I. Title.

BR121.3.J46 2011
270.8'30112—dc22   2010046058

5 7 9 8 6

Printed in the United States of America
on acid-free paper

CONTENTS

ACKNOWLEDGMENTS

As so often in the past, I thank Cynthia Read of Oxford University Press for all her encouragement and support.

Thanks to my colleagues at Baylor University, especially Byron Johnson, Tommy Kidd, Jeff Levin, David Jeffrey, Gordon Melton, and Rodney Stark. I greatly appreciate the support of Baylor president Ken Starr.

And once again, thanks to my wife, Liz.

LIST OF TABLES

PREFACE

The first edition of *The Next Christendom* appeared in 2002. I wrote the book in response to what seemed to me a critically important historical development, namely, that the worldwide geography of Christianity had shifted fundamentally, and that this change had enormous implications for politics and culture, no less than for religious life.

Christianity has in very recent times ceased to be a Euro-American religion and is becoming thoroughly global. In 1900, 83 percent of the world's Christians lived in Europe and North America. In 2050, 72 percent of Christians will live in Africa, Asia, and Latin America, and a sizable share of the remainder will have roots in one or more of those continents. In 1900, the overwhelming majority of Christians were non-Latino whites; in 2050, non-Latino whites will constitute only a small subset of Christians. If we imagine a typical Christian back in 1900, we might think of a German or an American; in 2050, we should rather turn to a Ugandan, a Brazilian, or a Filipino. We can argue about the detailed projections of numbers, but in broad detail, this is a reliable description of a religious revolution, much of which has occurred since the mid-twentieth century. Everything else in my book grew from this basic observation.

Although just nine years have passed, a great deal has happened since the appearance of the first edition. For authors, the most traumatic stage of producing a book is the day they return the final page proofs. After that no further corrections or additions are possible, and any mistakes are set in stone. I returned the proofs of my first edition on a historic date, which was in fact the last day of the old world, namely September 10, 2001. That date explains several features of the original book, including my repeated calls for the need to understand religious influences in politics and to appreciate the dangers of global religious strife; these are not points that need much stressing these days.

In the present edition, I have omitted most such remarks because they now seem so glaringly obvious. Nobody now needs to be alerted that, as I stated in my original opening paragraph, "it is precisely religious changes that are the most significant, and even revolutionary, in the contemporary world. Before too long, the turn-of-the-millennium neglect of religious factors may come to be seen as comically myopic, on a par with a review of the eighteenth century that managed to miss the French Revolution." Nor, in this edition, do I need to reiterate that "the lack of global ideological conflict that we have witnessed since the fall of Soviet communism could represent only a temporary respite." Several wars later, that comment is superfluous.

Apart from changes in relations between religions, much has happened within Christianity worldwide. Just in the past decade, one of the world's largest Christian entities, the Anglican Communion, has lumbered inexorably toward an agonizing global schism along North-South lines. And the influence of global South nations continues to grow within the Roman Catholic Church: by 2030 at the latest, Africa will have more Catholics than Europe. Across the globe, too, upstart charismatic and Pentecostal churches continue their dramatic advances. Meanwhile, Christians in many parts of the world continue to suffer violence and persecution, most notoriously in African nations like Nigeria and the Sudan, but also in Asian countries like Indonesia. In its most ancient heartlands, in Iraq and elsewhere in the Middle East, Christianity seems close to extinction. Despite the customary media focus on confrontations between Christianity and Islam, organized Hindu groups in India have been responsible for some of the most egregious persecution.

These events demanded coverage in this new and thoroughly updated revision. Among other things, I have taken full account of the many new quantitative and survey data that have become available since earlier editions, and these give an even more solid foundation to the figures that I offered there. These newer figures suggest that the global population shift is actually proceeding a good deal more rapidly than I initially suggested.

In this past decade, moreover, the volume of research and writing on worldwide Christianity has expanded impressively. Apart from some splendid national and regional case studies, we also have wide-ranging surveys that explore the implications of the new forms of emerging Christianity. Central to these studies is often the familiar question of the relationship between Christianity and culture. When, for instance, we look at new African churches, how far can we interpret their distinctive beliefs and practices in terms of older local worldviews? Is their emphasis on healing and spiritual warfare a reassertion of pristine New Testament beliefs, or an alarming concession to syncretism? In 2008, this theme even intruded on the U.S. election campaign, when a widely seen video clip showed a Kenyan bishop praying that vice-presidential candidate Sarah Palin be protected from every form of witchcraft. Just how are Western Christians meant to respond to modern-day churches that hold firm opinions about the reality of witchcraft—beliefs, of course, that are by no means confined to Africa?

Other observers ask to what extent global South Christianity bears the imprint of Euro-American churches, of mission agencies, or pressure groups? This issue attracted fierce debate in 2009–2010 when the nation of Uganda attempted to pass strict laws against homosexuality, laws that could in certain circumstances carry the death penalty. Allegedly, the incentive for this morality crusade came from conservative U.S.-based evangelicals, whose views profoundly influenced Ugandan Christians. More generally, and less controversially, when we see the spread of global Christianity, is this in fact a diffusion of American methods and approaches?

Such questions about religion and culture are not merely academic in nature, as they affect the potential expansion of newer churches in the global North. If such churches are, in fact, purely African or Asian in inspiration, that would severely limit their likely growth. If on the other hand they represent a vibrant new manifestation of authentic Christianity, their chances of adapting to surrounding cultures would be vastly greater.

How, moreover, is the new Christianity likely to affect the poor, among whom it finds its most devoted adherents? How, in particular, should we interpret the enormous success of prosperity churches across the global South? Are these movements just a form of cynical hucksterism, or do they offer worthwhile values that genuinely help bring believers out of poverty? Politically, what will be the impact of new Christian movements? Will Christianity contribute to liberating the poor, giving voices to the previously silent, or, does it threaten only to bring new kinds of division and conflict? Does Christianity liberate women or introduce new scriptural bases for subjection? Finally, as global South societies become more prosperous, will they secularize on the model of Europe?

For many reasons, then, I felt that a new edition of *Next Christendom* was needed, both to take account of what has happened in the emerging Christian world and also to provide fuller coverage of those newer interpretations and debates. We are living through a revolution, and the world is changing so very rapidly.

That remark about rapid change also points to the dangers of writing about strictly contemporary affairs. On several occasions, this book refers to the nation of Sudan, which now seems on the verge of a decisive split between a Muslim Sudan and a mainly Christian South Sudan. My remarks about that region should be adapted accordingly.

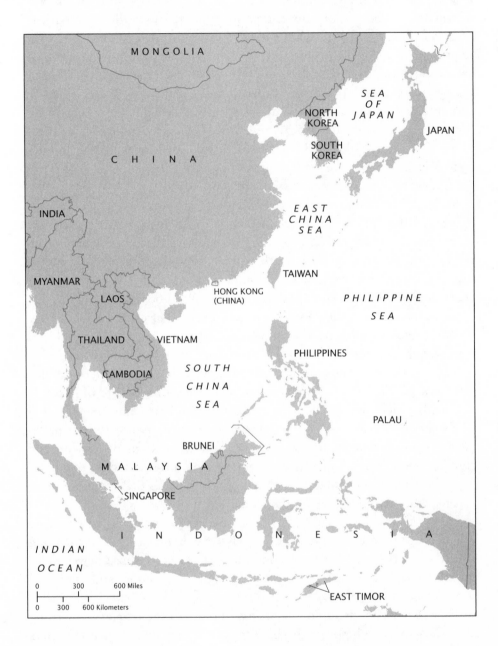

MONGOLIA

CHINA

NORTH
KOREA

SEA
OF
JAPAN

SOUTH
KOREA

JAPAN

INDIA

EAST
CHINA
SEA

MYANMAR

TAIWAN

LAOS

HONG KONG
(CHINA)

PHILIPPINE
SEA

THAILAND

VIETNAM

CAMBODIA

SOUTH
CHINA
SEA

PHILIPPINES

PALAU

BRUNEI

MALAYSIA

SINGAPORE

INDONESIA

INDIAN
OCEAN

0   300   600 Miles

0   300   600 Kilometers

EAST TIMOR

MOROCCO

WESTERN
SAHARA
(MOROCCO)

TUNISIA

MEDITERRANEAN SEA

ALGERIA

LIBYA

EGYPT

MAURITANIA

MALI

NIGER

CHAD

ERITREA

SUDAN

DJIBOUTI

SENEGAL

GAMBIA

GUINEA-
BISSAU

GUINEA

SIERRA LEONE

LIBERIA

IVORY COAST

BURKINA FASO

GHANA

TOGO

BENIN

SÃO TOME
& PRINCIPE

EQUATORIAL
GUINEA

NIGERIA

CAMEROON

CENTRAL
AFRICAN
REPUBLIC

ETHIOPIA

SOMALIA

UGANDA

KENYA

RWANDA

GABON

CONGO

DEMOCRATIC
REPUBLIC
OF THE
CONGO

BURUNDI

TANZANIA

CABINDA
(ANGOLA)

ANGOLA

ZAMBIA

MALAWI

ZIMBABWE

MOZAMBIQUE

NAMIBIA

BOTSWANA

SOUTH
AFRICA

SWAZILAND

LESOTHO

ATLANTIC

OCEAN

INDIAN

OCEAN

MADAGASCAR

0   500   1000 Miles

0   500   1000 Kilometers

ATLANTIC

OCEAN

Gulf of Mexico

BAHAMAS

MEXICO

DOMINICAN REPUBLIC

CUBA

ST. KITTS AND NEVIS
BARBUDA
BELIZE
ANTIGUA
JAMAICA
DOMINICA
PUERTO RICO
HAITI
GUADELOUPE
MARTINIQUE
GUATEMALA
CARIBBEAN SEA
ST. LUCIA
BARBADOS
EL SALVADOR
GRENADA
ST. VINCENT AND THE GRENADINES
HONDURAS
TRINIDAD AND TOBAGO
NICARAGUA
COSTA RICA
VENEZUELA
GUYANA
PANAMA
SURINAME
FRENCH GUIANA
COLOMBIA

ECUADOR

PERU

BRAZIL

PACIFIC

BOLIVIA

OCEAN

PARAGUAY

CHILE
ARGENTINA

URUGUAY

ATLANTIC

OCEAN

0   500   1000 Miles

0   500   1000 Kilometers

BELIZE

GUATEMALA

HONDURAS

EL SALVADOR

NICARAGUA

COSTA
RICA

PANAMA

CARIBBEAN

SEA

PACIFIC

OCEAN

| 0 | 100 | 200 Miles |
| 0 | 100 | 200 Kilometers |

THE NEXT CHRISTENDOM

ONE

The Christian Revolution

Europe is the Faith.
—*Hilaire Belloc*

As I travel, I have observed a pattern, a strange
historical phenomenon of God "moving"
geographically from the Middle East to Europe, to
North America, to the developing world. My theory is
this: God goes where He's wanted.

—*Philip Yancey*

We are currently living through one of the transforming moments
in the history of religion worldwide. Over the last five centuries, the story of Christianity has been inextricably bound up
with that of Europe and European-derived civilizations overseas, above all
in North America. Until recently, the overwhelming majority of Christians
have lived in white nations, allowing some to speak of "European Christian"
civilization. Conversely, radical writers have seen Christianity as an ideological arm of Western imperialism. Many of us share the stereotype of
Christianity as the religion of the West or, to use another popular meta-
phor, the global North. It is self-evidently the religion of the haves. To
adapt the phrase once applied to the increasingly conservative U.S. elec-
torate of the 1970s, the stereotype holds that Christians are un-black,
un-poor, and un-young. If that is true, then the growing secularization
of the West can mean only that Christianity is in its dying days. Globally,
perhaps, the faith of the future will be Islam.

Over the last century, however, the center of gravity in the Christian
world has shifted inexorably away from Europe, southward, to Africa and
Latin America, and eastward, toward Asia. Today, the largest Christian
communities on the planet are to be found in those regions. If we want to
visualize a "typical" contemporary Christian, we should think of a woman

living in a village in Nigeria, or in a Brazilian *favela*. In parts of Asia too, churches are growing rapidly, in numbers and self-confidence. As Kenyan scholar John Mbiti has observed, "the centers of the church's universality [are] no longer in Geneva, Rome, Athens, Paris, London, New York, but Kinshasa, Buenos Aires, Addis Ababa and Manila."[1] Whatever Europeans or North Americans may believe, Christianity is doing very well indeed in the global South—not just surviving but expanding.

This trend will continue apace in coming years. Many of the fastest growing countries in the world are either predominantly Christian or else have very sizable Christian minorities. Even if Christians just maintain their present share of the population in countries such as Nigeria and Kenya, Mexico and Ethiopia, Brazil and the Philippines, there are soon going to be several hundred million more Christians from those nations alone. Moreover, conversions will swell the Christian share of world population. Meanwhile, historically low birthrates in the traditionally Christian states of Europe mean that these populations are declining or stagnant. In 1950 a list of the world's leading Christian countries would have included Britain, France, Spain, and Italy, but none of these names will be represented in a corresponding list for 2050. In 1900 Europe was home to two-thirds of the world's Christian population; today, the figure is about 25 percent, and by 2025 it will fall below 20 percent.

Christianity should enjoy a worldwide boom in the coming decades, but the vast majority of believers will be neither white nor European, nor Euro-American. According to the statistical tables produced by the respected Center for the Study of Global Christianity, some 2.3 billion Christians were alive in 2010, about one-third of the planetary population. The largest single bloc, some 588 million people, is still to be found in Europe. Latin America, though, is already close behind with 544 million, Africa has 493 million, and 352 million Asians profess Christianity. North America claims about 286 million believers. Now, we need not accept these numbers in precise detail, and I believe the Asian figures, present and future, are too high; but even so, these estimates supply a broad outline. Already, then, a large share of the Christian world is located in Africa, Asia, and Latin America. Just as striking are the long-term trends. The number of African Christians is growing at around 2.5 percent annually, which would lead us to project a doubling of the continent's Christian population in thirty years.[2]

If we extrapolate these figures to the year 2025, the Southern predominance becomes still more marked. Assuming no great gains or losses through conversion, then there would be around 2.6 billion Christians, of whom 695 million would live in Africa, 610 million in Latin America, and

TABLE 1.1
The Changing Distribution of Christian Believers

	Number of Christians (millions)			
	1900	*1970*	*2010*	*2050*
Africa	10	143	493	1,031
Asia	22	96	352	601
North America	79	211	286	333
Latin America	62	270	544	655
Europe	381	492	588	530
Oceania	5	18	28	38
TOTAL	*558*	*1,230*	*2,291*	*3,188*

Source: World Christian Database, http://www.worldchristiandata-base.org/wcd

480 million in Asia. Europe, with 574 million, would have slipped to third place. Africa and Latin America would thus be in competition for the title of most Christian continent. About this date, too, another significant milestone should occur, namely that these two continents will together account for half the Christians on the planet. By 2050 only about one-fifth of the world's 3.2 billion Christians will be non-Hispanic whites.[3] Soon, the phrase "a white Christian" may sound like a curious oxymoron, as mildly surprising as "a Swedish Buddhist." Such people can exist, but a slight eccentricity is implied.

This global perspective should make us think carefully before asserting "what Christians believe" or "how the church is changing." All too often, statements about what "modern Christians accept" or what "Catholics today believe," refer only to what that ever-shrinking remnant of *Western* Christians and Catholics believe. Such assertions are outrageous today, and as time goes by they will become ever further removed from reality. Europe is demonstrably *not* the Faith. The era of Western Christianity has passed within our lifetimes, and the day of the Southern churches is dawning. The fact of change itself is undeniable: it has happened, and will continue to happen.

LOOKING SOUTH

The concept of a rising global South is fairly recent in historical terms. In the 1950s, emerging African and Asian nations tried to distinguish themselves from what then seemed the rigid separation of the globe between capitalist West and communist East, proclaiming their membership in a nonaligned Third World. Tragically, that term soon became synonymous not with prosperous neutrality but with grinding poverty and uncontrollable population growth, and that fact led some observers to see the critical global division as one of economics, rather than political ideology. In 1980, at the height of a renewed Cold War, the Brandt Commission portrayed the world mired in a Common Crisis that involved both global North (Europe, North America, Japan) and global South, a term that comprised the remaining societies—by no means all of which are located in the Southern Hemisphere. In this context, the term "South" is characterized less by geographical location than by relative access to wealth and resources, by poverty and dependency.[4]

Even in 1980, the "Southern" category was overbroad. It included some heavily developed regions, such as South Korea, as well as many countries characterized by cataclysmic poverty and underdevelopment, such as the Congo. Over time, these distinctions have grown still greater as many nations once characterized as Third World have now become prosperous and influential. Just a year after the Brandt Commission released its report, fund manager Antoine van Agtmael created the more optimistic term "emerging markets" to characterize rising nations such as China and Brazil, whose emergence has been impressive. In the 1970s and 1980s, the world's economic powerhouses comprised the so-called Group of Seven or G7, which included the four largest European economies, as well as the United States, Canada, and Japan. Today, the equivalent elite club is the G20, in which Euro-American nations share the table not only with China and India (of course) but also Brazil, South Africa, Mexico, Argentina, Saudi Arabia, South Korea, and Indonesia. Clearly, the Southern category is problematic, but as I will argue, in terms of classifying religious patterns, the concept of the South does have its value.[5]

Since the 1950s Christian leaders and religious studies scholars have grown accustomed to the vision of Christianity literally going South, in the sense of an ever-larger share of Christians being found in the teeming poverty of Africa, Asia, and Latin America—the Tricontinental world. The theme is well known in Europe, where African affairs are more noticed than they customarily have been in the United States. In the 1970s, this global change was discussed in well-known works by European scholars such as Andrew Walls, Edward Norman, and Walbert Buhlmann. Meanwhile, African and Asian thinkers explored the intellectual implications in works such as Kosuke Koyama's *Water-Buffalo Theology* and John

S. Pobee's *Toward an African Theology*. By 1976 African and Latin American scholars joined to form an Ecumenical Association of Third World Theologians. Walbert Buhlmann's term "the Third Church" drew the obvious comparison with the Third World and further suggested that the South represents a new tradition comparable in importance to the Eastern and Western churches of historical times. Walls likewise sees the faith in Africa as a distinctive new tradition of Christianity comparable to Catholicism, Protestantism, and Orthodoxy. It is "the standard Christianity of the present age, a demonstration model of its character…anyone who wishes to undertake serious study of Christianity these days needs to know something about Africa."[6]

Yet outside the ranks of scholars and church bureaucrats, commentators were slow to recognize these trends, to what I have described as the creation of a new Christendom, which for better or worse may play a critical role in world affairs. Until quite recently, materials either from or about global South churches were rarely in evidence in the catalogues of North American religious publishers, with a couple of conspicuous exceptions such as Orbis Books. This relative absence did not mean that publishers willfully suppressed the information for sinister motives, but they knew from experience that Third World topics rarely attracted enough of a general audience to make a new title profitable. For whatever reason, the emerging religious markets of the global South remained almost invisible to mainstream Northern observers.

The imbalance was just as evident in the Western academic world, in which published studies of Third World religion represented only a tiny fraction of scholarship on Christianity. At the same time, the volume of academic studies coming out of Africa and Latin America actually shrank as universities in those regions were crippled by lack of resources. To quote John Mbiti once more, "It is utterly scandalous for so many Christian scholars in [the] old Christendom to know so much about heretical movements in the second and third centuries, when so few of them know anything about Christian movements in areas of the younger churches."[7] Happily, matters have changed greatly since Mbiti wrote in the 1970s, and the last decade has witnessed an outpouring of excellent scholarship. While scholarly works are appearing too quickly to be listed comprehensively, some demand attention, especially the volumes of the recent *Cambridge History of Christianity*, with its strongly global focus, and its pervasive theme of World Christianities. It is now impossible for any worthwhile "History of Christianity" to omit the epochal developments in the newer Christian lands.[8]

Among secular commentators too, the global shift of Christianity is only gradually gaining recognition, although the underlying questions raised are profound. Just what does Western civilization mean when what were once its critical religious aspects are now primarily upheld outside the "West"? One influential work that paid serious attention to changing religious patterns was Samuel P. Huntington's book *The Clash of Civilizations and the Remaking of World Order*. Even Huntington, though, understated the rising force of Christianity. He argued that the relative Christian share of global population will fall steeply as the twenty-first century progresses, and that this religion will be supplanted by Islam: "In the long run...Muhammad wins out." But far from Islam being the world's largest religion by 2020 or so, as Huntington suggested, Christianity should still have a substantial lead and will maintain its position into the foreseeable future. By 2050, some 34 percent of the world's people will be Christian, roughly what the figure was at the height of European world hegemony in 1900.[9]

While Muslim countries are indeed experiencing rapid rates of population growth, similar or even higher rates are also found in already populous Christian countries, above all in Africa. Alongside the Muslim efflorescence Huntington rightly foresaw, there will also be a Christian population explosion, often in the same or adjacent countries. If we look at the nations with the fastest demographic growth and the youngest populations, they are evenly distributed between Christian- and Muslim-dominated societies. I therefore dispute the assertion that "Christianity spreads primarily by conversion, Islam by conversion and reproduction." Even today, in numerical terms, the preponderant religion of the world's poorest is Christianity, rather than Islam or Hinduism.[10]

BACK TO THE FUTURE

The numerical changes in Christianity are striking enough, but beyond the simple demographic transition, there are countless implications for theology and religious practice. To take a historical parallel, Christianity changed thoroughly when a movement founded in a Jewish and Hellenistic context moved into the Germanic lands of Western Europe during the early Middle Ages. Although it is only a symbolic example, we can learn something from the way in which the English language imported its large Christian vocabulary. Such familiar words as "church" or "bishop" are borrowed from Greek originals, though in radically mutated forms. "Church" derives from *kyriakos oikos* (house of the Lord), "bishop" from *episkopos*, "supervisor," or one who watches over the community. We can imagine the Roman and Greek missionaries to the Anglo-Saxons confronting the notorious English incapacity to deal with foreign tongues and hearing their elegant terms butchered into the words we have today.

In this instance, the substance of the words survived the cultural transition intact, but in other vital ways, a largely urban Mediterranean Christianity was profoundly changed by the move to the northern forests. In art and popular thought, Jesus became a blond Aryan, with the appropriate warrior attributes, and West European notions of legality and feudalism reshaped Christian theology. To take one potent example, modern Western interpretations of the Atonement (both Catholic and Protestant) can be traced to the writings of Saint Anselm around 1100. For Anselm, human sins were like grievous offenses committed against a great lord, debts that required a ransom or restitution of great price, which, in Christianity took the form of the death of God's Son. Although Eastern Orthodox theologians rejected this theory as overly legalistic, it made excellent sense to a Western society deeply sensitive to questions of honor, fealty, seigniorial rights, and acknowledging the proper claims of lordship. The biblical LORD became a feudal lord.[11] European Christians reinterpreted the faith through their own concepts of social and gender relations, and then imagined that their culturally specific synthesis was the only correct version of Christian truth. In fact, it was sometimes as far removed from its origins as the word "church" is from *kyriakos oikos*. As Christianity moves southward, the religion will be comparably changed by immersion in the prevailing cultures of those host societies.

But what would this new Christian synthesis look like? At least for the foreseeable future, members of a Southern-dominated church are likely to be among the poorer people on the planet, in marked contrast to those in the older, Western-dominated church. For this reason, some Western Christians have since the 1960s expected that the religion of their Third World brethren would be fervently liberal, activist, and even revolutionary, that they would follow the model represented by liberation theology. In this view, the new Christianity would chiefly be concerned with putting down the mighty from their seats, through political action or even armed struggle. All too often, though, these hopes have proved illusory. Frequently, the liberationist voices emanating from the Third World derived from clerics trained in Europe and North America, and their ideas won only limited local appeal. Southern World Christians would not avoid political activism, but they would become involved strictly on their own terms. While many espoused political *liberation*, they made it inseparable from *deliverance* from supernatural evil. The two terms are indeed related linguistically and often appear together in biblical texts. Despite this, the juxtaposition of the two thought-worlds of liberation and deliverance seems as baffling for many Euro-Americans as it is natural for global South Christians.[12]

Generally, we can say that many global South Christians are more conservative in terms of both beliefs and moral teaching than are the mainstream churches of the global North; this is especially true of African churches. The denominations that are triumphing all across the global South are stalwartly traditional or even reactionary by the standards of the economically advanced nations. The churches that have made most dramatic progress in the global South have either been Roman Catholic, of a traditionalist and fideistic kind, or radical Protestant sects, evangelical or Pentecostal. Indeed, this conservatism may go far toward explaining the common neglect of Southern Christianities in North America and Europe. Western experts rarely find the ideological tone of the new churches much to their taste.

Of course, we must be careful about generalizations concerning the vast and diverse world of Southern Christianities, and I stress the plural. The concepts of "South" and "Third World" are enormous generalizations, which ignore not only the distinctions between countries but the regional differences within such vast states as China or Brazil. What do new Protestant megachurches in Brazil have to do with independent congregations in Africa, or rising denominations in China? In Africa, the new Christianity defines itself against a pagan society, while Latin American Pentecostalism emerges from a matrix that is thoroughly Christian. In economic terms, too, the divergences are evident. A South Korean, for example, might have far more in common with a German or American, a resident of an advanced industrial society, than with a Peruvian or Kenyan. There is no single Southern Christianity, any more than there is such a thing as European or North American Christianity: each of these terms involves numerous components, some strongly at odds with the others. Consider the diverse European religious scene that includes, for instance, Polish Catholics, German Lutherans, and Greek Orthodox, and each of those labels comprehends both elite and popular interpretations of faith. Why should (say) African Christianity be any more monolithic, and why should it have any resemblance to faith in East Asia? What has Seoul to do with Kampala?

Yet it is not absurd to compare churches in very dissimilar societies, provided that they share significant features that distinguish them from the traditional Christian heartlands. In many African and Asian countries, for instance, churches are largely made up of Christians relatively new to the faith, either first or second generation converts; this characteristic affects styles of worship and faith. The same holds true for recent Latin American converts to surging evangelical or Pentecostal denominations. Furthermore, across the global South, Christians live alongside numerous members of other creeds, possibly as small minority populations, therefore they always have to bear in mind the risk of hostility from these neighbors. New Christians, moreover, carry with them a substantial cultural baggage from these other religions, whether that means traditional primal worship, or one of the great world faiths. In all these ways, Christians in the newer churches operate on assumptions very different from believers in the United States or Germany.[13]

And as we will see, African and Asian churches know the concept of martyrdom as a recent historical reality. These stories of conflict have a palpable political impact. Even in a society in which religious leaders strive for good interfaith relations, there is always a recollection of injuries done in the not too distant past, by the Buddhists of this temple, or the Muslims of that town. Stories of persecution always underlie views of contemporary governments, in ways that recall the ambivalent attitudes of early Christians to secular power. Memories of martyrdom shape faith and conduct.[14]

FIRES FROM HEAVEN

Making all allowances for generalization, then, global South Christians retain a strong supernatural orientation and are by and large far more interested in personal salvation than in radical politics. Often, Christianity grows and spreads in highly charismatic and Pentecostal forms, ecstatic religious styles that are by no means confined to classical Pentecostal denominations, but which span churches with very different origins and traditions. Pentecostal expansion across the Southern continents has been so astonishing as to justify claims of a new Reformation.[15]

In addition, rapid growth is occurring in nontraditional denominations that adapt Christian belief to local tradition, groups that are categorized by titles such as "African indigenous churches." Their exact numbers are none too clear, since they are too busy baptizing newcomers to be counting them very precisely. By most accounts, membership in Pentecostal and independent churches already runs into the hundreds of millions, and congregations are located in precisely the regions of fastest population growth. Within a few decades, such denominations will represent a far larger segment of global Christianity, and just conceivably a majority. These newer churches preach deep personal faith and communal orthodoxy, mysticism, and puritanism, all founded on clear scriptural authority. They preach messages that, to a Westerner, appear simplistically charismatic, visionary, and apocalyptic. In this thought-world, prophecy is an everyday reality, while faith-healing, exorcism, and dream-visions are all fundamental parts of religious sensibility. For better or worse, the dominant churches of the future could have much in common with those of medieval or early modern European times.[16]

The theological coloring of the most successful new churches reminds us once more of the massive gap in most Western listings of the major trends of the last century, which rightly devoted much space to political movements such as fascism and communism but ignored such vital religious currents as Pentecostalism. Yet today, fascists or Nazis are not easy to find, and Communists are becoming an endangered species, while charismatics and Pentecostals are flourishing around the globe. Since there were only a handful of charismatics and Pentecostals in 1900, and several hundred million today, is it not reasonable to identify this as perhaps the most successful social movement of the past century? According to current projections, the number of charismatic/Pentecostal believers should cross the one billion mark before 2050. In terms of the global religions, there will be by that point roughly as many charismatics/Pentecostals as Hindus, and twice as many as there are Buddhists. And that is just taking one of the diverse currents of rising Christianity: there will be even more Catholics than Pentecostals.

These trends must make us think carefully about the character of what we consider normative or typical Christianity. Not just is the "normal" Christian in the modern world no longer Euro-American, she is unlikely to bear much resemblance to American mainline Protestantism. The media, however, may be slow to recognize that fact. In 2005, the *New York Times* published an obituary of the Rev. Dr. Paul Abrecht, a brilliant and committed thinker who served the World Council of Churches for many years. The *Times* remarked that he "took a leading role in formulating mainstream Christianity's response to modern ethical challenges," especially the nuclear threat. While no one would quarrel with the praise heaped upon Dr. Abrecht, the word "mainstream" must startle. In numerical terms alone, liberal Protestantism has never represented a mainstream of Christianity, or even a majority, and as time goes on, the relative significance of that tradition will decline ever further.[17]

THE TWILIGHT OF CHRISTIANITY?

As Southern Christianities continue to expand and mature, they will assuredly develop a wider theological spectrum than at present, and stronger liberal or secularizing tendencies may well emerge. For the foreseeable future, though, the dominant theological tone of emerging world Christianity is traditionalist, orthodox, and supernatural. This would be an ironic reversal of most Western perceptions about the future of religion. When I was working on the first edition of this book, I described its general theme to friends and colleagues, many of whom are well educated and widely traveled. When I said, though, that my theme was "the future of Christianity," a common follow-up question was, in effect "So, how long do you think it will last?" or specifically "How long can the Catholic Church survive?" In their own way, secular, liberal Americans have a distinctly apocalyptic view of the future, with a millenarian expectation of the uprooting of organized religion. At the least, there is a widespread conviction that Christianity cannot survive in anything like its present form.

For more than a century, the coming decline or disappearance of religion has been a commonplace assumption of Western thought, and church leaders have sometimes shared this pessimistic view. Every so often, some American or European writer urges the church to adjust itself to present-day realities, to become relevant by abandoning outmoded supernatural doctrines and moral assumptions. Some years ago, the Episcopal bishop John Spong of Newark advocated just such a skeptical and secularist New Reformation in his book *Why Christianity Must Change or Die*. Templeton Prize–winning scholar Arthur Peacocke urged that the church abandon the "incomprehensible and unbelievable" teachings of supernaturalism, and present the faith in a "credible" manner. Voices in the mass media regularly proclaim that Christianity has failed and is collapsing and will continue to do so unless and until the religion came to terms with liberal orthodoxies on matters of sex and gender. The need to rationalize seems all the more urgent in the face of the attacks by the so-called New Atheists.[18]

Viewed from Cambridge or Amsterdam, such pleas for accommodation may make excellent sense, but in the context of global Christianity this kind of liberalism looks distinctly dated. While some American churches have declined, it is the most liberal and accommodating that have suffered the sharpest contractions. It would not be easy to convince a congregation in Seoul or Nairobi that Christianity or "traditional faith" is dying, when their main concern is building a worship facility big enough for the ten or twenty thousand members they have gained over the last few years. And these new converts are mostly teenagers and young adults, by no means the graying reactionaries of media legend. Nor can these churches be easily told that, in order to reach a mass audience, they must bring their message more into accord with (Western) secular orthodoxies. While Westerners have to confront atheists and secularists, emerging Christians find their critical challenges come from the potent claims of rival faiths—from Muslims, Hindus, and Buddhists.

In contemplating this shift to traditionalism, a historical analogy comes to mind. In eighteenth-century Europe and America, secular Enlightenment ideas made enormous progress among social elites. Few traditional bastions of Christian belief escaped attack. The Trinity, the divinity of Christ, the existence of hell, all fell into disfavor, while critical Bible scholarship undermined the familiar bases of faith. Thomas Jefferson was confident that rational Unitarianism was destined to be the dominant creed of the new United States, and he generously offered his version of the New Testament shorn of miracles or supernatural intervention. Under assault from the European monarchies, the Roman Catholic Church dissolved the Jesuit order, which represented the aggressive confidence of bygone days. In 1798 antireligious French revolutionaries captured the pope himself. So alarming were the signs of the approaching end that orthodox Protestants were galvanized to undertake new missionary endeavors to try and compensate for the approaching collapse of Christian Europe. The missionary fervor of the early nineteenth century owed much to that crisis atmosphere.[19]

Any knowledgeable observer in the 1790s would have concluded that orthodox Christianity had reached its last days, and of course, this sensible opinion would have been absolutely wrong. In the early nineteenth century, orthodoxy and tradition made a comeback, as did the papacy and, indeed, the Jesuits. The rationalism prevailing in many Protestant churches was overwhelmed by a new evangelical revivalism, which received an enormous boost from the revivals that began in 1798. Far from dominating the American scene, Unitarian-Universalists today comprise around 0.2 percent of the U.S. population. So thoroughly was eighteenth-century liberalism obliterated that many modern writers tend to assume that its ideas were invented anew by Victorian skeptics and rationalists, or perhaps grew out of the controversies over Darwinian evolution. Then as now, the triumph of secular liberalism proved to be anything but inevitable.

CHRISTENDOM

For many modern readers, the term "Christendom" carries undesirable implications. The English word "Christendom" is archaic, and of its nature refers to a bygone era in which the Christian religion represented the central justification and organizing force of society. Augustine's *City of God* is the best-known source for the idea that the Christian world should also be a political order, which in the context of the early Middle Ages implied some version of the Christianized Roman Empire. For modern Christian thinkers, "Christendom" evokes a medieval European age of faith, of passionate spirituality, and of a pervasive Christian culture. As G. K. Chesterton wrote, "Christendom is in the literal sense a continent. We come to feel that it contains everything, even the things in revolt against itself."[20]

But "Christendom" also implies an intimate alliance between church and state, the use of secular mechanisms to implement church policies, and the institutionalization of religious intolerance. To characterize part of the world as Christendom of necessity also implies a stark contrast with some other regions or cultures that espouse different faiths. In the medieval context, Christendom stood in a tense relationship with *dar al-Islam*, an image that bears uncomfortable parallels to strictly contemporary circumstances. In a modern context, also, the term "Christendom" suggests a picture of Christianity as the religion of one part of the world—white, wealthy, and technologically advanced—spreading its faith as part of the package of imperial exploitation. Surely, Christendom connotes a theocratic historical nightmare that no sensitive modern would care to see reenacted?

But, of course, I use the word "Christendom" in a more neutral sense. My original scholarly background is in early medieval history, an age when states and kingdoms were notoriously transient things, and when European Christians placed their primary loyalty in the seemingly eternal institution of the church. They were members of Christendom first, and only after that were they subjects of nations. That is the sense in which I use the concept of "Christendom," rather than as a political or militarized entity. In its origins, then, "Christendom" has supranational and even antinational implications quite different from the term's use in common parlance.

Medieval people spoke readily of "Christendom," the *Res Publica Christiana*, as a true overarching unity and a focus of loyalty transcending mere kingdoms or empires. Kingdoms such as Burgundy, Wessex, or Saxony might last for only a century or two before they were replaced by new states and dynasties, but any rational person knew that Christendom simply endured. This perception had political consequences. While the laws of individual nations lasted only as long as the nations themselves, Christendom offered a higher set of standards and mores, which alone could claim to be universal. Though it rarely possessed any potential for common political action, Christendom was a primary form of cultural reference.[21]

Ultimately, Christendom collapsed in the face of the overwhelming power of secular nationalism. Later Christian scholars had to come to terms with this new age of post-Christendom, when one could no longer assume any connection between religion and political order.[22] By the start of the twenty-first century, however, the whole concept of the nation-state was itself under challenge. When the U.S. intelligence community imagines the world that we must confront within fifteen or twenty years, this theme of fragmentation features prominently. In the coming decades, "governments will have less and less control over flows of information, technology, diseases, migrants, arms, and financial transactions, whether legal or illegal, across their borders.... The very concept of 'belonging' to a particular state will probably erode." Already by 2025, "in areas of Africa and Asia, states as we know them might wither away, owing to the inability of governments to provide for basic needs, including security." "Although states will not disappear from the international scene [by 2025] the *relative power* of various nonstate actors—including businesses, tribes, religious organizations and even criminal networks—will grow as those groups influence decisions on a widening range of social, economic and political issues"[23]

To use Benedict Anderson's phrase, nation-states are imagined communities of relatively recent date, rather than eternal or inevitable realities. In recent years, many of these communities have begun to reimagine themselves substantially, even to unimagine themselves out of existence. In Europe, loyalties to the nation as such are being replaced by newer forms of adherence, whether to larger entities (Europe itself) or to smaller (regions or ethnic groups). If even such once-unquestioned constructs as Great Britain are under threat, it is not surprising that people are questioning the existence of newer and still more artificial entities in Africa or Asia, with their flimsy national frontiers dreamed up so recently by imperial bureaucrats. As Paul Gifford notes, many Africans live in mere quasi states:

"though they are recognized legal entities, they are not, in a functional sense, states."[24]

When social scientists analyze the decline of states in the face of globalization, they note parallels with the cosmopolitan world of the Middle Ages. Some scholars have even postulated the future emergence of some movement or ideology that could in a sense create something like a new Christendom. This would be what political scientist Hedley Bull called "a modern and secular equivalent of the kind of universal political organization that existed in Western Christendom in the Middle Ages." Might the new ideological force be environmentalism, with a mystical New Age twist?[25] Yet the more we look at the global South in particular, the more we see that while universal and supranational ideas are flourishing, they are not secular in the least. The centers of gravest state weakness are often the regions in which political loyalties are secondary to religious beliefs, either Muslim or Christian, and these are the terms in which people define their identities. The new Christian world of the South could find unity in common religious beliefs.

That many Southern societies will develop a powerful Christian identity in culture and politics is beyond doubt. Less obvious is whether, and when, they will aspire to any kind of global unity. In this matter, the Atlantic Ocean initially seems to offer a barrier quite as overwhelming as it was before Columbus. Very soon, the two main centers of Christianity will be Africa and Latin America, and within each region there is at least some sense of unity. Latin American ecclesiastics meet periodically, scholars treat the region as a whole (albeit a diverse one), and a similar canon of authors is read widely. The same can be said of Africa in its own way. However, next to no common sense of identity currently unites the churches and believers of the two continents. Even in terms of worldwide Christian networks, the two continents belong almost to different planets, and Asian nations represent a still different reality. For many Protestant Africans, the World Council of Churches offers a major institutional focus of unity, but because the Roman Catholic Church abstains from membership in the Council, this forum is closed to the majority of Latin Americans. When African and Latin American church leaders and scholars do meet, all too often it is at gatherings in Europe or the United States, pursuing agendas conceived in the global North.

The resulting segregation of interests and ideas is remarkable, since the churches in Africa, Asia, and Latin America share so many common experiences. They are passing through such similar phases of growth, and are, independently, developing such very similar social and theological worldviews. All, also, face similar issues, of race, of inculturation, and, still, of how to deal with their respective colonial heritages. All these are common hemispheric issues that fundamentally separate the experiences of Northern and Southern churches.

Moreover, churches on all three continents share a passionate enthusiasm for mission and evangelism that is often South-South, organized from one of the emerging churches, and directed toward some other region of Africa, Asia, or Latin America—we think of Brazilian missionaries in Africa, Ugandans in India, Koreans in the Middle East. Although poorly studied, South-South evangelism represents one of the most impressive phenomena in contemporary Christianity: the topic cries out for a major book-length survey.[26]

Given the lively scholarly activity and the flourishing spirituality in different regions of the global South, a period of mutual discovery is inevitable. When it begins—when, not if—the interaction should launch a revolutionary new era in world religion. Even though many see the process of globalization as yet another form of American imperialism, it would be ironic if an early consequence was a growing sense of identity between Southern World Christians. And once that axis is established, we really would be speaking of a new Christendom, based in Africa, Asia, and Latin America.

CLASHING CIVILIZATIONS?

The archaic term "Christendom" conjures some potential nightmares about the future we are imagining. The last Christendom, in the Middle Ages, was anything but an unmixed blessing for either church or society. While it offered a common culture and thought-world, the era was also characterized by widespread intolerance, symbolized at its very worst by aggressive crusades, heresy hunts, and religious pogroms. Critically, Christendom was defined in terms of what it was not, since the Christian world existed in unhappy conjunction with neighboring Muslim states.[27]

According to some scenarios, this Christian-Muslim conflict may in fact prove one of the closest analogies between the Christian world that was, and the one coming into being. No less than Christians, the Muslim world will be transformed by the epochal demographic events of the coming decades, the shift of gravity of global population to the Two-Thirds World. Muslim and Christian nations will expand adjacent to each other, and often Muslim and Christian communities will both grow within the same country. Based on recent experiences around the world—in Nigeria and Indonesia, the Sudan and the Philippines—we face the likelihood that population growth will be accompanied by intensified rivalry, by struggles for converts, by competing attempts to enforce moral codes by means of secular law. Whether Muslim or Christian, religious zeal can easily turn into fanaticism.

When the U.S. intelligence community imagines the near-future world, it is acutely concerned about developments in the so-called Arc of Instability, a vast area of the globe stretching from sub-Saharan Africa through the Middle East and into Central and Southern Asia. Nations within this arc are characterized by surging population growth and an alarming youth bulge, as well as by political fragmentation and extremism, and border conflicts and ethnic disputes. Frequently, the endemic violence and discontent of these regions takes on a religious character, commonly scapegoating minorities, or accusing rival believers of belonging to pernicious global conspiracies. This is a disastrous recipe for relations between different religions, and especially between Christians and Muslims. In extreme cases, social and political pressures reach the point that state mechanisms fail altogether, commonly leaving power in the hands of nonstate actors—militias or religious groups.[28]

Domestic violence and civil wars could in turn provoke international conflicts. This development is quite likely when one of the competing ideologies is shared passionately by a neighboring country, or by an international religious-oriented alliance. Across the Muslim world, many believers have shown themselves willing to fight for the cause of international Islam, with far more enthusiasm than they demonstrate for any individual nation. Putting these different trends together, we have a volatile mixture that could provoke appalling wars and confrontations.

Such a clash is anything but inevitable. Around the world, Christians and Muslims often have lived contentedly side by side, learning to respect each other's sensitivities. This remains true today, after all the influence of growing militancy and foreign incitement. While Islam and Christianity are both demanding ideologies, they do not necessarily trump all other potential human connections, such as the bonds of community and local tradition as well as of village and family. In Africa, we regularly hear that a particular nation or region is 50 percent Christian, 50 percent Muslim, and 100 percent traditional African. In much of sub-Saharan Africa today, any discussion of religious relations commonly begins with a Christian speaker noting how many of his or her closest kin belong to the other faith. This is not a case of a bland "some of my best friends are Muslims," so much as a factual observation that one's brother, aunts, and several cousins follow Islam, so that any potential conflicts must be settled within a family context.

Yet despite powerful forces for harmony, it has in recent years been tragically common for conflicts to erupt even in those societies that were long cited as models of peaceful coexistence. Worldwide, religious trends have the potential to reshape political assumptions in a way that has not been seen since the rise of modern nationalism. While we can imagine any number of possible futures, a worst-case scenario would include a wave of religious conflicts reminiscent of the Middle Ages, a new age of Christian crusades and Muslim jihads. In responding to this prospect, we need at a minimum to make sure that our political leaders and diplomats pay quite as much attention to religions and to sectarian frontiers as they ever have to the distribution of oilfields.[29]

USING THE FUTURE

This scenario may well be too pessimistic, but there can be no doubt about the underlying realities, demographic and religious, which ensure that Christianity will flourish in the near future. The question is just how to respond to that fact. While political leaders must make their own agendas, current changes also pose questions for anyone interested in the state of religion.

The greatest temptation—and maybe the worst danger—is to use future projections as a club in present-day arguments. Northerners rarely give the South anything like the attention it deserves, but when they do notice it, they tend to project onto it their own familiar realities and desires. If in fact the global South represents the future, then it is tempting to claim that one's own ideas are more valid, more important, because they coincide with those of the rising Third World.

Over the past half-century or so, whenever global South Christianity has gained attention in North America or Europe, it has been through the form of what might be termed two dreams, two competing visions, each trying to deploy that new religious movement for its own purposes. For the Left, attracted by visions of liberation, the rise of the South suggests that Northern Christians must commit themselves to social and political activism at home, to ensuring economic justice and combating racism, to promoting cultural diversity. Conservatives, in contrast, emphasize the moral and sexual conservatism of the emerging churches, and seek to enlist them as natural allies. From their point of view, growing churches are those that stand farthest from Western liberal orthodoxies, and we should learn from their success. A Liberation Dream confronts a Conservative Dream. For both sides, though, the new South is useful, politically and rhetorically. Even if activists hold an unusual or unpopular position, it can be justified on the basis that it represents the future: if they wait long enough, they will be vindicated by the churches of Africa (or Asia or Latin America). Like any true-believing Marxist, one is claiming to be on the side of history, which will absolve its faithful disciples.

Both expectations, liberal and conservative, are wrong, or at least, fail to see the whole picture. Each in its different way expects the Southern churches to reproduce Western obsessions and approaches, rather than evolving their own distinctive solutions to their own particular problems. One difficulty is deciding just what that vast and multifaceted entity described as the Third World, or the Two-Thirds World, actually does want or believe. The South is massively diverse, and conservatism and liberalism are characterized quite differently from the customary usages of North American or European churches. Conservative theological or moral stances often accompany quite progressive or radical economic views. And the North-South divergence will probably grow as time goes on. As Southern churches grow and mature, they will increasingly define their own interests in ways that have little to do with the preferences and parties of Americans and Europeans.

We must be cautious about seeing such new movements through the lens of our own conflicts. As an analogy, we might imagine the situation in the seventh or eighth centuries in what was still, numerically and culturally, the Near Eastern heart of Christianity, in Syria or Mesopotamia. We picture a meeting of church leaders who have gathered to hear a report from a traveler from a not so antique land, from the remote barbarian world of Western Europe. The traveler delights his listeners by telling them of the many new conversions among the strange peoples of England or Germany, and the creation of whole new dioceses in the midst of the northern forests. Impatiently, the assembled hierarchs press him to answer the key question: this new Christianity coming into being, is it the Christianity of Edessa or of Damascus? Where do the new converts stand on the crucial issues of the day, on the Monothelete heresy, on Iconoclasm? When the traveler tells them, regretfully, that these issues really do not register in those parts of the world, where religious life has utterly different concerns and emphases, the Syrians are alarmed. Is this really a new Christianity, they ask, or is it some new syncretistic horror? How can any Christian not be centrally concerned with these issues? And while Syrian

Christianity carried on debating these questions to exhaustion, the new churches of Europe entered a great age of spiritual growth and intellectual endeavor.

And as in those times, it is extremely difficult to envisage the future trajectory of the faith. Who in that age could have foreseen the global expansion of that poor hatchling, Western Christianity? Today, similarly, we see promising signs of growth, as Southern Christians begin evangelizing the North, especially Europe, and in the process they transform many familiar aspects of belief and practice, exporting cultural traits presently found only in Africa or Latin America. We can only speculate what this future synthesis might look like. But underlying all these possibilities is one solid reality. However partisan the interpretations of the new Christianity, however paternalistic, there can be no doubt that the emerging Christian world will be anchored in the Southern continents.

++++++++++ TWO ++++++++++

Disciples of All Nations

> Europe is taught the way to scale Heaven, not by
> mathematical principles, but by divine verity. Jesus
> Christ is their Way, their Truth, their Life; who hath
> long since given a bill of divorce to ingratefull Asia
> where he was born, and Africa the place of his flight
> and refuge, and is become almost wholly and only
> European. For little do we find of this name in Asia,
> less in Africa, and nothing at all in America, but later
> European gleanings. Here are his scriptures, oratories,
> sacraments, ministers, mysteries.
>
> Samuel Purchas, 1625

As Christianity moves South and East, it is returning to its roots. To use the intriguing description offered by Ghanaian scholar Kwame Bediako, what we are now witnessing is "the renewal of a non-Western religion."[1] Founded in the Near East, Christianity for its first thousand years was stronger in Asia and North Africa than in Europe, and only after the fourteenth century did Europe (and Europeanized North America) decisively become the Christian heartland. This account challenges the prevalent view of Christianity as a white or Western ideology that was foisted on the rest of an unwilling globe, under the auspices of Spanish galleons, British redcoats, and American televangelists.

In this popular image, Christianity becomes not just an aspect of Western imperialism but an essential justification for that whole era. When twentieth-century African Americans sought religious roots distinct from the mainstream culture that spurned them, a substantial minority opted for the Muslim faith that they regarded as authentically African. Christianity, in contrast, was seen as the tool of the slave-masters. (Few Westerners pay any attention to the long history of Arab Muslim slaving enterprises in Africa.)[2] As "everyone knows," the authentic religions of Africa and Asia are faiths such as Hinduism, Buddhism, animism, and above all, Islam. Not just among African Americans, a common assumption holds that when we do find Christianity outside the West, it must have been brought there from the West, probably in the last century or two. Images of Victorian missionaries in pith helmets are commonly in the background.

The power of this hostile picture is all the more surprising when we realize how easily available are the historical sources and modern scholarly studies that utterly contradict it. We do not have to excavate obscure scholarly collections in order to read the rich and ancient histories of African and Asian Christianity. Based on this large literature, we can see that at no point did the West have a monopoly on the Christian faith. Even at the height of the missionary endeavor, non-Western converts very soon absorbed and adapted the religion according to their own cultural needs.

THE MYTH OF WESTERN CHRISTIANITY

The whole idea of "Western Christianity" distorts the true pattern of the religion's development over time. The conventional picture of Christian origins, presented in any number of popular history books and television documentaries, is commonly illustrated by a graphic of the Mediterranean world and Europe, with Jerusalem at an eastern extreme. Christianity grows from its roots in Palestine, spreads through Asia Minor and Greece, and ultimately arrives in Italy, the center of the map—and presumably of the world. The faith then spreads through the Roman world, until by the fourth century it becomes coterminous with the Roman Empire.

Tracing later developments from the seventh century on, animations or sequences of maps show Eastern Christianity being overwhelmed by the forces of Islam. As Muslim forces conquer each territory of the eastern or southern Mediterranean, the land affected is often depicted, literally, fading into darkness. For a modern viewer, it is easy to understand why Egypt, Syria, and Palestine would quickly be lost to the faith, since anyone can see that they were only clinging lightly to the far skirts of the Roman (and Christian) world. After the rise of Islam, maps generally shift their focus to the lands of Western Europe, especially to what will later become France and Britain. The Christian center of gravity shifted decisively from the Jordan to the Rhine, from Antioch to Chartres. In the East, all that remains by this point is the long-enduring, if ultimately doomed, presence of the Byzantine empire, based in Constantinople. Barring this single bastion, the usual graphic representation implies that by 800 at the latest, the time of Charlemagne, Christianity was more or less synonymous with Western Europe and grew or shrank with European fortunes. Long before this point,

Christians had abandoned their perverse habit of writing sacred texts in
Greek, Syriac, and Coptic, and confined themselves to good Christian
Latin.

Popular histories always oversimplify, but in this instance the inaccu-
racies are serious. To imagine the early history of Christianity, we would
do much better to use the standard map of the world that was regularly
offered in medieval times. In these older pictures, the then-known continents of Europe, Africa, and Asia all appeared as more or less equal lobes
conjoined at a central location, which was Palestine, with Jerusalem at its
center. This image made splendid theological sense, in that Jesus's sacrificial self-giving occurred at the very center of the world that he was saving.
Theology apart, the tripartite model is far more useful for understanding
Christian expansion, which occurred simultaneously into the three continents.[3] When we think of the missionary endeavors of the early apostles,
we think first of Paul's career in the eastern Mediterranean, because this
happened to be recorded in the Acts and Epistles that form so large a part
of the New Testament. Appropriately enough for the modern Europe-
centered view, the book of Acts ends once Paul established himself in
Rome. This Pauline movement became all the more important in hindsight because of the relative success of the Gentile churches after the
Jewish revolt of 66–73. At the time, though, the richest fields for missionary expansion were unquestionably in Africa and Asia, rather than
Europe. During the first century or two of the Christian era, Syria, Egypt,
and Mesopotamia became the Christian centers that they would remain
for many centuries. Christian art, literature, and music all originated in
these lands, as did most of what would become the New Testament.
Monasticism is an Egyptian invention.

By the time the Roman Empire granted the Christians toleration in the
early fourth century, there was no question that the religion was predominantly associated with the eastern half of the empire, and indeed with territories beyond the eastern border. Of the five ancient patriarchates of the
church, only one, Rome, clearly stood in the West: the others were at
Constantinople, Antioch, Jerusalem, and Alexandria. If we can imagine a
Christian center of gravity by around 500, we should still be thinking of
Syria rather than Italy. Africa, too, had its ancient Christian roots. Apart
from Egypt, much early Christian history focuses on the Roman province
known as Africa, roughly modern Tunisia. This was the home of such great
early leaders as Tertullian, Cyprian, and Augustine, the founders of
Christian Latin literature. When the Anglo-Saxons adopted Christianity
during the seventh century, they learned literacy and scholarship from

mentors such as "an abbot called Hadrian, by nation an African, well versed in Holy Scripture, trained in monastic and ecclesiastical teaching, and excellently skilled both in the Greek and Latin tongues." Hadrian founded the tradition of learning at what would become the great ecclesiastical center of Canterbury.[4]

THE EASTERN CHURCHES

Christianity has never been synonymous either with Europe or the West. In fact, theological controversies of the fourth and fifth centuries tended to isolate European or Western Christianity from the traditional Christian lands, and thus leave it on a geographical and cultural limb. Repeatedly, Christians engaged in furious arguments over the nature of Christ, debates that seem arcane to most modern observers but would be vital for defining cultural frontiers.

At issue was the relationship between the divine and human natures of Christ. The Catholic or Orthodox position, which ultimately triumphed, held that there were indeed two natures, which were conjoined and commingled. But other approaches were possible and could be grounded surprisingly well in scripture. Monophysites held that Christ had only one nature and was purely divine. At the opposite extreme, Nestorians accepted the two natures but held that these were not absolutely united, so that it was blasphemous nonsense to speak of the Virgin Mary as Mother of God. Between these extremes lay many shades of opinion, some of which could be reconciled with orthodoxy, but which were often labeled in more extreme terms than they really deserved. When we look more closely at his own writings, we see that even Nestorius himself—supposedly the founder of the—ism—was not a true Nestorian, and was actually very close to mainstream orthodoxy. Nor were most of the so-called Monophysites strict followers of that extreme position: they rather asserted particular aspects of mainstream doctrine in ways that the Catholic/Orthodox found dangerous.

For convenience though, and ignoring these important nuances, let us use those names—Orthodox, Nestorian, and Monophysite—for the different political/religious factions that splintered the Christian world. Broadly, the churches of Mesopotamia and Persia were Nestorian, while Egypt and Syria/Palestine became staunchly Monophysite. Following violent controversies, the Nestorians were cast out of the fold in 431, while the Monophysites were deemed heretical at the great ecumenical council at Chalcedon in 451. This left the Orthodox in command of the empire and the mainstream church apparatus. Over the next two centuries, many of the traditional centers of Christianity saw themselves as oppressed by the tyrannical rulers of Rome and Constantinople. Already, Christianity was bitterly divided between Western (European) and Eastern (Asian and African) models. Denominations arising directly from these theological squabbles survive today and have only barely patched up their differences.[5]

This mutual hostility helps to explain why European Christians had little sympathy or knowledge of some of the truly ancient Christian societies of the East, and why our historical view of the Eastern churches is often blinkered. When we refer to Christianity forming a relationship with the secular state, Western historians think of Constantine, who granted toleration within the Roman Empire in 313. Far less celebrated are the other early states that established Christianity as their own official religion in the fourth century, namely Ethiopia and Armenia. Almost certainly, Armenia was the first state anywhere to establish Christianity as an official faith, which it did around the year 300. Armenian Christianity became increasingly separated from the Western tradition in the fifth century after it adopted the Monophysite position. Even so, Christianity survived and flourished here up to the present day, developing a rich literary, musical, and architectural culture.[6]

The Ethiopian church is equally ancient, and an Ethiopian court official is one of the pioneer Gentile converts identified in the book of Acts. Like its Armenian counterpart, the organized church in Ethiopia owed much to Syrian missionaries of the third and fourth centuries. By the time the first Anglo-Saxons were converted, Ethiopian Christianity was already in its tenth generation. Though scarcely known by Westerners, the Ethiopian church offers one of the most heroic success stories in Christianity. Not surprisingly given its location, the church drew heavily on Egyptian influence. Through the Middle Ages, the symbolic center of the Christian kingdom was at the ancient capital of Aksum, long a point of contact with Pharaonic Egypt. An episcopal see was founded here around 340, and this remained the "home of the Ark of the Covenant, Ethiopia's original New Jerusalem." The Egyptian connection created a potent monastic tradition that endures to this day. It also meant that, like the Armenians, Ethiopians followed the Monophysite teaching, which reinforced their separation from European Christianity. Far from being concerned with the opinions of Rome, the story of the Ethiopian church for most of its history constitutes a battle between local control (the monastic leadership) and the *abunas*, the representatives of the Coptic Patriarchs in Alexandria. On every side, this was a wholly African affair.[7]

The Ethiopian church has many aspects that would surprise a Westerner, including practices that stem from Judaism. Believers practice circumcision, some keep a Saturday Sabbath, and many churches feature an ark. The ruling dynasty claims descent from Solomon and the Queen of Sheba, and their son, Menelik; based on this Solomonic tradition, the kings practiced polygamy. We really do not know whether early Ethiopians had been converted to Judaism before they found Christianity, or if (more likely) they just treated Old Testament models with much more reverence than would European Christians. As we will see, many modern-day African Christians likewise feel very comfortable with the world of the Old Testament and try to revive ancient Hebrew customs—sometimes to the horror of European Christians.[8]

But for all the apparent quirks of the Ethiopian church, only a daring outsider would venture to suggest that the faith for which Ethiopians have struggled and died for more than seventeen hundred years is anything less than a pure manifestation of the Christian tradition. In 1970, in the last days of the old royal regime, the church had "61,000 priests, 12,000 monks, 57,000 deacons, 31,000 *debteras* (choir leaders) and 827 monasteries."[9] Even today, after lengthy conflicts with Muslims and, more recently, anti-clerical Marxists, the church claims some 25 million members. To put this in Western terms, that is roughly the number of North American Methodists of all denominations combined.

SURVIVAL

Both Armenia and Ethiopia maintained a stubborn independence for most of their history. Ethiopia was one of the last portions of Africa to be swallowed by European imperialism. It was another king bearing the glorious Solomonic name of Menelik who in 1896 inflicted a crushing military defeat upon the invading Italians, one of the rare instances of successful armed resistance against the colonization of Africa. Only briefly, during the 1930s, did Ethiopia fall under European rule.

Yet Ethiopia and Armenia were far from unusual in keeping their distinctive religious identity alive through the Middle Ages. Even in those African and Asian regions subjugated by Islam, Christian loyalties survived for centuries. Contrary to the historical maps with which we are familiar, Christian lights did not just fade out following the arrival of the Muslims.

Initially, Muslim rulers made little effort to encourage conversion, partly for the solid, practical reason that converts to Islam ceased to pay the special taxes levied on unbelievers, so that it literally paid to keep Christian subjects Christian. The persecutions that did occur were sporadic and usually directed against monks and clergy rather than ordinary believers. Not until the later Middle Ages did the mystical Sufi orders begin the process of popular evangelism for Islam, and they did this by offering former Christians a package of familiar practices that included saints, shrines, relics, and pilgrimages, and a veneration for the ascetic prophet Jesus. The genius of the Sufis was to present the Muslim faith in catholic forms.[10]

Under Muslim rule, the patriarchates of Alexandria, Constantinople, and Antioch continued to be vital centers of ecclesiastical authority, still commanding the allegiance of millions of followers. Through the tenth century, the Patriarchs of Alexandria occupied a powerful role under the Muslim rulers, and when the royal capital moved to the upstart city of Cairo, so did the patriarch's residence. Christian primates "were often used as ambassadors, consulted for political advice, or even solicited for prayer." Between the eighth and eleventh centuries, Christians, and especially Christian clergy, played a critical role in absorbing the cultural riches of the ancient Hellenistic world into the emerging Muslim societies. These Christians—Melkites (Orthodox), Jacobites (Monophysite), Nestorians—preserved and read ancient texts, which they translated into Arabic. For centuries after the rise of Islam, the greatest intellectual center of the Middle East was the Nestorian university at Nisibis, before it was succeeded by Muslim Baghdad and Córdoba. The scholars of Nisibis kept alive the works of Plato and Aristotle that would ultimately be transmitted to Christian Western Europe.

The other great Christian center was the Persian university of Jundaisapur, which became the foundation of Muslim learning in Baghdad itself. When modern observers rhapsodize about the glories of medieval Islamic culture, few acknowledge the indispensable Christian foundations of Arabic learning. In turn, Muslim rulers generally respected the countless distinctions they found among their Christian subjects. The Ottoman Turks recognized each denomination or theological tradition as a separate *millet*, a community under its own laws and courts, and governed by its own particular clerical structures.[11]

Christians enjoyed nothing like what modern Americans construe as religious liberty, and there were stringent limits on any kind of Christian expansion. Seizures of church property are painfully symbolized by the fate of Constantinople's church of Hagia Sophia, once the greatest church in the world, but which in the fifteenth century became a mosque. (Today, it is secularized as a museum). Still, most Christian groups survived quite successfully into modern times. For many so-called heretics, such as the Monophysites, Muslim rulers were no worse than Christian Byzantine emperors, and less intrusive.

Egypt offers a telling example of Christian persistence. Partly, the Egyptian church retained such a mass following because of its enthusiastic adoption of the native Coptic language. At least the Gospels and Psalter were already available in Coptic by around 300. Elsewhere in North Africa, the church's insistence on speaking Latin meant that it never evangelized far beyond the cities, so that Christianity did not long survive the Muslim conquests. But Egypt offered a very different picture. At the start of the twentieth century, the Coptic Christians here comprised 10 or 20 percent of that nation's people, and perhaps more. Today, the official figure is around 5 percent, but most observers believe that is an underestimate. The modern Coptic church claims 10 million members.[12]

The fact of Coptic survival is all the more remarkable when we recall just who these Copts are. Their name is a corruption of *Aigyptos*, that is, native Egyptians, and their language descends from the tongue of the pyramid builders. When modern scholars translated the hieroglyphics on the Rosetta Stone, they did so by using the language they found spoken in the liturgies of the Coptic church. The Syrian Orthodox churches, similarly, still use a kind of Syriac that is close to the Aramaic spoken by Jesus himself. At so many points, the living Christianity of Egypt, Syria, Palestine, Ethiopia, and Armenia takes us back to the earliest centuries of the faith, a time when the followers of Jesus were developing cells of believers within a still vibrant Roman empire.

NEW HORIZONS

In some areas, Eastern churches actually expanded through missionary successes beyond the bounds of the Muslim world. Most spectacular among the growing churches were the Nestorian Christians, who had been labeled as heretical in late Roman times. They identified themselves as the Church of the East, and in 498, they erected their own patriarchate at the Persian capital of Seleucia/Ctesiphon (after the rise of Islam, the patriarchs moved their seat to the new metropolis of Baghdad). The church developed a thriving network of churches and monasteries across Persia and especially Mesopotamia, or modern Iraq. From these strongholds, missionaries penetrated deep into Central Asia by the seventh century. Along the Silk Route, the Church of the East erected new metropolitan centers—at Merv and Bukhara, Samarkand and Kashgar. The Nestorians and their "luminous doctrine" were welcomed at the Chinese imperial court, and in 638, a church was erected in China's capital of Ch'ang-an, then perhaps the largest city in the world.

Around 780, Nestorians recounted the Christian message in terms that were designed to appeal to Taoist or Buddhist scholars, just as contemporary European Christians had tried to make the faith acceptable to the Greco-Roman Mediterranean. The Nestorian tablet told how

> the illustrious and honorable Messiah, veiling his true dignity, appeared in the world as a man; angelic powers promulgated the glad tidings, a virgin gave birth to the Holy One in Syria... he laid down great principles for the government of families and kingdoms; he established the new religion of the silent operation of the pure spirit of the Triune; he rendered virtue subservient to direct faith; he fixed the extent of the eight boundaries, thus completing the truth and freeing it from dross; he opened the gate of the three constant principles, introducing life and destroying death; he suspended the bright sun to invade the chambers of darkness, and the falsehoods of the devil were thereupon defeated; he set in motion the vessel of mercy by which to ascend to the bright mansions, whereupon rational beings were then released, having thus completed the manifestation of his power, in clear day he ascended to his true station.

The intellectual categories used here would have startled a first-century Jew, but would have seemed no more alien than the Latin formulations of Anselm or Thomas Aquinas. The Church of the East was fully living up to its name, and Christians were interacting closely with other world religions. In both India and China, many Christians used a symbol that combined the Christian cross with the Buddhist lotus, which signified triumph over ignorance and the material world. Some Chinese regimes saw Christianity as a sect within Buddhism.[13]

By the tenth century the Nestorian church in China had enjoyed two hundred years of peace and toleration, before succumbing to persecution. Even so, the church revived in China in the twelfth and thirteenth centuries, and launched missionary efforts still farther afield, probably into southeast Asia. Indeed, the oriental triumphs of the Nestorians gave rise to the persistent Western myth of Prester John, a great Christian priest-king dwelling beyond the Muslim world. Christianity has thus been in China for a long time—about as long, in fact, as Buddhism has been in Japan.

In southern India, the ubiquitous Syrian missionaries founded native Christian communities that claimed to follow St. Thomas, *Mar Thoma*. Since long-established trade routes connected southern India with the Mediterranean world, Christianity may indeed have reached India as early as the second century, or perhaps even the first. Reflecting the vast breadth of Eastern Christianity, these Indian Christians spoke Syriac and retained their links with the Nestorian patriarch of Babylon, who resided at Baghdad. Today, the Indian state of Kerala has some seven million Thomas Christians, divided among Catholic, Protestant, and Orthodox traditions.[14]

NUMBERS

Just how numerous were the Christian communities that survived under Muslim rule? Modern images of medieval Christianity draw heavily on images of France and Western Europe, which are portrayed as priest-ridden, theocratic states, with little tolerance for Jews or heretics. Yet through much of the Middle Ages, a large proportion of the world's Christians themselves lived as despised minorities, under the political power of a hostile faith. In prerevolutionary Russia, the common word for "peasant" was *Krest'ianin*, which derives from "Christian," recalling a time when the rural masses stubbornly preserved their faith in the face of Tatar and Muslim invasion. As was so often in medieval times, the Christians were the oppressed poor and ignorant, rather than the sophisticated town-dwellers.

As late as the twelfth and thirteenth centuries, Christians still made up a large proportion of most former Roman territories that had fallen under Muslim rule, in Syria, Mesopotamia, and Egypt, and it is not easy to tell when Muslims actually gained majority status in these communities. A reasonable guess would place the transition around the time of the Crusades, about 1100 or 1200. In 1280, the patriarch of the Jacobite sect still "oversaw twenty metropolitans and about a hundred bishops from Anatolia and Syria to lower Mesopotamia and Persia." By way of comparison, the English church at the same time had just two metropolitans (Canterbury and York) and twenty-five bishops. And the Jacobites were just one Christian denomination among several.[15]

The size of the Christian communities in the East is significant because in the Middle Ages the Eastern lands were more densely populated than those of Europe. Medieval England and France were Christian states, while the regimes of Egypt and Syria were solidly Muslim, but there may have been more Christians all told in the Eastern nations than the Western, and the Easterners possessed at least as active a cultural and spiritual life. When assessing the population of "Christian Europe," we should also recall that large parts of the continent did not even nominally accept Christianity until well into the Middle Ages. Russia and the Scandinavian lands were both converted around 1000, but Lithuania, then a major state dominating much of Eastern Europe, did not formally accept Christianity until 1387. In the thirteenth century, the height of medieval Christian civilization in Europe, there may have been more Christian believers on the continent of Asia than in Europe, while Africa still had populous Christian communities.

My estimates differ from those of the standard reference source, namely the *World Christian Encyclopedia*, which has made a valiant effort to quantify Christian strength through history (see table 2.1).[16] According to the first edition of this work, Europe gained its preeminence earlier than I have suggested, probably around the tenth century. It is hard to be too confident about any of this. Historical demography is a painfully uncertain science, especially where religious minorities are concerned. Even today, governments underplay the size of inconvenient minorities, and in earlier times it was much easier for dissidents to live far removed from centers of government, from elite agencies and census takers. But the numbers offered by the *Encyclopedia* pose problems. The Christian population of Egypt alone in 1200 was probably around 3 million, and that takes no account of Ethiopia and Nubia, so the figures suggested for Africa might understate Christian strength by about a half. The undercount for Asia may be just as serious. On balance, I would argue that at the time of Magna Carta or the Crusades if we imagine a typical Christian, we should still be thinking not of a French artisan but of a Syrian peasant or Mesopotamian town-dweller, an Asian not a European.

The persistence of Christian communities under Islam challenges contemporary attitudes toward historical conflicts between the two faiths. In recent years, a powerful social movement has demanded that the West and specifically the churches apologize for the medieval crusading movement. In this view, the Crusades represented aggression, pure and simple, against the Muslim world, and nobody can deny the resulting wars involved their share of atrocities. Underlying the movement for apology, though, is the assumption that religious frontiers are somehow carved in stone, and that the Muslim-ruled states of the Near East must always and infallibly have been destined to form part of the world of Islam. An equally good case can be made that the medieval Middle East was no more inevitably Muslim than other regions

TABLE 2.1
Distribution of Christians in Ancient and Medieval Times

Continent	Christians (millions)			
	500	1000	1200	1500
Africa	8	5	2.5	1.3
Asia	21.2	16.8	21	3.4
Europe/Russia	14.2	28.6	46.6	76.3
GLOBAL TOTAL	43.4	50.4	70.1	81

Source: David B. Barrett, World Christian Encyclopedia (Nairobi, Kenya: Oxford University Press, 1982), 796.

conquered by Islam and subsequently liberated, such as Spain and Hungary. Much of what we today call the Muslim world was for a thousand years the heartland of Christianity. Westerners, though, rarely suggest that Muslims apologize for the aggressive acts that gave them power over these various lands in the first place. Westerners, including Western Christians, have simply forgotten the once-great Christian communities of the Eastern world.

CRISIS

Substantial Christian communities survived until modern times in other nations besides Egypt: in Syria, Lebanon, Palestine, Iraq, and Turkey. Since Christian numbers certainly had not grown from medieval times, we must conclude that these communities must have been still more numerous in bygone years. Even in 1900, Christians and Jews combined made up 30 percent of the total population of the Ottoman Empire. In the core Ottoman lands of Anatolia, the area that we today call Turkey, a substantial Christian population lasted until the early twentieth century, and Muslims were not even a majority in Constantinople itself.

Middle Eastern Christian communities flourished until they were devastated by a series of wars, expulsions, and population exchanges between 1915 and 1925, during and immediately following World War I. Nor have later eras been kind to the region's Christians. At the time of the establishment of the state of Israel, perhaps 20 percent of Palestinian Arabs were still Christian, though today, most of those live in exile, chiefly in North America or Australia. Iraq, too, had a venerable Christian community that in the 1980s might have accounted for some 4 percent of the population. Since that point, though, it has been gravely reduced by the combined effects of war, sanctions, and persecution, and many Christian leaders have been murdered. Quite conceivably, Christian life in Iraq might entirely disappear within a few decades. Even in Lebanon, a Christian community that once constituted a majority of the population is probably now reduced to 30 or 35 percent of the whole. The last Christian bastion in the region is Syria, where numbers have actually been strengthened by the arrival of exiles and refugees from elsewhere in the region. Conceivably, Christians make up perhaps 10 percent of Syria's population.[17]

In light of these repeated catastrophes, it is impressive to see how significant these Christian communities would be to the life of the ever-more solidly Muslim Middle East. Although numerically they were a tattered remnant of ancient glories, Christians would on occasion emerge as cultural leaders within the Middle East, and seldom more so than in the twentieth century. Some of the best-known Arab writers were (and are) Christian, including the celebrated Khalil Gibran, author of *The Prophet*, wide-ranging thinker Edward Said, and contemporary novelist Elias Khoury. In politics too, as Arab countries struggled to respond to the dual challenges of modernization and Western domination, it was mainly Christian activists who created a ferment of ideas and policies, who initiated the various nationalist and socialist movements that swept the region in midcentury. Christians founded the Arab nationalist Ba'ath movement that still rules Syria, as well as other nationalist groups such as the Syrian Social Nationalist movement. In Syria in the 1990s, five of the seven closest advisers of the late President Hafez al-Assad were Christians, and Christian influence remains disproportionately strong under his son and successor. Christians led the Arab Communist parties, which have always had their strongest support in the Christian areas of countries such as Palestine and Iraq.[18]

Christians also founded and led many of the most militant groups in the Palestinian nationalist cause, at least before the *intifada* of the late 1980s. Across the socialist and nationalist spectrum, we regularly find Arab leaders bearing such characteristically Christian names as Michael, Anthony, and George. For many years, for instance, George Habash remained the soul of the militant Palestinian resistance against Israel. Arab Christians remained politically powerful until the rise of a new Muslim fundamentalism in the 1980s and the growth of Islamist sects such as *Hamas*.

Except for Egypt and Syria, then, the Middle East has lost its ancient multireligious character over the past century—but the change is only that recent. From the seventh century through the twentieth, much of the Christian story took place in the lands of the Middle East, where it was at best sporadically observed by Western eyes.

RUIN

We have seen that Christian communities would long be influential minorities across the Middle East, but just how did their position so deteriorate that they slid into minority status? If they survived the initial Muslim conquests so well, when did Christians lose their once-overwhelming position in such ancient homelands as Egypt, Syria, and Iraq? The answer must be sought in political events of the later Middle Ages, when interfaith relations were transformed swiftly, and horribly. The change was heralded promisingly enough in the early thirteenth century when rumors told how Prester John's forces were on the march, and were on their way to assist the West against the Muslims. Great military forces were indeed operating in Asia, but they were in fact the Mongol hordes, the first of a wave of invasions that over the next two hundred years would devastate most of the centers of civilization in the Middle East. In the process, some of the most ancient Christian communities would be eliminated. The ruin of Mesopotamia in the 1250s was a catastrophe for Christians no less than Muslims.

Yet Christians could still take hope from these events. Middle Eastern Christians initially saw the Mongol invaders as potential liberators from the Muslim yoke, and they took the opportunity to revenge themselves on their Muslim conquerors. The Mongol king who sacked Baghdad in 1258 had a Christian queen, and at her behest, the Mongols destroyed many mosques. There were many prominent converts at the Mongol court, due in large measure to Nestorian efforts, and it was quite feasible that the whole nation could be converted. Seeing glorious prospects, Western Crusaders allied with these Asian invaders. Christian hopes culminated during the Mongol invasion of Palestine in 1260, which was led by a Christian Turkish warlord. This campaign ended though with the battle of 'Ayn Jalut, where the Muslim Mamluk Turks won decisively. 'Ayn Jalut has escaped the attention of those counterfactual historians who like to ask "what if?" and who imagine alternate scenarios. Had the Mongols won, their victory could well have consolidated Christian power across much of Asia, virtually destroying Islam in the process.

In reality, it was the Christians who suffered ruin. The Mongols were driven out, and the last Crusader states perished shortly afterward. When the Mamluk sultan Baybars took Antioch in 1268, he wrote triumphantly to its Christian ruler that, had he not escaped, "You would have seen the crosses in your churches smashed, the pages of false Testaments scattered, the patriarchs' tombs overturned. You would have seen your Muslim enemy trampling over the place where you celebrate Mass, cutting the throats of monks, priests and deacons upon the altars, bringing sudden death to the patriarchs, and slavery to the royal princes." Seeing the wave of Muslim victories, the Mongols came to believe that it was the God of Islam who was favoring his worshippers, and they accepted conversion. Meanwhile, the remaining Middle Eastern Christians found their situation dreadfully changed, as they were persecuted as quislings for their actions during the Mongol onslaught.[19]

Conditions grew still worse for Christians in the early fourteenth century, when Asia was struck repeatedly by plague and a general population contraction. Climate change contributed mightily to the general catastrophe. As global cooling shortened growing seasons and restricted trade routes, populations contracted and famine raged. The cumulative disasters resulted in the rise of new regimes, which tended to be intolerant and inward-looking. While European Christians blamed Jews for the disasters of the age, Muslim governments turned against Christians, who suffered repeated pogroms and forced mass conversions. In China, too, Christians were associated with the Mongol regime and fell victim to a nationalist reaction when the Ming dynasty came to power in 1368. This movement was disastrous for Christian communities, who at their height may have been several hundred thousand strong, counting both Nestorians and Roman Catholics. In the early fifteenth century, the bloody career of Timur (Tamerlane) uprooted Christian societies across Eurasia, marking the end of the Nestorian adventure.

By the sixteenth century, there is no evidence for any organized Christian activity in China and precious few remnants of the faith anywhere in Central Asia. Table 2.1 indicates the catastrophic decline of Christian populations across "ingratefull Asia" between 1350 and 1500. In Africa also, Christianity stood in deep peril. The Christian state of Nubia succumbed to Muslim pressure around 1450, and Ethiopia itself was almost wiped out in a deadly jihad in the early sixteenth century, "a systematic campaign of cultural and national genocide." Although the church and kingdom survived, Ethiopian culture was devastated.[20]

Even in Europe, the late Middle Ages witnessed a steep decline in Christian power in the face of Muslim expansion under the Ottoman Turks. Ever larger numbers of Christians found themselves under Muslim rule, and the trend did not begin to be reversed until the 1680s. This point deserves stressing in view of the modern image of a predatory Christian West ever seeking to expand its dominion over an unsuspecting world. In the seventeenth century, Muslim power was pressing hard on the frontiers of Germany, and Muslim pirates regularly raided the coasts of northern and western Europe, taking thousands of Christian slaves—perhaps a million through the whole era. When Martin Luther wanted to argue that faithful Christian communities should be able to choose their own clergy, he imagined a situation that seemed painfully likely to the Germans of his time: "If a little company of pious Christian laymen were taken prisoners and carried away to a desert and had not among them a priest consecrated by a bishop, and were there to agree to elect one of them...this man would as truly be a priest as if all the bishops and all the popes had consecrated him." Realistic Christians had to consider how they would maintain their faith if, as might well occur, they were carried off into Muslim servitude. Around 1700, the Moroccan royal court at Meknes was home to anywhere between 5,000 and 25,000 European Christian slaves at any given time.[21]

If we want to picture the lights of Christianity fading on an imaginary map of the world, with the Christian faith largely confined to Europe, then this is the era in which we should do so, a full thousand years after the fall of the Roman Empire in the West.

THE CATHOLIC MISSIONS

From about 1500, we can first glimpse the pattern of Christian expansion familiar from popular stereotypes, namely a religion borne by European warships and muskets to vulnerable natives in Africa or South America. Yet even then, these missions (if we can so dignify them) succeeded only to the extent that they created a religious structure that meshed with local cultures and beliefs. Even when carried by the armed force of European empires, the newly planted Christianity in Africa, Asia, and South America swiftly acquired local roots.

From about 1500, Spain and Portugal began a global expansion, ostensibly under the flag of Christianity. By the end of the sixteenth century, the Roman Catholic Church looked more like a genuinely global institution than at any time in its previous history, and far more so than during the time of the Roman Empire, which it had long outlived. Whereas the Romans merely dominated the Mediterranean world, the standards of Catholic Spain and Portugal were flying in Asia, Africa, and the Americas. By 1580 the Iberian powers had largely completed their conquest of the New World to their west, while soldiers and merchants were pushing eastward from Europe into the Indies. When the Spaniards established an imperial sea route from Mexico to Manila, the twin ventures were merging into a global strategy on a scale never before witnessed on the planet. This was the world's very first global empire, in contrast to the merely Eurasian ventures of the Persians, Romans, or Mongols. The popes supported Iberian missionary endeavors, above all in South America and the Philippines. In 1579, Manila became a diocese, a suffragan see of Mexico City. By 1595, Manila was an archdiocese in its own right, and over the next century the nation would be extensively Christianized. To put this chronology in context, Mexico, the Philippines, and the Kongo first received their Christianity only a century or so after the submission of Lithuania completed the conversion of Europe.[22]

In religious terms, the greatest long-term Catholic successes would be in Central and South America, where the conquered peoples accepted forms of Catholicism, heavily mixed with local beliefs. This particular expansion of Christianity remains one of the most controversial, since it was associated with a brutal conquistador regime at least as interested in winning treasure as in saving native souls. When challenged with his failure to convert and teach the natives of Peru, the conquistador Pizarro replied, frankly enough, that "I have not come for any such reasons; I have come to take away from them their gold." As far as we can reconstruct the voices of the native peoples, they saw the coming of Christian civilization as an undiluted disaster. One Mayan prophetic book records of the coming of the Spanish, "Here they arrived, with the true God, the true Lord, the cause of our misery." When the conquerors tried to destroy every written remnant of the ancient Meso-American civilization, all its literature and science no less than its religious materials, they were perpetrating one of the gravest crimes in the history of civilization. To understand the cultural impact, we would have to imagine foreign invaders deliberately annihilating European Christianity by seeking out and burning every copy of the Christian gospels. Burning a Bible might be shocking enough, but imagine being present at the destruction of what one knew to be the very last extant copy of the Gospel of John. Even natives friendly to the conquistadors wept bitterly when they saw what had become of their ancient documents.[23]

It is a mild defense to say that at least some the worst charges about the conquest are false. Twentieth-century scholars produced vastly inflated estimates of the pre-Columbian native population, which implied that the European contact had caused one of the worst acts of genocide in human history. More realistic population figures show that while the new Catholic world was initially founded upon conquest and exploitation, the "American genocide" charges are no more than a contemporary academic myth. Yet the new Christianity was unquestionably associated with robbery and tyranny, leaving a sinister heritage over the coming centuries.[24]

In formal terms, the conversion of Central and South America was steady and impressive. As early as the 1520s there were eight bishoprics in the Antilles, and the earliest sees were appearing in Mexico itself. By the 1570s the continent had an extensive network of bishoprics looking to metropolitan sees at Mexico City and Lima, and Lima was ruling congregations spread over what would later be the nations of Peru, Ecuador, Bolivia, and Chile. Natives were baptized in vast numbers, on occasion running to thousands in a single day. Some religious orders, especially Dominicans and Jesuits, struggled heroically to prevent natives being exploited by greedy European colonists.[25]

Yet at least in the initial decades, the depth of these conversions was questionable. For the first century or two after the conquest, the church made little effort to educate or evangelize, once native peoples had given formal assent to the faith. This severely limited penetration outside the cities and provincial towns. Moreover, native converts were granted admission to communion only on the rarest occasions, a policy that acknowledged the shallowness of conversions. Just as seriously, natives were almost never ordained to the priesthood. Learned councils reserved ordination for purebred Europeans, who were untainted by Indian or African blood. This excluded not just Indians but also the growing population of mixed-blood *mestizos*. Papal instructions tried to overrule these prohibitions, but in practice they were not entirely lifted until the end of the eighteenth century. We also know that many of the old pagan practices survived surreptitiously. Pope John Paul II canonized the so-called Martyrs of Cajonos, two Mexican natives who exposed the fact that many in their community were secretly worshipping the harvest god Huitzilopochtli and who were lynched for their deed. The martyrdom occurred in 1700, 180 years after the conquest.[26]

Far from being a formula for effective conversion, the record of colonial Latin America sounds potentially like a story of disaster, so much so that it is baffling that Catholicism would ultimately plant such deep roots in this continent. Yet gradually, Catholic clergy succeeded in adapting the liturgy and sacraments to the native worldview and its customs, in a highly successful act of inculturation. Complementing this movement, the ordinary people who were so often ignored and despised by the churches created their own religious synthesis, which became the focus of devoted loyalty. Lacking priests and access to some church sacraments, Latin American people concentrated instead on aspects of the faith that needed no clergy, on devotions to saints and the Virgin, and they organized worship through lay bodies such as the confraternities, the *cofradías*. These practices flourished in the magnificent churches built by the conquerors at once to inspire and overawe their subjects. As a result, Catholicism not only established itself, but became an integral part of the cultural identity of Latin Americans, in all parts of that very diverse landscape. As an institution, the impact made by the church was partial and often inadequate, but Christianity itself flourished. It is a distinction we will often note.[27]

BEYOND THE BORDERS

It is easy to see the Catholic expansion efforts in terms of imperial arrogance, of imposing European standards upon the rest of the globe, but in many cases, the missionaries found themselves in no position to enforce their will politically. Catholic missionaries also sought converts beyond the immediate reach of the European empires, in lands where they could not call on fleets and armies to protect them. Naturally, the Christianity of these other regions developed very differently from that of Peru or the Philippines.

Portuguese Catholics introduced Christianity into the territories they dominated along the western coast of Africa, but in most areas European control was confined to trading and military centers. Yet missionaries also penetrated into independent kingdoms inland, as in Angola. In the powerful realm of Kongo, a king was baptized in 1491. Observers over the next two centuries remarked on how widely the people of Kongo and Ndongo knew and accepted Catholic Christianity, at least as thoroughly as their South American counterparts. This was no mere conversion for convenience, for the purpose of securing European guns and gold. One of the first Christian Kongo rulers, Mvemba Nzinga, has been described as "one of the greatest lay Christians in African church history." In 1516 a Portuguese priest wrote of Kongo's king Afonso that "Better than we, he knows the prophets and the Gospel of our Lord Jesus Christ, and all the lives of the saints, and all things regarding our Mother the Holy Church." In the sixteenth century, a Kongo monarch received the papal title "Defender of the Faith," which had hitherto been bestowed on England's Henry VIII a few years earlier. Unlike Henry's family, though, the Kongolese monarchy devotedly upheld the Catholic religion. In 1596 São Salvador became a diocese in its own right.[28]

During the next century, Christianity thoroughly penetrated the local society and thought-world, though without supplanting traditional African lifestyles. The kingdom was dominated by "a literate elite, dressing partially in European clothes, and professing Catholicism." Native kings and dukes bore such names as Andrew, Peter, John, and Alfonso, and the state capital was named São Salvador, for the Holy Savior. Kongolese artists and metal-workers created miracles of native Christian art, making crucifixes and images in wholly traditional African style. By 1700 Kongolese Catholicism was already in its sixth generation. This story would have an intriguing American aspect. Most accounts of American history give special place to the moment in 1619 when two ships arrived in English Virginia and sold "twenty and odd Negroes," the first known victims of the Anglo-American slavery system. Only in the last decade or so, though, have we discovered who these unfortunates were. Originally part of the cargo of a Portuguese slave ship en route to Mexico, these slaves suffered a new abduction at the hands of the English pirates who brought them to Virginia. These "twenty and odd" slaves were natives of Ndongo or Kongo, and they must have been baptized Catholic Christians. At least some African Americans today can trace some descent from this pioneering form of indigenous African Christianity.[29]

THE SILK STRATEGY

Catholic missionaries became particularly creative when they encountered the unfamiliar social environments of China, Japan, and the Indian states. Lacking imperial backing, the missionaries (above all, the Jesuits) had to insinuate themselves into local societies, and in so doing they had to deal with many of the later dilemmas about adapting the traditions of a European church to a non-European reality. Christian leaders were forced to redefine the relationship between Christianity and Europeanness, and to ask whether accepting the faith implied a need to take on board the assorted cultural baggage. How far should strict ideals of orthodoxy be sacrificed in pursuit of a successful missionary strategy? And how many of the church's accepted practices were in reality reflections of European custom and prejudice, rather than essentials of the faith? Equally sensitive, then and now, was the matter of European political control. Time and again, missions collapsed when those being introduced to the new faith feared that they might be subjecting themselves to some kind of foreign imperial domination.

Issues of accommodating local customs and practices surfaced repeat-edly. In seventeenth-century India, the Jesuit Robert De Nobili succeeded by effectively posing as a Hindu guru, who instructed his disciples in the mysteries of Christianity. He wore local dress and respected the complex Indian caste system. This was indeed controversial because caste symbols implied a belief in reincarnation and former lives. Also, acknowledging caste meant refusing to treat the poorest on terms of equality, violating the teachings of Jesus—an issue that is still desperately contentious for Indian Christians today. Still, this represented a successful missionary strategy, and perhaps the only one that could have worked in the setting of the time. Illustrating the potential of religious harmony and interaction, the great Muslim rulers of India's Mughal empire were at this very time deeply devoted to the figures of Jesus and Mary, and their court artists drew heavily on European styles in depicting them. In the 1580s the Mughal emperor Akbar welcomed Portuguese Jesuits, to the point of prostrating himself before the Christmas crèche they were allowed to erect in his palace.[30]

For future missionaries, the lesson was obvious. Adapting the gospel to local cultures was the path to growth, while trying to force Asians or Africans into a Western straitjacket invited disaster. The enlightened Jesuit position was that as long as converts accepted Catholic Christianity, it could certainly be Catholicism of a Chinese, Indian, or Japanese variety, just as Europe had its French and Spanish species of the common truth.

A similar cultural dilemma arose in Japan over the seemingly trivial issue of preference in dress: should Christian priests wear silk or cotton? If cotton, missionaries were identifying with the poorest and most despised, following appropriate rules of Christian humility, but priests dressed thus would not be welcomed into the homes of the upper classes. If they chose silk—as they ultimately did—this identified them as members of the social elite, who could win the respect of lords and gentry. The silk strategy worked splendidly in gaining the adherence of Japanese elites, who would in turn order the conversion of their followers and tenants. For some decades, success followed success, so that by about 1600 it seemed that Japan would soon be a Catholic nation. Nagasaki became a bishopric in 1596, and the first ordinations of Japanese priests followed in 1601. Hundreds of thousands of Japanese were baptized.[31]

Disastrously, though, the extent of Catholic successes provoked a nationalist reaction. Hostility was all the more intense when the Japanese heard some European Catholics talk wildly of turning the nation into a Spanish colony as subservient as the Philippines. Catholic hopes of mass conversion were dashed by a severe persecution, which claimed thousands of lives. Japan's Catholic Century, which began so auspiciously in the 1540s, ended in blood and chaos. The story is familiar from the novels of Shusaku Endo, one of the greatest Christian authors of the past century. Japanese Catholicism survived clandestinely into the twentieth century, when its vestiges received a far greater blow than could have been inflicted by all the native regimes. In 1945 the second atomic bomb used against Japan destroyed the city of Nagasaki, the country's great Catholic stronghold.

Despite the Japanese debacle, Catholics found that another door opened promptly as Jesuit missions began to achieve stunning successes in China, then as now the world's most populous nation. Here too, Catholics followed the silk approach, presenting themselves in the familiar garb of scholars, and converting nobles and intellectuals. They offered prospective converts whatever Western learning might be of interest to the sophisticated Chinese civilization. The pivotal figure in the missions was the celebrated Matteo Ricci, who arrived in China in 1589. The Jesuit venture survived the collapse of the Ming regime in 1644 and won at least equal favor from the succeeding Manchu dynasty.[32]

Jesuits were very sensitive to issues of cultural adaptation and spurned attempts to impose European values. From the first, the missionaries tried to transform Christianity into a form that would be comprehensible and relevant to the Chinese, just as the Nestorians had done nine centuries earlier. The liturgy and scriptures were translated into Chinese, which meant choosing one of several possible Chinese terms for God. In the event the sixteenth-century missionaries chose *T'ien*, a term familiar in Chinese philosophy, and usually translated as "heaven"; they addressed God as *Shang-ti*, Lord of Heaven. The Jesuits took a relaxed attitude to deep-rooted Chinese customs and practices, preferring to absorb peacefully anything not flagrantly contrary to Christian teaching. The missionaries were supported by the Vatican and its *Propaganda* office, which in 1659 asked, perceptively, "What could be more absurd than to transport France, Spain, Italy or some other European country to China? Do not introduce all that to them but only the Faith. It is the nature of men to love and treasure above everything else their own country and that which belongs to it. In consequence, there is no stronger cause for alienation and hate than an attack on local customs, especially when these go back to a venerable antiquity."[33] This principle meant respecting the Chinese veneration for ancestors and the philosophy of Confucius. If European aristocrats lavished such wealth on creating sumptuous family tombs within the churches, why should Chinese gentlemen not pay due respects to their illustrious forebears?

The late seventeenth century was a glorious time for the Chinese missions, and in 1692, Christians earned an edict of toleration from the ruling emperor Kang Xi. The prospects were intoxicating: Kang Xi was arguably the world's most powerful sovereign at that time: he ruled perhaps 150 million subjects, a population equivalent to that of the whole of Europe, including Russia. Historically minded Catholics recalled that the conversion of the Roman empire had also begun with such an edict of toleration from a friendly emperor. Yesterday Rome; tomorrow China? Winning many converts, the missionaries advanced Chinese clergy, and Luo Wenzao, the first Catholic bishop of Chinese origin, was consecrated in 1685. By 1700 China had around 200,000 Catholics, a small fraction of the whole, but many were well-placed politically.

The Catholic missions in China can be regarded as one of the great might-have-beens in world history. If China had been converted in the seventeenth century, the impact on the future history of Christianity would have been incalculable, as would the effects on the religious balance in Europe itself. And a converted China would have provided a cultural beacon for Japan, Korea, Vietnam, and ultimately the whole of Asia. But of course, it was not to be.

The Jesuit cultural compromise fell apart at the end of the seventeenth century, when the Society's enemies succeeded in turning the popes against them. Within a few years, Jesuits came under repeated attack for permitting the Chinese to worship ancestors, for canonizing Saint Confucius, and including the names of pagan gods in the translated scriptures. By 1704 the Vatican ruled decisively against the Society of Jesus, prohibiting the Chinese Rites and ordering the suppression of recent Bible translations. Henceforth, religious services were to be held strictly in Latin. Worse, the papal envoys who declared the new regulations also made high claims for the political role of the Vatican, a foreign presence that could not be tolerated by the Chinese emperors. As the emperor understood, prophetically, "I know that at the present time there is nothing to fear, but when your ships come by thousands, then there will probably be great disorder." In 1724 the Chinese government responded to these accumulated insults by proscribing the Christian faith. The edict asked, "How can we expect foreigners to understand the Chinese culture? None of them really understands the Chinese language in the first place. Their words and philosophy are often laughable. Their preaching is similar to Buddhism, Taoism and other cults. Thus there is no need for these foreigners to preach to us. Consequently, we can ban this altogether."[34] As the Catholic Church became ostentatiously a foreign body, it invited persecution on a scale that eliminated most of the Jesuits' successes by the end of the eighteenth century.

The effects of the new policy were not confined to China. In the same years, the church began to insist on similar conformity among the Catholic

Christians of India, and the effects here were almost as severe. From about 1700 too, the Kongolese church began a long period of decline, which represents one of the greatest wasted opportunities in the story of African Christianity. Political fragmentation in the Kongo state was partly to blame, but much more significant was the church's refusal to approve native liturgies, and its reluctance to ordain African clergy. Nor was the Vatican willing to grant other key concessions to African values, including a married clergy, although this model was accepted elsewhere, in parts of Eastern Europe and the Middle East. The Chinese Rites fiasco, and the cultural rigidity it symbolized, crippled the progress of Catholic missions worldwide for more than a century.

THE GREAT CENTURY

Up to the end of the eighteenth century, large-scale missionary efforts were strictly the preserve of the Catholic powers, a point of superiority proudly stressed by Catholic controversialists. How could the upstart Protestants claim to be a true church since they self-evidently neglected Jesus's command to preach the gospel to all nations?

In fact, Protestant missionary endeavors were making significant advances from about 1700. In 1698, the Society for Promoting Christian Knowledge was founded in England, while the Society for the Propagation of the Gospel in Foreign Parts followed in 1701. At this stage, though, the Protestant movement was strictly limited, not least because British authorities were reluctant to have controversial Christian proselytizing disrupt their highly profitable ventures in India and elsewhere. It was left to the Danes to begin a significant Protestant mission in their Indian colony at Tranquebar, where two Pietist clerics were dispatched in 1705, and where they began translating the scriptures into Tamil. In retrospect, we note the coincidence of date, just a year after the Vatican made its fateful decision in the Chinese Rites affair.[35]

The great age of Protestant missions effectively began in the 1790s, partly as a consequence of the evangelical revival, and partly due to the unprecedented power and reach of the British Empire. Protestants, particularly from the British Isles, now entered the missionary movement in earnest. In the space of a decade, global missions acquired the kind of enthusiastic backing that they would retain through the colonial era. In 1792 modern missionary work began with the formation of London's Baptist Missionary Society, a venture that was soon challenged by the

London Missionary Society (Congregationalist, 1795) and the Anglican-sponsored Church Mission Society (1799). The new United States shared in the missionary excitement, with its own newly founded missionary Boards and Societies.[36]

Missions now became a major focus for Protestant activists. In 1793 William Carey began his passionate campaign to convert India, under the famous slogan that would inspire countless successors: "Expect great things from God, and attempt great things for God." China, too, attracted the rapt attention of European evangelicals. By 1807 the first Protestant missionary had set up shop in Canton. Africa likewise attracted fervent interest, partly due to the greatly enhanced knowledge of the continent's geography. In 1799 Mungo Park's *Travels in the Interior Districts of Africa* alerted European Protestants to the vast mission field waiting for harvest in the western parts of the continent. Also, new political footholds now developed. Colonies for freed slaves were created—at Sierra Leone in 1787 and Liberia in 1821—and in each case, the new settlers had had extensive first-hand contact with Christianity. When the British established themselves at the Cape of Good Hope in 1806, Protestant mission work began in earnest across southern Africa.[37]

These events began what is justifiably regarded as the great missionary century. As we have seen though, this was quite different from the sudden Christian expansion so often portrayed in modern accounts of European imperialism. In many cases, as in India, China, and large parts of Africa, Christian missionaries were not so much breaking new ground as reopening ancient and quite familiar mines. In the 1880s missionaries in the Kongo met with mass enthusiasm that would be difficult to explain if we did not realize that the people were rediscovering what had been the national religion only a century or so earlier. The response of those peoples was not "Thank you for bringing us this startling new message" but rather "Welcome back." White Christians were treading where African and Asian believers had been before, and where they had left deep marks in local cultures. Their ghosts still walked.[38]

Undeniably, the Christian missions of this new historical phase were intimately connected with political and imperial adventures, and Protestant and Catholic fortunes followed the successes of the different empires. Protestant expansion across Africa neatly followed the spreading rule of the Union Jack, while the French led the way for the Catholic cause in both Africa and Asia. The linkage between religion and empire is neatly epitomized by the experience of southern Uganda, where Catholics were colloquially known as *baFaransa* ("the French") and Protestants were *baIngerezza* ("the British"). Both British and French colonial authorities combined missionary endeavors with struggles against African slavery, so that imperial power was justified by both religious and humanitarian activities.[39]

By the mid-nineteenth century, the missionary impulse reached new heights as most of the African continent came within European reach, and the military defeat of China opened that country to new activity. Hudson Taylor, legendary missionary to China, popularized the term "the Great Commission" to describe Christ's command in the Gospel of Matthew to carry the gospel to all nations. In 1858 a new generation of prospective missionaries was inspired by the appearance of David Livingstone's book *Missionary Travels and Researches in South Africa*. Many of the legendary missionaries of this era began their career in midcentury, while whole new areas of Africa were opened in the 1870s by the establishment of missions around Lake Malawi and in Uganda.[40]

Catholic evangelism also flourished, institutionalized in new orders such as the Holy Ghost Fathers (Spiritans) and the White Fathers. The French even tried to evangelize in the Muslim world, and a bishopric was created at Algiers in 1838. It was an archbishop of Algiers, Cardinal Charles Lavigerie (1825–1892) who probably had the most systematic vision of a concerted imperial campaign to convert the whole of Africa. For Lavigerie, Christianity was resuming its ancient dominance in Africa, in which the Muslim age had been merely an unhappy interval, a thousand-year night that was now ending. Reinforcing this claim to ancient continuity, the pope gave him the title of archbishop of Carthage, and Primate of Africa. Lavigerie dreamed of a kind of modern-day crusading order, a well-armed *militia Christi* that would wander Africa defending pilgrims and suppressing slave-traders.[41]

In later decades, these Anglo-French successes attracted jealous imitators. Across Africa, each new entrant into the imperial stakes sought to justify its existence by the rhetoric of missionary endeavor: Germans, Italians, Belgians, all were ostensibly there to convert the poor heathen. Elsewhere in the world, American Christians in particular saw their destiny in China. By the 1920s, at the height of the Euro-American adventure in China, perhaps eight thousand Western missionaries were active in that country. Americans claimed their nation had a special role in the divine plan. In 1893 a World Parliament of Religions that met in Chicago proclaimed the triumph of Christianity in its liberal, Protestant, and quintessentially American form. In this view, the age to come would be the American century, and also, inevitably, the Christian century (the magazine of that name was founded in 1902). If anyone doubted the truth of this vision, they would be reassured by the vast achievements of American missionaries throughout Africa and Asia, and especially in China. By the 1950s the United States would be supplying two-thirds of the 43,000 Protestant missionaries active around the world.[42]

ESTABLISHED IN THE SOIL

For all the hypocrisy and the self-serving rhetoric of the imperial age, the dedication of the missionaries was beyond question. Knowing as they did the extreme dangers from violence and tropical disease, it is inconceivable that so many would have been prepared to lay down their lives for European commerce alone, and many certainly viewed missionary work as a ticket to martyrdom. Both their numbers and their zeal grew mightily after each successive revival in the West, especially when such an event coincided with a spectacular tale of exploration and martyrdom.

Also, for all their association with imperialism, nineteenth-century missionaries did make important concessions to native cultures (as opposed to native religions). Crucially, Protestants from the beginning recognized the absolute necessity of offering the faith in local languages, so the Bible was now translated, in whole or in part, into many African and Asian tongues. In many ways, Protestant missionaries were just as shortsighted as the Catholics in their attitudes toward colonized peoples, but in the matter of language, Protestants had a clear advantage. Both Protestants and Catholics were often realistic about the cultural problems they faced in presenting a universal faith in a colonial European guise. In fact, they faced exactly the same debates that their predecessors had encountered over how far they should go native in order to win converts. Particularly when venturing into dangerous territories, the temptation was to rely on the protection of European bureaucrats and soldiers, but a Christianity established by those means was not likely to gain many converts. At its worst, this policy threatened to create a segregated veranda Christianity, in which paternalistic clergy literally refused to admit native converts into their European houses. Farsighted evangelists recognized this peril. The founder of the Holy Ghost Fathers warned trainee missionaries that "You are not going to Africa in order to establish there Italy or France or any such country.... Make yourselves Negroes with the Negroes.... Our holy religion has invariably to be established in the soil."[43]

On the same principle, some Protestant missionaries in China abandoned the European clothing and lifestyle that gave them protection and prestige but which separated them from ordinary people. One of the great Protestant movements of this period was the China Inland Missions (CIM), founded in 1865. Members wore Chinese dress and sported the pigtail or queue that symbolized submission to the imperial dynasty: they were to be "all things to all men." By 1900 the CIM was directing some 800 missionaries. In India too, Methodist missionary E. Stanley Jones claimed success in separating the gospel from its imperial connotations: "The Indian is making an amazing discovery, namely that Christianity and Jesus are not the same—that they may have Jesus without the system that has been built up around Him in the West."[44]

In their openness to native cultures, missionaries were sometimes far in advance of secular politicians. Imperialist statesmen were slow to imagine a future in which the colonized peoples might be emancipated to independence. Even in the 1950s, few British or French leaders thought they would live to see the end of direct European control of Africa. In contrast, at least some early missionaries happily accepted that their own contributions represented only a temporary phase. In the 1850s, Henry Venn of the Church Mission Society asserted that missions would give way to churches on the banks of the Niger or the Congo, just as they once had in the lands of the Rhine and the Thames. Venn spoke, unforgettably, of the coming "euthanasia of the mission." The transition would come through a Three Self policy, in which the church should be built on principles of self-government, self-support, and self-propagation. The result would be "a native church under native pastors and a native episcopate." Most English missionaries realized that, in Jeffrey Cox's words, "The Empire of Christ could never be identified with the Empire of Britain in the long run, for the Empire of Christ was a multiracial, multinational empire that not only transcended the provisional (if providential) boundaries of the British Empire, but transcended the boundaries of time itself."[45]

These visions became clouded during the years of highest imperialist fervor, when, drunk with sight of power, some church leaders were speaking of an indefinite period of global white supremacy. Even so, ideas of future native autonomy never vanished entirely. Because they were so thoroughly acquainted with the situation on the ground, missionary writers were often influential critics of colonial abuses, and became prime sources for journalists and politicians seeking to expose those horrors. Without the work of at least some missionaries, Western anticolonial movements would never have emerged as robustly as they did.[46]

For any missionary venture, the ordination of native clergy must be the acid test of commitment to moving beyond an imperial context to leaving the veranda. In this regard, the churches of the Great Century offered a mixed picture. Some bodies recorded early successes. In 1765 the Church of England ordained Philip Quaque of the Gold Coast as its first African priest. A century later, in the 1860s, the same church chose the Yoruba Samuel Adjai Crowther as its first non-European bishop and deputed this learned "black Englishman" to found a missionary diocese in West Africa. Other churches followed suit in their respective territories, particularly the Protestant missions, and Chinese clergy were being ordained by the 1860s. Yet although the principle of native leadership was well established, it was not followed with any consistency. In 1914 the Roman Catholic Church worldwide had no bishops of non-Euro-American origin, except for a handful serving the Indian Thomas Christians in communion with Rome. In the whole of Africa, the Catholic Church ordained only a handful of native priests before 1920.[47]

Yet for all the uncertainties about native clergy, all the mixed messages about presenting Christianity in native terms, the successes were very striking. In 1800 perhaps 1 percent of all Protestant Christians lived outside Europe and North America. By 1900 that number had risen to 10 percent, and this proved enough of a critical mass to support further expansion. Today, the figure stands around two-thirds of all Protestants. Catholics also reaped their harvest. In 1914 the Catholic Church in Africa had 7 million baptized believers and an additional million catechumens: these figures doubled by 1938. Put another way, in the late nineteenth century, Africa had about 10 million Christians of all denominations, including the Copts, about 9 percent of the continental total. By 1950 that figure had risen to 34 million, or 15 percent; by 1965, there were 75 million Christians, a quarter of the whole. And though less spectacular, expansion in China nevertheless achieved more than in any previous age of Christian evangelization. Taking Protestants and Catholics together, China's Christian population stood at around 1.2 million in 1900, but 5 million or so by 1949.[48]

In 1910, some 1,200 representatives from a wide range of churches and missionary societies gathered in Edinburgh, Scotland, for the World Missionary Conference. This event represents the highwater mark of the Euro-American Protestant missionary movement. The conference took its theme from a phrase popularized by conference chair John R. Mott, and in the atmosphere of the time, the goal seemed realistic: "the evangelization of the world in this generation." But far from being an exercise in triumphalism, the conference heard speakers offer a sober and perceptive reckoning of both the strengths and the weaknesses of the missionary endeavor. While they had many advantages, missionaries had to tackle many different jobs around the globe. They must, above all, integrate preaching with a range of other approaches. They must offer Western-style education to prospective believers, while "medical work also constitutes a necessary factor in the great work of evangelizing the world." Literary work was also critical—not just translating scriptures, but creating local traditions of indigenous Christian literature. Moreover, few participants had any illusions about the huge obstacles facing missions in large sections of the world, where Christianity was so often associated with colonialism and Westernization. They understood just how difficult it would be to advance further in China or Japan, and above all, to spread the gospel among "fanatical Mohammedans." In its willingness to learn from a century of tumultuous experience, the Edinburgh Conference stands as an invaluable stocktaking of the state of Christianity as it faced an emerging world order.[49]

Most modern Europeans or Americans cringe at the claims their ancestors made about their "civilizing mission" to the rest of the world. Still, where the Victorian enthusiasts proved more right than they could have dreamed was in their belief that Christianity would indeed make enormous strides in the years to come. In most ways, the twentieth century was anything but a Christian century, since the tyrannies and warfare of those years made it look more like a new dark age than a golden age for any religion. Even so, Christianity would indeed enjoy worldwide success. To quote Stephen Neill, one of the great historians of the missionary movement, "in the twentieth century, for the first time, there was in the world a universal religion—the Christian religion."[50] In the third millennium, like the first, the faith would once again be a truly transcontinental phenomenon.

THREE

Missionaries and Prophets

If we had power enough to communicate ourselves to
Europe we would advise them not to call themselves
Christendom but Europeandom.
                              —*Charles Domingo, 1911*

I t is one thing to talk about missionary successes and numbers, but quite
another to determine the nature of the religious changes involved. The
act of joining a church or sect is not necessarily the same as the internal
process of conversion. While we can more or less measure the numbers
declaring themselves Christian, the inner dynamics of religious change do
not lend themselves to counting of any kind. Missions succeeded for different reasons in different times and places, and some new churches planted
much deeper roots than others.[1] Yet many of these churches enjoyed
remarkable success, to a degree that is impossible to understand if the new
Christians were responding only to fear or envy of the imperial conquerors.
Amazing as it may appear to a blasé West, Christianity exercises an overwhelming global appeal, which shows not the slightest sign of waning.

"THE FAITH OF EUROPE"

The runaway successes of Christian missions to Africa or Asia are all the
more striking in view of the extraordinarily poor image that such activities
possess in Western popular thought. For many contemporary observers,
the whole missionary enterprise epitomizes so much of what is wrong with

Western culture. At their worst, missions are presented as a cynical arm of ruthless, racist, colonial exploitation. American television's Arts and Entertainment network once showed a major documentary on the second millennium of Christianity, AD 1000–2000. In the segment on the sixteenth century, the narration recounted how "Europeans sail the world, and wherever they go, whatever they explore, they bring with them the faith of Europe—Christianity.…However, Christian explorers bring more than just their faith. They also bring a profound sense of cultural superiority, and a lust for wealth." By the nineteenth century, "the missions became inseparable from the expanding western empires and their seemingly insatiable desire for profit."[2]

Plenty of modern observers share this view. Kenyan leader Jomo Kenyatta complained that "When the missionaries came to Africa they had the Bible and we had the land. They said 'Let us pray.' We closed our eyes. When we opened them we had the Bible and they had the land." (The remark has been quoted by Archbishop Desmond Tutu, who is usually assumed to have originated it.) The Gikuyu people in Kenya had a saying that states, "There is no difference between missionary and settler." Ngugi wa Thiong'o describes the missions as part of the imperialist project: they

> Held the Bible in the left hand,
> And the gun in the right hand.
> The white man wanted us
> To be drunk with religion
> While he,
> In the meantime,
> Was mapping and grabbing our land
> And starting factories and businesses
> On our sweat.[3]

Chinua Achebe agreed that Christianity was part of the larger package of colonial intrusion. As one of Achebe's characters remarks, "The white man, the new religion, the soldiers, the new road—they are all part of the same thing." Achebe's books often play on the idea of "whiteness," which in traditional African thought was an inauspicious color, connected with leprosy: "But now Ezeulu was becoming afraid that the new religion was like a leper. Allow him a handshake and he wants an embrace."[4]

As European colonial empires were collapsing in the mid-twentieth century, it was fashionable for Third World writers to dismiss the Christian venture solely as misguided imperialism, and to argue that the effects were barely skin deep. Christianity, it seemed, could make little impact on

African social and especially sexual mores. To quote the disillusioned narrator of Mongo Beti's classic novel of colonial religion, *The Poor Christ of Bomba*, "I'm beginning to wonder myself whether the Christian religion really suits us, whether it's really made to the measure of the Blacks." In her scathing account of Western cultural imperialism, *Almanac of the Dead*, Native American novelist Leslie Marmon Silko writes that "The Europeans...had gone through the motions with their priests, holy water, and churches built with Indian slave labor. But their God had not accompanied them. The white man had sprinkled holy water and had prayed for almost five hundred years in the Americas, and still the Christian God was absent." Many Westerners sympathize with these views, seeking missionary Christianity as a kind of cultural leprosy. As journalist Nicholas Kristof remarks, "Mention the words 'evangelical missionary,' and many Americans conjure up an image of redneck zealots forcing starving children to be baptized before they get a few crusts of bread." Challenging such stereotypes, Kristof himself has written positively of the missionary presence in contemporary Africa.[5]

At best, in the suspicious modern view, the missionary impulse manifested ignorant paternalism. Discussion of missions today is all too likely to produce lame sexual jokes about "the missionary position," a phrase that raises powerful if unjust images about the whole endeavor. The phrase conjures a whole mythology, of repressed young Victorians attempting to spread their corrosive moral and sexual notions among a more liberated native population, who do not need such Western inhibitions, and would only be harmed by them. For a modern secular audience, the notion that the missionary enterprise might involve any authentically religious content, or might in fact be welcomed, seems ludicrous.[6]

Of course, it is not long since that missionaries attracted deep respect, and even veneration: recall the heroic accounts of Dr. Livingstone. Twentieth-century stories in this tradition included *The Inn of the Sixth Happiness* (1958) and the fictional portrait of the China missionary played by Gregory Peck in the classic 1944 film *The Keys of the Kingdom*. In stark contrast to these works, we think of the many negative depictions of missionaries in later film and fiction, in *Hawaii* (1966), *Black Robe* (1991), or *At Play in the Fields of the Lord* (1991). Such recent works all offer a broadly similar view of the missionary enterprise. Above all, missions are wrongheaded, since all religious traditions are of roughly equal value, so what is the point of visiting the prejudices of one culture upon another? The vision of perfect relativism breaks down somewhat when Western Christianity is concerned, since it is seen as ipso facto a less valid and desirable model than those which it is seeking to replace. Commonly, Christianity is less an authentic religion than a package of Western prejudices and inhibitions. In Barbara Kingsolver's successful novel *The Poisonwood Bible* (1998), a missionary girl in the Belgian Congo recollects how "We came from Bethlehem, Georgia, bearing Betty Crocker cake mixes into the jungle." Like the rest of her family, she is in Africa solely to humor her fanatical preacher father.[7]

Western attempts to export their own cultural sickness are all too obvious in matters of sexuality. In *Black Robe*, a young French Jesuit struggles with massive temptation after watching the frank sexual activities of the Native Canadian people he is trying to convert. When the missionary's daughter of *The Poisonwood Bible* arrives in the Congo, she is appalled by the overt sexuality she finds. African women sing joyous hymns of welcome, "with their bosoms naked as a jaybird's egg...all bare-chested and unashamed....Am I the only one getting shocked to smithereens here?" Her father denounces "Nakedness and darkness of the soul! For we shall destroy this place where the loud clamor of the sinners is waxen great before the face of the Lord."[8] In these fictional works, this latter-day Dark Legend, the missionaries are so obsessed with their losing battles against temptation that they float on the edge of insanity. In *At Play in the Fields of the Lord*, the religious fanaticism and sexual repression of a woman missionary bring her to psychic collapse. Missionaries, we see, bring a gospel of shame and hypocrisy.

Recently, a British author teaching in China recorded his horror at discovering that Western missionaries had introduced dozens of Christian-oriented books into a local school. Worse, his students' journals showed that these works had had a powerful effect in drawing many Chinese to Christianity. Appalled, he burned the books. He sternly upbraided the local missionaries: "What is it I object to? The Christian faith? Not per se. It's more the arrogance of coming into another culture, one with its own existing traditions, imagining that you have so much to teach instead of learn, and furthermore, the deceit, getting people when they're down, giving them false hope, taking spiritual advantage of them."[9]

Hostility to missionary activities is almost as intense within the churches themselves, or at least most of the liberal mainstream bodies. Whereas successful missions were once considered the richest ornament of an American or European church, the whole endeavor had become deeply suspect by the 1960s, the years of fastest decolonization. By 1970, African churches in particular were calling for a moratorium on Western missions because they stunted the growth of local initiatives. The equation seemed clear: missions were an arm of colonialism, and once the colonial governments were withdrawn, so also should their religious manifestations. Mainline U.S. churches such as the Lutheran and Episcopal severely pruned their funds for missionary work, preferring to spend money on social programs at home. The change of mood was obvious during the 2010 centennial commemorations of the great World Missionary Conference. At Fuller Theological Seminary, Dean C. Douglas McConnell remarked that "At Edinburgh [in 1910], people thought they were going to take over the world. And now many of our students wonder if they should even try."[10]

SOMETHING FELT IN THE MARROW

If the modern missionary stereotype had any force, we can scarcely understand why the Christian expansion proceeded as fast as it did, or how it could have survived the end of European political power. There must have been a great deal more to global South Christianity than the European-driven mission movement. In some cases, the appeal of Christianity might indeed have been linked to a desire to emulate the West. Christianity was inextricably bound up with the all-conquering imperial nations, and thus with an image of success and modernity. This appealed to local elites, who could begin the conversion of their societies from the top down. Around the world, even cultures that rejected the full religious package tried to absorb some aspects of Christianity as part of a wider effort to modernize, and thus better to compete with the West. Nineteenth-century Hinduism was revolutionized by reform movements that explicitly borrowed from Christian thought, practice, and worship styles.[11]

But emulation cannot be the whole answer. If the faith had been a matter of kings, merchants, and missionaries, then it would have lasted precisely as long as the political and commercial order that gave it birth, and would have been swept away by any social change. In many instances, though, Christianity grew as a grassroots movement, appealing to a rich diversity of groups. In some cases, this meant those on the margins of traditional societies. In his nuanced account of the conversion of the Igbo people of eastern Nigeria, Chinua Achebe describes how the faith gained its initial successes among the marginalized: "None of the converts was a man whose word was heeded in the assembly of the people. None of them was a man of title. They were mostly the kind of people that were called *efulefu*, worthless, empty, men.... Chielo, the priestess of Agbala, called the converts the excrement of the clan, and the new faith was a mad dog that had come to eat it up." Gradually, though, an increasing number of converts are drawn in from major families. (Today, the Igbo are overwhelmingly Christian.)[12]

In its early days, African Christianity was conspicuously a youth movement, a token of vigor and fresh thinking. Commonly, the key African converts were the younger members of society, teenagers and young adults, the ones most likely to travel to cities, ports, or trading posts during this first great age of globalization between about 1870 and 1914. These were the migrants, laborers, traders, and soldiers. In these border communities, they encountered the Christian faith that they subsequently brought home to their villages. Whatever the initial audience, what made Christianity succeed was the networking effect, as the word was passed from individual to individual, family to family, village to village. In their epic survey of African Christianity, Sundkler and Steed repeatedly stress the role of African converts themselves in passing on what they had received: "The new convert did not keep the discovery for individual consumption but took the message to others.... Thus it was that the message could spread as rings on the water."[13]

These native converts were the indispensable pillars of the spreading network of missionary organizations. Although popular accounts portrayed the missionary in Africa or elsewhere as a dauntless white man, native staff made up a sizable majority of the mission agencies (not to mention the fact that many of the missionaries themselves were, of course, women). Besides lacking popular recognition, these local activists were commonly denied formal positions or prestige, and were at best granted titles such as lay catechist, but the missions could not have succeeded without them. One celebrated African martyr was catechist Bernard Mizeki, who epitomizes the restless young convert of this era. When he was about twelve, he migrated from Portuguese East Africa to Cape Town, where he became a Christian in his early twenties. Working with an Anglican mission agency, he then founded a mission base in what is now Zimbabwe, until his murder in 1896. Dana Robert neatly pairs his life story with that of Ireland's St. Patrick, and perhaps in future years, the two will be equally renowned in the history of Christianity.[14]

The fact that women played such a significant role in spreading the new faith left a lasting imprint on emerging Christianities. Women missionaries often combined their evangelizing message with a wide-ranging concern about the education, health, and social role of their new women converts, a concern that might have a condescending tone, but which transformed colonized societies. As native churches developed, women leaders explored and adapted Christian doctrine in their own terms, assisted by the formation of different organizations, including the influential Mothers' Unions. As we will see, in modern times, global Christianity is inconceivable except in terms of the role played by women, as spiritual leaders and prophets, as hymn writers and key converts. From a great many examples, we might choose Agnes Okoh, a poor Nigerian widow, who in 1943 believed she had received a prophetic call. Returning from market one day, she heard a voice announcing "Matthew Ten." A friend read her the gospel passage, which begins "And when he had called unto him his twelve disciples, he gave them power against unclean spirits, to cast them out, and to heal all manner of sickness and all manner of disease." By 1947, she had begun a career as a preacher and claimed powers of healing and prophecy. Today, a denomination of some 850 congregations follows her inspiration, under the name Christ Holy Church International.[15]

We can suggest all sorts of reasons why Africans and Asians adopted Christianity, whether political, social, or cultural; but one all-too-obvious explanation is that individuals like Bernard Mizeki and Agnes Okoh came to believe the message offered and found this the best means of explaining the world around them. Achebe, again, describes the impact of the new preaching on one young Igbo man: "It was not the mad logic of the Trinity that captivated him. He did not understand it. It was the poetry of the new religion, something felt in the marrow.... He felt a relief within as the hymn poured into his parched soul. The words of the hymn were like the drops of frozen rain melting on the dry palate of the panting earth. Nwoye's callow mind was greatly puzzled."[16] For the fictional Nwoye, and for millions of his real-life counterparts, Christianity was accepted because it spoke to them, because they found it to be true. In Kenyatta's parable, quoted earlier, the African, not the European, ends up owning the Bible.

FAITH OF THE MARTYRS

Just how deeply, and how quickly, the new Christians appropriated the religion can be illustrated from the many stories of zeal in the face of persecution. In the Madagascar of the 1850s, thousands of Christians were "speared, smothered, starved or burned to death, poisoned, hurled from cliffs or boiled alive in rice pits."[17] In the British colony of Uganda, Anglicanism was established in 1877, and African clergy were being ordained by the 1890s. Also in this decade, Roman Catholic missionaries started making their own converts. From its earliest days, Ugandan

Christianity has produced its share of martyrs, whose stories demonstrate how firmly the faith has rooted itself in African soil. Some of the worst persecutions occurred in the kingdom of Buganda, which was later absorbed into the British colony. Christianity made rapid progress at the royal court, to the horror of the king. Among other things, he found that his Christian male courtiers now refused his sexual demands. He ordered his subjects to renounce the new faith upon pain of death, and hundreds of native Bugandans were executed in 1885 and 1886. On a single day, thirty-two Christians were burned alive. With such examples in mind, it was ludicrous to claim that the new religion was solely for white people, and the faith spread quickly in both Uganda and Madagascar. In the 1890s, Buganda experienced a mass conversion of astonishing speed. Today, perhaps 75 percent of Ugandans are Christian, as are 90 percent of the people of Madagascar.[18]

In terms of the number of victims, the bloodiest persecutions of these years occurred in Asia. During the nineteenth century, Christian missions were often associated with the aggressive power of colonial empires, which meant that they were believed to pose a threat to native regimes. Some of these were highly developed states in their own right, with the will and the means to defend themselves against suspect foreign influences. As a consequence, the great age of imperial expansion was a dreadful time for Christian believers unlucky enough to live beyond the protection of British gunships or French armies. One violent purge occurred in the native-ruled states of Indo-China during the mid- and late nineteenth century. The persecution claimed the lives of a hundred or so Catholic priests, but as in Africa, ordinary lay believers made up the vast majority of the victims— perhaps a hundred thousand in all. Korean Christianity was likewise born in blood, as that nation's Buddhist/Confucian regime killed some eight thousand Catholics. Thousands of Catholics perished during the nineteenth century, the savagery reaching its greatest ferocity during the 1860s and 1870. Considered globally, the second half of the nineteenth century must be seen as one of the great ages of Christian martyrdom. The Japanese occupations of the 1930s and 1940s added hideous new chapters to the stories of Asian believers.[19]

CROSSING THE RIVER

Once the religion was accepted, what remained was to purge away from that essential truth the foreign cultural trappings with which it was originally presented, and to let the message speak in intelligibly African or Asian terms. This process has been a lively theme for the rich tradition of fiction writing that has emerged in postcolonial Africa. One of the continent's most powerful writers is Kenya's Ngugi wa Thiong'o, whose book *The River Between* describes the conversion of his own Gikuyu village during the 1920s. The river in question refers to the literal and symbolic water dividing two villages, one newly converted, the other staunchly traditional-minded. At first, the book looks like a simplistic night-and-day account of how intrusive colonialist Christianity ruthlessly destroys the ancient way of life. The leading Christian convert, Joshua, is depicted in the most bigoted and fanatical terms, while traditionalist Waiyaki is a noble pagan, perhaps a native messiah. As the story develops, though, matters become more complex. One of Joshua's daughters rebels against her father by demanding the pagan circumcision that marks her entry into womanhood.

Although the ritual causes her death, her last vision is of Jesus. Joshua's other daughter falls in love with Waiyaki, and their union suggests the need for a cultural synthesis, in which Christianity would be acclimatized to African ways. For all its failings, there was something true in the white man's religion, but it "needed washing, cleaning away all the dirt, leaving only the eternal. And that eternal that was the truth had to be reconciled to the traditions of the people. A people's traditions could not be swept away overnight." A religion that failed to synthesize old and new "would only maim a man's soul." Joshua had erred when he "clothed himself with a religion decorated and smeared with everything *white*."[20]

From the earliest days of the missionary enterprise, indigenous peoples found aspects of Christianity exciting, even intoxicating, to the extent that they tried to absorb them into local culture, without waiting for the blessing of the European churches. In some instances, the zeal to accept and naturalize Christianity resulted in movements far removed from any customary notion of Christianity. I do not wish to exaggerate their numerical importance, since so much of the Christian history in Africa and Asia was, is, and shall be bound up with mainstream churches, Catholic and Protestant, rather than with the newer indigenous movements. The independent churches are critical, though, in demonstrating the real spiritual hunger that Christianity encountered and sought to satisfy.

To illustrate the passionate response to early Christian contacts, we might look at the Taiping movement that won enormous influence in nineteenth-century China. This might seem an unprepossessing example to illustrate Christian successes, since the movement became so deeply involved in politics, and failed so thoroughly. It incited a rebellion that resulted in tens of millions of deaths and set the stage for the ultimate destruction of the imperial regime. Although Chinese Communist historians prize the movement as a precursor to national liberation, the Taiping's roots were unmistakably Christian. The movement was founded by one Hong Xiuquan, who experienced a visionary ascent to heaven—the same story told by so many other first-generation converts. Here Hong met his true family, which included God, the Virgin Mary, and his elder brother, Jesus. His prophetic mission to redeem China was institutionalized in a new Society of Worshippers of Shang-ti (God). The group launched a rebellion intended to establish a regime of perfect communism, known as the Taiping, or "Great Peace." To put this term in its (Chinese) biblical context, the angels had proclaimed the birth of Christ with the words "Glory to God in the highest, and on earth, *Taiping* and good will towards men." Throughout its brief history, the movement maintained aspects of Christianity, but in a curious and deviant form. Recruits were required to learn the Lord's Prayer within a set period, upon threat of death.[21]

Such visionary movements have been remarkably common in world history and not just within the bounds of Christianity. Visionary prophets and messiahs were a frequent occurrence in medieval Europe, while similar stories have erupted regularly in Southern lands during the process of Christianization. Arguably, such charismatic prophets are an inevitable by-product of the conversion process, and their appearance in large numbers marks the transition from a grudging and formal acceptance of Christianity to the widespread internalization of Christian belief among the common people. In a sense, this is how Christianity goes native.

Going back to the early colonial period, Latin America has a long tradition of messianic, millenarian, and utopian movements, many of which appealed to dispossessed natives. Against this background, frequent reports of miracles and Marian visions could scarcely be politically neutral, and colonial regimes rightly suspected that desperate native peoples saw their best hope for liberation in the Virgin and saints, viewed in Indian guise. In the eighteenth century, native revolts in Central America usually took the form of apocalyptic "Virgin movements." The critical figures in Mexico's independence movement were priests like the legendary Father Miguel Hidalgo, who demanded justice in the name of the Virgin of Guadalupe. To this day, the Mexican church struggles over how to commemorate such figures whom it excommunicated as seditionists and heretics at the time, but who are now venerated as the nation's greatest heroes.[22]

Many such movements have used the idea that God's purposes would be fulfilled on the frontiers of this new continent rather than in corrupt Europe.

This idea is far from extinct today, not least in contemporary liberation theology. One Latin American messiah was Antônio Conselheiro ("the Counselor"), who led an apocalyptic social movement on the Brazilian frontier of the 1890s. The revolt has entered continental mythology, to the point of being commemorated by two of the region's greatest writers, namely Euclides Da Cunha (*Rebellion in the Backlands*) and Mario Vargas Llosa (*The War of the End of the World*). For Da Cunha, the affair demonstrated that Brazil was heir to "a multitude of extravagant superstitions" perhaps dating back to the fervent mysticism of the first Catholic settlers, who were so fascinated by miracles, visions, and "mysterious tongues of flame." These ideas were reinforced by the beliefs of various immigrant communities, especially the descendants of African slaves. Da Cunha saw Antônio's movement as a kind of social and racial atavism, a throwback to primitive religion. At best, "his teachings were no more than an approach to a Catholicism which he did not thoroughly understand."[23]

But from a contemporary perspective, Antônio's movement looks surprisingly modern. His claims to direct access to the Holy Spirit make him a forerunner of thousands of modern Pentecostal preachers in Brazil and many other Latin nations, who have successfully channeled the mystical impulse into a spate of flourishing denominations. We find many modern parallels for his millenarian preaching, in what Da Cunha disparagingly termed his "mixture of dogmatic counsels, the vulgar precepts of Christian morality, and weird prophecies," the whole entangled with a stern puritanism and strong measures of anticlerical and anti-Catholic fervor, and thorough distrust of secular modernity. The sermons were "barbarous and terrifying, calculated to send chills down the spines of his listeners." His hearers, overwhelmingly poor, were drawn from traditionally excluded racial and ethnic groups: "all ages, all types, all shades of racial coloring." As in a modern Pentecostal congregation, women believers were much in evidence.[24]

Another figure from the region's revolutionary canon is the Nicaraguan guerrilla leader Augusto Sandino, the inspiration for the later Sandinistas. In the 1920s, he was driven by a classic millenarian belief that the old order of the world would soon perish in fire and blood, to be replaced by a new system of justice and equality. He wrote that "The oppressed people will break the chains of humiliation.... The trumpets that will be heard will be the bugles of war, intoning the hymns of the freedom of the oppressed peoples against the injustice of the oppressors." In his vision, oppressed Indian, Latino, and *mestizo* peoples would serve a messianic role in the struggle against North American oppression.[25]

No single religious denomination traces its roots to these various revolts, although the spirit of Antônio the Counselor still pervades countless congregations. Some movements, though, that developed on or beyond the Christian fringe would develop into thriving independent churches. Under various names, these newer autonomous churches represent one of the most notable aspects of Southern Christianities. It is above all in Africa that such groupings would gain most significance. Often, the new indigenous denominations arose exactly in those regions that are likely to be experiencing the most striking population growth in the near future, so their traditions can be expected to play an increasing role in world Christianity.

OUT OF AFRICA

If the rising independent churches ever decide to identify a patron saint, they could do no better than to choose a seventeenth-century woman named Kimpa Vita, who was baptized by Italian Capuchin missionaries in the kingdom of Kongo.[26] Renamed Beatrice, she began her life as a Christian in the mode preached by the European Fathers, but she became disturbed as the priests attacked traditional ritual societies and initiations. She herself was a *Nganga*, a medium to the Other World, what colonial administrators might have called a medicine woman or witch doctor. About 1703, in a dream, she received a vision from St. Anthony, one of the most beloved saints in the Kongo, who warned her that the colonial churches were deeply in error. Jesus, she now learned, was a Black Kongolese, as were the apostles and beloved saints such as St. Francis. In fact, Jesus had been born in the Kongo capital of São Salvador. Her overarching message was that African Christians needed to find their own way to God, even if that meant using traditional practices condemned by the white priests. Kimpa Vita came to identify herself with St. Anthony, "the restorer of the kingdom of Kongo...the second God," whose spirit possessed her.

As so often in the African churches, a dream served as the conduit for a transforming spiritual message, with profound political implications. Kimpa Vita led a movement to reconcile the warring factions in her country, and she struggled to support the Kongolese monarchy. Time and again, we see analogies to Joan of Arc, and, as in Joan's case, her revelation led to a tragic encounter with the colonizers. In 1706 Dona Beatrice Kimpa Vita was burned as a heretic and witch. Her "Antonian" followers were suppressed, and many thousands were sent as slaves to the New World, chiefly to Brazil and South Carolina. Millions of North and South Americans alive today must trace some degree of descent from this pioneering form of indigenous African Christianity. Coincidentally or not, the nineteenth-century followers of Antônio Conselheiro sang that "It is Saint Anthony in the flesh (*Santo Antonio Apparecido*) to save us from punishment!"[27]

Although her sect would not long outlive her, Kimpa Vita would have many successors who tried to translate Christianity into terms intelligible for the Two-Thirds World. Across Africa, a common prophetic pattern has recurred frequently since the late nineteenth century. An individual is enthusiastically converted through one of the mission churches, from which he or, commonly, she, is gradually estranged. The division might arise over issues of church practice, usually the integration of native practices. The individual receives what is taken as a special revelation from God, commonly in a trance or vision. This event is a close imitation of one of the well-known New Testament scenes in which God speaks directly to his people, as at Pentecost or on the road to Damascus. The prophet then begins to preach independently, and the result might well be a new independent church. Particularly where the movement originates from a founder's revelation, such churches place a heavy premium on visions and charismatic gifts. Repeatedly, we find attempts to restore the splendors of primitive Christianity, supposedly lost or suppressed by mainstream church institutions. Everywhere, we see what Euclides Da Cunha termed "the same thunderings, the same rebellion against the ecclesiastical hierarchy, the same exploitation of the supernatural, the same heavenly longings, the same primitive dream which lay at the heart of the old religion before it had been deformed by the canonized sophists of the Councils."[28]

One of the greatest of these prophets was William Wadé Harris, a potent figure in modern African religion. Harris was a Liberian, who in the early years of the twentieth century was instructed by the angel Gabriel in a vision that had strong physical manifestations. He received "a triune anointing by God: he was tapped three times on the head and the spirit descended upon his head, feeling and sounding like a jet of water." Now, he was a prophet, the watchman of the apocalyptic dawn, he was Elijah. The angel also ordered him to abandon his prized European clothing. In so doing, he was rejecting not just the power of white colonialists but also of the Americanized black elite that monopolized power in his homeland. In 1913, clad in a white robe and turban, Harris began his wildly successful preaching journeys across West Africa: symbolizing the African nature of his mission, he bore a bamboo cross, a Bible, and a gourd rattle. Reportedly, he converted a hundred thousand people over a two-year period. He taught a message that was largely orthodox Christianity, teaching obedience to the Ten Commandments, and demanding strict observance of the Sabbath.[29]

What made Harris particularly African was his emphasis on dealing with the people's ancient cult-figures or fetishes, which European missionaries had scorned or ignored. Harris, on the other hand, like his listeners, believed that the fetishes contained vast spiritual force, which he combated by burning the objects. Legend tells how pagan shrines actually burst into flames as he approached, and their priests fled before the coming of such supernatural power. Unlike the white missionaries, who called witchcraft a delusion, Harris knew its power all too well and called upon his hearers to spurn occult practices. Nor did Harris condemn polygamy, and he traveled in the company of several wives. Although many of his followers eventually joined conventional mission churches such as the Methodists, Harrist churches survive in West Africa. Today, they appeal to transient immigrant communities such as Ghanaian workers in the Ivory Coast, the poorest of the poor.[30]

The First World War era was fertile for the creation of such movements, perhaps because events in Europe stirred apocalyptic expectations around the world and aroused hopes for a new religious/political order. The intensity of religious activism in these years suggests how wholeheartedly, how impatiently, the new African Christian communities tried to absorb the message into their own societies. We recall the stubborn faith of the Ugandan martyrs, just a decade or so after the arrival of Christianity in that country. In 1915, Baptist missionary John Chilembwe launched an armed revolt against British rule in the province of Nyasaland (later Malawi). This was the first modern African challenge to imperial rule presented in terms of nationalism and social justice, and it was built firmly upon Christian foundations. One of its key goals was the creation of a National African Church.[31]

Another contemporary prophet was Simon Kimbangu, who lived in what was then the Belgian Congo. At the time of the worldwide influenza epidemic in 1918—additional evidence that the world was undergoing an apocalyptic transformation—he received visions calling him to be a prophet and healer. Although he tried to resist his call, he ultimately began his preaching and healing ministry in 1921, attracting such a vast following that the terrified Belgian authorities sentenced him to be flogged and executed. The death sentence was commuted, but he remained in prison until his death in 1951. Even though Kimbangu preached an orthodox puritanical Christianity, he was distinctively African in his invocation of the help of the ancestors, and his focus on himself as a charismatic leader and mediator between God and the people. He also preached an African political message. One of his prayers promises, "The Kingdom is ours. We have it! They, the whites, no longer have it." Many of Simon Kimbangu's followers regarded him as an African savior and messiah, whose hometown of Nkamba was seen as a New Jerusalem. His church's calendar commemorates the key dates of his life, including the beginning of his ministry and the day of his death in prison. The more extreme messianic claims were not accepted by the official Kimbanguist Church that flourished after his death, the Church of the Lord Jesus Christ on Earth of the Prophet Simon Kimbangu, the EJCSK (*Église de Jesus Christ sur la Terre par son Envoyé Spécial Simon Kimbangu*). Believers do, however, see him as fulfilling Jesus's prophecy that "one who believes in me will also do the works that I do and will do greater works than these." The current size of this organization is very uncertain, but some claim numbers as high as 6 or 8 million.[32]

Harris and Kimbangu were by no means isolated figures. With their stress on spiritual healing, the new African churches gained strength because of the wave of epidemic diseases that swept most parts of Africa in the early years of the twentieth century, claiming millions of lives. In the Yoruba lands of Nigeria, the dreadful influenza epidemic led to the foundation of the faith-healing churches known as *Aladura* ("the Owners of Prayer"). From the 1920s on, the *Aladura* movement spawned many offshoots, usually under the leadership of some new charismatic leader or prophet. Such were the Cherubim and Seraphim Society, Christ Apostolic Church, and the Church of the Lord, Aladura. In some cases, the new bodies saw the divine messages received in trances and dreams as equal to the inspired word of the Bible.[33]

The tide of prophetic gifts was not confined to the astonishingly creative years of the 1910s and 1920s. Over the past century, many African believers have announced that God has chosen them for a special prophetic mission, and most have sought to Africanize the Christianity that they had received from European sources. As a final representative of this tradition, we might take Alice Lenshina. While a candidate for baptism in the Presbyterian church of Northern Rhodesia in 1953, Alice received visions in which she was taken up to heaven and ordered to destroy witchcraft, which was seen as so pressing a danger in many African societies. She formed a church, the *Lumpa* ("better than all others"), of which she became Lenshina or queen. The group attracted hundreds of thousands of followers, who formed a utopian community in order to await the Second Coming of Christ. As they rejected worldly regimes to the point of refusing to pay taxes, *Lumpa* members were persecuted by the newly independent Zambian regime, and a small war ensued between church and government. Alice Lenshina died in 1978, and while her church seems to have died with her, nobody would be surprised if clandestine followers reemerged someday.[34]

Reading all the seemingly endless stories of Africa's modern-day prophets and visionaries, and the revivals they are credited with, we are tempted to identify certain decades as ages of revival, ages of prophecy. The decade after 1910 certainly seems to fit this profile. The problem is that really no era since the 1890s has lacked this kind of passionate prophetic activism, so there are no real troughs to set besides the peaks. We can usefully draw parallels with American religious history. Traditionally, the nation's religious past has been interpreted as a series of great revivals, the first in the 1730s, second in the 1790s, and so on, right up to the present day, but these events can also be seen as convenient historical fictions. In reality, we can always find some kind of revival or great evangelical movement at work somewhere in North America, and only in retrospect do historians tie together a few of these events to portray them as "great revivals." In Africa similarly, it is more helpful to see the various revivals and prophetic movements as overlapping and more or less continuous events. To use the language of revivalism, Africa has now for more than a century been engaged in a continuous encounter with Pentecostal fires, and the independent churches have been the most obvious products of that intensely creative process. In American terms, much of the continent has served as one vast burned-over district.

AFRICAN AND INDEPENDENT

The various new congregations are today described as the African Independent Churches, or AIC's, which collectively represent one of the most impressive stories in the whole history of Christianity (in some accounts, the acronym stands for African Initiated Churches, or "African Indigenous"). The term covers a wide range of groupings, from strongly Africanized variants of recognizably European or American churches, all the way to tribal groups that borrow loosely and selectively from Christian thought and language. Although very diverse in ideas and practices, African independent churches use certain common themes, above all the adaptation of Christianity to local cultures and traditions. They are African churches with African leaders for African people.[35]

Independent denominations sprang up in many parts of Africa from the late 1880s on, as racial segregation in European-founded churches drove many activists to defect. For many, the age of the so-called Scramble for Africa rather marked a scramble out of inhospitable white churches and into the formation of new independent denominations. Many used words such as "Native" or "African" in their titles, and some claimed a distinct Ethiopian heritage. One of the earliest was the Ethiopian Church founded in Pretoria, South Africa, in 1892 by Mangena Mokone, a refugee from Wesleyan Methodism. This Ethiopian connection needs some explanation. African churches since Mokone's time are fond of quoting a verse from Psalm 68, which proclaims, "Let Ethiopia hasten to stretch out her hands to God." In North America, black churches were already claiming an Abyssinian identity from the start of the nineteenth century, and black American missionaries spread these ideas to Africa. Ethiopia gained a still greater appeal following the Emperor Menelik's resounding victory over the Italians at the battle of Adowa. By describing themselves as Ethiopian, the new denominations were not only justifying departures from white Christian models, but also claiming a pan-African Christian identity.[36]

Apart from the Ethiopian groups, some other independent churches are termed "prophetic" because they follow a modern-day charismatic leader like Kimbangu, Harris, and the rest. Finally, there are the important Zionist churches that grew ultimately from charismatic sects in late nineteenth-century North America and which practiced faith healing and speaking in tongues. They take their name indirectly from Mount Zion in Jerusalem, but more immediately from Zion City in Illinois, the headquarters of an influential American charismatic movement. Zionist churches were already operating in southern Africa in the 1890s, and they boomed in the early twentieth century. It was in 1910 that Engenas Barnabas Lekganyane established what would be one of the most successful—South Africa's Zion Christian Church, the ZCC. Despite the American influences in their origin, Zionist and other independent churches soon developed purely African leaderships. They enthusiastically adopted African customs, including polygamy and in some cases ritual taboos. They also resemble traditional native religions in their beliefs in exorcism, witchcraft, and possession. Some closely follow the customs of particular tribes, such as the Zulus, and have to some extent become tribally based churches. Many groups practice distinctive pilgrimages and ritual calendars, which intertwine with older tribal cycles.[37]

The grievances that gave rise to the new African churches are generally long gone, but the churches themselves are flourishing. Just how significant these groups might become we will see in the next chapter. For present purposes though, churches such as the Harrists and Kimbanguists, the Zionist and *Aladura* traditions, are significant because they suggest the real fervor that Christianity inspired outside the West. They confound the standard modern mythology about just how Christianity was, and is, exported to a passive or reluctant Third World. Over the last two centuries, at least, it might have been the European empires that first kindled Christianity around the world, but the movement soon enough turned into an uncontrollable brushfire.

FOUR

Standing Alone

We carry with us the wonders we seek without us;
there is all Africa and her prodigies in us.

—*Sir Thomas Browne*

As the spread of Christianity had closely coincided with imperial expansion, it seemed certain that the fate of the religion would be affected by the breakup of the old European empires. Just as these empires were built up in a slow and piecemeal fashion, so they did not disintegrate overnight. Although decolonization was at its most rapid in the late 1950s and early 1960s, the process extended for about half a century after the end of World War II, which so weakened the European powers. The British withdrew from India and Pakistan in 1947, and the Dutch recognized Indonesian sovereignty in 1949. It was in 1955 that the Bandung conference symbolized the emergence of a Third World, the community of new nations that aspired to be independent of both capitalist West and communist East. In sub-Saharan Africa, the decisive phase began with the independence of Ghana in 1957 and proceeded rapidly over the next decade. Landmarks in this process included the independence of Congo/Zaire and Nigeria in 1960, and of Algeria in 1962. However, the process continued long after this date. The Portuguese empire did not disintegrate until 1975, Zimbabwe gained its independence in 1979, and white rule survived in South Africa until 1994. The Soviet empire in central Asia continued as the greatest vestige of European colonialism until the USSR collapsed in 1991.

During the heady years of decolonization in the 1950s and 1960s, Western Christians were concerned about how the new African and Asian churches would survive the rapid transition. After all, Christianity in these regions had developed its essential framework by midcentury, but it was still "a skeleton without flesh or bulk, a mission-educated minority who were leading nascent Christian institutions."[1] There were also some severe political tests. In Kenya during the 1950s, Mau Mau rebels targeted the Anglican church as an arm of the imperial regime, and anarchy in the Belgian Congo during the 1960s led to widespread violence against believers and clergy. The Muslim insurgency in Algeria all but uprooted the old-established Catholic missions. Churches also suffered under new Asian Communist regimes.

Yet with a few exceptions, the new churches survived and flourished. Since midcentury, "the skeleton...had grown organs and sinew," as millions of new members have poured into the churches. It was precisely as Western colonialism ended that Christianity began a period of explosive growth that still continues unchecked, above all in Africa. Just since 1965, the Christian population of Africa has risen from a quarter of the continental total to about 46 percent, stunning growth for so short a period. Sometime in the 1960s, another historic landmark occurred when Christians first outnumbered Muslims in Africa. Adrian Hastings has written that "Black Africa today is totally inconceivable apart from the presence of Christianity."[2]

Whatever their image in popular culture, Christian missionaries of the colonial era succeeded remarkably. Much of this growth could be explained in terms of the churches' elastic ability to adapt to local circumstances. Across the global South, we see a common pattern of development. Initially, Westerners try to impose their own ideas of Christianity as it should be, often backed up by the force of colonial political power. This evangelism gains some followers, usually for an approved or state-run church, and a striking number of believers are contented to remain within that fold. Gradually, though, other people move beyond the colonial matrix, as they demand ever more accommodation with local ways: this is what happened with prophets such as William Wadé Harris.

This pressure can have various outcomes, depending on just how flexibly the old bottles can accommodate the new wine. In many cases the major European-oriented churches successfully adapt and incorporate native ways into local liturgies and worship styles. In other instances, though, the result is the formation of wholly new churches, in a way that might have disturbed the missionary founders. This can mean adopting some rival established denomination, as when millions of Latin American Catholics began converting to Protestant and Pentecostal churches. In yet other cases, believers form wholly new churches, so different from existing models that traditional-minded observers debate worriedly whether these upstarts have moved beyond the bounds of Christianity itself.

THE MISSION CHURCHES

Some of the greatest triumphs have been won by precisely the structures created by colonial authorities, which retain the passionate loyalty of indigenous peoples long after the empires themselves have dissolved. Despite all the scholarly attention justifiably paid to the distinctive Pentecostal and African indigenous churches (Zionist, Ethiopian, prophetic), the most successful structures across the global South are still easily recognizable to any North American. After decades of Protestant growth in Latin America, the Roman Catholic Church is still overwhelmingly the largest single religious presence on that continent, and the great majority of people still define their religious life in Catholic terms. If 60 or 70 million Latin Americans are Protestant (a fair estimate) then 490 million are not: most are, at least nominally, Catholic. In Africa, likewise, the leading churches are Roman Catholic, Anglican, Methodist, and so on, and will likely be so for the foreseeable future.

The continuing power of the mainstream churches must be emphasized because many Westerners are understandably fascinated by the insurgent movements. Kenneth Woodward, for instance, writes that "In Africa alone, the collapse of European colonialism half a century ago saw the wild proliferation of indigenous Christian cults inspired by personal prophecies and visions."[3] That is true as far as it goes, but the overall statistics must be borne in mind. Although African Independents today claim an impressive 100 million members, that represents only one-fifth of all African Christians. Africa's Roman Catholics alone outnumber its Independents by two to one. Members of Africa's mainstream Catholic and Protestant churches often resent the attention that European and American academics pay to the independent churches. It is far easier to find scholarly studies of the independent or prophetic churches than of the Catholic or Anglican congregations that define religious life for hundreds of millions. Just as understudied is the important Evangelical Church of West Africa, ECWA, which claims some five million worshippers. This church is orthodox in its beliefs and sober in its practices, very much like a mainstream conservative

Protestant church in North America. ECWA has little sympathy for charismatic or prophetic excesses, which explains why it attracts so few Western researchers.

However well intentioned the emphasis on strongly Africanized forms of faith, this slant tends to make African Christianity look far more exotic and even syncretistic than it really is. And all the emphasis on "Independents" suggests that the other churches are somehow dependent, lying under the neocolonial yoke. In Latin America similarly, books on Pentecostal congregations are now commonplace, but we have few descriptions of everyday life in a regular Catholic parish. For academics and journalists alike, the ordinary is just not interesting.

The European colonial empires that flourished in the nineteenth century have left a global religious heritage. The idea that religions might actually represent the afterlife of dead empires is scarcely new. In the seventeenth century, Thomas Hobbes described the papacy as "no other than the ghost of the deceased Roman Empire, sitting crowned upon the grave thereof: for so did the papacy start up on a sudden out of the ruins of that heathen power." The Hellenistic empire founded by Alexander the Great offers another historical parallel. Although this political entity lasted only briefly, it left a millennium-long heritage in terms of the widespread dispersion of Greek language, thought, and culture. Unwittingly, the Greek dynasts created the world in which early Christianity could spread so quickly.[4]

The present map of Catholicism around the world can be seen as a ghostly remnant of several empires, the French and Portuguese, but above all, the Spanish. According to official figures, some ten countries account for around half the world's Catholic believers. Brazil was once the crown jewel of the Portuguese empire, while Mexico, Colombia, Argentina, and the Philippines all owe their Catholic roots to Spain. As of 2010, Latin America had 470 million baptized Catholics—41 percent of the global total—more than in the whole of Europe and North America combined. A good number of North American Catholics are also of Latino heritage.

Catholic growth has been particularly dramatic in Africa, usually in former French and Belgian territories. As recently as 1955, the church claimed a mere 16 million Catholics in the whole of Africa, but the growing availability of air travel permitted missionaries access to whole areas of the continent that were hitherto beyond reach. Africa's Catholic population grew to 55 million in 1978, and to around 170 million today. John Allen puts the expansion in perspective: "Africa in the twentieth century went from a Catholic population of 1.9 million in 1900 to 130 million in 2000, a growth rate of 6,708 percent, the most rapid expansion of Catholicism in a single continent in two thousand years of church history." Today, Africans account for one-eighth of the world's Catholics, and by 2025, the 230 million African Catholics will represent one-sixth of all members of that church worldwide.[5]

These numbers, incidentally, may actually be understating Catholic growth past and present. The African church is likely undercounting its followers as it lacks the institutional framework to track what's happening on the ground. According to the Gallup World Poll, the number of Africans claiming to be Catholic is already approaching 200 million, which is 20 percent larger than any official church figure. By 2050, Africa will have far more Catholics than Europe. By this point, in fact, Europe will account for just 15 percent of the world's Catholics—and many of those will be immigrants from Africa, Asia, and Latin America.[6] African church structures have grown correspondingly. According to the church's *Statistical Yearbook*, just in the brief period 2001–06, "the Catholic population in Africa increased 16.7 percent, with a 19.4 percent increase in priests and a 9.4 percent increase in graduate- or theologate-level seminarians." Already today, Africa has 500 bishops and more than 35,000 priests, and vocations are in a far healthier state than in most of Europe or North America, though they are still not enough to cope with demand. Nigeria has what may be the world's largest Catholic theological school, Bigard Memorial Seminary in Enugu, with a thousand students on three campuses: to put this in perspective, the largest U.S. seminary has only two hundred students. In Nigeria, which has around 21 million Catholics, even parish churches that offer five or six Sunday masses still find large numbers forced to listen to the services

TABLE 4.1
The World's Largest Catholic Communities

Nation	Number of Catholics (millions)
Brazil	160
Mexico	97
Philippines	72
United States	68
Italy	57
France	47
Spain	42
Colombia	41
Poland	37
Argentina	36
TOTAL	657

Source: Catholic Almanac 2010

from outside the doors. John Allen reports interviewing the Catholic archbishop of Nairobi, Kenya, who complained about the pressing challenges
facing his church: "We have so many vocations!"[7]

The expansion can be illustrated from any number of countries. The
number of Tanzanian Catholics grew by 419 percent between 1961 and
2000, and the country today is 30 percent Catholic. Overseeing this growth
is a strong ecclesiastical structure, with 5 archbishops and 32 bishops.
Whereas in 1965 less than one-quarter of Tanzania's bishops were native
Africans, by 1996 local men headed all the dioceses.[8] During the 1960s,
archbishops of African stock emerged in many of the new nation-states,
and today, Africa has fourteen cardinals. Somewhere, the shade of Cardinal
Lavigerie is smiling contentedly.

The church's message has an appeal completely separate from the
imperial power by which it was originally carried. There are eerie parallels
here to the original spread of Christianity in Europe, which enjoyed its
greatest successes after the collapse of the Roman political regime. To quote
Kenneth Woodward, some church historians now "see history doing a second act: just as Europe's northern tribes turned to the church after the
decay of the Roman Empire, so Africans are embracing Christianity in face
of the massive political, social and economic chaos."[9] In modern Africa, as
in medieval Europe, the religion of the old master races became most attractive when the formal political bonds were severed, so that accepting
Christianity did not imply submission to a foreign political yoke. At that
point, subject peoples were delighted to appropriate not just the beliefs but
also the old administrative and cultural forms of empire.

Also haunting world Christianity is the specter of the defunct British
Empire. The Anglican Communion now claims some 80 million members
worldwide, a figure that significantly overestimates the number of practicing
church members in the United Kingdom proper. By more plausible estimates, Anglicans in the British Isles are massively outnumbered by those
overseas, and the so-called Anglican (literally, "English") Communion
looks ever more African. The world's best-known Anglican cleric is probably former Cape Town archbishop Desmond Tutu, who (alongside Nelson
Mandela) became the symbol of the South African liberation movement.
Having said this, recent divisions in the Anglican world mean that another
African is running close to Tutu in the celebrity stakes, namely conservative
Nigerian primate Peter Akinola, who presided over a church some 21 million strong. By 2050, the global total of Anglicans could be approaching
150 million, of whom only a minority will be white Euro-Americans. The
imperial heritage is evident from other British-derived churches such as

Methodists and Presbyterians, which similarly used the imperial frame-work to spread their distinctive messages.[10]

The church in the former British colony of Uganda illustrates the process of autonomous growth. This promises to be an enormously significant development, since Uganda is one of the fastest-growing countries in Africa, with a current population of around 34 million. We have seen how Ugandan Christianity established its local credentials during the great persecutions of the 1880s. Anglicanism easily survived the transition from imperial rule, and the church became a separate province in 1961, a year before national independence. Christianity's role as a truly native faith was reinforced again in 1977, when Anglican archbishop Janani Luwum was martyred for opposing the dictatorship of General Idi Amin. Today, Anglicans make up perhaps 35 percent of the total population. There are twenty dioceses and seven thousand parishes, and by any measure of church attendance and participation, Anglicanism is considerably healthier in Uganda than in what was once the mother country.[11]

One prominent church leader of Ugandan origin is John Sentamu, who in 2005 became the archbishop of York. This is the second see in the Church of England and a venerable diocese originally founded in the year 627. Sentamu himself is not shy about denouncing racism, imperialism, or offi-cial abuses, but on the missionary achievement, he is unequivocal. He has said,

> My late parents always said to me whenever you meet a group of people who may be interested in hearing what you have to say, always tell them how grateful we are for the missionaries who risked their lives to bring the good news of God's salvation to Uganda. It is because of that mis-sionary endeavor that I am standing in front of you. A fruit of their risk-taking and love.[12]

The Ugandan story suggests how the old colonial churches succeeded in adapting to local styles of worship and belief, which made the transition to political independence much easier. As early as the 1920s, the East African "mission churches" were transformed by a strongly evangelical revival movement that had its heart in Uganda and Rwanda but which affected many neighboring states (this was also the time of the great West African revivals that gave rise to the *Aladura* churches). In East Africa, followers were known as the *balokole*, the "saved ones," and the *balokole* became a major force in the new church: one disciple became the first archbishop of the Ugandan Anglican church after that nation's independence. The *balokole* movement gave the East African churches a charismatic tone, which endures to the present and which reduced the boundaries dividing the established churches from the newer Independents and Pentecostals.[13] The revivalist emphasis on healing and visionary experience made the churches attractive to members of traditional animist faiths. Even though older and newer churches disagree on issues of theology and structure, they share many common cultural assumptions.

SECESSION

Across the South, the older churches and missions remain the primary fact in the Christian story, yet they do not represent the whole picture. In many areas, older groupings proved inadequate for a changing society. Much of the most spectacular Christian expansion in recent decades has occurred not within either the Protestant or Catholic realms but in new independent denominations. We can see a proliferation of churches with affiliations that might be termed "none of the above." The relative strength of Christian traditions, according to the Center for the Study of Global Christianity, can be seen in table 4.2.

Regardless of the precision of any of these figures, we must be struck by the fact that almost one Christian in five worldwide is neither Protestant, nor Catholic, nor Anglican, nor Orthodox. For the average Western Christian, this idea is puzzling: apart from Mormons, possibly, what else is there? Just what is an Independent? In some sources, the same figure is given even more confusingly as "Other." These Other churches represent a

TABLE 4.2
Strength of Christian Megablocs

Ecclesiastical Megabloc	Adherents (millions)	
	2005	2025
Roman Catholics	1,119	1,361
Independents	427	582
Protestants	376	469
Orthodox	220	253
Anglicans	80	114
Marginal Christians	34	50
TOTAL	2,256	2,834

Source: www.globalchristianity.org/resources.htm

wide variety of denominations, often (but not always) included under the general label of Pentecostal. Some are affiliated with Northern world denominations such as the (Pentecostal) Assemblies of God, but many are not. Some of these Other congregations are indigenous churches with roots entirely in Africa, Asia, and Latin America, sometimes in regions where Christianity was planted within the last century or so.

Driving this growth has been a global revival movement that is one of the most important religious stories of the past century. As church historian Mark Shaw describes in his important study of *Global Awakenings*, revival movements often began in North America, but they soon spread around the world, freely crossing cultural and geographical frontiers, and driving religious revolutions in nations as diverse as Nigeria, Korea, and Brazil. Although revivals as such are not necessarily tied to any theological movement, the new churches that grow out of them tend to be highly charismatic, as well as evangelical. As Shaw remarks, these are

> charismatic people movements that seek to change their world through the translation of Christian truth and the transfer of power. These grassroots movements are a combination therefore of a spiritual factor (the Spirit of God), a people factor (the transfer of power to the marginalized), a truth factor (the application of the gospel to the pressing questions of a people group and culture) and a justice factor (a mission to change one's world in response to the gospel).[14]

These movements also maintain the imprint of their U.S. initiators, in the sense of promoting familiar American values of autonomy and democratization. As Mark Noll remarks,

> The American tendency has been to see authority as self-created rather than inherited; to read the Bible for oneself rather than just to accept biblical interpretation from others; to create organizations to meet a need rather than simply to inherit organizations; to empower laypeople, first laymen and then laywomen, as opposed to being super-clerical; and to use the forces of the market for the church rather than to worry about the forces of the market. The American tendency has been populist, and sometimes democratic, rather than aristocratic.[15]

Putting those trends together, we see an upsurge of newer churches that transgress long-established boundaries.

Growth outside the traditional churches has been very evident in Latin America. Roman Catholicism represented the religion of the overwhelming majority of the people as recently as forty years ago, but since that time, there has been a marked defection to Protestantism. (I am here including Pentecostals as a subset of Protestants, but as we will see, the two terms are not identical.) In 1940, barely a million Protestants were recorded in the whole of Latin America. Since 1960, though, Protestant numbers in the region have been growing at an average annual rate of 6 percent, so that today Protestants make up between 10 and 15 percent of the whole population, 60 or 70 million people.[16]

In terms of their share of the population, Protestants or *evangélicos* are strongest in Guatemala and Chile, in each case representing around one-quarter of the whole. Brazil alone might have as many as 30 or 40 million *crentes* or believers—that is, Protestants. If it were a separate country, then the most Protestant region of Latin America would be the U.S. territory of Puerto Rico, where numbers stand at around 35 percent. These proportions are so important because Protestants also tend to be more religiously committed, more likely to be active churchgoers, than most of their nominally Catholic neighbors. Just how much stronger the new churches can become is an open question and remains a matter of alarm for the Catholic hierarchies of the region. Observers of the region are also intrigued by conditions in Cuba, where Pentecostalism could well emerge as a potent force when the Communist regime eventually falls.[17]

Mexico illustrates the upsurge of Protestant practice over the last half-century. The nation traditionally was divided between a vigorous Catholicism and an equally dedicated current of secularism and anticlericalism. For much of the twentieth century, successive Mexican governments were deeply hostile to the Catholic Church, and there were periods of intense persecution: we recall Graham Greene's novel of a martyred priest, *The Power and the Glory*. While not actually favored by the authorities, Protestants were relatively free to operate, and by 1970 they were about 1 million strong, representing 2 percent of the population. Since that date, Protestants have flourished by appealing to two quite different constituencies, respectively urban and rural. In the cities, like elsewhere in Latin America, Protestantism particularly appeals to migrants and the marginalized. One remarkable development is the conversion of rural Indian communities in southeastern Mexico, in provinces such as Chiapas, Tabasco, and Veracruz, often among Maya peoples. In Oaxaca, the evangelical share of the population grew from 1.5 percent to 7.3 percent between 1970 and 1990, and the absolute number of evangelicals swelled by 531 percent. Of 110 million Mexicans today, around 6 percent are Protestants, compared with 89 percent who nominally identify themselves as Roman Catholic.[18]

We have to be careful about judging the exact scale of the movement to Protestantism, which not too long ago was described in rather inflated terms. In the 1980s, it was common to read claims that Protestantism was sweeping the continent, that many countries would be half Protestant by the year 2000, and so on. In 1990, David Stoll published a carefully argued book that sought to answer the question *Is Latin America Turning Protestant?* He found that while evangelicals were certainly making great strides, the more extreme claims stemmed from partisan agencies with a strong theological agenda. One influential trend was known as Discipling the Nations, and advocates had an apocalyptic commitment to achieving evangelical majorities in previously non-Protestant countries by the end of the second millennium. This optimism did much to shape statistical estimates. We can also discern an element of anti-Catholicism, since the claim being made was that millions of new believers were being rescued from this supposedly nonbiblical and non-Christian faith. Enthusiastic missionary agencies rarely paid enough attention to the chronic difficulties in measuring church membership and relied on optimistic self-report data.[19]

Special problems apply to Third World societies in which it is not easy to collect information from remote rural areas. Figures claimed for Latin America relied too heavily on projections from major churches accessible to scholars, mainly in large urban concentrations. And however transforming they may appear at the time, conversions are not always a permanent and life-changing event: Latin America has plenty of ex-evangelicals as well as ex-Catholics. But even when we take these problems into account, evangelical achievements are remarkable enough, and we can properly see this religious shift as one of the great religious revolutions over the past few centuries. Its importance is all the greater given population growth in Latin America and the likely significance of the region in decades to come.[20]

THE DAY OF PENTECOST

In addition to growing in overall numbers, the nature of Protestantism itself has changed substantially over the last half-century, with the expansion of Pentecostal sects. The Pentecostal boom worldwide was little known to the lay public in the West before the publication of Harvey Cox's important book *Fire From Heaven* (1995), but the "rise of Pentecostal spirituality" has to be seen as truly epoch-making. According to reputable observers, by 2000, charismatic/Pentecostal numbers worldwide were increasing at the rate of around 19 million each year. The Center for the

Study of Global Christianity states that the number of charismatic/ Pentecostal believers was 582 million in 2000, potentially rising to over 800 million by 2025.[21]

A word about definition is in order here. Historically, the chief religious division in the Western Christian world was between Roman Catholics and Protestants, the latter term including all those groups that descended from the great ideological split of the Reformation. The key difference is that Protestants rely on the Bible alone as the source of religious authority, rather than on tradition or the institutional church. In this broad division, the Pentecostal movement should logically be considered Protestant, since it grew out of other Protestant churches, namely Methodism and the Holiness tradition, and it preaches a fundamentalist reliance on scriptural authority. Across Latin America, the term *evangélico* refers indiscriminately to both Protestants and Pentecostals. Increasingly, though, observers differentiate Pentecostals from Protestants because of growing divergences between the two in matters of faith and practice. One central division is that Pentecostal believers rely on direct spiritual revelations that supplement or even replace biblical authority. Across the continent, Protestants and Pentecostals remain at arm's length, because they appeal to different audiences. While Protestants serve a largely middle-class audience, Pentecostals derive their support chiefly from the poor, sometimes from the very poorest sections of society.

Pentecostalism has deep roots in Latin America, where some independent churches were founded before World War II. Their numbers were tiny until the 1950s, when growth began in earnest. Since that date, Pentecostals account for 80 or 90 percent of Protestant/Pentecostal growth across Latin America. Chilean Protestantism has a heavy Pentecostal majority, and this tradition has also become very strong in Central America. Some of the new Pentecostals adhere to international denominations, such as the U.S.-based Assemblies of God. Today, this church claims at least 15 million members in Brazil, in contrast to only 2 or 3 million in the United States itself. The same denomination is now the largest non-Catholic community in Guatemala. However, much of the Pentecostal growth has occurred in wholly new denominations, with roots in Latin America. Chile is home to the Jotabeche Methodist Pentecostal church, which boasts eighty thousand members, and its cathedral in Santiago can seat eighteen thousand.[22]

Brazil represents a particular success story for Pentecostals, appropriately enough in the land of Antônio Conselheiro. The Brazilian Pentecostal movement was founded in the early twentieth century by missionaries of the Assemblies of God, a church that continues to boom. The denomination

might have 15 or 18 million Brazilian adherents, and there are more followers of the Assemblies of God in the greater São Paulo region alone than
in the entire United States. Pentecostal conversions surged during the 1950s
and 1960s, when native Brazilians began founding autonomous churches.
The most influential included *Brasil Para o Cristo*, Brazil for Christ,
founded in 1955 by Manoel de Mello. His spiritual roots lay in the
Assemblies of God, and his colorful evangelization tactics included
American-style mass rallies and crusades. Today, the movement's main
temple claims 1 million members. Other groupings from this time include
God Is Love, founded in São Paulo in 1962, and the Church of the Four
Square Gospel (*Igreja do Evangelho Quadrangular*), which traces its roots
to U.S.-based evangelist Aimee Semple McPherson.[23]

A third wave of Pentecostal evangelism has made massive gains over the
last thirty years, and again it clearly builds on local foundations. Of the
fifty-two largest denominations in the Rio de Janeiro area in the 1990s,
thirty-seven were of local Brazilian origin. Their successes have been striking—they would say, miraculous. Harvey Cox cites a study of Rio de
Janeiro in the early 1990s, where over a three-year period, no less than
seven hundred new Pentecostal churches opened. In the same period, an
impressive 240 Spiritist temples also appeared, mainly of the African-
derived Umbanda tradition—and just *one* new Roman Catholic parish.
According to one recent estimate, some forty new Pentecostal churches are
opening in Rio each and every week. In the 1990s alone, Brazilian
Protestants and Pentecostals grew from 9 to 15 percent of the population,
while Catholic strength fell from 84 to 74 percent.[24]

One controversial example of the new Pentecostalism is the Brazilian-
based Universal Church of the Kingdom of God, the *Igreja Universal do
Reino de Deus,* or IURD. The Universal Church was founded by Edir
Macedo de Bezerra only in 1977, but today it claims 8 million members.
Other estimates were much lower, but in any case the expansion was awe-
inspiring, and the church operates in forty countries besides Brazil. After so
brief an organizational existence, the IURD now controls one of the largest
television stations in Brazil, has its own political party, and owns a Rio de
Janeiro football team. In Brazil alone, it operates 4,500 "temples," and it
is presently attempting to build a full-size replica of the ancient Jewish
Temple of Solomon in São Paulo. Its wealth comes from the fervent devotion of members, who tithe faithfully.[25]

The IURD has been widely attacked, and it is classified as a cult by some
European governments and by media exposés in the United States. The
Universal Church has been criticized for superstitious practices that exploit

its largely uneducated members. The church sells special anointing oil for healing, and television viewers are encouraged to place a glass of water near the screen so it can be blessed by remote control. The IURD's website promises that "A miracle awaits you." Sometimes, this miracle takes the form of release from demonic powers, since the church offers "strong prayer to destroy witchcraft, demon possession, bad luck, bad dreams, all spiritual problems" and promises that members will gain "prosperity and financial breakthrough." Believers are told, in effect, that prayer and giving operate on the same crass principle as secular investments: the more one gives to the church, the more material benefit could be expected in this life. Some critics denounce the IURD as an irresponsible moneymaking scheme. The *New York Post* exposed the church under the headline "Holy-Roller Church Cashes in on Faithful." One embarrassing videotape showed Macedo gloating over his profits and urging lieutenants to squeeze more out of the flock. A new indictment in 2009 suggested that Macedo's illicit takings had run into hundreds of millions of dollars. Financial abuses, albeit on a much smaller scale, were also directed against Brazil's second largest Pentecostal church, the Reborn in Christ, *Renascer em Cristo*, which has some 1,200 churches in Brazil, in addition to a sizable media operation.[26]

We should not use these cases, however, to generalize about the possible flaws of the rising churches, still less about religion in a Third World context. All organizations can become deviant or exploitative: witness the scandals in American mainline churches over the last two decades, over financial fraud as well as sexual abuse. From the nature of the mass media, we do not hear about the other responsible churches that are not involved in abuse and exploitation, and which work faithfully for their members. And whatever our view of the IURD, its growth indicates that it is catering to a vast public hunger, so that even if this group were to disappear tomorrow, new movements would arise to take its place. In most cases, we would presumably hear nothing about them in the North unless they fell prey to outrageous scandal. Without this kind of reporting, we would remain unaware of the religious revolution that is in progress across the Southern world. In Africa too, charismatic revival has spread beyond the ranks of recognized Pentecostal denominations. In Ethiopia, for instance, the Meserete Kristos Church is one of the largest national denominations within the global Mennonite faith, with around 150,000 baptized members. It has grown largely by adopting worship styles and a commitment to healing that would surprise most North American Mennonites, yet the results have been impressive. Canadian visitors were delighted to hear that the church was reporting growth of 10.6 percent for the previous year, but were bemused by the response of the local administrator noting this claim: "Ten-point-six percent! We are embarrassed about that. It means we are already stagnant. The assembly will not be happy to hear that. It should be 30 percent." Such are the expectations of contemporary African Christianity.[27]

Equally charismatic is the Kale Heywet ("Word of Life") Church, which grew out of the old European-based Sudan Interior Mission, and whose orientation was originally Baptist. Today, though, the church is thoroughly Ethiopian and charismatic. It is moreover the nation's largest Protestant denomination, with four or five million adherents. Not surprisingly, the Ethiopian word for Protestant is simply *Pentay*, or Pentcostal. How could there be any other kind?[28]

Also successful has been another church that some Northern observers would consider only a semi-Christian movement, the Latter-day Saints (LDS), or Mormons. Only a generation ago, Mormons were mainly concentrated in the United States, but matters have now changed completely. Of 11 million Mormons today, less than half now live in the United States and Canada, while over one-third live in Central and South America: there could soon be thirty temples in Latin America. Mexico and the nations of Central America account for 1.3 million church members. As a personal observation, the globalization of the LDS faith was brought home to me by the visit of two missionaries to my home in Pennsylvania. Of itself, such an occurrence is nothing new, but on this occasion, both the Mormon evangelists were young women, one from Mongolia, the other from the Pacific nation of Tonga. The church well recognizes its Southern markets, and its recruiting literature effectively emphasizes the distinctive New World and Native context of this faith. In keeping with the Mormon scriptures, the group's posters and videos depict Jesus preaching before what are clearly Meso-American and Maya pyramids, to awed Native hearers. By present projections, the proportion of Mormons living in Europe and North America will fall steadily over the next thirty or forty years, while African and Latin American contingents will grow apace.[29]

THE CATHOLIC RESPONSE

In the long term, the Catholic response to these changes may be as far-reaching as Protestant expansion itself. The desperate lack of Catholic priests across the global South meant that the church initially failed to keep up with shifts in population and popular taste, and no amount of condemnations from the hierarchy could keep the faithful from drifting to the new sects. Once the evangelical churches began to flourish, though, Catholics themselves had to compete by developing alternatives offering a far greater sense of popular commitment and lay participation. These include the famous *comunidades eclesiales de base*, the base communities, which rely on heavy lay involvement and participation in liturgy and church life, and which are deeply involved in community organizing. These groups have served as an inspiration for radical First World Christians. Also important have been charismatic Catholic groups, which revive the mystical and visionary aspects of the faith. In fact, conservative Catholics have been disturbed to note just how much these new institutions look like their Protestant counterparts, and the base communities attracted particular hostility.[30]

Although they have received far less attention in the West than the base communities, Catholic charismatic organizations may well be more influential in the long run. According to some estimates, the Catholic charismatic movement could have 75 million followers in Latin America, where they follow celebrity priests like Brazil's Marcelo Rossi. Rossi speaks, sings, and acts exactly like a Pentecostal pastor, and like them, he commands audiences of many thousands, rising to half a million for Holy Week services. While he has in no sense reconquered Brazilian cities for the Vatican, at least he has helped stem the rate of defections.[31]

Several such Catholic charismatic movements operate in the Philippines, where Protestants currently comprise around 8 percent of what was historically an overwhelmingly Catholic nation, and there are surging Pentecostal groups such as the Jesus Is Lord movement. But they may have met their match in Catholic groups like *Bukas Loob Sa Diyos* ("Open in Spirit to God"), and Couples for Christ. Particularly successful in combating Protestant penetration is the El Shaddai movement, a lay charismatic group that takes its name from a Hebrew term for the face of God. El Shaddai was founded in 1984 by Brother Mike Velarde, who strikes an American observer as a megastar televangelist. The group's meetings, hundreds of thousands strong, look like nothing so much as a 1960s rock festival. Audiences are predominantly made up of women, but many whole families are in evidence. As in Pentecostal churches, there is a firm belief in God's direct intervention in everyday life, which observers interpret in different ways. Some see this belief as a childlike faith in the divine presence; for others, the new groups are teaching a crass materialism. El Shaddai followers raise their passports to be blessed at services, to ensure that they will get the visas they need to work overseas. Some open umbrellas and turn them upside down as a symbolic way of catching the rich material blessings they expect to receive from on high. This suggests a materialistic thought-world not too far removed from the Brazilian IURD. The movement probably has 7 million members across the Philippines, making them a potent political force, and it also has the nucleus for a truly global presence. The sizable army of expatriate Filipino workers worldwide permits El Shaddai to operate congregations or chapters in over twenty-five countries, including the United States and Canada, in most nations in western Europe, and the Persian Gulf region.[32]

Occasional warnings about the group's possible excesses show that the Philippine Catholic hierarchy does not see El Shaddai as an unmixed boon, but there is little doubt that the movement has done much to prevent the kind of mass defections that have occurred in Brazil and elsewhere. This experience offers sobering lessons for other Catholic nations alarmed at an upsurge of "sects." One way or another, inside the Catholic Church or outside it, Christianity worldwide is becoming steadily more charismatic.

AFRICAN INDEPENDENTS

The same lesson emerges from the success of the newer churches in Africa. In recent years, some of the most successful congregations have been Pentecostal, and here too the Assemblies of God are growing fast. Throughout, we can see many analogies to the new Pentecostalism of Latin America. In Tanzania, charismatic services are marked by "rapturous singing and rhythmic hand-clapping, with ... prayers for healing and miraculous signs." "Announcements of the meetings and the so-called power crusades can be seen on more or less every second house in the larger cities." In most of Africa, Pentecostals have overtaken the independent or indigenous churches in popularity, but such groups remain powerful in some areas. The Independents vary widely in their belief and practice, but these too should be comprehended under the flexible Pentecostal label. Many indigenous churches do not like the Pentecostal title, which implies a reliance on American mission activities rather than spontaneous local growth. Independents fully deserve their name: they are nobody's puppets. Still, Harvey Cox makes a convincing case that we should also place the African Independent Churches (AICs) firmly within the Pentecostal landscape, on account of their "free wheeling, Spirit-filled" worship style. Their worship "exhibits all the features of Pentecostal spirituality we have found from Boston to Seoul to Rio de Janeiro." The founders of the various prophetic churches also fit well into the Pentecostal mode, and their conversion experiences are classic Pentecostal narratives.[33]

Also successful have been "health-and-wealth" churches, practicing varieties of spiritual warfare but also promising their adherents material blessings here and now. These churches have proved very attractive to the middle classes as well as the poor. Perhaps the best example is the Winners' Chapel founded by Bishop David Oyedepo in the mid-1980s. Its great showplace is Faith Tabernacle, which reportedly seats fifty thousand worshippers. Other flourishing institutions are vast open air "evangelical campgrounds" with names such as Mountain of Fire and Miracles, Deeper Life, and Redemption Camp (the last spreads over some twelve thousand acres).[34] These new churches thrive across Africa, although there are huge regional variations. In some countries, such as Uganda, major traditional churches still predominate, while in west Africa, traditional "mission" churches coexist with indigenous groups like the Cherubim and Seraphim. In southern Africa, Independents seem to be carrying the day, but they face serious competition from newer Pentecostal churches. Over the last half-century, the Zionist churches have been phenomenally successful in South Africa, above all in the poorest urban areas.[35] By the year 2000, there were four thousand independent churches in South Africa, and nine hundred congregations operating in the city of Soweto alone.

The largest such body, the Zion Christian Church (ZCC), is a vital religious and political force in South Africa. Government figures suggest that it commands the loyalty of around 11 percent of South Africans, perhaps six million in all, but other sources claim that the combined strength of the church's two competing branches might run to twelve million or more. Whatever the actual numbers, the ZCC demonstrates its power in its vast seasonal pilgrimages. Every Easter, more than a million ZCC pilgrims gather for several days of celebrations at Zion City, the church's chief shrine in South Africa. To put this in perspective, the crowd gathered at the ZCC's pilgrimage is larger than that which greets the pope in St. Peter's Square on Easter morning. Another powerful independent group is the amaNazaretha, the Nazarite Baptist Church founded by the messianic Zulu prophet Isaiah Shembe in 1912: this too has its great pilgrimage gatherings.[36]

The growth of independent churches in South Africa neatly corresponded with the growing political and racial crisis in this nation between the 1960s and the 1990s. As a result, many black Africans felt uncomfortable belonging to mission churches associated with a colonialist regime. This distaste may explain why the Independents have done so well across the far southern nations. Another country in which AICs have enjoyed comparable success is Zimbabwe, which as "Rhodesia" was the scene of a bloody liberation war from 1965 to 1979. Newer churches have also done well in Botswana, which is presently half Christian. Only about 30 percent of Botswana's church members belong to such familiar denominations as the Anglicans, Methodists, and Roman Catholics. Seven percent more adhere to Pentecostal groups, while the remainder, almost two-thirds of Christian believers, belong to AICs.[37] In this region at least, independent groups continue to grow quickly, while membership in the mission churches stagnates.

CHINA

Protestant and Pentecostal expansion is not limited to Latin America. Christian numbers have also been growing apace in societies around the Pacific Rim, though the exact scale of this phenomenon is open to debate, and as in Latin America, we have to be wary of overly optimistic claims. But Asian churches too demonstrate a real excitement about the prospects for future growth, a sense of standing at the beginning of a new Christian epoch. To quote one enthusiastic observer of modern Asian missions, "Europe is in the times of Jesus with anti-establishment protests against an aging religious institution tottering under the weight of its wealth, property and privileges. Asia is in the times of Paul, planting a convert church in virgin soil."[38]

The greatest statistical mystery concerns the People's Republic of China, which prior to the communist victory in 1949 was seen as the world's richest single mission field. Conditions for Christians deteriorated sharply under a communist government that was both antireligious and xenophobic. All foreign missionaries were soon (1951) expelled as agents of imperialism. While Chinese Christians were grudgingly tolerated, they were expected to join organizations officially registered with the government. Catholics were required to join a Catholic Patriotic Association, while Protestants were to accept the Three-Self principle: self-government, self-support, and self-propagation. That scheme was originally meant to create a tougher and more autonomous Chinese Christianity, and whatever the Communists may have wanted, that was exactly the effect. As Mark Noll remarks, "forcing the missionaries to leave was the birth of Christian China. Even though there was tremendous suffering and momentous persecution, what was left was Chinese Christianity, and Chinese Christians knew how to do the gospel in China without the missionaries. In a strange way, losing China was how the gospel took root in China."[39] Current estimates of Chinese Christian numbers vary enormously, from 25 million or so, to an incredible 200 million. If present-day numbers are so contested, then so, evidently, are future growth projections. The minimum realistic figure is that of the Chinese government itself, which to say the least has no vested interest in exaggerating the tally of religious believers. The government publicly admits to a combined Catholic and Protestant number of some twenty million, 1.5 percent of all Chinese. Beyond those, of course, there are the unregistered Christian communities, the famous house churches, and their numbers are a total mystery. The World Christian Database suggests 70 million house church believers; others say 50 million, still others far fewer. Putting the various estimates together, the Pew Forum gives a Christian population of 4 or 5 percent; the CIA's *World Factbook* gives 3 or 4 percent. The differences may sound insignificant, were we not dealing with a colossus like China, where just 1 percent of the population means an impressive thirteen million souls.

The best evidence we now have comes from extensive opinion surveys undertaken over the past decade, material that is now being made available through a Templeton Foundation–supported project at Baylor University. At first sight, this evidence portrays Chinese Christianity more modestly than some recent accounts, with a mere 35 or 40 million adherents. However, the researchers stress that these numbers are minimal, and that they identify only those who are prepared to admit openly to Christian faith. Depending on the attitudes of zealous local officials, such an overt admission might be suicidally rash. Pew survey evidence also finds many additional Chinese who might not describe themselves overtly as Christian, but who are prepared to accept the existence of "God/Jesus." Perhaps these are converts en route to full belief.[40]

Putting the Templeton and Pew materials together, we can reasonably place the number of Chinese Christians at around 65 to 70 million, around 5 percent of the population. That falls a good deal short of any vision of "converting China." Christians comprise just a small minority within that country, roughly comparable to the Muslim percentage of modern Western European nations. Even viewed in these somewhat reduced terms, though, the Chinese number still demands attention. Those 65 or 70 million Christians outnumber the *total* population of major nations like France, Britain, or Italy and the level of Christian commitment is awe-inspiring. As in Africa, we find a broad range of denominational styles, from the "mainline" Three-Self churches to the strongly charismatic approach of the house church movement. Put another way, China has about as many Christians as it does members of the Communist Party.

The Christian figure represents a phenomenal growth from the five or so million who witnessed the Communist takeover back in 1949, and the subsequent decades of massacre and persecution. Christians have not merely survived under such adverse conditions but have actually experienced a population boom through two generations of often vicious antireligious persecution, particularly during the sadistic horrors of the Cultural Revolution. Patchy evidence indicates healthy Christian growth in certain areas, as disaffection with communism grew in the 1980s. For national authorities, one of the most alarming signs of this religious upsurge is the number of defections to Christianity by party cadres, and even officials, after the 1989 democracy protests intensified the ideological crisis. Of the twenty-one most wanted student leaders following the Tienanmen protests, two have now been ordained as priests. Describing his conversion, another movement leader said, "In China we have traditionally followed Buddhism. We had quite a deep religion. But Communism destroyed everything. When Communism became this corrupted thing which failed everybody, people still needed a belief. I think that's the reason for Christianity in China." In a daring analogy, David Jeffrey suggests that "Among those disappointed true-believer Marxists, it may well be that Marxism has served as a kind of John the Baptist to the rapid emergence of Christianity among Chinese intellectuals." Trying to explain the mass appeal of Chinese Christianity, other observers stress its strongly charismatic nature, its promise of healing in body and mind: many who survived the Cultural Revolution are quite ready to credit the notion of demonic evil.[41]

Surveying the state of Chinese Christianity, David Aikman argues that the faith may within coming decades achieve within China the same kind of cultural hegemony that it has already achieved in South Korea—not a wholesale national conversion, but a permeation of national life and culture. If true, this would have sweeping implications for international relations, no less than for the state of democracy and human rights in the world's most populous nation. Catholic China-watcher Francesco Sisci suggests that "we are near a Constantinian moment for the Chinese Empire."[42]

ASIAN DAWNS

Christianity has made rapid progress in the Chinese diaspora, the flourishing network of Chinese communities scattered around the Pacific Rim, in nations such as Indonesia, Malaysia, Hong Kong, and Singapore. By no means are all Christians in these areas ethnic Chinese: Indonesia's large Christian minority is especially diverse. Even so, the assumed linkage between Chinese origins and Christianity has been apparent during episodes of anti-Chinese protest, when Muslim mobs have targeted both Chinese businesses and Christian churches. As we will see, the ethnic-religious equation potentially places religion at the heart of future battles in nations such as Malaysia and Indonesia.[43]

One Christian success story in Asia is South Korea. Christianity first arrived in Korea in the 1590s, originally as part of the wider Catholic missions to the Far East. The earliest Catholics in Korea were invading Japanese soldiers, which hardly augured well for the faith's reception. Soon, though, Korean scholars encountered Catholicism in more promising circumstances at the Chinese court. Protestant missionaries appeared later, in the nineteenth century. The number of Christians in the whole of Korea was only 300,000 or so in 1920, but this has now risen to at least 15 million, about a third of the national population.[44]

Christians represent a solid majority of those declaring any religious affiliation, quite an achievement for a society that for centuries defined its identity in terms of Buddhism and Confucianism. Korean Protestants outnumber Roman Catholics by about three to one, and as in Latin America, Protestant growth has been largely Pentecostal. At the time of the Korean War, the nation's Pentecostal believers could be counted only in the hundreds, but by the early 1980s, their ranks had swelled to almost half a million. The Yoido Full Gospel Church in Seoul now has 850,000 members, earning it a place in the *Guinness World Records* as the world's largest single congregation. The Kwang Lim Methodist Church reported 150 members in 1971, but 85,000 by the end of the century. Mainstream Protestant churches have also succeeded remarkably. The Myung Sung Presbyterian Church is the world's largest congregation in that tradition, and there are almost twice as many Presbyterians in South Korea as in the United States. Korean Christianity has a deep commitment to evangelism and mission work. Today, some fourteen thousand South Koreans are on mission overseas, a figure second only to the United States. Many of these missionaries work in China, while others target North Korean exiles as a means of reaching the hermetically sealed, and fanatically anti-Christian, Democratic People's Republic.[45]

Even in the grimmest political circumstances, the churches have been resilient. Communist Vietnam offers quite as powerful an example as China. Perhaps 10 percent of the country's 80 million people are Christian, most of whom are Catholic, and Catholicism is surviving well. In 2005, the

Vatican created a new diocese in Vietnam, breaking up the existing see of Xuan Loc that had swollen to an unmanageable population of more than 1 million, spread over 262 parishes. The announcement was accompanied by the ordination of fifty-seven priests. As in China, moreover, the estimate of Christian numbers does not include Protestant churches that are not registered with the government. Sometimes, nonregistration is a matter of principle, but the authorities also make the process extremely burdensome in order to discourage Christian growth. Unregistered churches face a perpetual struggle, and local bureaucrats and police can consign believers to prisons or re-education centers on little more than a whim. The scale of these catacomb churches is open to debate, but internal government documents suggest mushroom growth in some areas, notably those inhabited by tribal minorities such as the Montagnards. On occasion, Christians have been accused of involvement with widespread rural unrest across the country. Years after the communist victory, Christianity is still a force to be reckoned with.[46]

Elsewhere in Asia too, Christianity has a significant presence, rarely recognized by Westerners. India's Christian roots run deep, and the country has attracted successive waves of missionaries, although the rate of growth has fallen short of Chinese or Korean standards. The nation's Christian population is today estimated at a slim 2.3 percent of the whole, 25 million individuals. Even if that number represented the whole story, then India's Christians would still outnumber other better known minority religions, such as the Sikhs. Yet all observers recognize that that government figure for Christians is too low, given the government's vested interest in denying the power of "foreign" faiths, especially those that appeal chiefly to those of low or no caste. Plausible numbers are hard to come by, but Indian Christian observers generally speak of perhaps 40 million believers in India today, or 3.7 percent of the total population.

In absolute numerical terms, then, India has more Christians than most European nations, and more than half of these would be Independents, members of devoted charismatic churches affiliated to neither historic Protestant nor Catholic denominations. Among the more familiar churches, the Roman Catholic Church alone claims some 21 million Indian faithful. Moreover, although Christianity remains marginal to the larger Hindu cultural tradition, Indian churches have produced innovative theologians who have explored the interaction between Christianity and Asian faiths, and confronted the dilemmas of Christian existence as a tiny minority faith.[47]

Christianity has made deep inroads into regions once closely associated with other religions such as Hinduism, Buddhism, and Chinese traditional faiths. The great exception to this statement has been Islam, and the historically Muslim lands into which Christian missions have rarely penetrated. Evangelical Christians speak of the great missionary territory of the future as the "10–40 window," a vast and densely populated rectangle stretching across Africa and Asia, from ten degrees north to forty degrees north of the equator. In practice, Christianity has made huge strides in much of this so-called Resistant Belt, far more successfully than might once have been dreamed, but the Muslim world remains difficult territory. Suggesting just how intractable the problems are for hopeful Christians, we recall that the U.S. intelligence community has labeled this region the Arc of Instability.

It is open to debate what opportunities might be open to Christian evangelism if Muslim countries ever were persuaded to accept greater religious pluralism, but given that such a transformation seems impossible, it is scarcely worth speculating. In addition, Islam's powerful grip on these lands does not only rely on the mechanisms of state power; it is efficiently preserved by strong clerical structures and powerful loyalties of tribe and clan. In consequence, conversion to any non-Muslim religion can be a deeply perilous undertaking, making it all the more impressive that Christianity has made any strides whatever.

As we will see, the definition of Islamic-Christian frontiers will be a vital and contentious matter in future politics. For present purposes, though, we should note that the current general advance of Christianity is not, for the foreseeable future, going to affect every part of the globe.

EXPLAINING SUCCESS

Christian numbers have been growing in many diverse cultures, and the reasons for this expansion are equally complex. As I noted earlier, I do not claim that we can speak of "Southern" Christianity in any homogeneous way, both because of the very diverse cultures in which the faith has grown in recent years, and the many different social, economic, and political settings. Having said this, though, many of the new churches do have certain features in common, which set them apart from the traditional Christianity of Europe and North America. And in this regard, we can understand the African independent congregations in very much the same context as the Pentecostal movements of Asia and Latin America.

One common factor is that the various Southern churches are growing in response to similar economic circumstances. Their success can be seen as a by-product of modernization and urbanization. As predominantly rural societies have become more urban over the last thirty or forty years, millions of migrants are attracted to ever larger urban complexes, which utterly lack the resources or infrastructure to meet the needs of these "post-industrial wanderers." More than a billion people—one-sixth of the world—are illegal squatters living on the fringes of a Third World city. Sometimes people travel to cities within the same nation, but often they find themselves in different countries and cultures, suffering a still greater sense of estrangement. In such settings, the most devoted and fundamentalist-oriented religious communities emerge to provide functional alternative arrangements for health, welfare, and education.[48] This sort of alternative social system has been a potent factor in winning mass support for the most committed religious groups, and it is likely to become more important as the gap between popular needs and the official capacities to fill them becomes ever wider.

Medieval Europeans developed the maxim that "town air makes free," and for all its horrors, urbanization today does promise a new political and religious autonomy. In Latin America especially, the move to the cities over the last half-century has liberated ordinary people from traditional religious structures. No longer were they restricted to the only churches that landowners would permit on their estates, which in virtually every case were Catholic. Yet while liberating themselves, people were also seeking social structures not so very different from what they had previously known when they had lived in small villages, or on landed estates: there were features of village life that they missed badly. One theory holds that the new Latin American churches provide the uprooted with the kind of familiar structure to which they were accustomed. In Africa too, the independent churches find their firmest support in the swollen cities, among migrants and the dispossessed. On both continents, the pastors of the new churches exercise a paternalistic role reminiscent of familiar figures from rural society, of landlords in Latin America, of tribal authorities in Africa. The congregations replace the family networks that prevailed in the older villages.

We have already seen the linkage between urban growth and church expansion in a megalopolis like Rio de Janeiro, but we could easily choose other examples. Also in Brazil, the São Paulo metropolitan region has some 20 million people, and the city's growth has been virtually unplanned: at least 1.5 million live in the dire poverty of the *favelas*, the shantytowns. But alongside the poverty, we also find dramatic evidence of church growth. As a *Washington Post* report observed,

Throughout many of São Paulo's poorer neighborhoods, where abandoned industrial buildings are tattooed by graffiti and surrounded by patchwork fences, newly built evangelical churches rise from the ruins in walls of mirrored glass. Sometimes, the churches have expanded faster than their surroundings allow, requiring creative solutions. At the Agua Branca Baptist Church, the congregation outgrew its rented brick facility, so it bought a giant blue-and-white-striped tent from a circus, big enough to accommodate the crowds of 1,500 it attracts most Sundays.

São Paulo's annual March for Jesus attracts some 2 to 3 million participants, organized by such thriving evangelical denominations as *Renascer em Cristo*.[49]

Similar urban pressures have had similar consequences elsewhere in Latin America. In Chile, one of the great centers of Protestant expansion, the greater Santiago area has over 6 million people, over 40 percent of the national total. The population of Peru, again, has grown from 10 million in 1960 to around 30 million today. This growth has been disproportionately urban and in fact concentrated in one city, namely Lima, with its 8.5 million people—more than a quarter of the national total. (No other Peruvian city approaches a million in population.) Urbanization has been particularly rapid in Central America, driven by the dual forces of natural disaster and rural guerrilla wars, so that some 60 percent of Salvadorans now live in cities. And as elsewhere, urbanization is generally accompanied by evangelical expansion.

Africa offers similar stories of speedy urbanization. One of the most important, in terms of the future significance of the region, is the vast Nigerian city of Lagos. In 1950, Lagos was a ramshackle port community with around a quarter of a million people. The official population in 1990 was 1.3 million, but the surrounding metropolitan region had then grown to 10 million people, and today it approaches 20 million. Today, the population density of Lagos is about 20,000 people per square mile, and the city suffers desperately from congestion and pollution. Although Lagos is divided between Christians and Muslims, the city has played host to some of the largest evangelical gatherings in world history, with the biggest revivals claiming attendance running into the millions. Revivals organized by the Redeemed Christian Church of God have gathered congregations running into the millions. On one night in 2000, 1.6 million turned out to hear German Pentecostal evangelist Reinhard Bonnke, who advertised through the enticing slogan "Come and receive your miracle."[50]

RADICAL COMMUNITY

Churches provide a refuge during a time of immense and barely comprehensible social change. Cox aptly writes of modern urban centers that "sometimes the only thriving human communities in the vast seas of tar-paper shanties and cardboard huts that surround many of these cities are the Pentecostal congregations." A study of new Pentecostal churches in the barrios of Bogotá, Colombia, notes that "the *compañerismo* (fellowship) of the believers is comparable to the intimacy of a large family gathering."[51]

This sense of family and fellowship is crucial for understanding the wide and remarkably diverse appeal of the new Christian congregations. As we have seen, by no means all draw from the very poorest. The older Protestant denominations in Latin America and East Asia commonly appeal more to middle-class groups, who have expanded as a result of modernization, but whose goals and aspirations were hard to fulfill within older social structures. For David Martin, the older Protestantism of Latin America "provided a vehicle of autonomy and advancement for some sections of the middle class, conspicuously so in Brazil, and provided channels of mobility for some who would otherwise have been condemned to poverty."[52]

Yet it is among the very poor that the churches have won some of their greatest recent victories. Christian growth in India has drawn heavily on people of low caste or indeed from the outcastes, the Dalits or Oppressed, and that emphasis has aggravated conflict with traditional-minded Hindu authorities. In Latin America, Pentecostalism has appealed particularly to the very poorest, including Brazil's black population and the Maya Indians of Central America. Indian peoples alone constitute a potential base of real strength, accounting for perhaps 40 million of the continental population—20 million in the Andean nations, 16 million more in Mexico and Guatemala. The traditionally disfranchised find in the churches a real potential for popular organization. Based on his study of new churches in Belém, Brazil, Andrew Chesnut notes that "in late twentieth-century Brazil, Pentecostalism stands out as one of the principal organizations of the poor." The churches provide a social network that would otherwise be lacking and help teach members the skills they need to survive in a rapidly developing society.[53]

Given the history of much of Latin America, any movement that makes inroads among the poorest must of necessity be crossing racial boundaries, and much of the recent revivalism in Brazil has occurred among those of African descent. Despite the nation's vaunted multiracialism, Brazil's blacks and *mestizo* people have been largely excluded from political and social power, and that fact has been reflected in religious institutions. Broadly speaking, darkness of skin directly correlates with poverty and political weakness. Though blacks make up about half the national population, they represent only 2 percent of congressional representatives and a tiny fraction of the corporate elite. In the Roman Catholic Church too, Afro-Brazilians supply only 1.5 percent of bishops and priests. Not surprisingly, blacks provide willing recruits for new churches in which they can rise to leadership positions and to which they can bring their own cultural traditions. According to Paul Freston, the typical Brazilian Catholic is elderly, rural, white, and male; the typical Protestant is young, urban, dark, and female.[54]

The growth of black spirituality has powerful implications for the wider picture of world Christianity in the next half-century. Not only will Africa itself be the religion's spiritual center within a few decades, but hundreds of millions of other Christians will belong to the wider African diaspora in the Americas and the Caribbean, and on the soil of Europe itself. As one Nigerian Pentecostal pastor declared, "This is the time of the African. The Europeans have had their time, the Asians have had their time, the Americans have had their time. The black man is going to read the last Gospel before the coming of Christ. That is why the most vibrant churches in the world are pastored by blacks. It's our time." It may not be too long before some enthusiast modifies Belloc's celebrated phrase to boast that "Africa is the Faith."[55]

The new churches are succeeding because they fulfill emerging social needs, and this is as true in matters of gender as of race. No account of the new Southern movements can fail to recognize the pervasive role of women in these structures, if not as leaders then as devoted core members. Carol Ann Drogus writes of Latin America that "most Pentecostal converts are women…women are crucial to the maintenance and expansion of Pentecostal churches." Especially in this continent, much of the best recent scholarship on Pentecostalism stresses the sweeping changes that religious conversion can make in the lives of women and their families. A North American audience is accustomed to seeing religious believers as reactionary on issues of women's rights, but the new churches play a vital role in reshaping women's lives, in allowing them to find their voices. As in nineteenth-century England or North America, evangelical religion has encouraged a new and exalted view of the family and of domesticity, placing much greater emphasis on male responsibility and chastity. The reshaping of gender roles echoes through global South Christianity, and Latin American churches often present Jesus as divine Husband and Father.[56]

In practical terms, the emphasis on domestic values has had a transformative and often positive effect on gender relationships, what Elizabeth Brusco has memorably called a "reformation of machismo."[57] Membership in a new Pentecostal church means a significant improvement in the lives of poor women, since this is where they are more likely to meet men who do not squander family resources on drinking, gambling, prostitutes, and even second households. Drogus quotes one Pentecostal woman who reports that "I met a wonderful man. He never drinks, never smokes, he is polite, and he has a good job."[58] As in matters of race, Christianity is far more than an opium of the disinherited masses: it provides a very practical setting in which they can improve their daily lives.

At so many points in our story, we can see impressive analogies to the rise of early Christianity in the days of the Roman Empire, and it is tempting to use the scholarship on the older period to help us interpret the present day. As historian Peter Brown observes of the third and fourth centuries, "The appeal of Christianity still lay in its radical sense of community: it absorbed people because the individual could drop from a wide impersonal world into a miniature community, whose demands and relations were explicit." Every word in this sentence could be wholeheartedly applied to modern Africa or Latin America. The provision of social services that were otherwise unobtainable also goes far to explaining the growth of urban Christianity during Roman times, just like today. Brown suggests that

> The Christian community suddenly came to appeal to men who felt deserted. At a time of inflation, the Christians invested large sums of liquid capital in people; at a time of increased brutality, the courage of Christian martyrs was impressive; during public emergencies, such as plague or rioting, the Christian clergy were shown to be the only united group in the town, able to look after the burial of the dead and to organize food supplies.... Plainly, to be a Christian in 250 brought more protection from one's fellows than to be a *civis Romanus*."[59]

To be a member of an active Christian church today might well bring more tangible benefits than being a citizen of Nigeria or Peru.

Other more recent historic analogies come to mind. What we are now witnessing in the global South is very much what occurred in the North when it was passing through a comparable stage of social development. We can trace countless parallels between Pentecostal growth today and the much-studied story of English Methodism in the century after 1760, the most rapid stage of that nation's industrialization. Then as now, popular sects arose to meet the needs that could be filled neither by secular society, nor by the established churches, which had scarcely a foothold in the burgeoning cities. The new Dissenting churches were a triumph of cooperative endeavor, at once providing material support, mutual cooperation, spiritual comfort, and emotional release in the bleak wastes of the expanding industrial society.[60]

RECEIVE YOUR MIRACLE

When trying to understand religious movements, scholars apply the familiar techniques of social science and see change as a function of such familiar categories as modernization, race, class, and gender; but such an approach always runs the risk of missing the heart of the matter. People might join churches because, consciously or otherwise, they see these institutions as a way of expressing their social aspirations, but other elements also enter into the equation. Members join or convert because they acquire beliefs about the supernatural realm, and its relationship to the visible world.[61] Just what are these teeming masses seeking from their churches and revivals? What kind of miracle are they looking for?

The seemingly diverse Southern churches have in common many aspects of belief and practice, and these characteristics differentiate them from older Northern Christianity. Just what these distinctive beliefs are, we will explore in more detail in chapter 6, but for present purposes we have to stress the critical idea that God intervenes directly in everyday life. For both Pentecostal and independent sects, and often, for mainstream churches as well, the sources of evil are located not in social structures but in types of spiritual evil, which can be effectively combated by believers. Southern religion is not otherworldly in the sense of escapist, since faith is expected to lead to real and observable results in this world. The believer's life in this world is transformed through conversion, and the change echoes through every aspect of their lives, from ethics of work and thrift to family and gender relations.

Audiences respond enthusiastically to a gospel that promises them blessings in this life as well as the next—recall the upturned umbrellas at El Shaddai meetings, or the blessing of passports. To quote an observer of Brazil's emerging churches, "Their main appeal is that they present a God that you can use. Most Presbyterians have a God that's so great, so big, that they cannot even talk with him openly, because he is far away. The Pentecostal groups have the kind of God that will solve my problems today and tomorrow. People today are looking for solutions, not for eternity." As a Pentecostal pastor in the same country explained, "We have salvation, but salvation is in heaven. We are here on earth. Jesus will come but he's not here yet."[62] Much the same points could be made about the rising churches across most of Africa and Asia. Over the past decade, aggressively marketed prosperity churches have enjoyed a real boom, especially in West Africa. Paul Gifford, for instance, has published an excellent (and often disturbing) analysis of the most prominent leaders, such as Bishop David Oyedepo of Nigeria's Winner's Chapel, or Nicholas Duncan-Williams of Ghana's Action Chapel.[63]

People want prosperity—or at least, economic survival—but just as critical is the promise of health, and the desperate public health situation in the new cities goes far toward explaining the emphasis of the new churches on healing of mind and body. Apart from the general range of maladies that affect North Americans and Europeans, the Third World poor also suffer from the diseases associated with deprivation, hunger, and pollution, in what has been termed a "pathogenic society." Child mortality is appallingly high by Northern standards. The attacks of these demons of poverty are all the graver when people are living in tropical climates, with all the problems arising from the diseases and parasites found in those regions. As well as physical ailments, many psychiatric and substance abuse problems drive desperate people to seek refuge in God. Although shantytowns and *favelas* were never easy places to live, they became infinitely more dangerous when drug use and trafficking expanded from the 1980s, with all the attendant perils of gangs, drug wars, and easy access to heavy weaponry. Taking all these threats together—disease, exploitation, pollution, drink, drugs, and violence—it is easy to see why people might easily accept the claim that they were under siege from demonic forces, and that only divine intervention could save them. The promise of healing must of necessity extend to communities and societies, no less than the individual.[64]

At its worst, a Faith Gospel of success and health can promote abuses and materialism, and it is easily mocked. Nigerian author Wole Soyinka presents a wonderful satire of such a health-and-wealth sermon in his play *The Trials of Brother Jero,* in which the preacher promises: "I say those who dey walka today, give them their own bicycle tomorrow...I say those who dey push bicycle, give them big car tomorrow. Give them big car tomorrow." The doctrine also excuses corruption. If a pastor lives luxuriously, if he owns a very big car, he is simply living proof of the wealth that God has given him, while presumably someone who remains poor is just lacking adequate faith. The moral perils are all too obvious. Yet a doctrine promising glory in this world as well as the next has undoubted appeal.[65]

For the foreseeable future, the characteristic religious forms of Southern world Christianity—enthusiastic and spontaneous, fundamentalist and supernatural-oriented—look very different from those of the older centers in Europe and North America. This difference becomes critically important in light of current demographic trends. In the coming decades, the religious life characteristic of those regions may well become the Christian norm.

The Rise of the New Christianity

> After this I looked, and there before me was a great
> multitude that no one could count, from every nation,
> tribe, people and language, standing before
> the throne and in front of the Lamb.
>
> —*Rev 7:9*, NIV

Projecting demographic changes forty or fifty years in the future seems like a risky venture, and perhaps this chapter should really be titled "Fools Rush In." Yet the process of Christian expansion outside Europe and the West does seem inevitable, and the picture offered here is based solidly on current trends, religious and demographic. In this instance, the foolishness seems justified. To borrow the remark credited to sociological pioneer Auguste Comte, demography really is destiny.

One central fact in the changing religious picture is a massive relative decline in the proportion of the world's people who live in the traditionally advanced nations. If we combine the figures for Europe, North America, and the lands of the former Soviet Union, then in 1900, these Northern regions accounted for 32 percent of the world's population. Viewed over the span of world history, that may have been an atypically large proportion, which reflected the explosive demographic growth of the industrial revolution years. Throughout the course of the twentieth century, matters reverted to what was likely a more typical preindustrial norm, as the proportion of peoples living in the advanced nations fell, slowly at first, but then more dramatically. By 1950 the share had fallen a little to 29 percent, but the rate of contraction then accelerated, to 25 percent in 1970, and around 18 percent by 2000. By 2050 the figure should be around 10 or 12 percent.[1]

Relative growth rates in the South have been just as impressive. Africa and Latin America combined made up only 13 percent of the world's people in 1900, but that figure has now grown to 21 percent, and the rate of change is accelerating. By 2050 Africa and Latin America will probably be home to 29 percent of the world's people. In 1900 Northerners outnumbered these Southerners by about 2.5 to 1; by 2050 the proportions will be almost exactly reversed. Overall, global population stands at 6.9 billion today, and should reach 9 billion around 2050, but that increase will not be equitably distributed around the globe. Southern nations are growing very rapidly, while their Northern neighbors are relatively static.

There are many ways to look at statistics of this sort, and one's use of language inevitably reflects value judgments. It is tempting to speak of European rates of population growth as weak, stagnant, or anemic, while African rates are strong or booming, implying that Europe is somehow losing a contest, or failing to achieve. We rarely speak of decline as a good thing. As Josef Stalin famously remarked, quantity has a quality all of its own. Yet one does not have to be a Malthusian to be alarmed by uncontrolled population growth, and most observers would praise the changes in social structure and gender relations that have permitted Europeans to achieve demographic stability. One person's stagnation is another's stability.

Being one of the world's largest nations can be a mixed blessing. The fact of size offers the potential of a huge domestic market for goods and services, and implies political clout. A fast-growing population is also a young community, with a large labor force, a thriving pool of military recruits, and at least the potential of a solid tax base. At the same time, large countries face intense pressure on energy and natural resources, as well as the dangers of social and political turbulence. Demographically stable European nations face an exactly opposite range of costs and benefits, with declining markets and labor forces, and all the problems of an aging community requiring ever more expenditure on pensions and health care. It is an open question whether modern governments are worse prepared to face the emerging problems of the booming South or the stable North.

Such predictions are open to detailed criticism, and the demographers who produce these figures make no claims about their absolute reliability. Projections only work so long as people maintain their present behavior unchanged, and societies adapt to changing circumstances. Extrapolating present-day trends far enough down the road can lead to ludicrous results. Carrying current trends to their logical conclusion, the Japanese will literally have bred themselves out of existence by the year 2500. In reality, "logical" conclusions are far from inevitable. Populations can and do rebound from decline, while what seems like exponential growth can taper off. If the United States had maintained the growth rates of the eighteenth and early nineteenth century, then it would today be as populous as China, but of course it did not. In the same way, United Nations demographers predict that global population will eventually level off in a hundred years or so, at a new plateau of around 10 billion.[2]

Crucially, population change is conditioned by economic circumstances. The history of the West indicates that as a community becomes more prosperous, people tend to have fewer children, and these trends should eventually be replicated in the global South. The decline in family size reflects greater confidence in the ability of medicine to keep children alive, and to ensure that the babies who are born will actually grow to adulthood. Also, couples who have faith in social welfare arrangements have less need to create large families who will maintain them in old age. Gender relationships play a critical role. As economies become more sophisticated, more women participate in the workplace, and employed women cannot afford to devote as much of their lives to bearing and rearing children as do women in traditional societies. This fact encourages a trend toward smaller family size. In the long run, feminism may be the most effective means of regulating population.

As Southern economies develop, their demographic patterns come to resemble those of the older industrial nations, and we already see a steadying or decline of fertility rates in much of the world. Yet it will take some decades for the full effect of those changes to become apparent. For present purposes, we can be confident that in the middle term—say, the next fifty years—we will indeed be seeing a spectacular upsurge in Southern populations, and a decisive shift of population centers to the Southern continents, and especially to Africa.

DECLINING EUROPE

The stagnation of Northern and particularly European populations will be one of the most significant facts of the coming decades. If we take what are currently the eight most populous nations of Europe, then their combined populations amounted to 536 million as of 2000. (These nations are Russia, Germany, Britain, France, Italy, Ukraine, Poland, and Spain.) By 2025 that total will have fallen slightly, to about 529 million, most of the reduction occurring in Russia and Ukraine. Western Europe will retain a fairly stable population. But the rate of decline becomes more marked in midcentury, when these major European nations will have shrunk to 490 million.[3] If we expand our focus to the European Union as a whole, then its combined population would contract by about one-sixth between 2000 and 2050. In 1950 a list of the world's twenty most populous states would have included six European nations, apart from the USSR; on a comparable list in 2025, only Russia and Germany would still be ranked among the leaders.

In order to keep a population stable, a nation needs an overall fertility rate of 2.1 children per woman (the rate would have to be higher in countries with worse infant mortality rates). Today, many countries are reporting rates well below that, and twenty-three recorded fertility rates below 1.5, so all are likely to contract over coming decades. All but three of these nations are European, and we see historic lows in countries such as Germany (1.4), Italy (1.3), and Spain (1.3). All the members of the former Soviet bloc are also in sharp decline: the Russian rate now stands around 1.4. In the Russian case, historically low birth rates are compounded by soaring death rates and the revival of infectious diseases, including AIDS. The United Nations projects that the present-day Russian population of 145.6 million could fall to 121 million by 2050, but some pessimists imagine an even worse decline, to 80 million or so. If true, that would bring the Russian population back to where it stood before the revolution of 1917. In 2000, the Ukraine had a population of 49 million, but by 2050 that figure could fall to just 33 million.[4]

The main non-European member of this declining cohort is Japan, which as a long-established industrial nation shares many European social patterns. If present trends continue, the Japanese population that today amounts to 126 million will fall below 100 million by 2050, and to 67 million by 2100. By 2015 a quarter of Japanese will be sixty-five or older. The demographic contraction in Europe and the advanced nations would be even more advanced if not for the fertility of recent immigrant groups, mainly from Africa or Asia. Conversely, the absence of mass immigration in Japan goes far toward explaining the perilous condition of that country.[5] Although debates over immigration policy are often framed in humanitarian or altruistic terms—"We should help poor people by letting them come here"—for many countries, mass immigration represents the only possible means of maintaining a viable society.

SOUTHERN BOOM

In contrast to Europe and Japan, we can consider the experience of sub-Saharan Africa. In 1900, Africa had around 120 million people, or 7 percent of the global population. In 2005, the number of Africans reached one billion, or 15 percent of humanity. By 2050, Africa's population will be between two and two and a quarter billion, which will then be about a quarter of the world's people, and those numbers do not count millions of African migrants in Europe and North America. In 1900, Europeans outnumbered Africans by four to one; by 2050, Africans should have a three to one advantage over Europeans.

Population growth comes into even sharper focus when seen in a local context. By contemporary standards, just a century ago, human beings were sparsely distributed across large stretches of Africa. Consider the three East African nations that would become Kenya, Uganda, and Tanzania: in 1900, they were occupied by just seven or eight million people, in an area not much smaller than Western Europe. By 2000, the three countries had a combined population of 90 million. By 2050, they might have 260 million. The Ethiopian kingdom that repulsed an Italian invasion in 1896 had some twelve million subjects. Today there are 88 million Ethiopians, and by 2050 there could be 280 million. Growth in West Africa was comparable. In 1900, the lands that would become Nigeria had around 16 million people, rising to 150 million today, and probably to around 270 million by 2050.[6]

To take another focus, consider the nine nations that are on course to be the most populous in Africa by midcentury: Ethiopia, Nigeria, Congo-Kinshasa, Uganda, Sudan, Tanzania, Kenya, Madagascar, and Niger. In 1950, the combined population of these nine nations was around 100 million, rising to almost 400 million by 2000. By 2050, though, those nine nations will have a combined population of 1.2 billion. That would represent a twelvefold increase in raw numbers in just a century.

Obviously, AIDS has had a devastating effect in this region, and the eventual population totals may be somewhat less than this. AIDS-related deaths have dramatically slowed population growth in southern African nations such as South Africa and Zimbabwe, and over the next decade or so, Central and West African nations will suffer dreadfully from the epidemic, with the roster of deaths peaking before 2020. But even taking this ongoing catastrophe into account, the estimates cited here all explicitly allow for the disease factor, and demographers can still confidently predict very large population growth across the region.

Latin America and Asia both experienced sharp population growth during the second half of the twentieth century. Mexico, for instance, grew from just 15 million people in 1900 to around 100 million by 2000. Having said this, projected growth rates for both continents have slowed somewhat, reflecting the influence of greater prosperity and greater access to contraception. The demographic shift is particularly marked in Latin America. In 1970, for instance, more than 46 percent of Mexicans were under the age of fifteen, compared to around 29 percent today, and some Latin American nations even grapple with the problems of a graying population. Uruguay, in fact, is "older" than the United States or Canada, in the sense of having a larger share of its population over sixty years of age. Even so, Latin American growth rates still exceed European figures, and will continue to do so for some decades to come. Between 2000 and 2050, population growth in the eight largest nations in Latin America will be around 40 percent. The combined population for these countries was 429 million in 2000, potentially rising to 600 million by 2050.

According to the U.S. Census Bureau, several nations around the world are projected to double their populations in the next quarter-century, even after we have allowed for the effects of AIDS. These countries of super-rapid growth are all located in either sub-Saharan Africa (Uganda, Madagascar, the Democratic Republic of the Congo) or in Asia (Afghanistan, Bangladesh). The highest fertility rates in the world are found in Afghanistan, Burundi, Liberia, and the Democratic Republic of the Congo, all of which report astonishing fertility rates between 6.7 and 7.2. These are followed closely by nations such as Uganda, Angola, Somalia, and Yemen. Certainly, not all African and Asian countries are exploding at anything like this rate, and growth rates have declined steeply in China, Thailand, Vietnam, and Indonesia. Nevertheless many global South nations are still very fertile.

The contrast between growth and stagnation can be seen from the respective age-profiles of North and South. In a typical European country, the number of people aged sixty-five or over normally runs at around one-sixth of the population: the figure is 16 or 17 percent in France, Britain, and Spain. Yet people over sixty-five make up only 3 or 4 percent of most Southern nations. At the other end of the age spectrum, the proportion of people aged fourteen or under normally runs at 16 to 20 percent or so of the population in European nations. Across the global South, in contrast, the figure is usually around a third, and it rises much higher in some African countries. In Uganda, half the people are below this age, a level also approached in neighboring countries like the Democratic Republic of the Congo. The world's youngest nations are African, namely Uganda, Niger, and the Congo, countries in which the median age of the population is around sixteen. By the same measure, the oldest countries are all in Europe or Japan—*forty* is the median age of the people of Italy, Germany, Sweden, and Japan.

These trends can only lead to an ever-larger proportion of the Earth's people living in what have long been the economically less advanced regions, in Africa, Asia, and Latin America. Table 5.1 suggests the growing predominance of Southern nations over the next half-century or so.

By 2050, six of the world's twenty most populous nations will be on the African continent. Among Northern nations, apart from the United States, only Russia and Japan will retain their positions among the world's largest nations, and neither of these is likely to remain on the list for much longer. Equally striking is the emergence of more and more nations with what presently seem inconceivably vast populations ranked in the hundreds of millions. In 1950 only four nations boasted populations of a hundred million or more, namely the United States, the USSR, China, and India. By 2025, at least fifteen will fall into this category, and these leading large nations will account for two-thirds of the human race. By the end of the present century, fourteen states could each have 200 million people or

TABLE 5.1
The Most Populous Nations in the World, 2025 and 2050
Nations are listed in order of their projected rankings as of 2050
(all figures are in millions)

National Population in: Nation	1975*	2000	2025	2050
1. India	619	1,006	1,396	1,657
2. China	918	1,264	1,395	1,304
3. United States	215	282	358	439
4. Indonesia	135	214	279	313
5. Pakistan	76	152	228	291
6. Ethiopia	33	64	140	279
7. Nigeria	64	123	197	264
8. Brazil	109	176	231	261
9. Bangladesh	76	132	198	250
10. Congo (Kinshasa)	25	52	110	189
11. Philippines	44	81	129	172
12. Mexico	61	100	130	148
13. Egypt	37	65	104	138
14. Uganda	11	24	57	128
15. Vietnam	48	79	102	111
16. Russia	135	147	128	109
17. Turkey	41	67	90	101
18. Iran	33	69	90	100
19. Sudan	16	34	63	97
20. Japan	112	127	118	94

Note: 1975 figures for Russia refer to the RSFSR, the Russian Socialist Federated Soviet Republic, and not to the Soviet Union of which it then formed part.
Source: http://sasweb.ssd.census.gov/idb/ranks.html.

more, and of these, only the United States will represent what is presently the advanced Western world.

These projections are markedly different from the perceptions that prevail in the contemporary West. Asked to name the world's largest countries either now or in the near future, most Americans or Europeans would probably think of China, India, Pakistan, Nigeria, and some other obvious names on the list. But how many would include lands such as Ethiopia, Uganda, or the Sudan? The rankings also include some extreme incongruities for anyone who grew up in the mid-twentieth century. For those of us who remember the Vietnam War era, it is inconceivable that "heroic little Vietnam" might soon outpace Russia itself in population.

DAMNED LIES AND STATISTICS

These demographic changes will inevitably have their impact on the world's religious structures. The difficulty is, though, that religious patterns are far harder to quantify than those in other areas of life. We can be reasonably sure *where* the bulk of the world's people will be living in 2050, but do we dare make statements about what they will believe? When we collect statistics for birth or marriage, we are measuring specific and provable events, which are biological or legal in nature, and we have some grounds for making projections. Equally, we can at least attempt to predict changes in economics or environmental conditions, though in neither area can experts claim a terribly impressive record of accuracy. As the saying has it, economic forecasting was invented for the purpose of making astrology look respectable. But religious matters are still more intractable. What, exactly, do we mean if we say that a given country has 10 million Christians, or even more questionable, that the number of Christians is likely to double over the next twenty or thirty years?

Since so much of this book concerns numbers and focuses on present and future religious statistics, it is important to say what can and cannot be done with the evidence that we have. As another saying goes, you can prove anything with statistics, even the truth. Most social statistics can be challenged or modified depending on the definitions used, and the means by which information is collected. These problems become acute when matters of religion are concerned, and even the definition of "Christian" can be controversial. Talking with an American evangelical in the 1980s, I mentioned the grim plight of the Christian community in Lebanon, only to be sternly corrected on the grounds that that country, in fact, had virtually no

Christians. This was surprising because by most accounts, the population of Lebanon at that point was 40 or 50 percent Christian, in a line of tradition that dated back to Roman times. In my friend's view, though, the term "Christian" could be used only for someone who had experienced a personal born-again conversion, and basically applied to evangelicals in the North American mold. This is the same attitude that produced the notorious comment that the nation of Poland contained only a hundred thousand or so Christians, and the rest of the population were all Roman Catholics.

These restrictions can seem overly narrow or bigoted, but the "Christian" title becomes more problematic in other cases. Many denominations around the globe have no doubt of their own claim to this status, yet have been attacked for theological peculiarities that seem to put them beyond the Christian pale. Are Mormons Christian?[7] Latter-day Saints spend not a moment in doubting or arguing the fact, yet conservative and evangelical believers reject them quite as assuredly, since Mormons use additional scriptures over and above the Bible and espouse doctrines far removed from traditional Western Christianity. Similar caveats would remove from the Christian fold at least some of the African and Asian independent churches that are presently at the cutting edge of Christian expansion (see chapter 6). Also problematic are the millions of Latin Americans who define themselves confidently as Catholic, yet whose religious practice draws on African-derived spiritualities such as Santeria, Umbanda, or Candomblé. Denying that Mormons are Christians does not raise too many statistical problems for overall numbers, but excluding these other groups could make a sizable difference to our picture of religious loyalties.

But if some observers underclaim Christian numbers on grounds of theological strictness, others are just as likely to make exaggerated claims. The reasons are clear enough. Religious statistics often rely on overly optimistic reports by church bodies themselves. Some churches have well-controlled mechanisms to measure types of involvement in a given community, and they carefully collect numbers for baptisms, confirmations, or marriages, but literally have no way of detecting when a church member leaves for any reason other than death. Missionaries place a high premium on recording conversions, which are the primary means of measuring success, but do not count converts who slip away, those who become indifferent or actively hostile.

Nor are problems of counting confined to the new Christian lands. In any country, when you have once been a member of a particular Roman Catholic parish, it is all but impossible to convince that church that you have resigned from it, even if you have demonstrated full commitment to another denomination. A Mother Church does not abandon her errant children. In various European countries, it is just as hard to remove yourself from the registers of the various state churches that act as if they still had the established role they possessed centuries ago. Some churches count as members everyone baptized within that tradition, so that "Christian" becomes a default status in official surveys and virtually means "none of the above." "You're not a Catholic? Not a Muslim? Not a Jew? Fine, I'll put you down as a Lutheran"—or an Anglican, or some other group, depending on the country in question. This tactic accounts for the inflated numbers claimed by English Anglicans, German Evangelicals, or Italian Catholics. The Church of England claims the loyalty of 25 million baptized Anglicans, even though less than a million of those are ever seen within the precincts of a church.

Different churches measure membership in different ways. One church includes as a member every person baptized in infancy, while another confines the term to those who have made some kind of adult commitment. When we are trying to interpret a claim about the numerical strength of any denomination, our first question should usually be "Are they counting children?" Some churches count active participants who share regularly in ritual life, for instance by taking Communion every Easter or Christmas, so that anyone who failed to meet this standard would be purged from the rolls. Others (like Roman Catholics) simply never remove a supposed member. We could easily imagine two denominations with roughly the same number of "real" active members, although one less careful about record keeping could report numbers ten times larger than the other. Most churches do not actively lie about their membership statistics; they genuinely do not know the figures. This helps explain why indigenous churches in Africa are so often credited with five or six million members: the number is not so much a real statistic as a symbolic statement implying "a great many people."

Problems of evidence become particularly tricky when international issues are involved. Generally, though, estimates of Christian populations are actually more likely to be accurate in countries that lack an official or established church. In the newer Christian cultures, practices such as baptism do not yet have the same role as obligatory social rituals that they do in England or Spain, while church membership is likely to be more active and less formal. In this sense, church statistics for, say, Uganda or Nigeria are actually likely to be *more* reliable than those reported for Britain or France.

With all these issues in mind, it is tempting to ask whether any religious statistics at all are worthwhile, but I believe that they are, provided certain commonsense guidelines are followed. First, for working purposes, we cannot be too precise about defining Christianity. Ever since the movement began two thousand years ago, the range of groups describing themselves as followers of Jesus has always been very diverse, and we should acknowledge and accept that broad range of self-conceptions. For the purposes of this book, a Christian is someone who describes him- or herself as Christian, who believes that Jesus is not merely a prophet or an exalted moral teacher, but in some unique sense the Son of God and the Messiah. Beyond that, we should not inquire into detailed doctrine, whether a person adheres to the Bible alone, accepts the Trinity, or has a literal belief in Jesus's bodily resurrection. The vast majority of self-described Christians worldwide do in fact meet most of these criteria for membership in the faith, but for present purposes we cannot exclude those who do not.

Equally, we have to pay attention to the sources of the numbers we are offered, whether, for instance, they represent "none of the above" choices, or the more plausible estimates of actual religious involvement in given communities. Even so, with all due awareness of the problems involved, I will in many cases be using official definitions of religious loyalty, the admittedly exaggerated statements about numbers of adherents put out by various governmental and ecclesiastical bodies. With whatever qualms, this means accepting the statistics that suggest that for all its evident secularization, Europe is still overwhelmingly Christian and appears to remain the world center of Christianity.

This approach acknowledges that people often do retain a lingering cultural loyalty to a church label, even when actual religious involvement is nonexistent. The fact of living under the hegemony of a particular tradition inevitably tends to shape one's consciousness, so that even a not-very-enthusiastic believer can appropriately be seen as a cultural Christian, or a cultural Muslim, or whatever the tradition in question. Even when someone claims to abandon religion, it is this predominant religion that they are rebelling against and which largely shapes the form taken by that rebellion. As the old joke holds, everyone in the American South is Baptist, even including atheists, as the God in whom they do not believe is the Baptist God. Rejecting fears of a mass conversion to Protestantism in Latin America, one Catholic responded that in that continent, "you are Catholic just by breathing the air. The Catholic faith has so permeated the life of the people—the courtroom, the kitchen, the plaza, the architect's eye—that it would take centuries for Latin America to sweat it out." That is as good a description of "cultural" religion as we are likely to find.[8]

Surveys regularly indicate that millions of Americans describe themselves as Catholic even though they reject many or most of that church's positions, often on what most would consider essential doctrine. Are these people "really" Catholic? It all depends who you ask. For present purposes, my view is that if they consider themselves Catholic, then that is what they are.

As a final obstacle, religious trends simply do not develop as logically and predictably as demographic factors. To take what should be one of the world's pivotal nations in the near future, at least 45 percent of Nigerians are currently Christian, some 72 million people, but how will that number change in future decades? No church or religion has a guaranteed market share in any country. It is quite possible to imagine a scenario in which the proportion of Nigerian Christians could fall as low as 10 percent, in the event of persecutions, or a successful jihad by the nation's Muslims. The figure could rise far higher, if a sweeping Christian revival were to occur.

THE FUTURE DEMOGRAPHICS OF RELIGION

Although we might be tempted to despair about any attempt at prediction, we are still observing major trends in the development of global South Christianity, and in every case, these suggest surging growth. In Africa especially, experience over the last half-century indicates that the Christian share of the population will rise substantially across most of the continent, making deep inroads in the center and east. This trend is so marked that any projections offered here might be overly conservative. Religious maps may change, the frontiers shift, but Southern world Christianity will be growing.

To illustrate this, let us visualize the shape of the Christian world in another twenty or forty years: where will the bulk of Christians live? What should be the largest Christian communities in the year 2025 or 2050? For present purposes, we will make the conservative assumption that Christian communities will remain relatively stable as a proportion of national populations (see table 5.2). If these figures are even close to correct, then this list would comprise the leading Christian centers in the world of 2050. By that point, these eleven nations will account for half the world's Christian population.

One uncertainty about this table is the political integrity of the states named, and it is possible that countries such as the Democratic Republic of

TABLE 5.2
The Largest Christian Communities, 2025 and 2050

Nation	Estimated Christian Population (millions) in:		
	2000	2025	2050
USA	225	270	350
Brazil	164	190	234
Philippines	77	116	162
Ethiopia	36	65	160
D. R. Congo	34	70	150
Mexico	95	127	130
Nigeria	50	83	127
Uganda	20	47	106
China	65	75	85
Russia	90	85	70
Germany	58	61	52

Note: Information about religious affiliations is based on U.S. government statistics, found, respectively, in the *Annual Report on International Religious Freedom* (http://www.state.gov/g/drl/irf/) and the *CIA World Fact Book* (http://www.cia.gov/cia/publications/factbook/index.html).

the Congo will no longer exist in that form and may have disintegrated into two or more smaller entities. Nevertheless, the regions in question will be major Christian territories, and this fact confirms a powerful southward shift. By 2050 eight nations could each have a hundred million Christians or more, and of these, only one represents what is presently the advanced industrial world, namely the United States. Equally striking, perhaps, are the nations that are not found on this list, such traditional heartlands of Christian loyalty as Britain, France, and Italy.[9] The most striking element here is the rise of Christian Africa. Not only were there far more Africans, but a much larger share of them were Christian. In consequence, the absolute number of African believers soared, from just 10 million in 1900 to a projected 500 million by 2015 or so, and (if estimates are correct) to a billion by 2050. Put another way, the number of African Christians in 2050 will be almost twice as large as the total figure for *all* the Christians who were alive anywhere on the planet back in 1900. About a third of the world's Christians by 2050 will be African, and those African Christians will outnumber Europe's by more than two to one. The Christian world will have turned upside down.

Uganda is representative of the fast-growing Southern countries. The country's population in 1950 was just 5.5 million people, in a land the size of Oregon, but the number of people was roughly doubling every quarter-century or so. To put this in context, this was the same stunning growth rate that North America experienced during the colonial and early national period. There were 11 million Ugandans by 1975, 24 million by 2000. The U.S. Census Bureau suggests that there might be 128 million Ugandans by the middle of the present century. The country currently records an annual growth rate of 3.6 percent, which sounds impressive enough until we recall that that is not the birth rate, but the actual rate of annual growth. The *birth* rate is four times that of most European nations. The rate of overall growth would be even higher if not for the effects of AIDS and civil violence.[10]

In religious terms, Uganda represents one of the triumphs of the missionary movement. Christianity was newly planted in the mid-nineteenth century, yet today, about 41 percent of the population is Protestant, 42 percent Catholic, and 12 percent Muslim, while the rest follow traditional African religions. If we assume no further expansion by means of conversion, then Uganda's Christian population should grow from around 27 million today to 47 million in 2025, and—if the high projections are correct—to 106 million by midcentury. This last figure is probably too high, and the present birth rate may well fall substantially. But even if it does, Uganda will still be a major presence on the world map, with considerably more self-described Christians than in nations such as Germany or Britain.

To take an even more remarkable example, look at neighboring Kenya, a land that in 1900 had a mere 1.5 million residents. Today it has 40 million, and by 2050 it could have 65 million. Today, around 80 percent of Kenyans are Christian (approximately 32 million Christians), while 4 or 5 million are Muslim. Assuming those proportions remain constant, we could expect to see 50 million Kenyan Christians by 2050.

The Philippines offers a comparable Asian example. By 2050, it will be home to the third or fourth largest number of Christians on the planet.[11] The current population of around 88 million will expand quickly due to a high rate of population growth, currently estimated at 2 percent each year. It is also, like Uganda, a very young country, in which 35 percent of the population is currently under the age of fifteen. By 2050 there could be 170 million Filipinos. The city of Manila reports a population of around 1.8 million, but the larger metropolitan area contains perhaps 12 million. By 2050 the Manila metropolitan area could easily have 18 or 20 million inhabitants.

In religious terms, Christianity has deep roots in the Philippines, which was part of the Spanish colonial expansion of the sixteenth century. About

85 percent of the nation presently has some degree of identification with the Roman Catholic Church, while another 8 percent are associated with various Protestant groups (a further 5 percent are Muslims). If we assume that these proportions will remain constant, then by 2050 we will be speaking of around 160 million Filipino Christians. This growth will have major implications for the shape of global Catholicism. Today, the Catholic Church of the Philippines reports 72 million members, which represents a larger Catholic population than that found in any individual European state, and the number of Catholics is growing swiftly. At present, the Philippines reports 1.7 million Catholic baptisms each year, a number larger than the *combined* totals for the four leading Catholic nations of Europe, namely France, Spain, Italy, and Poland.[12] By 2025 the number of Filipino Catholics could grow to 110 million, and to 145 million by 2050.

That the Philippines will continue to represent a major Catholic state is a reasonably safe bet, but we can be far less confident about another emerging super-state, namely Brazil. Here too, the country has grown enormously, and this pattern will continue. There were 53 million Brazilians in 1950, there are around 200 million today, and by 2050 there should be around 260 million. An upsurge of AIDS-related deaths means the rate of increase is lower than it would have been otherwise, but even so, we are still dealing with a classic Third World population profile. Almost 27 percent of Brazilians are age fourteen or less. But religious statistics are much more tenuous than secular demographics. Today, about 74 percent of Brazil's population is reported as Catholic, while a further 15 percent are Protestant or Pentecostal. If we extrapolate those figures into the mid-twenty-first century, then we see a society with more than 150 million Catholics, and 30 or 40 million Protestants. But can we make this projection with any confidence? The non-Catholic population has swelled so very quickly in recent years as to make any such predictions moot, and it would not be astonishing if Brazil by this stage was half-Protestant. That Brazil will be a key center of world Christianity is beyond doubt, but the precise contours of its religious life are unknowable.

THE UN-SECULAR CITY

None of the reasons why churches have been growing so astonishingly in the global South is likely to change in the near future. These emerging churches work so well because they appeal to the very different demographics of their communities, and do best among young and displaced migrants in mushrooming cities. The most successful new denominations target their message very directly at the have-nots, or rather, the have-nothings. Again, demographic projections suggest that the environment in which they have flourished will continue to exist well into midcentury. By 2050, there will be an ever-growing contrast between the age profiles of the global South and North, between one world of the young and very mobile, and another of the old and static.

Most of the global population growth in the coming decades will be urban. Today, around 45 percent of the world's people live in urban areas, but that proportion should rise to 60 percent by 2025, to 66 percent by 2050. In another epochal change, these urban centers will be overwhelmingly Southern. In 1900 all the world's largest cities were located either in Europe or North America. Today, only three of the world's ten largest urban areas can be found in traditionally advanced countries, namely Tokyo, New York City, and Los Angeles (see table 5.3). Currently, 80 percent of the world's largest urban conglomerations are located in either Asia or Latin America, and African cities will become much more prominent by midcentury. China in particular continues to urbanize. Already, China has 160 cities with populations over a million, and as early as 2015, over half of the nation's population will be urban. The metropolitan area of Chongqing alone, a name scarcely known to most Westerners, already has over 30 million people, more than the entire nations of Iraq or Peru.

TABLE 5.3
The World's Largest Urban Concentrations in 2025

Metropolitan Area	Population (millions)
Tokyo	37.1
Delhi	31.8
Mumbai	28.8
São Paulo	23.2
Dhaka	23.1
New York/Northern NJ	22.9
Mexico City	22.9
Calcutta	22.3
Shanghai	22.2
Karachi	20.7
Lagos	17
Beijing	16.6
Manila	16.5
Kinshasa	16.4
Cairo	15.2

Source: World Christian Database.

China is of course a highly organized state, but much of the urban growth will take place in much weaker social and political environments, even of failed or failing states. The proportion of Africans living in urban areas will grow from around 40 percent today to almost 66 percent by 2050. Worldwide, the result will be a steadily growing number of huge metropolitan complexes that could by 2050 or so be counting their populations in the tens of millions. Megacities such as Cairo, Mumbai (Bombay), Dhaka, Karachi, Jakarta, Lagos, and Mexico City each have perhaps 30 or 40 million people, and next to nothing in terms of working government services. Tens of millions of new urban dwellers will in effect be living and working totally outside the legal economy or any effective relationship with officialdom. Still other colossi will arise in the future, giant cities with names hitherto unfamiliar to Westerners, centers such as Kampala, Kinshasa, Dar-es-Salaam, and Sana'a. By midcentury, still other African names will soon be joining the roster of megacities—Bamako, Lubumbashi, Niamey, and Maputo.[13]

Rich pickings await any religious groups who can meet the needs of these new urbanites, anyone who can at once feed the body and nourish the soul. Will the harvest fall to Christians or Muslims? And if to Christians, will the winners be Catholics or Pentecostals?

EUROPE

Demographics alone cannot tell the full story of the broadening gap between the numerical strength of Christians in the First and Third Worlds, since cultural shifts too will play their part. Not only are there going to be far more Christians in the global South than the North, but the Southerners are also likely to be much more committed in terms of belief and practice. The cultural change is evident in Europe, which notionally has a present-day Christian population exceeding 500 million. To say the least, that number looks optimistic. Over the last century or so, massive secularization has seriously reduced the population of European Christians, whether we judge "Christianity" by general self-description or else demand evidence of practice and commitment. Rates of church membership and religious participation have been declining precipitously in a long-term trend that shows no signs of slowing.[14]

Great Britain offers a model example of institutional collapse. In a population of around 60 million, the number adhering to non-Christian religions is still not large. Jews, Muslims, Sikhs, and Hindus combined total no more than 5 percent of the British total, roughly the same non-Christian proportion as in the United States. But we cannot safely conclude that the remaining 95 percent of British people should be classified as Christian. Depending on the survey, between 50 and 75 percent of British people identify themselves as Christians, but the degree of this identification is often slight. Based on baptismal records, Great Britain claims to have 25 million members of the Church of England, which has long enjoyed an established status. As we have seen, though, few of these supposed Anglicans show any enthusiasm for the faith. As Theo Hobson observes, "The English inhabit the ruins of the greatest national religion of modern times." Extrapolating current trends would leave English churches literally abandoned within a generation or two. The proportion of British people claiming "no religion" now stands at 40 percent.[15]

Similar situations can be found in most other west European nations and in the former Communist countries of Eastern Europe. In Germany, the situation of the Evangelical Church is comparable to that of British Anglicans. In theory, the church claims the loyalty of most German Protestants, around a third of the population, but out of 27 million notional members, only a million or so demonstrate any regular religious participation. Activity is higher among German Catholics but still represents only a small share of reported members. About a quarter of the population claim no religious affiliation, not even a residual Christianity.[16]

Declining religious identification is just as obvious in the historically Catholic nations. In France, as in Britain, many report some notional affiliation with Christianity, but only 8 percent, some 5 million, emerge as practicing Catholics. According to a survey taken in 2007 fewer than half of French people claim even a notional loyalty to Catholicism, and that poll was taken before the wave of sex abuse scandals that have so traumatized Europe's churches. It is difficult to see in what sense France can still be described as a Catholic country, other than by force of ancient habit.

Italy offers a similar story. Because of the church's long-standing hegemony, it is still customary for most Italians to acknowledge some vestigial Catholic identity, and indeed most Italians are baptized as Catholics. According to church statistics, some 97 percent of Italians count as Catholics, some 55 million adherents. Based on this figure, Italy is now the only European country listed among the world's five most populous Catholic nations. However, religious practice in Italy has declined steeply in recent years, and a more reasonable estimate of belief and loyalty would suggest an active Catholic population far below this level.

Worries about religious decline in Catholic Europe became acute follow-ing the clerical sex abuse scandals that emerged in 2010. European media commonly presented the picture of a systematic church crisis, and asked how or if the church can recover. Would the scandals irreparably destroy Catholic authority? Would they drive millions away from the church? Would they lead believers to divert their giving to secular causes, devas-tating church finances? To some extent, these questions were confusing cause and effect. While abuse scandals may well thin church numbers and subvert the Vatican's political influence in Europe, they are symptoms of secularization as much as causes. If the Catholic consensus had not been so badly undermined already, stories of clerical abuse would not have appeared in the media, and would have had nothing like the effect they did. As we have seen, Catholic countries have been becoming steadily more secular for at least a generation, quite independent of any claims of priestly deviance. Recent events will only accelerate these trends.

Now, the picture of Christian decline needs to be qualified somewhat. As scholars such as Grace Davie remind us, falling observance cannot simply be equated with pure secularism. Even in the relatively secular countries, survey evidence still shows surprisingly high levels of belief, suggesting that people are believing without belonging, and a majority still characterize themselves, however indecisively, as Christians. Just when observers are writing the obituaries of the continent's Christian heritage, Europeans offer startling manifestations of faith when (for instance) they turn out in hun-dreds of thousands to greet a papal visit, or when millions visit pilgrimage shrines. Yet having said this, these arguments do not necessarily offer com-fort for Christians in the longer term, as it is not clear how long a religion can survive as a generalized social memory. Residual Christianity may be surviving a generation or so after institutional structures went into free fall, but the situation in thirty or forty years might be much grimmer. Contemporary churches are surviving on accumulated capital, which is evaporating at an alarming rate.[17]

Both Anglicanism and Roman Catholicism are global communions, so that declining loyalties in Europe should be more than compensated by gains elsewhere in the world, but that pattern will not hold true for all denominations. The Eastern Orthodox churches will suffer acutely from demographic changes, given that the church's numbers are so heavily con-centrated in declining Europe. Presently, the Orthodox church worldwide claims about 220 million followers, almost all in countries of eastern and southeastern Europe that are likely to be losing population steadily over the next fifty years. Although postcommunist Russia has experienced a substantial Orthodox revival, demographic trends mean that the long-term future of that church must be in doubt. Falling birth rates will ultimately be more destructive to Orthodox fortunes than Muslim or communist persecutions ever were. Taking an optimistic population projection, Orthodox believers will by 2050 have shrunk to less than 3 percent of the world's population, dismally smaller than the early twentieth-century figure. In the worst-case scenario, the total number of Orthodox believers in the world by 2050 might actually be less than the Christian population of a single nation such as Mexico or Brazil.[18]

THE NEW EUROPEANS

A largely secularized First World confronts a rapidly growing South in which religion thrives and expands. We can illustrate this point by comparing Uganda with Britain, or Brazil with Spain. But this contrast does not just involve societies separated by oceans, since the interaction of North and South will be reproduced within the individual countries of North America and Europe themselves. This will occur as a consequence of mass migrations.

The far-reaching ethnic transformation of Europe was largely an accidental by-product of the Cold War. As western European industries boomed during the 1950s and 1960s, the natural source for cheap labor would have been the poorer (white) countries of southern and eastern Europe, but the rigid nature of Cold War boundaries forced employers to turn elsewhere. Industrial states recruited in Asia and Africa, often in former colonial territories: the British drew labor from the Caribbean and Pakistan, the French from North and West Africa. These immigrant populations have grown steadily, since these groups have experienced far higher birth rates than the older populations of the metropolitan countries. People of African and Asian stock now play a crucial part in European societies, especially in major cities. About half of London's people are now nonwhite, and by 2050, around 20 percent of the population of Great Britain will be from ethnic minorities, with origins in Africa, Asia, or the Caribbean. The empires have struck back.

Across Europe, mass immigration has been deeply controversial for decades, but it is difficult to see how else European nations could cope with what otherwise would be sharply declining (and aging) domestic populations. If Germany ceased to accept immigration, then its current population of 82 million would shrink about one-quarter by 2050: in the same years, the working population would fall from around 41 million to only 26 million.

Yet the problems would become acute long before this. Europe's baby-boom generation is already beginning to retire, and over the next decade the vast demands on social security could well crash fiscal systems across the Continent. The gravity of the burden facing public finances was already becoming apparent before the economic crisis of 2010. A report issued by the French government argued that Europe would have no alternative but to admit 75 million immigrants by 2050, with the frank admission that this would mean becoming a racially hybrid society and accepting "cross-fertilization."[19]

The U.S. intelligence community sees the demographic decline as a serious potential brake on global economic progress. Discussing the prospects for 2020, a recent report comments that "over the next 15 years, West European economies will need to find several million workers to fill positions vacated by retiring workers. Either European countries adapt their workforces, reform their social welfare, education, and tax systems, and accommodate growing immigrant populations (chiefly from Muslim countries) or they face a period of protracted economic stasis that could threaten the huge successes made in creating a more united Europe."[20]

Looking at the supply side of the equation, Southern peoples will face continuing pressures to move northward en masse, due to poverty and environmental catastrophe. Presently, Western Europe alone has between 10 and 20 million illegal immigrants from Africa and Asia, over and above the legally settled communities. One enormous and continuing incentive will be water resources, since the regions of fastest population growth are often those in most acute danger of drought and drought-related famines. Today, twenty-one countries are "either cropland or freshwater scarce," a potentially disastrous condition that presently affects some 600 million people. By 2025, the number of countries affected would rise to thirty-six, with a combined population of 1.4 billion. Just to take one regional example, several of the world's fastest growing nations survive on the finite water resources of the Nile. In coming decades, accumulating pressure on these waters will certainly drive regional conflicts, which in turn will force ever more North and East Africans to seek new homes in Europe.[21]

Demographic changes naturally have religious consequences, since the new immigrant groups follow cultural patterns more akin to their home societies than to the host nations. Islam of course is a long-established force in Europe, and many Muslims are of ancient stock, particularly in the southeastern parts of the continent. Europe as a whole, from Ireland to Russia, had 18 million Muslims in 1970, rising to some 35 million in 2010, and some Western European nations have acquired sizable Muslim minorities (see table 5.4).

TABLE 5.4
Muslim Populations in Western Europe

	Muslims (millions)	Total Population (millions)	Percentage
France	5	60	8.3
Germany	3.5	82	4.3
Britain	1.6	60	2.7
Italy	1	57	1.8
Spain	1	41	2.4
Netherlands	1	16	6.3
Belgium	0.4	10.3	3.9
Austria	0.35	8	4.4
Switzerland	0.31	7.2	4.3
TOTAL	14.16	341.5	4.2

Source: Adapted from David B. Barrett, George T. Kurian, and Todd M. Johnson, World Christian Encyclopedia, 2nd ed. (New York: Oxford University Press, 2001).

By 2050, Europe as a whole will have a Muslim minority of at least 15 percent, possibly as high as 20 percent.

The most visible aspect of religious change has been the upsurge of mosques and Muslim community centers across most western European nations. French cities such as Marseille have acquired a strongly North African flavor. In contrast to the United States, poorer migrants concentrate not in decayed urban cores but in working-class suburbs, the *banlieues*, which have become notorious as centers of multiple social deprivation, of crime and disorder.[22]

Looking at the spread of mosques across urban Europe, it would be easy to believe that Islam might indeed be Europe's future religion. Yet a great many other European immigrants are Christian, and they raise the prospect of a revitalized Christian presence on European soil. As we will see, Southern influence grows through two related but distinct phenomena. In some cases, Third World churches undertake actual mission work in secularized North America and especially Europe. Commonly, though, the evangelism is an incidental by-product of the activities of immigrant churches, an important phenomenon given the large African and Asian communities domiciled in Europe.

The emergence of a new Christianity was symbolized for me by an encounter while researching the first edition of this book, as I was visiting Amsterdam, which is at the heart of one of the world's most secular societies. Being there on a Sunday morning, one becomes aware of how little religious activity, Christian or otherwise, takes place in or near the center city. It was all the more interesting, then, to venture into a working-class suburb to see a swelling stream of individuals all clearly bound for the same destination. Each was an African, clearly not terribly well-off, but each was in his or her Sunday best, and everyone clutched a well-thumbed Bible. Some families were in evidence, but most of the passersby, obviously en route to an African church, were single men, presumably immigrants separated from homes and families. The overwhelming impression that the churchgoers gave was one of decency and dignity.

That encounter actually leads to a larger story, which neatly indicates the limitations of the secular dream, even in the Netherlands. In the 1960s, Dutch planners laid out a sprawling landscape of streets and apartment complexes in the area of Amsterdam known as South-East, a working-class zone that tourists never penetrate. As the planners envisioned a wholly Godless future, the section would clearly have no need for a church. But then the African Christian immigrants arrived, in their thousands. Today, South-East has perhaps a hundred booming churches, although none comes vaguely close to the architectural glories of the medieval buildings in Amsterdam's Centre. A number of the new churches, in fact, are in converted garages and back rooms. Even so, the humble circumstances do little to cool the enthusiasm. Those congregations perhaps represent the future face of Christianity in Western Europe.

The effects of immigration can be seen across the denominational spectrum. People of African and Caribbean stock have revived Catholic communities in the metropolitan countries. Other churches are of a type quite different from local traditions, including Pentecostals, Baptists, and independents. Even in Germany and Switzerland, there are now enough independent African churches to form their own separate federation or Conference.[23]

Great Britain is home to a substantial network of African and Caribbean churches, heavily charismatic and Pentecostal in worship style. London's 400,000 Africans now outnumber Afro-Caribbean residents, and some regions of the city have a strongly African cast. Describing a successful African church, a correspondent in the British *Guardian*—the sacred scripture of liberal secularists—noted how "London, the cynical capital of the unbelieving English, must be one of the least religious places in the world.... *Yet, as the city continues to be Africanized, so it is being evangelized.* Charismatic and Pentecostal churches like this one do things differently, and they have flourished."[24] Currently, about half of all churchgoers in London are black.

Yet outsiders get a sense of the scale of this activity only when a scandal erupts. In Britain, African and Latin American churches hit the headlines during exposés of exorcism and spiritual warfare, in which children have been harmed, sometimes after they were accused of being witches or demon-possessed. Following one quite well-documented instance of African human sacrifice in London, the media began, incredibly, linking such activity to Pentecostal churches. In what was almost a revival of the notorious ritual abuse panic of the 1980s, African-rooted spiritual practices were presented as a form of bloodthirsty child abuse, derived from jungle superstition.[25]

Little attention need be accorded to such tabloid sensationalism, and incidents of abuse and child maltreatment are of course wildly untypical. But even such scabrous reporting did have the incidental benefit of alerting mainstream readers to the scale of African and Southern religion on offer in what was once the capital of the British Empire. One spectacular manifestation of the new churches would be London's Kingsway International Christian Centre, KICC, founded by Nigerian pastor Matthew Ashimolowo. He began in 1992 with only three hundred members, and now the KICC seats five thousand worshippers at its main facility, the Miracle Centre, as well as several satellite churches. The KICC is claimed as the largest church to be created in Britain since 1861, and the Miracle Centre's auditorium offers double the capacity of Westminster Abbey or St. Paul's Cathedral. Although the church has been hit by financial scandals, the ministry continues to be a powerful force in Britain and beyond. Matthew Ashimolowo uses cable television and radio to speak to a wider audience in the United Kingdom and beyond—in Nigeria, Ghana, and Europe. He has attracted controversy by urging, logically enough, that the Anglican church should just "die gracefully" in the United Kingdom and hand its buildings over to newer groups like his own.[26]

In Canada, as in Europe, immigrant groups have slowed the general decline in churchgoing. Also as in Europe, changes in religious practice may not exactly reflect a decline in Christian beliefs or loyalties, but the figures are nonetheless depressing. In 2005 a study of actual church membership—as opposed to notional adherence—found that between 1961 and 2001, Canada's Anglican Church lost 53 percent of its following, and that if losses continued at that rate, the church would be reduced to a single member as early as 2061. Also between 1961 and 2001, the United Church of Canada lost 39 percent of its membership, and other mainline groups also shrank rapidly. The most serious slippage occurred in the once solidly Catholic province of Quebec. Today, around 30 percent of Canadians report that religion is very important to them, compared with 59 percent of Americans. Again, as in Europe, the numbers would have been still worse for churches of all denominations if not for the vigorous religious life of Caribbean and Asian immigrants. Montreal's Catholic churches would be poorly attended if not for the enthusiasm of new Canadians of Vietnamese and Haitian stock. Elsewhere, immigrants are the mainstays of the rising Pentecostal churches.[27]

It is hard to predict how the newer ethnic communities will continue to affect the religious life of the host societies. Aside from the usual difficulties in assessing religious loyalties, there is also the issue of harmonization, of judging how far the children of immigrants will adopt the laxer and more "modern" thought-ways of Europe. Based on the American experience, sociologists of religion argue that new immigrants are commonly more religiously active than their forebears at home, and this pattern may well be followed in Europe. To take an extreme example, British authorities identify thousands of British-born South Asian people as actual or potential recruits for Islamist terror movements. On the other hand, many children of British Muslims see their family religion mainly as a matter of ethnic and cultural pride, rather than a powerful motivating ideology. Girls, in particular, chafe at traditional restraints. The next generation might conceivably be as religiously lukewarm as their white neighbors. Already, birth rates of Muslim populations across Europe are beginning a steep decline that is comparable to the record of older-stock Christian communities in the last generation.

Yet having said this, the process of secularization is not yet that advanced, and for the next few decades, the face of religious practice across the face of Europe should be painted in brown and black. When we measure the declining strength of Christianity in Europe, we must remember how much leaner the statistics would be if not for the recent immigrants and their children—the new Europeans.

THE UNITED STATES

The contrast between population trends in Europe and the global South could hardly be more marked. The United States, though, offers a more complex picture. Though in most senses the heart of the West, demographically the United States has less in common with Japan or Western Europe than with the developing nations. Critically, the U.S. population will continue to grow, if not at Ugandan rates, then far more impressively than any European nation. Today, there are about 310 million Americans. That number should grow to 439 million by 2050, possibly to 570 million by 2100.

The main driver for population growth will be immigration, which reached amazing heights during the 1990s. At the peak of the boom in 1999–2000, the nation was receiving 1.5 million new legal migrants each year, not counting illegals. Soon, the foreign-born portion of the U.S. population will be 15 percent, exceeding the previous record set in 1890: by 2050, one American in five will be foreign-born. And those statistics lead us to draw interesting historical parallels. As we think of the ethnic groups that dominated the previous immigration surge around 1900, the Jews, Italians, and Slavs, we recall how they revolutionized American life through the following century. We must assume that the social (and religious) transformation over coming decades will be no less complete.

As the nation grows, its ethnic character will become less European and less white, with all that implies for religious and cultural patterns. For most of American history, the racial question essentially concerned two groups, black and white, people of African and European descent. In 1930 the nation comprised 110 million whites, 12 million blacks, and just 600,000 "Others," meaning Native Americans and Asians. From the 1960s on, the Otherness of America developed apace, largely due to a relaxation of immigration controls. As we gain greater distance from the event, the passage of the Immigration Reform Act in 1965 increasingly looks like the most significant single event of that much-ballyhooed decade.

American society is steadily moving from a black-and-white affair to a multicolored reality. Today, 50 million Americans are counted as Hispanic, 64 percent of them of Mexican ancestry. Nearly 15 million more Americans are East and Southeast Asian, of Chinese, Japanese, Filipino, Vietnamese, and Korean stock. Asians and Hispanics combined make up 20 percent of the population today, but this share is projected to grow to over a quarter by 2025, and to at least 35 percent by 2050. Although expert projections change over time, the current best bet is that the United States in 2050 will be 25 to 30 percent Latino, and 8 or 9 percent Asian. As recently as 1970, Asian and Hispanic Americans accounted for only 8 percent of total births in the United States, but today that number has increased to more than a quarter. One reason for this transformation is that Latinos are generally much younger than longer-established populations.[28] By mid-century, over 100 million Americans will claim Hispanic origin. They will then constitute one of the world's largest Latino societies, more populous than any actual Hispanic nation with the exception of Mexico or Brazil.

Although the ethnic change will ultimately affect all parts of the country, it is already evident in some regions. Presently, four states (California, Texas, New Mexico, and Hawaii) have achieved majority-minority status, in that non-Latino whites have ceased to form an absolute majority of the population, and other states will soon join the list. Soon, Latinos alone will constitute a majority of California's people, while Latinos make up 40 percent of the population of Texas, the second largest state. By the 2050s, the United States as a whole will be a majority-minority nation.[29]

Looking at these changes makes us reconsider our whole view of American history. In the nineteenth century, Manifest Destiny led Anglos to overwhelm the whole continent, leaving the older Hispanic cultures shrinking islands of language and faith within the new U.S. borders. At best, they were treated as quaint tourist attractions. In retrospect, those islands look rather more like bridgeheads from which new advances would someday occur. Such changes must also make us reconsider the nation's religious trajectory, which was once described mainly in terms of Protestant and Puritan expansion. An America in which the population's center of gravity is so rapidly shifting to the south and west inevitably has a greater appreciation of the non-Puritan, non–New England, Christian traditions that have so influenced other parts of the nation. When one daily passes Spanish missions on the way to work, and when so many other drivers have bumper stickers of the Virgin of Guadalupe, there is something unconvincing about the assumption that America's Christian culture radiated outward from Massachusetts Bay.

That story has profound religious implications. As historian Oscar Handlin wrote in 1952, "Once I thought to write a history of the immigrants in America. Then I discovered that the immigrants *were* American history." That remark can easily be adapted to characterize American religion. Far from what anyone could have dreamed at the time, the 1965 Immigration Act had vast consequences for American religion, especially Christianity. At least 66 percent of recent immigrants are Christian, compared to just 8 percent Muslims. Catholics alone account for over 40 percent of new immigrants, representing the equivalent of a substantial new Catholic diocese arriving each and every year. And as in Europe, it is the newer "Southern" populations who will account for much of what denominational growth will occur in coming decades. Just to take an East Coast example, around half the congregations active today in the Boston–Cambridge area worship in languages other than English. Since immigrant congregations are often small, this does not imply that anything like a half of all believers are non-Anglophone, but it does suggest a vigorous growth. When the Greater Boston Baptist Association used posters on subway trains to spread its evangelistic message, the languages used included English, French, Spanish, Portuguese, and Korean.[30]

Though the ethnic change can be illustrated from many churches from across the country, one *New York Times* story from 2005 provides a perfect example. Under the headline "If a Diverse Congregation Were Cash, This Church Would Be Rich," the story reported conditions in Spring Valley:

> As immigrants have settled in this working-class Rockland County village, the weekly attendance at Saint Joseph's has ballooned to nearly 4,000 people, spread among services in English, Spanish, Haitian-Creole and Polish each week. With the crowds bigger than ever on Sunday, it was possible to hear Easter greetings in any of those languages—sprinkled with a bit of Tagalog, Bengali and Vietnamese.[31]

Such diversity poses real challenges (and opportunities) for U.S. churches, which must acknowledge the specific cultures from which these new believers stem: they are not just immigrants, or Latinos, or Asians. When the Los Angeles Catholic parish of St. Cecilia faced declining numbers, its priest restructured church life to take into account major local constituencies. That meant seeing parishioners not (for instance) as Mexicans and Nigerians, but as members of specific regions and communities, with their own devotions and customs, their own ways of venerating the Virgin Mary. Parish life accommodated the ways of African Igbo people, of Guatemalans, of Mexicans from the province of Oaxaca. As the local priest remarked, "This church now is the definition of a parish—which is the communion of communities." Even finer distinctions can be seen in St. Anne's church in Santa Monica, where members of several separate Oaxacan villages celebrate their particular local saints with the appropriate rituals and festivities.[32]

Latinos represent the most obvious aspect of religious change. Perhaps a third of all U.S. Catholics are Latino, and some 4,000 parishes have some kind of Hispanic ministry, including Spanish-language masses. Some projections suggest that by 2050, more than 80 percent of U.S. Catholics will have Latino roots. A century ago, an upsurge in the American Latino population would have been seen as part of a general Catholic menace, since Hispanics were assumed to be automatically, and blindly, members of the Roman Catholic Church. Yet the overall picture is much more complex, and more controversial. Already, 20 percent of U.S. Latinos are evangelical Protestants, and many believe that the evangelical share will expand significantly in coming decades. Among first-generation Latinos in the United States, Catholics massively outnumber Protestants, by 74 to 18 percent, but among the third generation, the Catholic share has shrunk to a 59–32 majority. At least two thousand Pentecostal churches in New York

City cater to predominantly Latino congregations.[33] Contributing to Catholic decline is the shortage of Latino priests. While church authorities worry about the ratio of U.S. Catholic believers to priests, the ratio of Hispanic believers to Hispanic priests is eight times worse. No wonder, then, that evangelical pastors can exercise such an appeal. Also, mainstream congregations have been slow to adapt to Latino culture. In contrast, notes Catholic authority Ronaldo Cruz,

> Many of these [evangelical] churches are storefronts, and they don't ask you whether you've been through sacrament. They accept you as you are. Often they are lay people and they speak the language. They provide music and social service right away, so they are quick to respond. They work to make you feel part of the community immediately.[34]

The U.S. Catholic hierarchy understands how perilous the situation may be. To try and reduce the continuing hemorrhage of believers, Latino Catholics in the United States have tried very much the same solutions as their counterparts in the Philippines or South America, importing Pentecostal customs such as familiar music and instruments during services, and encouraging emotional expressions of spontaneous praise and thanksgiving. Over half of Latino Catholics now describe themselves as Pentecostal or charismatic, combined to just 12 percent of non-Latinos. The effects of this charismatic trend can be startling. Reporting on one southern California *Catholic* parish, the *Los Angeles Times* told how

> an evangelical zeal filled the air. As a band belted out lively salsa rhythms, hundreds of Latino worshipers waved their arms and swayed, singing praises to Jesus. Then the preacher strode forward. For nearly an hour, he delivered passionate words of God as he built up to the service's climax: the altar call, when he invited worshipers, mostly immigrants from Central America, to step forward to accept Jesus' love and forgiveness. Nearly a hundred men, women and children came forth, dropping to their knees, some weeping, while prayer leaders laid hands of healing on them.

In the Washington, D.C., area, a recent *Encuentro Catolico* offered an opportunity to "pray, weep and dance." In the words of one observer, the event showed that "God made the salsa, God made the merengue." Such ecclesiastical tactics may or may not succeed, but in any case the Latino religious scene has been so volatile in recent decades that detailed predictions of any kind are rash. But whatever the exact denominational balance may be, the changing racial picture is only going to strengthen overall Christian numbers.[35]

Predicting the religious loyalties of Asian Americans poses similar problems. Some follow traditional Asian religions such as Buddhism, but many others are Christian. In some cases, immigrant communities derive from strongly Christian homelands, such as the Philippines, or from countries with large Christian minorities, such as Vietnam or South Korea. Other Asian migrants are recent converts. In this sense, the Asian American communities of Los Angeles or San Francisco can usefully be seen in the same religious context as other Pacific Rim cities like Manila, Seoul, or Jakarta. In addition to strengthening Christian numbers in the United States, such migrant communities transmit American ideas to home countries, because of the constant interchange between Asian American communities and their ancestral nations. Family and social links thus help promote Pentecostalism in Korea or the Philippines. And as in Europe, the presence of migrant churches is likely to introduce the practices of the newer churches into the religious mainstream of the host nation. Transnational groups such as El Shaddai have a solid presence in the United States. For all the writing over the last decade or so on the enormous cultural and economic significance of the Pacific Rim region, few observers have noted that this region would increasingly become a Christian Arc.[36]

The Christian presence is powerfully evident in any Asian community in North America. Vancouver, for example, has such a sizable Asian presence that it sometimes seems like a thriving Chinese city accidentally misplaced on the wrong side of the Pacific. Inevitably, the city has its quota of Asian temples and holy places, including sumptuous Buddhist and Hindu temples, and some evocative and cherished Taoist sites. These are the places that tourists visit when they want to seek out characteristically "ethnic" religion. Yet the greater Vancouver area also has around fifty Christian congregations labeled with some Asian ethnic title, such as Chinese Pentecostal or Korean Baptist, and that number does not count distinct services in ethnic languages offered by mainstream Catholic or Protestant churches. Roughly half of these Christian congregations and special services cater to the Chinese community, while the remainder are directed toward Koreans, Japanese, and Filipinos. In addition, thousands of Vancouver residents of Asian descent attend mainstream Christian services in the English language. A similar picture can be found in Chinatowns and Little Saigons across the United States, where Christianity has made particular progress among people of Chinese stock. The number of Chinese American churches has grown from around sixty-six in the 1950s to more than a thousand today, and nearly two-thirds of Chinese Americans attend Christian churches.[37]

The experience of Korean Americans illustrates the dimensions of Asian American Christianity. Though Korean immigration to the United States began in the late nineteenth century, virtually all the 1.2 million or so Americans who today claim Korean ancestry trace their roots in the new land to the last thirty years. The Korean community in the United States is deeply imbued with Christian teaching: Christians outnumber Buddhists by ten or twenty to one. In many cases, immigrants were already Christian upon their arrival, so that a sizable majority of first-generation Korean Americans is Christian, and these are usually enthusiastic church members. Of seven thousand Asian Protestant churches in the United States, four thousand are Korean. In southern California alone, an association of Korean Protestant churches has 1,359 congregations, representing 39 denominations. In addition to mainstream churches—Presbyterian, Methodist, and Catholic—there is also a large parachurch network of small group and Bible-study activity, especially on university campuses, where some talk of an Asian Awakening. Over time, many of these cells will evolve into full-scale churches that will draw ever closer to the cultural mainstream. The example of European ethnic churches on American soil suggests that Korean Christian communities will become progressively less ethnically centered as time goes by. Korean churches already realize that they will have to make greater use of English in order to retain the loyalty of younger members.[38]

CHRISTIAN AMERICA?

The strength of American Christianity, present and future, contradicts much received wisdom. Americans like to think of their land as one of diversity, perhaps a diversity unparalleled anywhere in the globe, but in religious matters at least, such a view is far from the truth. America remains today substantially what it has always been, namely a Christian country. That observation can sound aggressively partisan or intolerant, since some extremists believe that Americans are a Christian people who require a Christian government, with all that implies about religious exercises in schools and public displays. I make no such assertion, since I believe that religion flourishes best when it is kept farthest away from any form of government intervention, even the best-intentioned. But while the United States is home to a remarkable number of religious denominations, overwhelmingly, these are traditions within the broader stream of Christianity.[39]

The number of adherents of non-Christian religions in the United States is strikingly small. If we combine the plausible estimates for the numbers of American Jews, Buddhists, Muslims, and Hindus, then we are speaking of about 4 or 5 percent of the total population. According to the *World Christian Encyclopedia*, even by 2025 the combined strength of the non-Christian religions will only be about 7 percent (I am of course counting Mormons as Christians). This makes the United States about as religiously diverse as most European nations, and less so than some. We have already seen the swelling of Muslim populations in Western Europe, and we add to that the influx of Hindus, Sikhs, and Buddhists. All told, adherents of non-Christian religions presently make up 10 percent of the population of France, 6 to 8 percent for Germany and the Netherlands, 5 percent for Great Britain.

The degree of religious diversity in the United States is limited compared to what we find in many African and Asian nations, where religious minorities commonly make up 10 or 20 percent of the people, often more. Ironically, in terms of American perceptions, some of the most diverse lands are to be found in the Middle East, which Westerners often imagine in terms of Muslim homogeneity. In fact, Egypt and Syria are more diverse than the United States. So, of course, is Israel, which is avowedly a Jewish state. Nevertheless, the population of the core pre-1967 state of Israel is only 80 percent Jewish, and this proportion falls steeply when we take account of the occupied territories.

Political factors help explain why Americans tend to misunderstand the religious complexion of their society. Projections about the possible future of American religion have become an important weapon in debates concerning the separation of church and state. When conservatives demand school prayer, for instance, liberals object that the present Christian predominance will not last much longer, and that demographic trends might well lead to Islam or Buddhism growing quickly in the United States. The political implications are clear. Would those Christians who want school prayer or public displays of religion really make the same demands if they were forced to listen to Muslim prayers, to see Asian Buddhist shrines on public grounds? Do Christians want to see tax moneys flowing to faith-based charitable organizations if the faiths in question are Muslim or Buddhist? Partly because of this political agenda, liberals offer unrealistically high projections of Muslim or Buddhist numbers in the United States, and activists from those religions echo these optimistic figures.

In reality, the number of new immigrants who practice non-Christian religions is far less than is often supposed. The powerful Christian presence among East Asians means that Buddhist or Taoist numbers are smaller than they might appear, and the numbers commonly given for American Muslims are likewise exaggerated. Even though we read suggestions that the United States is home to as many as 8 million Muslims, actual numbers remain a good deal smaller than this, probably 4 million or so, at most 1.5 percent of the population. Though Americans tend to assume that all Middle Eastern immigrants must be Muslim, perhaps three-quarters of Arab Americans are in fact Christian. The United States has been a popular destination for better-off Arab Christians from lands such as Palestine, Lebanon, and Syria. And any likely Muslim growth through immigration will be far exceeded by the continuing Christian influx from Africa, Asia, and above all, Latin America.

For better or worse, in numerical terms at least, the United States is substantially a Christian country now, and Christian predominance is likely to be still more marked in decades to come. Out of all the leading Christian nations of the last two hundred years, the United States will be the last to occupy this role in the twenty-first century.

SIX

Coming to Terms

Cristianizar no puede ser equivalente de occidentalizar.
To Christianize cannot be the same as to Westernize.
—*Vitalino Simalox (Maya)*

Ecclesia semper reformanda.
—*Martin Luther*

If demographic change just meant that Christianity would continue to be practiced in more or less its present form, but by people of a different ethnic background, that would of itself be a fact of some historical moment. But the changes of the coming decades promise to be much more sweeping than that. The types of Christianity that have thrived most successfully in the global South have been very different from what many Europeans and North Americans consider mainstream. These models have been far more enthusiastic, much more centrally concerned with the immediate workings of the supernatural, through prophecy, visions, ecstatic utterances, and healing. In fact, they have differed so widely from the cooler Northern norms as to arouse suspicion that these enthusiastic Africans (for instance) are essentially reviving the pagan practices of traditional society. This view frankly challenges the authenticity of African Christianity, just as, in other settings, critics point to pagan or non-Christian parallels for practices in new Korean or Brazilian churches.

Nor is this question of authenticity just a matter of academic interest. If in fact the bulk of the Christian population is going to be living in Africa, Asia, or Latin America, then practices that now prevail in those areas will become ever more common across the globe. This is especially likely when those distinctive religious patterns are transplanted northward, either by migration or by actual missions to the old imperial powers, to what were once the core nations of world Christianity. When we look at the Pentecostal enthusiasm of present-day Brazil, or the indigenous churches of Africa, then quite possibly we are getting a foretaste of the Christianity of the next generation. Or—as some worry—might it be less than a pure Christianity? Just how much have the newer churches done to fit in with the cultures in which they find themselves?

Claims that the Southern churches have strayed from older definitions of Christianity are seriously exaggerated. However greatly Southern types of Christianity have diverged from older orthodoxies, they have in almost all cases remained within very recognizable Christian traditions. Far from inventing some new African or Korean religions that derive from local cultures, the rising churches usually preach a strong and even pristine Christian message. This approach has implications for future missionary efforts. While we can scarcely imagine a church having a global appeal if its faith was cloaked purely in, say, an African ethnic form, it is possible to see some of the newer bodies exercising an appeal across racial and national boundaries. Another new "missionary century" may dawn, but next time, the missionaries would be traveling northward.

WHOSE CULTURE?

In modern Christian writings, we often encounter the word "inculturation," which means interpreting the Christian proclamation in a form appropriate for particular cultures, usually with the implication of non-Western cultures.[1] The idea of adapting religious practice to local conditions sounds at worst harmless and, at best, essential for any evangelistic endeavor. People differ in their cultural expression, and what works in one cultural setting won't in another. To take an obvious example, many northern Europeans tend to view dancing or swaying as inappropriate for a solemn or religious setting, while Africans regard such physical movement as perfectly normal. Also, this dancing is not simply a display by a soloist or troupe; it is a truly communal activity that involves the whole congregation.[2] This attitude is evident from religious groups across the lands of the African diaspora, in Brazil, Cuba, and the United States. Churches that try and enforce practices from "back home" on unwilling locals are going to be displaced by more flexible groups. Adaptation as such is essential and attracts little criticism, so long as the fundamental truths of a faith are not compromised.

The issue then becomes determining just what are the core beliefs of Christianity, and what are cultural accidents. To take an obvious example from the modern West: is the ancient prohibition against women clergy a core belief or a cultural prejudice? What about ordaining homosexual clergy? The debate over substance and accidents goes back to the very origins of Christianity. The biblical book of Acts records the furious debate over whether Gentile converts were required to accept the rules of Judaism, complete with circumcision and dietary laws. Ultimately, the church, or at least the majority party, concluded that these practices were not essential to the faith. In varying forms, these issues have echoed through the history of Christianity and have surfaced on virtually every occasion when churches have come into contact with some hitherto unfamiliar society. We recall the Chinese Rites controversy of the seventeenth century. In Victorian southern Africa, the missionary bishop J. W. Colenso refused to order his Christian converts to renounce polygamy, since it was so obviously an integral part of their African culture (and the practice deterred adultery). Naturally, more conservative believers denounced Colenso, but the controversies remain.[3]

The dilemma was elegantly summarized by the Chinese emperor Kang Xi, who was open to hearing Christian arguments, but who was perplexed by the relationship between the new teachings and his familiar culture. "If all this be true," he asked, "how is it that God waits over 1600 years before giving us any knowledge of it; how is it that the Chinese are left out, and only the barbarians are mentioned?" Must the new preaching utterly replace everything that made him Chinese? Or as Andrew Walls has remarked, "This question is alive for Africans just as it was for Greek converts in the ancient Hellenistic world. Do we have to reject our entire history and culture when we become Christians?"[4]

Because of the long Western dominance of Christianity, debates over faith and culture often focus on attitudes to specifically European matters. When a Christian group acclimatizes to a new society, the common assumption holds that what is traditionally done in Europe or North America is correct and authentic, and provides the gold standard by which to assess local adaptations. The more we look at the Christian faith in its European guise, though, the more we can see this too represents a kind of inculturation, albeit an old-established example. This is not to say that there is no such thing as an unchanging "historic Christian faith," but we must be careful to distinguish the core idea from the incidentals.

The cultural assumptions of European missionaries and empire-builders become obvious when we see a great church in one of the old British or French colonies in the tropics. The visitor leaves the bright sunshine to enter into a dark Gothic chamber, which seems quite inappropriate for the local climate and environment. Still, Victorian builders knew in their hearts that a religious building had to follow certain cultural norms, and that meant using the Gothic styles that mimicked the brooding forests of medieval northern Europe. Its enthusiasts described the Gothic style simply as Christian architecture. Presumably if the course of Christian history had run differently, then other societies would have succeeded in spreading their distinctive cultural visions across the world, with equal confidence that these too were the only fit vessels for conveying Christian truth. To take an outlandish example: if Central America had become an early Christian heartland, then our religious literature and architecture would use the imagery of jaguars rather than lions. And who knows but that in another century or two, the jaguar will indeed become a primary Christian symbol for millions of believers?

Most observers today would agree that Gothic architecture was just a cultural manifestation, rather than a core element of Christianity, but other parts of so-called traditional Christianity can perhaps be treated just as flexibly. Western Christianity itself has changed greatly over the centuries, and grown and flourished precisely by incorporating ideas from various cultures. Walls describes Christianity as "infinitely translatable." Christianity became inculturated in different societies, and each in turn contributed to the larger package of Christian beliefs. Within the first few centuries of its existence, Christians in Egypt used figures of the goddess Isis with her child Horus as the model for devotional imagery of Mary and the infant Jesus. Across the Mediterranean, the functions of numerous local deities were transferred to Christian saints. Borrowings from paganism are well known, to the extent that the pope himself takes his title of *pontifex* from one of the chief priests of pagan Rome. Christianity has been flexible about these adaptations, and there is no obvious reason why the age of absorption should have ceased in the fifth or tenth centuries, or indeed the twenty-fifth.[5]

Historically, one of the greatest examples of accommodation to native religions occurred when the Mediterranean-based religion of Christianity expanded into the realms of the northern barbarians in the dark centuries following the fall of Rome. The Mediterranean Christians who converted northern Europe overtly tried to ensure that the new converts would see the continuities from their old religion. Writing to the missionaries to England in about 600, Pope Gregory the Great ordered that "the temples of the idols should on no account be destroyed. The idols are to be destroyed, but the temples themselves are to be aspersed with holy water, altars set up in them, and relics deposited there...and since they have a habit of sacrificing many oxen to demons, let some other solemnity be substituted in its place, such as a day of dedication, or the festivals of the holy martyrs whose relics are enshrined there."[6] Those converted temples became the sites of what would later become great Christian churches, though these origins were long forgotten: London's St. Paul's Cathedral almost certainly stands on the site of an ancient pagan structure. By the nineteenth century, perhaps some of these ancient temples were the spiritual homes of the Christian missionaries who set off to convert Africa and Asia. In their turn, these men and women worried about just how many of the pagan practices they found could possibly be reconciled with the new faith.

OLD AND NEW WAYS

Reusing buildings is one thing, but Pope Gregory's letter suggests that the missionaries were also compromising with the older religion to the extent of absorbing older ritual calendars. In the English language, even the greatest Christian festival, Easter, bears the name of a pagan spring goddess. This kind of adaptation explains why the ancient pagan seasonal festivals are so often blessed with the names of the greatest Christian saints: across Europe, Midsummer Day is associated with St. John the Baptist. Almost certainly, the newly venerated saints acquired some of the characteristics of the gods they were replacing.

The European Christianity that was exported from the sixteenth century on was already a magnificent example of successful inculturation, and the process continued in the lands encountered beyond the oceans. In fact, the Iberian clerics charged with converting the New World knew and often cited Pope Gregory's letter, and they applied its lessons wholeheartedly. Some of the greatest cathedrals and churches of Latin America rose on the sites of Aztec or Inca temples, commonly reusing the building stone.[7]

One of the best-known stories in New World Christianity concerns the Mexican Indian Juan Diego, who in 1531 reported a vision of a divine Lady whom the Spaniards believed to be Our Lady of Guadalupe. The Lady, the dark one (la Morena), soon attracted the passionate devotion of the Indian people and was recognized as patron of Mexico. In explaining her phenomenal popularity, scholars believe that she was initially identified not as the Virgin worshipped at the Spanish shrine of Guadalupe but as Coatlaxopeuh, "she who crushes the serpent." This was a title of the pre-Christian Aztec goddess Tonantzín, who was appearing on ground that had been sacred to her long before the coming of Christianity. Elsewhere in Latin America, too, the cult of the Virgin carries pagan associations. Cubans devote themselves to *La Caridad, La Virgen de la Caridad del Cobre*. The many West African slaves imported into that land viewed her as a goddess, and today her cult is part of Afro-Cuban Santeria. Another great Mexican saint was Santiago, Saint James the Greater, whose extravagant commemoration on July 25—complete with dancing, masks, and elaborate costumes—almost certainly derives from the veneration of a still older warrior figure, the god Quetzalcoatl.[8]

We might take these stories to indicate that Catholicism had only a tenuous hold on the native and African peoples, who carried on their ancient religions under a thin disguise. This may have been the case at first, but the cult of the Virgin in particular helped native people accept the full panoply of Catholic belief and ritual, and also served to Christianize the new slave populations. Ethnically as much as spiritually, she is *their* Virgin. Just as Guadalupe is usually seen in the company of the Indian Juan Diego, so images of *La Caridad* show her appearing to rescue black and *mestizo* sailors. In Ecuador, the equivalent of Guadalupe is the Virgin of El Quinche, who is so popular because her skin color is that of the local *mestizos*. Honduras is home to Our Lady of Suyapa, a tiny but enormously influential figure of the Virgin in dark wood, who is *la Morenita*—the little Dark One. In Indian Guatemala and southern Mexico, the Black Christ of Esquipulas is another divine figure whose color repudiated white claims to racial dominion. In Central America, meanwhile, ancient Mayan priestly dynasties maintained their spiritual power in the guise of Catholic confraternities. The church made large compromises with pre-Christian practices to accomplish its goals, but no more than it had done in northern Europe a millennium before. And as in those earlier lands, the Latin American church soon occupied a place as the authentic religious voice of the people.[9]

Nor is this process confined to Latin America. Older traditions shaped the rich devotional life of the Philippines, in the celebration of the Santo Niño, or the dark-skinned Jesus venerated as the Black Nazarene. Asian Catholics are equally inspired by the Virgin, who dominates the religious thought of the Philippines no less than that of Mexico. The Virgin has offered rescue and refuge during the times of persecution and massacre that have so often befallen the communities of China, Korea, and Vietnam. Here too, accounts of apparitions are central to popular piety: if Mexico has Guadalupe, Vietnam has its shrine at La Vang. In Asia too, the Virgin has assumed the attributes of older female divinities, especially the beloved figure of the Buddhist Guanyin. At the south Indian shrine of Vailankanni, the Lourdes of the East, Mary's image as Mother of Good Health makes her a congenial sister to the great female deities of Hinduism.[10]

LITURGY AND LANGUAGE

As Christianity becomes increasingly Southern, it cannot fail to absorb the habits and thought-worlds of the regions in which it is strongest. Much of that adaptation will be unconscious, as it was during the historic Christianization of Europe. Latin Christians did not hold learned theological debates over whether Gothic architecture should become a favored style for building churches, they just did what seemed natural given their physical and cultural environment. Much of what we think of as "normal" Western Christianity reflects the same type of unconscious absorption.

There is nothing deliberately racist or exclusive about the process that traditionally made white Northern Europeans portray Jesus as one of themselves, just as Africans and Asians use their own familiar imagery in their religious art. The process of absorption goes back at least as far as the ancient Ethiopian church, which naturally depicted Jesus in local guise, and Kongolese metalworkers of the seventeenth century similarly produced very African-looking crucifixes. Over the last century, the gallery of Christian imagery from Africa and Asia has expanded exponentially, and an image of Christ as an African or Asian scarcely causes any surprise for most observers.[11]

Perhaps the most important acts of assimilation occur in the area of language, as believers absorb the faith by translating its ideas into intelligible terms. We Westerners can easily see the need for such a quest, since the Bible is so foreign to us culturally. The New Testament emerged from a specific eastern Mediterranean society, and used language and metaphors that made excellent sense for the kind of societies and economic communities that prevailed across the Roman Empire. Suitably modified for different environments, the ideas also work well in most agricultural communities, but for modern urban or suburban dwellers, the language has lost its meaning. With the aid of a learned commentary, a modern reader can understand such concepts as separating wheat and chaff, grafting vines, new wine and old wineskins, but in becoming so remote, the metaphors have lost their relevance. We respond to their obsolescence by generating new figures and analogies that speak to us.

In the same way, the newer Christian societies have been creative in adapting religious language to local settings. Lamin Sanneh, one of the most perceptive scholars of worldwide Christianity, writes that the simple decision to translate the scriptures into local languages was in itself a key concession to native cultures, and one made by even the most obtuse Northern missionaries. The mere act of translation proved that no single language was privileged as a vehicle of salvation. This is important in light of modern postcolonial critiques of the tyranny of the European languages. According to this view, forcing subject peoples to speak English or French also requires them to internalize colonial worldviews, to accept their own submission with every word they utter. Yet this problem does not apply to religious matters, at least to anything like the same degree. Sanneh writes that "Much of the heat with which mission has been attacked as Western cultural imperialism begins to dissipate when we apply the vernacular principle."[12]

Through the act of translation, too, and the use of familiar local terms and concepts, the scriptures are forced to become relevant to each individual culture. To take an obvious problem, there is no point in using the phrase "as white as snow" for people who have never seen snow. Better to speak of "as white as a strand of cotton." Such minor changes can have complex effects. While the Bible has Jesus declare, "I am the true Vine," some African translators prefer to replace vine with fig. This botanical change introduces a whole new theological meaning, since "this African tree represents the ancestors, and is sometimes planted on tombs." Jesus now speaks as the voice of death and resurrection.[13]

However unconsciously, translation transforms Jesus and his followers into Africans for African hearers, makes them Chinese for a Chinese audience. When Nestorian Christians proclaimed their faith in China, they did it in terms that made the church sound much like a philosophical sect comprehensible to Confucians or Taoists:

> As a seal, [Christians] hold the cross, whose influence is reflected in every direction, uniting all without distinction. As they strike the wood, the fame of their benevolence is diffused abroad; worshiping toward the east, they hasten on the way to life and glory; they preserve the beard to symbolize their outward actions, they shave the crown to indicate the absence of inward affections; they do not keep slaves, but put noble and mean all on an equality; they do not amass wealth, but cast all their property into the common stock; they fast, in order to perfect themselves by self-inspection; they submit to restraints, in order to strengthen themselves by silent watchfulness; seven times a day they have worship and praise for the benefit of the living and the dead; once in seven days they sacrifice, to cleanse the heart and return to purity.[14]

Modern African Christianity offers many examples of such domestication. In her collection of "prayers and praises," Ghanaian Madam Afua Kuma offers this version of the feeding of the five thousand:

He is the one
Who cooks his food in huge palm-oil pots.
Thousands of people have eaten
Yet the remnants fill twelve baskets.[15]

The collection from which this passage comes is aptly titled *Jesus of the Deep Forest*. Another of her hymns proclaims

He is the great Grass Hut, the Shed which shelters mice
The "Thump thump" of the pestle, he beats down our hunger
Hard wood hoe-handle, which brings us our food
Onyankopon Amponyinam; God the provider.

Vernacular prayers and liturgies come to be associated with new holy places, with shrines or martyrdom sites drawing purely on local traditions. The independent churches of southern Africa have been very active in spiritualizing the landscape through vast ritual gatherings and pilgrimages. One of the great shrines is Ekuphakameni, in South Africa, the "high and elevated place" chosen by prophet Isaiah Shembe. The site has acquired all the cultural resonance of the biblical Zion, and it features in the hymns of the group's Nazarite Baptist Church:

I remember Ekuphakameni
Where the springs are
Springs of living water
Lasting for ever.[16]

Even though the language is biblical, its associations are purely African. Ekuphakameni may in time become as great a Christian shrine as Lourdes or Walsingham.

Once naturalized in a culture, such local imagery comes to be expected, while a conspicuously foreign Jesus arouses suspicion. Earlier, we looked at the phenomenal success of the independent African church founded by Alice Lenshina in the 1950s. Her followers were attracted by the many hymns she composed, which used local languages far more fluently and eloquently than the mission churches had ever attempted.

Where the Bible is concerned, freedom of translation is restrained by some sense of obligation to the sacred text, but liturgical texts and practices can be handled with greater freedom. Particularly since the 1960s, there has been an upsurge of locally oriented liturgies that use culturally relevant terms and practices. At their worst, these innovations have been forced and unconvincing, but some have been impressive. The much-admired New Zealand liturgy was developed to reflect both the local physical environment and the racial balance between native Maoris and white *pakeha*:

> Dolphins and kahawai, sealion and crag,
> coral, anemone, pipi and shrimp:
> give to our God your thanks and praise.
> . . . .
> You Maori and Pakeha, women and men,
> all who inhabit the long white cloud:
> give to our God your thanks and praise.[17]

Liturgical innovation became widespread in the Roman Catholic Church after the second Vatican Council of the 1960s encouraged the use of vernacular language and practice. As Cameroonian theologian Jean-Marc Ela urged repeatedly, inculturation is central to the church's mission: "If Christianity seeks to be anything more than an effort to swindle a mass of mystified blacks, the churches of Africa must all join to come to terms with this question." Some of the innovations were quite creative, and fitted well with local tradition. In Zaire/Congo, ancient custom held that distinguished visitors were to be greeted by spearbearers, and accordingly, spears were added to the liturgical procession as a means of acknowledging the presence of God. Some Catholic churches have tried to use local foodstuffs in the Eucharist, to make the communion meal a genuine banquet held by a powerful chief, rather than an imported symbolic affair. Millet and corn replace wheat in the host, while wine is made from palm or banana. In Brazil too, progressive Catholic clergy import African customs such as drumming and dancing in order to try to make the Mass relevant to the poorest believers, who are usually of African descent.[18]

THE LAW OF BELIEVING

An ancient Church maxim declares, *lex orandi, lex credendi*, that the law of prayer is the law of belief, that how we worship shows what we believe. As worship patterns change, so do the underlying beliefs, and changes in practice in the global South will inevitably have their consequences in terms of belief and theology. As one Catholic archbishop has remarked, "Our Namibian African people have accepted Christ. But this Christ walks too much among them in a European garment." Inculturation "must be carried deeper than just music, drums and clapping of hands." In recent years, we can trace the emergence of innovative Southern theologies.[19]

Steeped as they were in Jewish tradition, Jesus's first Palestinian followers portrayed him as the great High Priest. Modern Africans, in contrast, find more power and relevance in the vision of Jesus as great Ancestor, an idea that also resonates in east Asia. This Jesus exercises for all people the same care and love that the ancestor of a specific tribe would for his or her descendants. Integrating the idea of ancestors into the liturgy has been a primary goal of the newer African Catholic rites. In contemporary Eucharistic prayers, God the Father is firmly placed in this "ancestral" context:

> O Father, Great Ancestor, we lack adequate words to thank you....
> O Great Ancestor, who lives on the brilliant mountains...
> Our Father, father of our ancestors, we are gathered to praise you
>   and to thank you with our sacrifice.

Independent churches also stress Jesus's role as prophet and healer, as Great Physician. Although this approach is not so familiar in the modern West, this is one of many areas in which the Independents are very much in tune with the Mediterranean Christianity of the earliest centuries. The idea of the Holy Spirit has also gone through subtle changes. An intriguing trend in African churches has been to name this figure "the Earthkeeping Spirit," a term with vast implications for ecological aspects of religion. The notion also has a wider appeal, for instance in Native American Christian thought.[20]

Latin American churches have been creative in evolving new theologies based on the distinctive experience of those cultures. Given the historic social inequalities of the Latin countries, Hispanic theology is acutely concerned with issues of liberation, suffering, and social justice, while matters of race are also paramount. Some of the most active thinkers have been Latinos based in North America, and a key concept in these circles is that of *mestizaje*, "mixed-ness," the status of being *mestizo* or mixed blood. In contemporary theology, *mestizaje* is so critical because it transcends traditional racial hierarchies. It thus comes closer to the New Testament goal of a society without racial privilege or domination, in which there is neither Jew nor Greek, Latino nor Anglo. And while mixed-race people were traditionally marginalized and despised, newer theologians see this status as uniquely privileged.

Mestizaje allows a society to draw equally on its diverse cultural inheritances. "The mestizo affirms both the identities received while offering something new to both." Mestizos are uniquely qualified to question the arrogant claims to purity made by given races or states. Since they have no abiding city on earth, *mestizo* loyalty is neither to race nor nation, but to Christendom, the pilgrim church. To quote the title of a book by Mexican American theologian Virgilio Elizondo, *The Future Is Mestizo*. These ideas are important for other societies in various stages of racial mingling, notably in Europe, and are likely to gain in importance in coming decades. It is a potent theology for a world of deracinated migrants and wanderers, those who (in Paul Gilroy's phrase) define their identities in terms not of roots but of routes.[21]

This approach profoundly affects readings of the Bible. Elizondo memorably presents Jesus as a *mestizo* son of Galilee's mixed and marginalized society, who enters the great city of Jerusalem in order to challenge its wealth, to confront the racial arrogance of the pure-blooded elite. For Elizondo, the world's poor and marginalized have a distinctive role in the divine plan. His Galilee Principle asserts that "what human beings reject, God chooses as his very own." This idea has much in common with the Christian theologies of rejection formulated by other once despised groups, such as India's Dalits or untouchables.[22]

THE QUEEN OF THE SOUTH

Contemporary Hispanic theology raises challenging questions about the whole area of popular religious practices, the world of devotions, processions, and pilgrimages often dismissed by a term such as "folk Catholicism." In the context of Latin American history, though, these practices are quite central to popular religious identity, and it is no longer acceptable to regard them simply as a dilution of the superior European reality. "Popular religious expressions of the people" thus become "the living creed and primary sources of theology."[23] By European standards, these practices may be flawed or suspect, but who ever said that European criteria were absolutely valid for all times and places? Europe created its own religious identity through a lengthy process of mingling and adaptation.

This emphasis on popular belief and tradition has major implications for the veneration of the Virgin Mary and, consequently, for the whole approach to the divine. In Latin Catholicism, Mary is often portrayed as something like a feminine face of God. For Mexicans, the Virgin of Guadalupe is an absolutely central symbol, just as *La Caridad* is for Cubans. Modern theologians such as Elizondo proudly defend this veneration, citing the exalted biblical image of the woman clothed with the Sun in the book of Revelation. In his view, Guadalupe becomes a messianic symbol for the resurrection of the world's oppressed races, the "Galileans." "In the person of Juan Diego was represented the Indian nations defeated and slaughtered, but now brought to life." In every sense, she is the mother of all border-crossers. Repeatedly, Mexican popular and revolutionary movements have claimed to be directly serving *La Morena*, the weak woman who conquers the conquerors. But modern writers go well beyond just defending this devotion, and ask moreover why Northerners seem so appalled by it. Roberto Goizueta argues that simple racism causes Northerners to reject "the racial, cultural and religious *mestizaje* of the Guadalupan symbol.... And like Jesus, *la Morenita* continues to ask us today, 'Why be frightened?' "[24]

In this specific area of theology, a southward shift may already be having a global impact. In modern Catholicism, the figure of the Virgin has usually been associated with more conservative and traditional forms of religious practice, so the veneration of Mary has played a significantly smaller role in devotion in liberal Northern countries. This tendency was reversed somewhat under the conservative papacy of John Paul II, and during his reign, remarkable attention was paid to Marian shrines and visions. On his 1998 visit to Cuba, the pope made a special visit to the shrine of El Cobre to crown the statue of *La Caridad* and proclaim her queen and patron of the island. Exalting the Virgin to the highest possible degree fits very well with the Catholic traditions of Latin America, Africa, the Philippines, and other regions that are steadily assuming a more central position within the church. As we will see, the College of Cardinals is becoming steadily more Latin in complexion.

These Marian trends will assuredly be reflected within the United States itself. In a potent acknowledgment of the shifting ethnic foundations of world Christianity, the Church has proclaimed the Virgin of Guadalupe as patron of all the Americas. In 1988 the liturgical celebration of the Mother of the Americas, *la Morena*, was raised to the status of a feast in all dioceses in the United States.[25] Although I make no attempts to predict exact dates for the changes described in this book, one key date can be cited with confidence, namely December 12, 2031. This is the feast-day of Our Lady of Guadalupe in the year that marks the five-hundredth anniversary of the original apparition to Juan Diego. The event will unquestionably be commemorated with a vast celebration of Mexican and Chicano Catholic identity, both north and south of the Rio Grande. This year might in fact come to be seen as America's true and proper Quincentennial, in contrast to all the ambiguities associated with the celebration of Columbus's landing in 1992.

Some years ago, I observed at first hand the role of "the Queen of the South" in drawing together the various currents within American Catholicism. I was watching a Peruvian procession of the sort that occurs many times each year in the villages of the Andes. The centerpiece of the event was the ornately decorated figure of the Virgin, richly dressed and surrounded with flowers, and borne on a bier by the distinguished men of the vicinity. They were heralded by women beautifully dressed in traditional gowns, who strewed the way with flowers. Behind the figure of the Virgin came the band, enthusiastic and sometimes discordant, and behind them walked several hundred Peruvians, their faces proclaiming an ethnic identity that can be traced long before the Inca empire was born. The unusual thing about this celebration was its location, since the hilly path through which they marched was found not in the Andes but in the gentler slopes of western Maryland, and the pilgrims were en route to the national shrine of the Virgin at Emmitsburg. Emmitsburg has an excellent claim to be one of the birthplaces of U.S. Catholicism, as a missionary center that would become home to Elizabeth Seton, the first American-born saint. Watching this Peruvian pilgrimage, one could see the oldest and newest faces of Catholic North America confronting each other quite amicably.

A revived cult of Mary would have an appeal far beyond the Americas. Marian devotion is a powerful force in African Catholicism, and has been since the time of the earliest native converts. One of the first Catholic martyrs of sub-Saharan Africa was Isidore Bakanja, who was converted in the Belgian Congo in 1906, and whose fervent Marian piety led to his murder at the hands of secular-minded white colonists. In the 1980s, mystical visions of the Virgin were reported in Rwanda, Kenya, and Cameroon. Amazing reports of Marian apparitions have also occurred within the Coptic church. In Egypt, spectacular Marian visions and miracles were recorded at Zaytoun, near Cairo, in 1967 and 1968. The events at Zaytoun galvanized the Egyptian people during the grim period following the disastrous 1967 war, and the shrine attracted millions of seekers, Muslim as well as Christian (the Virgin Mary is a prominent and beloved figure in the *Qur'an*).[26] A Catholic church dominated by Latin Americans and Africans would prove receptive to new concepts of Marian devotion, which might serve as a bridge to other ancient Christian communities, and even to other faiths. A black or brown Mary would be a powerfully appropriate symbol for the emerging Southern Christendom. Although these new theologies might disturb some North Americans or Europeans, Northern views on religious matters should become less and less significant.

MARGIN AND MAINSTREAM

We could well be witnessing another example of a powerful trend in Christian history, namely the spread of ideas and practices from the margins or borderlands of the faith to the heartland. As Joel Carpenter remarks, "Christian theology eventually reflects the most compelling issues from the front lines of mission, so we can expect that Christian theology will be dominated by these issues rising from the global South." The modern ecumenical movement offers a potent example, inspired as it was by thinkers who had worked on the mission frontiers, where denominational differences mattered little, and the key test was whether or not one was a Christian. This theme of Christian unity was powerfully stated at the 1910 Edinburgh Mission Conference, and we see its inheritance in later movements to create global structures such as the World Council of Churches.[27]

If we do not immediately recognize examples of such a drift to the center, it is because the ideas are now so mainstream that it is incredible to think that they would ever have been viewed as odd or deviant. Innovations from the fringe become normal. To take one example, a majority of Christians around the world regularly recite a version of the Nicene Creed, which proclaims belief "in the Holy Spirit, the Lord and Giver of Life, who proceeds from the Father *and the Son*" (my emphasis). The phrase "and the Son," *filioque*, is not part of the original text, and is condemned by the Eastern Orthodox churches. The *filioque* originated in the distant borderlands of Christianity as it existed in the sixth and seventh centuries, as Catholics in Spain and Gaul confronted missionary issues unfamiliar to the mainstream church of the day, which was centered in Constantinople. Being forced to deal with Arians, who rejected the equality of Father and Son, local Catholics asserted the dignity of Christ, and they did so by taking what seems like a breathtakingly bold step. They simply altered the quasi-sacred text of the creed in order to reflect local needs and realities. By the eighth century, the *filioque* spread across Western Europe, and Charlemagne and his heirs popularized it as part of their campaign to spread Christianity throughout the Germanic world. Only in the eleventh century, though, was this weird border practice accepted by the papacy. By that time, this explosive word had become a proud symbol of the emerging Western church, and an assertion of its distinctiveness from the ever-more distant church of the East.

A vigorous emerging church thus formulates its beliefs, and even its basic theology, according to immediate local needs and pressures, rather than waiting for the approval of venerable but distant mentors. What the "mainstream" church thinks is not terribly important for them, and mainstream is a designation that changes over time. And also over time, those innovations seem so obvious that most people are unaware that things were ever different.

BEYOND CHRISTIANITY?

So far, we have been looking at forms of adaptation that clearly build on familiar Christian traditions, but some patterns in the emerging churches raise searching questions about the acceptable limits of accommodation. At what point does inculturation end, to be replaced by the submergence of Christianity into some other religion? When cultural assimilation reaches a certain point, Western observers complain that what is being transformed is not merely the trappings but the core of the faith. What is being practiced, it appears, is not inculturation but syncretism, the blatant adulteration of Christianity by elements of other religions.

The syncretist theme becomes particularly important when older religious practices survive in emerging churches that command the loyalties of millions, and which can be expected to expand in coming decades. Across southern Africa, some independent churches have retained a wide range of traditional practices, including polygamy, divination, animal sacrifices, initiation rites, circumcision, and the veneration of ancestors. By no means all the independent congregations accept the full range of older practices, but most African churches accept prophetic and visionary ideas that have long since fallen out of fashion in the West. Ideas of healing and prophecy have permeated the far more numerous mainstream denominations, such as Catholics, Anglicans, and Lutherans.

Sometimes, pagan parallels seem quite strong. Zulu Zionist churches, for instance, are led by charismatic prophets who lead the church, who pray for the sick, who determine the causes of disease and specify remedies. Even for sympathetic Western observers, these prophets should properly be seen as a later manifestation of the tribal diviners who played such a key role in pagan times. The new Christian prophets, like the pagan diviners before them, are healer figures who possess supernatural gifts and act as channels to the ancestors. In some cases, they seem to be superhuman and become messiah figures. Some of Simon Kimbangu's followers saw him in this role, while Isaiah Shembe's disciples presented him as a new incarnate God on Earth, who appeared to them after his death. Such extreme doctrines come close to elevating prophets to Christ-like status. The Rizalist sects of the Philippines preach the divinity or messianic status of Jose Rizal, the national hero of the struggle against Spanish rule in the 1890s. Even though they are influenced by Catholic ritual and liturgy, they also draw unmistakably on traditional Malay pagan practices.[28]

It is tempting for Western commentators discussing Southern forms of Christianity to focus on such seemingly odd features, partly to make an account more picturesque. Some years ago, a *Newsweek* account of "The Changing Face of the Church" accurately charted the southward shift of Christianity, but implied that the rising churches were recklessly syncretistic. Author Kenneth Woodward argued that "As in the past, today's new Christians tend to take from the Bible whatever fits their needs—and ignore whatever fails to resonate with their own native religious traditions....On the Chinese New Year, says Catholic bishop Chen Shih-kwang of Taichung, Taiwan, 'we do mass, then we venerate the ancestors'—a notion that is totally foreign to Western Christianity. In India, where sin is identified with bad karma in this and previous lives, many converts interpret the cross to mean that Jesus' self-sacrifice removes their own karmic deficiencies, thus liberating their souls from future rebirths." In this view at least, Christianity remains little more than a cultural veneer.[29]

Sometimes, rejecting the authenticity of Southern churches has a polemical purpose. As we will see, the Anglican Communion has in recent years suffered intense controversies over attitudes to sexual morality and particularly homosexuality, and it is the African and Asian churches that have been most resolutely opposed to liberalization. Yet just as global South churches charge Americans and Europeans with betraying the faith, so Northern world liberals respond by impugning the Christian credentials of the newer churches. Such a conflict arose at the 1998 Lambeth conference at which Anglican bishops voted heavily against a liberal statement concerning homosexuality. Bishop John Spong of Newark declared that the conservative African bishops had "moved out of animism into a very superstitious kind of Christianity," and this explained their failure to understand the issues at hand. Spong professed himself appalled by the whole tone of Third World spirituality, with its "religious extremism": "I never expected to see the Anglican Communion, which prides itself on the place of reason in faith, descend to this level of irrational Pentecostal hysteria." Spong was in effect suggesting that "Pentecostal" fervor was a thinly disguised continuation of ancient paganism, with all its unenlightened moral trappings.[30]

PREPARING THE GOSPEL

The indictment is clear. Many Southern churches are indeed syncretistic, they represent a thinly disguised paganism, and all in all they make for "a very superstitious kind of Christianity," even post-Christianity. Certainly there are parallels between the new Christianity and the older religious world, but these can be explained in different ways. While a puritanically inclined critic might believe that the Southern churches had simply sold out to the old pagan religions, a more benevolent interpretation is possible. Since the older traditions already included many elements that fit well with the faith that the missionaries were preaching, it was natural to draw upon them.

Christians have long practice at explaining their use of traditional (and even "pagan") ways of thought. When early Christians saw the many parallels between their own new religion and the ancient practices of Mediterranean paganism, they argued that God had already sowed the older cultures with ideas and themes that would grow to full fruition once they were interpreted in a fully Christian context. The traditional religions should be seen as a *preparatio evangelica*, a preparation for the gospel. Since potentially Christian themes were so abundant in older African cultures, it is scarcely surprising that the newer churches of the last century have so enthusiastically absorbed so many of the old ideas. Where such ideas went flagrantly beyond the pale of Christian doctrine—as in the apotheosis of the prophets—the independent churches themselves usually tried to restrain or suppress these ideas.[31]

In sub-Saharan Africa, European missionaries were excited to find how many of their ideas resonated with native cultures. There was little need to explain the idea of monotheism to societies that already venerated a high God, a being far more exalted than the common run of spirits and deities. As veteran missionary Diedrich Westermann wrote in 1926, "The African, apart from his magical practices, believes in God. He is not a tribal God, but Lord of the universe, and the Christian missionary can in most cases introduce himself as ambassador of the God the African knows."[32] The problem in this passage concerns the "magical practices," which are presented almost as an incidental irritant and which would fade away quickly. In practice, they certainly did not. The main problem the missionaries faced in Africa and much of Asia was not that they were trying to explain a bafflingly alien worldview, but that their message almost rang too true with local cultures. In the realm of spiritual and magical beliefs, Christian/pagan parallels opened the door for evangelism, but on the negative side, they also attracted charges that converts were just recycling the traditional out-look on this world and the next.

Unlike in modern Europe or North America, Christian preachers did not have to convince Third World audiences of the reality of the supernatural, of spirits and spiritual powers. In much of Africa or East Asia, older cultures had a powerful interest in spirits, particularly the souls of ancestors, and the real effects that these could cause in the human realm. Ancestors who were offended or neglected could cause problems for their living heirs. Misfortune, sickness, and death were attributed to the workings of mischievous spirits, commonly directed by ill-meaning neighbors. In the early twentieth century, American missionaries in Korea noted that "Many of the religious characteristics of the Korean people mark them for discipleship in the Christian faith. Believing as they do in the universal presence of spirits, it is not difficult for them to accept the doctrines of the spiritual nature of God."[33] While these ideas seemed superstitious to the early missionaries, they could easily mesh with older Christian ideas, and with the thought-world of the Bible itself.

AN UNSEEN WORLD

If there is a single key area of faith and practice that divides Northern and Southern Christians, it is this matter of spiritual forces and their effects on the everyday human world. The issue goes to the heart of cultural definition and worldviews. In traditional African society, various forms of divination were used to seek out the cause of evil, and to identify the wrongdoer as an essential first step toward neutralizing his or her evil powers. At every stage, this scheme of explanations offended the sensibilities of European missionaries, who saw themselves in a heroic struggle against the evils of superstition, fatalism, and witchcraft. How could churches possibly accept such ideas?

As in the earlier Chinese debates, the issue of ancestors generated fierce argument, and much mutual misunderstanding. While missionaries denounced what they thought was ancestor worship, native peoples in Africa and much of Asia believed they were only showing due veneration to past generations, who survived as a spiritual presence essential to the well-being of family and community. For decades, the white-dominated churches were simply baffled at the resilience of the older ideas. As Andrew Walls has remarked, "The role of ancestors and witchcraft are two important issues. Academic theologians in the West may not put witchcraft high on the agenda, but it's the issue that hits ordinary African Christians full in the face." What white missionaries failed to realize was that they were in reality at war with the whole foundations of a society, the most basic means of understanding the world. Conflicts between European and African ways were also inevitable when the missionaries challenged the ceremonies, initiations, and rites of passage that were so crucial to the cycle of life in traditional society.[34]

The dilemma faced by the European churches is illustrated by a parable told by John Mbiti, who imagines a brilliant African student going off to a European seminary. Here, he "learned German, French, Greek, Latin, Hebrew, in addition to English, church history, systematics, homilectics, exegesis and pastoralia." He reads all the great European Bible critics, such as Rudolf Bultmann. Returning home to his native village, the student is welcomed joyfully by his extended family but suddenly, his sister falls dangerously ill. With his Western training, he knows that her illness requires scientific medicine, but everyone present knows with equal certainty that the girl is troubled by the spirit of her dead great-aunt. Since this erudite student has so much theological training, the family knows that it is obviously up to him to cure her. The debate between the student and his family rages until "the people shout 'Help your sister, she is possessed.' He shouts back, 'But Bultmann has demythologized demon possession!'" The family is not impressed and nor, presumably, are the demons.[35]

Most churches eventually acknowledged that the older beliefs were too deeply embedded to be removed, and either made their peace with tradition or else made it an integral part of their own system. The influential African prophets won followers by acknowledging the older spiritual powers and absorbing them within a new Christian synthesis. Their examples have been followed enthusiastically by the African indigenous churches, with their beliefs in spirits and exorcism: "their very life and worship revolves around healing, visions, dreams, the overcoming of evil forces." The Zion Christian Church (ZCC) believes that ancestors intercede on the behalf of the living. A belief in spirits is also fundamental to the Aladura churches of West Africa. The Cherubim and Seraphim movement "claims to have conscious knowledge of the evil spirits which sow the seeds of discomfort, set afloat ill-luck, diseases, induce barrenness, sterility and the like." Exorcism is the common response. The group's prophets receive visions in trances, and offer dream interpretations.[36]

Far from being confined to backwoods preachers, such beliefs have in recent years been spread widely through the (mainly) Nigerian-made Christian videos and DVDs that are so widely available across Africa, and through the worldwide African diaspora. Such evangelical or charismatic video production stands at the forefront of evangelism in modern Africa, and represents a highly influential form of Christian media in the emerging churches. Looking at the Nigerian videos creates a sense of paradox, in that such modern technology is used to present ideas that appear so stubbornly premodern. Commonly, they preach the need for heroic Christian spiritual warfare against the forces of evil that permeate modern society, forces that often involve ancestral curses. West Africa, in this view, is uniquely subject to the assaults of evil because of the recent history of pagan and animist faiths in the region, the bloody history of sacrificial worship, and the widespread survival of those practices today. In consequence, demonic influences permeate the land and people. Typical titles include *Ide Esu* (*The Devil's Bondage*), *The Haunting Shadows*, and *Blood On the Altar*. The curses on the land can be combated and removed only by charismatic Christian prayer, worship, and exorcism, usually led by a faithful pastor.[37]

WITCHES

The witchcraft issue has long agonized the mission churches, and today it proves a major stumbling block for otherwise sympathetic observers of global South churches. Euro-Americans, after all, live in a society where witches are a romantic joke, celebrated on greeting cards at Halloween. American baby boomers grew up with the television situation comedy *Bewitched*. It is difficult, then, to take seriously the event that occurred during the 2008 election campaign when a video showed Kenyan Pentecostal bishop Thomas Muthee invoked blessings on vice-presidential candidate Sarah Palin. Among other things, Muthee asked that God "keep her safe from every form of witchcraft." This outlandish request, it appeared, discredited Palin's faith, and also the creeds of all churches so out of touch with modernity as to accept the reality of demons and witchcraft. For most Europeans and Americans, anyone holding such beliefs must be irredeemably premodern, prescientific, and probably preliterate.[38]

Without understanding witchcraft, though, the religious coloring of much of the world can make little sense. A century ago, missionary pioneer Rowland Bingham warned potential followers that, "[t]here is the constant invisible warfare that has to be waged against the powers of darkness...It is fashionable in the Western world to relegate belief in demons and devils to the realm of mythology, and when mentioned at all it is a matter of jest. But it is no jest in West Africa or any other mission field for that matter." So pervasive is belief in witchcraft that, according to Aylward Shorter, "at the popular level, the African believer is often more engrossed in the identification of human sources of evil, and in counteracting them, than in the acknowledgement and worship of superior forces of good." Far from declining as society modernized, witch-finding and witchcraft accusations actually flourish in the booming cities, and become rife during times of economic slump and political crisis. Even today, a single outbreak of witch-panic can lead to hundreds of murders in a period of weeks or months. Moreover, one of the main centers of modern witch-hunting activity has been South Africa, the most developed state on the whole continent. Less publicized but no less brutal are antiwitchcraft movements in Asian societies, including India and Indonesia.[39]

The attitude of the churches to such outbreaks is controversial. They must of necessity treat social fears very seriously, but without stirring or exploiting these concerns for their own ends. As they well know, if they do not respond appropriately, then the faithful will resort to vigilantes and mob violence. Having said this, some new Christian groups themselves shade into counter-witchcraft movements, which win popularity by identifying and persecuting alleged witches, including so-called witch children. For some preachers, like Nigerian "apostle" Helen Ukpabio, belief in witchcraft and possession becomes a dominant theme of their mission, with potentially harmful social consequences.[40]

Generally though, mainstream churches emerge very creditably, as they offer believers theologically sound means of dealing with alleged supernatural menaces. Above all, the mainstream churches teach that Christ has triumphed over all evil forces, so that believers can trust in his power. The means to safety and sanity are found in prayer and the proper forms of church life, rather than in witch-finding and the rituals of counter-witchcraft. In 2009, Pope Benedict XVI warned Angolan clergy of their absolute duty to liberate African Catholics from witchcraft beliefs: "So many of them are living in fear of spirits, of malign and threatening powers. In their bewilderment they end up even condemning street children and the elderly as alleged sorcerers. Who can go to them to proclaim that Christ has triumphed over death and all those occult powers?"[41]

SPIRITUAL WARFARE

Fundamental to such ideas is the concept of spiritual warfare, of confronting and defeating evil demonic forces. For African Christians, one of the most potent passages of the New Testament is found in the letter to the

Ephesians, in which Paul declares: "Our struggle is not against enemies of blood and flesh, but against the rulers, against the authorities, against the cosmic powers of this present darkness, against the spiritual forces of evil in the heavenly places." Although it may appear superstitious and irrelevant to many Northern Christians, the passage makes wonderful sense in most of Africa, as it does for believers in Latin America or Asia. Once again, we can draw parallels between the modern expansion of Christianity and the growth of the religion in ancient times. Writing of the Roman world, Peter Brown comments that, "[h]owever many sound social and cultural reasons the historian may find for the expansion of the Christian Church, the fact remains that in all Christian literature from the New Testament onwards, the Christian missionaries advanced principally by revealing the bankruptcy of men's invisible enemies, the demons, through exorcisms and miracles of healing."[42]

Brown also stresses the complexity of the early Christian universe, a far more hierarchical affair than is found in most contemporary Western visions. Christians of those times believed the world was under assault from a plethora of demons and evil forces, but also knew that the faithful could count on the help of armies of saints and martyrs, and legions of angels. From New Testament times on, much Christian writing was devoted to specifying just how much veneration should appropriately be paid to such heroic figures, and the exact nature of evil. Once again, emerging Christian churches are debating issues that hark back to the most ancient Christian times.

The cultural conflict over literal interpretations of exorcism and spiritual healing has in modern times found a face in former Roman Catholic archbishop Emmanuel Milingo. In 2001 Milingo won notoriety in the West when he not only violated his oath of celibacy by marrying a woman, but he did so in a service held under the auspices of the notorious Rev. Sun M. Moon. He subsequently tried to form an independent church with married priests, and in 2009, the church laicized him. Yet it would be unfortunate if the archbishop was to be remembered only through this bizarre event, since for many years, he epitomized African concerns within the Catholic Church.

In 1969 Milingo became archbishop of Lusaka, Zambia, and increasingly, he saw his religious vocation in terms of combating the all-too-real forces of evil. As he declared, "In my tradition, the society knew that these spirits could cause spiritual disorder in the community, even before the Christian period. They knew there was something in the community that could disturb." He placed spiritual healing and exorcism at the center of his ministry, combining traditional beliefs with the language of the charismatic revival. He was duly attacked for charges of heresy and witchcraft, all the more ferociously because his stern condemnations of political corruption had made him many enemies. The Vatican removed him from his see in 1982, but he was subsequently vindicated of most charges, and he gained the favor of Pope John Paul II. He later acquired an international reputation as an exorcist, whose powers are more in demand in Europe than in Africa. Although his views stand far outside the conventional spectrum of Western religious thought, Milingo has no doubts about his biblical roots. Speaking of the many possessed individuals who seek his help, he has remarked, "I found it a shame for us as Christians that we were not able to help them. Jesus Christ has given us authority and power to take care of these problems. Luke nine recalls Jesus giving his apostles authority over all demons and at the same time over all sorts of diseases."[43]

Also illustrating the cultural gulf that separates Northern and Southern churches is Moses Tay, formerly the Anglican archbishop of Southeast Asia, whose see was based in Singapore. Visiting the Canadian city of Vancouver, Archbishop Tay found himself in Stanley Park, where he encountered the totem poles that represent an important symbol of the city. He was deeply troubled. The archbishop concluded that as artifacts of an alien religion, these were idols possessed by evil spirits, and they required handling by prayer and exorcism. This behavior horrified the local Anglican church, which was committed to building good relationships with local native communities, and which regarded exorcism as absurd superstition. (Moreover, totem poles themselves should more properly be seen as symbols of status and power, rather than specifically religious objects.) Considering his own standards, though, it is difficult not to feel some sympathy with the archbishop. Considering the long span of Christian writings on exorcism and possession, he could summon many literary witnesses to support his position, far more than the Canadian church could produce in favor of tolerant multiculturalism.[44]

HEALING

In practical terms, the belief in spiritual powers has its most direct impact in terms of healing through spiritual means. The practice of healing is one of the strongest themes unifying the newer Southern churches, both mainstream and independent, and perhaps their strongest selling point for their congregations. Yet this emphasis should certainly not be seen as a compromise with paganism, since it is so thoroughly integrated into Christian practice, as well as with local cultures. As Walls describes the African experience, "Healing is being addressed to the person, as the center of a complex of influences. It is addressed to the person as target of outside attack, as sufferer from unwanted legacies, as carrier of the sense of failure and unfulfilled duty. It is the long established African understanding of the nature and purpose of healing that is at work. What distinguishes its Christian phase is that the central Christian symbol of Christ is identified as the source of healing."[45]

From the earliest days of the European missions, the promise of healing was at the heart of Christian successes. Prospective converts were excited by biblical accounts of healing miracles, stories that the missionaries themselves were already treating with some embarrassment. Fundamentally minded Europeans had no doubts about the reality of biblically recorded cures in apostolic times, but questioned whether miracles continued into the modern age. Their converts, though, were quite willing to accept modern miracles. In nineteenth-century China, an enthusiastic convert named Xi Liaochi began his own successful mission focused on exorcism and the spiritual treatment of opium addiction. His career led to bitter controversies with the Europeans, who saw him as little more than a witch doctor on the farthest fringes of the faith. The affair ignited a lasting feud within the missionary establishment.[46]

Yet there can be no doubt of the appeal of such healing activities. In Africa, the explosion of healing movements and new prophets in the first quarter of the century coincided with a dreadful series of epidemics, and the religious upsurge of those years was in part a quest for bodily health. Today, rising African churches stand or fall by their success in healing, and elaborate rituals have formed around healing practices. Typically, in the Church of the Lord (Aladura), a healing ritual involves confession, "followed by the exorcising or expulsion of evil spirits, priestly blessings, and administration of holy words." Many congregations use material symbols such as holy water and sanctified healing oils. The Aladura churches have debated for years whether believers should use any modern or Western medicine, or rely entirely on spiritual assistance. The same customs are found in what were the mission churches. In Tanzania, some of the most active healing work in recent years has occurred within the Lutheran church, under the auspices of a bishop who himself claimed prophetic powers.[47]

Healing is equally central in many of the new churches of Latin America. When Andrew Chesnut explored the upsurge of Pentecostalism in the

Brazilian city of Belém, he placed issues of health and sickness at center stage, since these issues so often occur in the conversion narratives told by believers. Addiction problems are usually to the fore: Chesnut argues that "More than any other reason, it is the desire to be cured of alcoholism that impels Brazilian men to convert to Pentecostalism." Issues of healing, whether of mind or body, dominate the everyday life of the churches of the poor. Accordingly, "in some churches, faith-healing so dominates the liturgy that the sanctuary resembles a hospital."[48] Nowhere in the global South do the various spiritual healers encounter serious competition from modern scientific medicine, since this is so far beyond the reach of most of the poorest. For most ordinary people, Western medicine implies the assembly-line treatment of public hospitals, where any chance of receiving adequate treatment is outweighed by the dangers of catching new infections.

Healing is the key element that has allowed Christianity to compete so successfully with its rivals outside the Christian tradition, with traditional religion in Africa, with various animist and spiritist movements of African origin in Brazil, with shamanism in Korea. To some extent, the churches are forced to share the same intellectual universe as their competitors.

In Brazil, the Pentecostal churches that recruit poor urban dwellers find their most intense competition from African-derived spiritist movements such as Umbanda, which promises cures and exorcism. Edir Macedo, founder of the Universal Church of the Kingdom of God, is a former disciple of Umbanda, and the two groups recruit from much the same populations. The Korean Pentecostal churches that have flourished in recent years offer spiritual healing, especially the megachurches with tens or hundreds of thousands of members. And here too, the newer congregations face charges that they are only dressing up older local traditions, in this case shamanism. To quote Harvey Cox, a sympathetic observer: "what one finds in the Yoido Full Gospel church of Seoul involves a massive importation of shamanic practice into a Christian ritual."[49] Although conditions in China are more difficult to observe, healing-oriented groups provide the key competitors for Christian growth. One fast-growing religious movement of recent years has been the Falun Gong sect, which owes its appeal to claims of miraculous healing.

Given the central emphasis on physical health, we have to ask how the rising churches have been affected by the AIDS crisis that has so devastated Africa as well as other Third World nations such as Brazil. Sub-Saharan Africa presently accounts for more than two-thirds of known cases of HIV infection. In some regions of the continent, perhaps 40 percent of inhabitants carry the AIDS virus. Since the late 1970s, nearly 17 million Africans have probably died of AIDS. In Kenya alone, perhaps a million and a half have already died from AIDS-related illnesses, and more than a million more carry the HIV virus.[50]

The chief Southern centers of Christianity are also the regions hardest hit by AIDS, in the Democratic Republic of the Congo, Uganda, and South Africa, as well as in Brazil. For a Western audience, it might be thought that AIDS would be a powerful deterrent to religion, in showing the futility of prayer or spiritual healing. In reality, the epidemic has had no such effect, largely because no other form of treatment has proved any more effective. Western medicine has not acquitted itself any better than prayer, because the treatments that have proved effective in North America are just not accessible to poor Africans or Asians. No church can credibly claim to be offering a cure for AIDS, though some Pentecostal congregations have significantly reduced the kind of risky sexual behavior that spreads the disease. On the other hand, other churches have arguably made the situation even worse by fighting the promotion of condoms. On balance, the churches have not contributed greatly to stemming the disease, but this does not mean they have ignored the crisis. Many congregations have exercised different kinds of ministry in the worst affected areas. In Uganda, for instance, churches focus on comforting the dying and offering help to bereaved families.[51]

THE OLDEST CHRISTIANITY

Considering the central role of healing and exorcism in Southern churches, it is tempting to look for older pagan roots, and to ask just how the emerging congregations justify their ideas. Of course, Southern churches thrive because of their appeal to distinctively African or Latin American ideas—their ability to work within traditional culture—but these examples of accommodation do not amount to a betrayal of the faith, still less to syncretism. The rising churches can plausibly claim to be following abundantly documented precedents from the founding ages of Christianity. The Bible itself so readily supports a worldview based on spirits, healing, and exorcism. When Jesus was asked if he was the Messiah, he did not give an abstruse theological lecture but pointed at the tangible signs and wonders that were being done in his name. "Go back and report to John what you hear and see: The blind receive sight, the lame walk, those who have leprosy are cured, the deaf hear, the dead are raised, and the good news is preached to the poor." When Paul took the Christian faith to Macedonia, the first known mission into Europe, he was responding to a vision received in a dream.[52]

In understanding what can look like the oddities of Third World churches, it is helpful to recall one basic and astonishing fact, which is that they take the Bible very seriously indeed. To quote Richard Shaull, "In Pentecostalism, poor and broken people discover that what they read in the Gospels is happening now in their midst." For Southern Christians, and not only for Pentecostals, the apostolic world as described in the New Testament is not just a historical account of the ancient Levant, but an ever-present reality open to any modern believer, and that includes the whole culture of signs and wonders. Passages that seem mildly embarrassing for a Western audience read completely differently, and relevantly, in the new churches of Africa or Latin America. As David Martin remarks of another region in which this type of faith has spread in recent years, "The Pentecostal emphasis in Korea is really to see 'The Kingdom' both future *and* present in the signs of the Kingdom, especially healing and the 'baptism of the Spirit.' "[53]

Against this background, we need to think exactly what we mean when we say that a given person "believes in" the Bible and its stories. It is possible to believe in the stories recorded as if they are literally correct narratives of events that really occurred, but this is quite different from seeing them as applicable to present-day conditions. In Southern charismatic and independent churches, though, belief goes much farther, to the stage of participation in a present event. It has been said of Prophet William Wadé Harris that after his conversion, "it was no longer a question of what Moses did, or what Elijah did, or the words and works of Jesus as reported in the Bible. It became a question of involvement—as with the ancestors, the living dead—with Moses, with Elijah, with the archangel Gabriel, and supremely with Jesus Christ."[54]

For many new believers, stories of miracles and healing are so self-evidently crucial to the early Christian message that some suspicion must attach to any church that lacked these signs of power. As one Old Testament passage complains, "In those days the word of the Lord was rare; there were not many visions." To quote a modern follower of the Shona prophet Johane Masowe, "When we were in these synagogues [the European churches] we used to read about the works of Jesus Christ...cripples were made to walk and the dead were brought to life...evil spirits driven out.... That was what was being done in Jerusalem. We Africans, however, who were being instructed by white people, never did anything like that....We were taught to read the Bible, but we ourselves never did what the people of the Bible used to do."[55]

Parallels with ancient Christianity are just as clear when we consider prophetic leadership. In most Western cultures, the word "prophecy" is much debased from its original meaning. Today, a prophet is basically a fortune-teller, whose reputation stands or falls by the accuracy of his or her predictions. For the world of the first century, though, a prophet was someone who spoke the inspired word of God, which might or might not be relevant to current worldly concerns. Often, then and now, the prophetic inspiration was conveyed by means of material symbols. Isaiah Shembe received his divine call when he was burned by lightning, leaving a scar on his thigh.[56] The vitality of prophecy in the contemporary South means that the rising churches can read biblical accounts with far more understanding and sensitivity than Northern Christians can. In the book of Acts, prophecy was a sign of the true church. And if that was true two thousand years ago, why should it not be true of a man or woman today, a Kimbangu or a Shembe? Prophetic powers are exactly what Jesus promised his disciples, without any caveat that these gifts might expire with the end of the first century.

OLD AND NEW TESTAMENTS

When Southern churches read the Bible as a document of immediate relevance, they are accepting not just the New Testament but also the Old. This often gives rise to beliefs and practices that look Jewish rather than Christian: we recall the distinctive features of the Ethiopian church. The taste for the Hebrew Bible is not hard to understand, since the patriarchal world looks so very familiar for many new Christian societies, above all in Africa. The first books of the Bible show us a world based on patriarchal clans that practice polygamy and circumcision, and which regularly honor God through blood sacrifice. African Christians also find it difficult to understand just why there are some parts of the Bible they are expected to believe with absolute literalism—for instance, the Resurrection—while stories about Moses and Solomon must be treated as no more than instructive fables. Who made that seemingly random decision?

When a modern church follows ancient Hebrew ways, we must ask whether it is subtly reviving paganism or just trying to observe the Old Testament in all its details. One active community in West Africa is the Musama Disco Christo Church (MDCC), which was founded in the 1920s by the inspired prophet Joseph Appiah. Following the Genesis story of Jacob, the group has erected a sacred pillar, it has an Ark of the Covenant, and a Holy of Holies, which may be entered once each year only by a high priest. The MDCC also practices animal sacrifice, and sacrificial blood is used in an annual ceremony modeled on Passover.[57] Other churches ordain a Saturday Sabbath, some prefer to call God by the name "Jehovah," and some, including the ZCC, ban the eating of pork. Even the ancient and thoroughly orthodox Ethiopian church has absorbed some aspects of biblical Judaism.

The question arises of how much farther the new churches might go in absorbing pre-Christian traditions, if they found warrant in the Old Testament. In 2000 the Roman Catholic archbishop of Bloemfontein, South Africa, not only suggested that Christians might be permitted to honor their ancestors through blood libations, but that a ritual sacrifice of sheep or cows might be incorporated into the Mass. The archbishop, Buti Tlhagale, saw his proposal "as a step toward meaningful inculturation." Critics reacted with horror, as much because the suggestion violated animal rights as on grounds of heresy. Animal sacrifice had explicitly been condemned by some of the most venerated leaders of African Christianity, including the Ugandan martyr Janani Luwum. Still, Archbishop Tlhagale was far from isolated, since blood is used in some of the liturgical practices that have developed across Africa since the 1960s. In keeping with traditional ideas of consecration, the Congolese church uses a profession rite in which a drop of the candidate's blood is placed on the altar cloth. Such practices make great sense in African terms, and it would be easy to justify the practice by an arsenal of biblical texts. The whole New Testament notion of atonement is presented in the language of ritual blood sacrifice, which is precisely why it has become ever more distant (and even repulsive) for many modern Christians. Bizarre though it might seem at first, the whole idea of sheep having their throats cut during a Christian service raises to an acute degree the whole question of the limits of inculturation. Archbishop Tlhagale himself remains a distinguished leader of the South African church and has subsequently been elevated to the crucial see of Johannesburg.[58]

THE ONCE AND FUTURE CHURCH

It is easy enough to find behaviors or rituals that seem to place the new churches beyond what Westerners see as the legitimate bounds of Christianity, but in so many critical ways the independent congregations undeniably lie within the great tradition. Even in some of the areas in which they might seem odd or deviant, they are not so much departing from the Christian mainstream as emphasizing some aspects that have become unfamiliar—for example, in their Hebraism.

Perhaps the best way of refuting charges that emerging churches are anything less than fully Christian is to cite the example of a movement that genuinely is syncretistic, and that has, by any imaginable standard, moved far outside Christianity. Northern Mexico is home to a native people called the Tarahumara, who have adapted elements of Christianity to a traditional mythology. They believe in God and his wife, the Virgin Mary, who correspond to the Sun and Moon, together with their son Jesus. The divine family created all Indians, while non-Indians are the offspring of the Devil and his wife. Holy Week is the centerpiece of the ritual year, since that is the one time of year at which the Devil can defeat God. The Devil gets God drunk and seduces God's wife by his splendid guitar playing. Throughout Holy Week, the Tarahumara flock to the churches to defend the dangerously weakened divine couple, and they demonstrate their strength through elaborate processions of Soldiers and Pharisees. The Tarahumara consider themselves the "saviors of God in the Sierra Madre."[59]

I am not citing this example to mock or criticize the beliefs of the Tarahumara people, but rather to provide a point of reference in the debate over what is or is not Christian, as against what has been appropriated from pre-Christian ideas. In the case of the Tarahumara, the Christian veneer is slight and mainly involves borrowing sacred names, together with some aspects of Catholic ritual. The contrasts with the vast majority of independent churches are obvious. These latter preserve all the fundamental beliefs that would be recognizable from any stage of Christian development, including strict monotheism, a sense of Christ's unique role, and a firm sense of the division between divine and human realms.

Members of the independent churches themselves have no doubts whatever about their claims to authentic Christian status. This assertion is proudly proclaimed in denominational titles: we are dealing with the Zion Christian Church of the Star, Mount Ararat Apostolic Church, or the Eleven Apostles Spirit Healing Church. Many churches include the word "Apostolic" in their title, indicating a sense of direct continuity to the believers of the New Testament era, and to the powers manifested by the Christians of that age. Among the Aladura churches of West Africa, typical denominations take their names from both apostles (Christ Apostolic Church) and angels (The Cherubim and Seraphim Society). These churches believe staunchly in the divinity of Christ, his miracles, and resurrection.

The belief statements of the different churches are classic statements of Christian doctrine. Botswana's St. Michael's Apostolic Church proclaims that "The *ecclesia* is a congregation of faithful men in which the pure word of God is preached and the sacraments are daily administered according to Christ's ordinances." In the words of Nigerian prophet Agnes Okoh, "*Obu na ife m na ekwu adiro na akwukwo nso?*" which means, "What I am saying, is it not in the Bible?"[60]

In many ways, the Christian texts and creeds make far more sense for the independent churches than they do in the West. Western churches might teach the doctrine of the communion of saints, and imagine the supernatural church as a union of living believers with those past souls who have already died. In other words, Christians gain immeasurable strength from the cloud of witnesses with which they are constantly surrounded. For the African churches, the notion of continuity with the world of the ancestors is not only credible, it is a fundamental component of the belief system. And while many Western Christians have difficulty in accepting notions of the afterlife or resurrection as literally rather than symbolically true, these theories find a powerful resonance in African or Asian independent churches. The fact that believers regularly see their dead ancestors in dreams and visions is taken to prove that the deceased are still alive in God. Closeness to native traditions gives a powerful relevance to corporate and communal visions of the church, the *ecclesia*.[61]

These beliefs have implications for liturgy and worship. Even African Catholic churches struggle to find ways of honoring these ancestors without straying into forms of worship. In one rite, a priest presents a consecrated host to a vase symbolizing the presence of the bygone generations, proclaiming the coming of Christ, and saying, "We join with you [ancestors] so that you also may attain the fullness of life in the new heaven." Burial rites have also been restructured to take more account of the continuity with the ancestors. To the casual observer, other rituals seem to come close to the idea of postmortem baptism for departed ancestors.[62]

INITIATES

Practical necessity has forced some newer churches to revive ancient customs long dormant in the older Christendom. One striking example is the catechumenate, the probationary stage through which new Christians were required to pass before earning full membership in the church. In the ancient church, this was a significant institution, associated with rigorous training and gradual revelation of the mysteries of the faith. The catechumenate largely died out in the European Middle Ages when it was assumed that all church members were born and brought up in a Christian community, but in modern times, the institution has enjoyed a resurgence. In many African and Asian societies, new Christians can reasonably be assumed to be coming from a pagan background or else from entirely different religions, so they require intense training and preparation as catechumens. In the late nineteenth century, Cardinal Lavigerie and his White Fathers demanded that converts go through a probationary period of four years, and this rigorous approach influenced Protestant counterparts. A catechumen was not automatically qualified to pass to full membership in the congregation, and a moral or disciplinary lapse could mean that the person was forced to begin the process anew.[63]

In some Congolese dioceses, the transition from catechumen to baptized Christian has taken on many of the features of traditional initiation rites. Candidates spend time away from their communities, learning both religious knowledge and new worldly skills, and the Easter baptism ceremonies may involve an exchange of masks, signifying the shedding of old pagan identities. The baptism is accompanied by an exorcism, which is given far more weight than the symbolic vestige that this rite occupies in the West. In twenty-first-century Africa, as in second-century Rome, baptism is an awe-inspiring symbol of the believer's separation from a failing pagan world, an act of divine rescue.[64]

The point about the catechumenate reminds us that in many ways, Southern Christianities today stand in much the same relationship to the wider society that the church did in the Roman Empire, before and during the great age of conversions. The new churches rise and fall for much the same reasons as their ancient predecessors, and the enemies they faced were much the same. Observers of contemporary Southern conditions often draw such ancient parallels. Andrew Walls notes that "Our knowledge of the early church prior to the Council of Nicea in 325 is fragmentary, but the fragments reveal many of the concerns African churches have today, from distinguishing between true and false prophets to deciding what should happen to church members who behave badly. Even the literary forms are often similar. . . . Reading the pre-Nicene literature and the literature of the European conversion period in the light of modern African experience cast floods of light. African and Asian Christians can vastly illuminate 'our' church history." Walls is "everlastingly grateful that . . . that second-century Christianity (and third-century, and even first-century) can still be witnessed and shared in."[65]

CHURCHES AND SECTS

The idea that global South churches are living in something like a renewed apostolic age inspires nothing short of awe, and it would be easy to write of all these developments in a thoroughly supernatural, and even credulous, way. (Not for a second am I suggesting that critical scholars like Walls fall into this category.) A religious believer might accept that God really is inaugurating a new era of signs and wonders, to give Christianity a kind of rebirth. Such a revival would be all the more miraculous because it so directly contradicts every secular assumption and undermines the values of the world's dominant social order. I am in no position to affirm or deny that miraculous quality, but solid secular reasons also go far to explaining the character of the rising churches. Placing the churches in a social context does not make them any less impressive, but it does help to explain why they have the beliefs and practices they do. Even more usefully, looking at Southern churches in this way might help us understand how they are going to evolve in coming decades. Just because these churches look and act a certain way now does not mean that this is how they will be for centuries to come.

Much of the success of the newer churches unquestionably reflects their adaptation to local traditions and thought-patterns, so that African Christianity has become quintessentially African, Korean Christianity thoroughly Korean, and so on. But accommodation with local ways is not the sole explanation of why the rising churches possess such a vital sense of the divine presence in everyday life. In fact, many of what initially seem to be characteristically African or Latin American ways of worship also appear regularly in Northern cultures, and these commonalities cannot simply be explained in terms of Africanness or Koreanness. If Africa's flourishing indigenous churches place a far greater weight on healing than do their northern neighbors, we might be tempted to explain this in terms of the functions expected of religion in traditional African society. On the other hand, spiritual healing has frequently characterized new and fringe religious movements in Europe and North America over the centuries, and the theme might be seen as a universal element in popular religion. Just as African churches often look to charismatic leaders and prophets, so do sects and new religious movements in any part of the world.

Even some of the allegedly "primitive" attitudes to the spiritual world found in Africa or Asia would in the late twentieth century acquire steadily growing credence among white Western evangelicals and Pentecostals, with their belief in spiritual warfare. One aspect of this is spiritual mapping, identifying localities in which evil forces are believed to lurk, so that they can be confronted by prayer and exorcism. It is not just in the global South that people read Paul's letter to the Ephesians and believe that they too are warring against vast powers of spiritual evil. A phrase from this very passage inspired the title of Frank Peretti's *This Present Darkness*, one of the best-selling American books of recent years. Even exorcism, the center-piece of the spiritual warfare idea, has enjoyed a massive revival in the contemporary West, usually among people of European descent.[66] One goal of Mel Gibson's influential film *The Passion of the Christ* was to restore to the narrative the centrality of Jesus's cosmic struggle with the Devil, and with ancillary evil forces. Indeed, the film begins with Jesus crushing the head of the serpent, a classic image of the Christian victory over the demonic. Looking at the widespread impact of such ideas, it becomes harder to draw a strict geographical or cultural boundary bet-ween "Northern" and "Southern" patterns of religious experience.

When we see such broadly similar churches growing in so many diverse regions, then the parallels cannot simply be explained just in cultural or racial terms. We would do better to see some of these practices as an aspect of the *newness* of the rising churches. In understanding the character of the new Christianity, it is helpful to use the division between "churches" and "sects" that is so basic to the academic study of religion.[67] A century ago, sociological pioneer Max Weber tried to define the differences between Europe's religious organizations, in passages that sound as if he is ana-lyzing the present-day religious realities of global North and South. *Churches*, in Weber's view, are formal bodies that intellectualize religious teachings and restrain emotionalism in their services. They offer believers a formal liturgy and set prayers, in ways that portray the divine as remote from daily life. *Sects*, by contrast, are overtly emotional and spontaneous, and encourage individual mystical experience; they tend toward funda-mentalism, while shunning the intellect as a possible source of danger. The prayers of the sects indicate a firm belief that the divine is ever-present, ever-ready to act in everyday life.

Sociologist Ernst Troeltsch further developed this theoretical division, and he contrasted the upstart quality of the sects with the deeper roots of the churches. The matter of recruitment was critical. Most sect members are voluntary converts, whose lives are largely controlled by the organiza-tion, so that the sect becomes a small exclusive fellowship of people seeking spiritual perfection. Churches, in contrast, are larger and better-established bodies, whose members are customarily born into the organization. Churches also attract members of higher social status and educational level than do the sects. Additionally, the two types of structure differ widely in terms of their leadership. Sects demand that leaders demonstrate spiritual and charismatic gifts; churches are run by formally trained ministers, who operate within a bureaucratic framework.

What most strikingly unites the otherwise diverse Southern churches is that in most cases, Christianity as a mass popular movement is a relatively new creation, so that first- and second-generation converts are well represented in the various congregations. They simply cannot assume that members are likely to be born into the group, hence the importance of the catechumenate. In terms of the sociology of religion, this means that they are classic sects, with all that implies for leadership, worship style, and degree of commitment. They are fundamentalist and charismatic by nature, theologically conservative, with a powerful belief in the spiritual dimension, in visions and spiritual healing. With their claims to prophetic status, figures such as Simon Kimbangu or Isaiah Shembe exactly fit the classic profile of sect leaders. In practice, leadership roles in Pentecostal and independent churches are open to anyone who is accepted as having spiritual gifts, regardless of any formal education or theological training.

The sociological model of the sect offers a useful means of understanding both independent and Pentecostal churches across the global South. When we see independent churches in South Africa or Nigeria, some of what initially appear to be their odd and African features are in reality no such thing. Yes, they are indeed distinctive when measured against the "mainline" churches of Europe or North America, but not when compared with countless smaller and fringe movements that largely attract white believers.

The literature on new religious movements not only provides good models for understanding the distinctive beliefs of such groups, but it may also predict their future development. As time passes, successful sects become more churchlike in their own right, more formal and bureaucratic. Crucially, they might insist that clergy acquire formal academic training, rather than merely being "called by the Spirit." The history of Methodism from the eighteenth century on provides a classic model of such a process.[68] As sects drift away from their origins, they in turn spawn a new generation of enthusiasts who seek to recapture the charisma and spiritual power that they believe to be integral to religious experience. Churches beget sects, which in turn become churches, until they in turn beget new and still fiercer sects. The cycle has recurred many times and will continue ad infinitum.

As Southern churches grow and mature, they will assuredly lose something of their sectarian character, and become more like the major churches, with all that implies for the nature of leadership, worship style, and so on. They will move toward the mainstream, just as Methodists and Quakers did in their day. One symbolic example of such a change occurred in 1969, when the Kimbanguist church, one of the largest indigenous churches, actually joined the World Council of Churches, then as now dominated by liberal and mainstream Protestants. The Church of the Lord (Aladura) took the same step in 1975, the Harrists and several other Independents in 1998. If past precedents are anything to go by, Southern religious organizations will become more formal and churchlike, and just possibly more skeptical toward claims about healings and prophetic visions.

A change from sects to churches accelerates as their host societies modernize, as Western medicine becomes more affordable and gains more credibility. African and Asian societies might undergo the same kind of secularization that Europe experienced in the eighteenth century, when concepts such as witchcraft and prophecy gradually fell out of favor. Conceivably, the new churches themselves could become key agents of modernization. Studies of Latin American Pentecostalism note how believers gain a new sense of individual respect and responsibility, together with habits of thrift, sobriety, and literacy, and similar observations can be made of their African counterparts. A growing Pentecostal community tends to create a larger public base for the growth of democratic capitalism and, in the long term, perhaps for greater secularism.[69] At the same time though, as churches become part of the establishment, newer and more radical bodies will spin off from them. In the coming decades, the newer Christian communities will develop at least as much diversity as those of the old Europe did in the Middle Ages, or the early modern period.

Yet all these changes are likely to occur over generations, and the transformation described here will not be anything like complete until well into the present century. For the foreseeable future, then, Southern churches should continue to offer a powerful and attractive package for potential converts, both North and South. They can plausibly present themselves as modern-day bearers of an apostolic message that is not limited by geography, race, or culture, and claims of signs and wonders will serve as their credentials. If and when the rising churches turn their attentions northward, they might well find a deeply interested audience willing to listen to these very old messages repackaged in such unexpected forms.

++++++++++ SEVEN ++++++++++

God and the World

Do not be afraid. I see God's hand in this.
—*Archbishop Janani Luwum of Uganda*

In the name of God, in the name of this suffering
people whose cries rise to heaven more loudly
each day, I implore you, I beg you, I order you,
in the name of God: stop the repression.
—*Archbishop Oscar Romero of San Salvador*

We can predict something of the beliefs and practices of the emerging Christianities, but what of the future relationship between God and the world? The greatest change from present assumptions is likely to involve our Enlightenment-derived assumption that religion should be segregated into a separate sphere of life, distinct from everyday reality. In the Western view, religion may influence behavior in what is often, revealingly, termed the real world, and faith might even play a significant political role, but spiritual life is primarily a private inward activity, a matter for the individual mind. For Americans particularly, the common assumption holds that church and state, sacred and profane, are wholly separate enterprises and should be kept as separate as oil and water. In most historical periods, though, such a distinction does not apply, and is even incomprehensible. Scholars studying medieval Europe are scathing about any attempt to draw lines between "religion" and ordinary life, and doubt whether anyone living in those times could actually have understood the modern distinction between church and state.

In this sense, many societies of the global South live in an intellectual world far closer to the medieval world rather than to Western modernity. In recent decades, the politics of much of Africa, Latin America, and Asia have been profoundly affected by religious allegiances and activism, as clergy have repeatedly occupied center stage in political life. This phenomenon is not unknown in the modern West, which so esteems clerical activists such as Martin Luther King Jr. and Dietrich Bonhoeffer, but it happens much more systematically in the global South. In these Christian communities, cardinals and bishops have emerged as national moral leaders in a way that really has not happened in the West since the seventeenth century. Also, as in the European Middle Ages, political interventions by the clergy have been explicitly religious in nature, drawing on ancient prophetic traditions, and on a powerful and innovative kind of biblical exegesis.[1] It is not just in the Muslim world that religious ideologies tend to trump political and national loyalties.

However unimaginable it may have appeared fifty years ago, not only is Christianity flourishing in the Third World but so are distinctively Christian politics. If in fact Christianity is going to be growing so sharply in numbers and cultural influence in coming decades, we can reasonably ask whether the faith will also provide the guiding political ideology of much of the world. We might even imagine a new wave of Christian states, in which political life is inextricably bound up with religious belief. If so, then the South will soon be dealing with some debates that have a very long pedigree in the traditional centers of Christianity, issues of the proper relationship between church and state, and between rival churches under the law. Other questions that inevitably arise in such settings involve tolerance and diversity, the relationship between majority and minority communities, and the extent to which religious-inspired laws can (or should) regulate private morality and behavior. However these issues are resolved, this political dimension will further intensify the enormous cultural gap between North and South, between secular and religious societies.

OUT OF COLONIALISM

The association between church and state has a very long history in the global South. Under colonial regimes, Christian churches enjoyed state support, which they reciprocated by their strongly conservative political stances. The church was in effect an arm of government. In Latin America, the preferential position enjoyed by the Catholic Church continued long after independence, and in some countries survives today. Only in 2000 did Chile end the church's legal hegemony over education and cultural life, a relic all the more surprising in a country with one of the largest Protestant minorities in the region. Prior to this, only Catholics could appoint chaplains

HALF PRICE BOOKS

EST. 1972

Half Price Books #014
626 South Whitney Way
Madison, WI 53711
608-273-1140

09-09-19 2:03 PM

Store #0014 / Cashier ESor014 / Reg 3
Sale # 221292

SALE TRANSACTION

The Next Christendom: The Co 2663877760
1 @7.98 $7.98
Michelangelo: Creation Hands 8197910205?
1 @2.49 $2.49

2 Items in Transaction

Subtotal $10.47
Sales Tax (5.5% on $10.47) $0.58
TOTAL $11.05

PAYMENT TYPE
Cash $51.05

CHANGE $40.00

Thanks for shopping at Half Price Books!

Get cash back when you sell your
books, music, movies & games!
We are bookish, but have a social life.
Find us @halfpricebooks on
Facebook, Twitter & Instagram

H02001400322129274

Cash refunds and charge card credits on all merchandise
are available within 7 days of purchase with receipt.
Merchandise charged to a credit card will be credited to
your account. Exchange or store credit will be issued for
merchandise returned within 30 days with receipt.
Cash refunds for purchases made by check are available
after 12 business days, and are then subject to the time
limitations stated above. Please include original packaging
and price tag when making a return. Proper I.D. and
phone number may be required where permitted.
We reserve the right to limit or decline refunds.

Gift cards cannot be returned for cash, except as required by law.

The personal information you provide is confidential and will
not be sold, rented or disclosed to a third party for commercial
or other purposes, except as may be required by law.

RETURN POLICY

Cash refunds and charge card credits on all merchandise
are available within 7 days of purchase with receipt.
Merchandise charged to a credit card will be credited to
your account. Exchange or store credit will be issued for
merchandise returned within 30 days with receipt.
Cash refunds for purchases made by check are available
after 12 business days, and are then subject to the time
limitations stated above. Please include original packaging
and price tag when making a return. Proper I.D. and
phone number may be required where permitted.
We reserve the right to limit or decline refunds.

Gift cards cannot be returned for cash, except as required by law.

The personal information you provide is confidential and will
not be sold, rented or disclosed to a third party for commercial
or other purposes, except as may be required by law.

to the armed forces, only Catholic organizations obtained tax exemptions on property and donations, and religious education in schools was purely Catholic. Bolivia ended the church's privileged role as recently as 2009. In the early twentieth century, Catholic thinkers were entranced by the theory of integralism, a neomedieval notion that Catholic social doctrine should pervade every aspect of social, economic, and political life, with the clergy exercising broad influence over secular matters. Although the theory was discredited by its association with ultra-right views and fanatical anti-communism, it maintains a subterranean existence.[2]

During political conflicts in Latin America, Catholicism was dependably on the side of the traditional ruling orders, often to the point of approving repression. During the Argentine dictatorship of the 1970s and 1980s, Catholic Church authorities were notorious for their acquiescence in official violence and for the brutal proceedings of the dirty war.[3] Radicals on the other side of the conflict were often strongly anti-Catholic and anticlerical. In Mexico, the church suffered violent persecutions at the hands of radical regimes through the first half of the twentieth century. In Africa too, the mission churches supported by the colonial powers were sporadically attacked during insurrections.

Increasingly during the twentieth century, Third World churches came to be identified with the cause of reform or, frequently, revolution. Although the ideological bent of the churches changed massively, we still find the idea that they should be thoroughly involved in politics, and even to lead the nation. In the early twentieth century, exponents of radical political Christianity were chiefly to be found on the fringes of the mission churches. The most visible leaders were African prophets such as John Chilembwe or William Wadé Harris, or radicalized Catholic priests like Brazil's legendary Father Cicero. From the 1950s on, however, such ideas penetrated the mainstream churches, in Europe and North America, and across the Third World. Protestants were deeply affected by memories of the churches' failure to confront Nazi Germany, and were radicalized by campaigns against racism and against the apartheid regime of South Africa. These ideas gained a stronghold in the World Council of Churches (WCC), which since the late 1960s has often espoused radical and left-wing political causes. The organization faced serious controversies over precisely how far to go in its opposition to unjust states. Resentment became public in the 1970s when the WCC's Special Fund regularly gave money to guerrilla fighters opposing the white Rhodesian regime. For critics, this funding uncomfortably crossed the boundary dividing the Church Militant from the Church Militarist.[4]

In the Roman Catholic Church, theologies of liberation spread widely following the second Vatican Council of 1963–65. At least for a while, the Vatican not only permitted but endorsed radical political action. In 1967 the papal encyclical *Populorum Progressio* called for "bold transformations" to redistribute wealth globally. Both Catholics and mainstream Protestants shared similar ideas about the right and obligation to oppose oppressive regimes, and to combat the structural racial and economic justices found across the global South. Both also found rich precedents in Christian history for such activism. They looked to the Exodus story of liberation from slavery, as well as to Old Testament prophets of justice such as Amos. In the New Testament too, liberationist readers found much ammunition for a radical social critique, especially in the Magnificat, the proclamation of God's coming reign by the Virgin Mary, in which the rich are cast from their seats and the humble exalted. No less incendiary—and just as popular—is the Epistle of James, which warns of the fiery judgments awaiting the wealthy and proud. Another potent theme was that of *Kairos,* the "Hour" of God's judgment on human injustice, and on exploitative social structures.[5]

In its various forms, liberation theology motivated individual believers to participate in political struggles, and made it clear that the churches were no longer on the side of oppressive regimes. This movement had real political consequences in repressive states, since clergy were allowed much greater latitude of speech and action than ordinary citizens, and so could serve as symbolic centers of resistance and activism. If an ordinary labor union member spoke out against torture and repression, then he or she was likely to be jailed or killed forthwith, but a government had to be more circumspect when a priest or bishop uttered the same words. Jailing a priest, particularly a Catholic priest, invited the condemnation of the Western media and a probable confrontation with the Vatican. Clergy became valued spokesmen for opposition movements. Similar constraints on official behavior applied when protests or organizational meetings were held under church auspices. At least when under the eyes of Western media, repressive regimes had qualms about storming churches or firing on religious processions that they would not have had if protesters were waving red flags. Moreover, in a society in which the government and military dominate all forms of media and mass communication, intrachurch networks provide an effective system of alternative media, ideal for rapid mobilization and communication.

Churches offered a kind of safe zone, as radical clergy effectively reinvented the medieval Christian notion of sanctuary. In the bloody aftermath of the 1973 coup d'état in Chile, the families of the persecuted had nowhere to turn, with the conspicuous exception of the *Vicaría de la Solidaridad*, a mission under the protection of the nation's Catholic Church. In the repressive Brazil of the 1970s, by far the most effective source of opposition was the Catholic Church under the leadership of São Paulo's Cardinal Paolo Arns, who freely exploited the fact that the military dictatorship would never dare touch a religious figure of his stature. His sister Zilda Arns was a legendary organizer of medical work among poor children, and was commonly described as Brazil's Mother Teresa. One does not lightly go to war against saints, or their families.

Of course, the church's immunity was strictly limited and applied only when governments cared about world opinion. The "sanctuary" principle worked in authoritarian South Korea, tied as it was to the Western world system, but not in isolated and paranoid North Korea, in which the churches were ruthlessly destroyed, and in which possession of a Bible is grounds for execution.[6] Even in the Western Hemisphere, governments under threat of collapse might strike at the church. A decent respect to the opinions of mankind did not save the life of Archbishop Oscar Romero, when in 1980 he issued his frontal challenge to the rightist regime of El Salvador. In 1989 six Jesuit priests were murdered as further victims in the ongoing savagery in that nation. In Guatemala too, murderous state violence reached even into the episcopal ranks, with the 1998 slaying of the auxiliary bishop who served as head of the archdiocese's human rights office.[7]

In practice, such violence has actually reinforced the church's reputation as defender of the exploited. In many countries, churches would acquire an enviable reputation for courageous and effective opposition to repressive regimes.

LATIN AMERICA AND LIBERATION

Liberation theologies took very different courses depending on the politics of the region where they took root. Liberationist ideas achieved their earliest successes in Latin America, and the story of Catholic radicalism is so central to Latin American history since the 1960s to the 1980s that it is scarcely possible to discuss it in any detail here. Catholic activism received a kind of charter in 1968, during the conference of the Latin American bishops (CELAM) meeting at Medellín, Colombia, an event that has been described as a kind of declaration of independence. Borrowing extensively from Marxist terminology, the assembled bishops condemned neocolonialism, exploitation, and the institutionalized violence of capitalist society, and demanded fundamental economic and social reforms. In 1971 the Peruvian theologian (and Catholic priest) Gustavo Gutiérrez published what was perhaps the best-known work of the new movement in his *Teologia de la Liberación*.[8]

Over the next twenty years, many church leaders took very seriously the call for a "preferential option for the poor." Radicalism was personified by activist bishops such as Helder Cámara, who from 1964 to 1985 served as archbishop of the Brazilian province of Recife and Olinda, where he was known as the bishop of the *favelas*. Dom Helder himself grew out of an integralist background, suggesting how naturally the new left-wing synthesis could be reconciled with older theocratic notions. Catholic radicals developed a popular constituency through the base communities, which some visionaries saw as the nuclei of a future church of the people. In what was loosely a Leninist model, the base communities were to be the seeds of the new society emerging within the shell of the old, until they eventually became strong enough to discard the old husk. By the late 1970s, there were said to be 80,000 such communities in Brazil alone.[9]

Catholic radicals remained in lively dialogue with Marxist groups, and Christians participated in some of the revolutionary movements of these years. Already in the mid-1960s, some priests working with the poor were becoming heavily politicized, and some wholeheartedly adopted a revolutionary agenda. The patron saint of this movement was Colombian priest Camilo Torres, who fought alongside a guerrilla group until he was killed in battle with the armed forces in 1966, becoming a martyr for the Far Left worldwide. He believed that "The revolution is the way to obtain a government which will feed the hungry, clothe the naked, teach the ignorant, fulfill the works of charity, of love of neighbor.... Therefore, the revolution is not only permitted but is obligatory for Christians."[10] Although he stood at a far extreme of Catholic politics, Torres represented a wider constituency in his belief that the church and clergy needed to reshape government for the good of the poor.

Liberationist hopes reached a new height in the late 1970s. When the Sandinista revolution triumphed in Nicaragua in 1979, several current and former priests served in the radical government. The following year, the assassination of Archbishop Romero created a popular martyr, as Central America became the focus for the Christian Left worldwide. The momentum, however, stopped here. In 1978 the election of John Paul II brought to the Vatican a conservative pope whose experiences in Poland had given him a deep distrust of Marxism in any form. Through the 1980s the new regime in the Vatican systematically silenced radical theologians, such as Brazil's Leonardo Boff. Meanwhile, revolutionary hopes in Central America were dashed by global conditions, in the form of U.S. intervention and the collapse of the Soviet bloc. The Sandinista regime lost power in 1990.[11]

[handwritten margin notes: JPII + U.S.A Soviet collapse ↓ dashed revolution hopes]

THE TRADITION TODAY

During the papacy of John Paul II, a series of new episcopal appointments brought the Latin American church into a much more conservative line. The new pattern was exemplified by Peruvian Juan Luis Cipriani, a member of the conservative Opus Dei organization and bishop of the diocese of Ayacucho. This position was so sensitive because Ayacucho was the storm center of the fierce guerrilla war waged by the nation's Maoist guerrillas, the Shining Path, who were suppressed by bloody military campaigns in the 1990s. Cipriani, like the Vatican, held that the regime was fighting for Christianity and civilization, and underplayed talk of military atrocities. In 2001 he became a cardinal.[12]

His counterpart in the Mexican church is Norberto Cardinal Rivera Carrera, archbishop of Mexico City, who investigated and suppressed seminaries that he believed to tilt toward Marxist doctrine. Like conservative prelates elsewhere in Latin America, he favored priests from strict new religious orders such as Opus Dei and the Legion of Christ. The theological zeal, however, cloaked a serious problem. The Legion of Christ was founded in 1941 by Mexican priest Marcial Maciel, and it won high favor in the Vatican by its strong theological and political conservatism. Gradually, though, it became clear that Fr. Maciel himself was tainted by numerous financial and sexual scandals, which involved his supporters in ever more elaborate cover-ups.[13]

Contrary to the extravagant hopes of the 1970s, Latin America would not become subject to a kind of left-wing theocracy, but it would be wrong to see recent changes exclusively in terms of a withdrawal from idealism. Nor have church leaders renounced a political voice, and they remain active in secular politics to a degree that would be unthinkable in the global North. Despite the rightward shift of the church in that region, Latin American clergy remain major political players, who often do intervene on the side of democracy and human rights. As a counterpoint to Peru's conservative Cipriani, we can cite Brazil's Cardinal Claudio Hummes, the successor to São Paulo's activist Paolo Arns. Though conservative on moral issues—he forbids his clergy from advocating or permitting condom use, even to prevent AIDS—his view of Christian doctrine strongly emphasizes social obligation and responsibility, and Hummes supports the landless peasants' movement, the *Movimento dos Sem Terra*. In his condemnation of globalization and corruption, Mexican cardinal Rivera Carrera represents a similar mix of theological Right and economic Left of a kind that puzzles non-Catholic commentators.[14]

Another cardinal elevated at the same time as Cipriani was Oscar Andrés Rodríguez Maradiaga, archbishop of Tegucigalpa, Honduras. Obviously approved by the Vatican, Cardinal Rodríguez nevertheless speaks freely on issues of social justice, and has emerged as a leading spokesman in the campaign to cancel the crushing debts owed by Third World nations. A foe of globalization, he has asserted that "neo-liberal capitalism carries injustice and inequality in its genetic code." Within Honduras, his work for political democracy resulted in an overenthusiastic parliament electing him as the nation's new chief of police. Although he declined the honor, the incident speaks volumes for continued assumptions about the moral ascendancy of the church and its proper role in secular life.[15]

CHURCH AGAINST STATE

Under such leadership, the popular organizations that had sprung up during the previous generation now entered a political ice age. Though some survived and flourished, many base communities withered and failed to become the nuclei of a radical Catholic Reformation. Much of the impulse that originally inspired the communities has been diverted into Pentecostalism, which appeals to similar constituencies among the urban poor. In part, Pentecostal growth can be seen as a response to the failed revolutionary expectations of earlier years, and in several countries, the newer sects expanded most rapidly during the political repression of the 1980s.

But the theme of religious radicalism survived and found new manifestations. Leftist regimes have risen to power in several nations—under such leaders as the demagogic Hugo Chávez, who has ruled Venezuela since 1998, Evo Morales in Bolivia, and the Paraguayan president Fernando Lugo. Each government in its way builds on older religious foundations. Lugo himself was a young Catholic priest in the late 1970s when he was exposed to liberation theology in its era of greatest zeal and intensity. In 2005, he resigned as bishop in order to run, successfully, for national office.

Naturally, then, he speaks the language of liberationist thought and favors land redistribution. Liberation-minded clergy advise and support both Chávez and Morales; in fact, Morales's radical-minded deputy interior minister is an ex-Jesuit.[16]

Other religious influences, however, can also be seen, illustrating the thoroughly confessional forms of the region's political struggles. Just as Catholic bishops have attacked both the Bolivian and Venezuelan regimes for being repressive or even anti-Christian, so those countries' leaders have struck back at the mainstream Catholic Church and hierarchy. Both Chávez and Morales claim to be struggling to empower the common people, and for both, Catholicism is the ultimate symbol of reaction and entrenched privilege. In 2009, Morales proclaimed that "Some members of the Catholic Church hierarchy used prayer as an anesthesia so the people would not become free. When they cannot dominate us with the law, then comes prayer, and when they cannot humiliate or dominate us with prayer, then comes the gun." Both leaders responded by reducing the official role of the church and withdrawing state support. They also enhance the privileges of other groups, both evangelical Protestants and also, in Bolivia, the ancient Indian religions (Morales makes much of his Indian heritage). Chávez himself ostentatiously cites biblical and religious references in his rhetoric and has publicly flirted with Protestantism. On the other side, the Catholic Church presents itself as resisting tyranny, fighting calls for class warfare, and defending human rights. For both sides though, for presidents and bishops, religion provides the inescapable framework for political thought and action.[17]

THE NEW CHURCH POLITICS

All too often the Catholic Church occupies such a prominent role because it is literally the only institution that can hope to speak for ordinary people, and this is especially true in nations in which the mechanisms of government and civil society have virtually collapsed. The church has thus spoken out in the nation of Colombia, which has come close to the noxious position of a failed state, assailed at once by corrupt and oppressive government forces, by narcoterrorists, and by lethal and sinister militias of both Left and Right. Groups of all political shades finance themselves by kidnapping. Only the most daring clergy can afford to speak publicly against such dehumanization, and it costs them dearly. In 2002 the violence claimed the life of Cali's archbishop Isaías Duarte Cancino, who had proclaimed that anyone who attacked civilians "lacks the virtues proper to a human being and becomes the most miserable of men... theirs is not a just war, but merely a repetition of the savage acts from the saddest times in human history." More recently, the upsurge of drug-related violence has undermined most civil institutions in large sections of Mexico, where dedicated clergy provide the only trustworthy resources for many ordinary people in a *tierra caliente*, a war-torn hot zone. Priests comfort and succor the bereaved, while helping civilians survive the conflict between the state and the traffickers.[18] If not exactly struggling for liberation in the sense advocated in the 1970s, modern church leaders do indeed find themselves struggling on behalf of the faithful and risking their lives in the process.

Also, as in North America, the past thirty years have witnessed a shift in the substance of politics, from matters of economics, class, and labor to questions of personal rights and morality, often involving debates over sexuality. Gay marriage has proved an especially sensitive theme. Mexico and Brazil have granted varying degrees of recognition to same-sex unions, while in 2010, Argentina gave equal marriage rights to homosexual and heterosexual couples. In all these matters—abortion, homosexuality, stem-cell research—the churches have been active, with the Catholic clergy supporting conservative moral stances. Often, Catholics have joined with Protestant leaders, with whom they are often at odds on other issues. Indeed, the presence of a firmly evangelical constituency means that Catholics have an added incentive to step forward as moral leaders, to maintain their position as the national conscience.[19]

Churches of all shades have been involved in such debates in Brazil, where religion permeates political thought and action. The country now has an explicit Protestant caucus, the Evangelical Parliamentary Front, whose goal is to ensure that public policy falls "in line with God's purposes, and according to his Word." One recent account of a Protestant congressman cites his desire to make the Brazilian statute book conform to the Bible: "I believe it's an obligation. You can't isolate church from society. The churches to which evangelicals belong have a mission, which is to promote the kingdom of God." Anthropologist Regina Novaes comments that "To understand Brazilian politics today, it's necessary to understand the field of religion. If you don't understand religion, you can't understand Brazilian politics." Even in Mexico, where the Catholic Church was long excluded from any public voice, the clergy have been visible activists in presidential contests, speaking out on such matters as euthanasia, abortion, morning-after contraception, and generally "respect for life and strengthening families."[20]

AFRICA'S REVOLUTIONS

Elsewhere in the world, too, the link between Christianity and popular politics is stronger than ever. In Africa, religion has been tied to liberation struggles since the 1960s. Most of the first generation of independent Africa's political leadership was Christian, commonly the products of mission schools, and these pioneers were often active church members in their own right. Zambian president Kenneth Kaunda was the son of a Presbyterian minister, while Senegal's leader Leopold Senghor had trained for the priesthood. Tanzanian president Julius Nyerere and Ghanaian leader Kwame Nkrumah had both taught in mission schools. Nyerere was a Catholic who worked closely with the churches, and for all his radical nationalism, he praised the missionaries who, he felt, "had brought the best they knew to Africa, their church and way of life." He drew heavily on Christian thought and language in formulating his radical variant of African Socialism, which he traced back to the early Christian communism described in the book of Acts.[21]

The linkage between Christianity and nationalism was enhanced over the next thirty years as church leaders of many denominations became prominent in the struggle against the entrenched white South African regime. In the process, the churches enthusiastically adopted the messages of liberation theology and tried to present a prophetic witness against secular evils. In 1985, Catholic and Protestant leaders agreed on the *Kairos* statement, which applied radical theology to modern politics. The statement was called forth by the shocking situation in which blacks and whites "sit in the same Church, while outside, Christian policemen and soldiers are beating up and killing Christian children, or torturing Christian prisoners to death, while yet other Christians stand by and weakly plead for peace." In the South African case, repression was an apocalyptic sign: "The god of the South African state is not merely an idol or a false god, it is the devil disguised as almighty God—the Antichrist." Having committed themselves so wholeheartedly to the idea of resistance, the churches enjoyed great prestige by the time of the fall of the white regime in 1994, when Anglican archbishop Desmond Tutu emerged as an unquestioned moral leader. Tutu tried to reconcile the nation's old rivals through a Truth and Reconciliation Commission, an innovative attempt to apply Christian ideas of repentance and forgiveness to national secular politics, rather than just individual relationships.[22]

Christian involvement in the South African struggle is well known in the West, but less celebrated is the key role that churches and clergy have taken in what has been called the second African revolution. Many of the new independent regimes that took power in the 1960s themselves became corrupt and oppressive, and these governments in their turn came under pressure to reform. In the worst cases, the independent governments became monstrous tyrannies, like those that successively ruled Uganda in the 1970s and 1980s. In the Ugandan case, the resulting struggle against oppression claimed the lives of many Christian protesters. We have already mentioned Archbishop Luwum, murdered on the orders of Idi Amin in 1977. The same year, political strife in the Republic of Congo (Congo-Brazzaville) led to the murder of a Catholic archbishop, Cardinal Biayenda.[23]

The leadership exercised by Archbishop Tutu was not unique in Africa, or even exceptional. In some cases, bishops and clergy led national movements against dictatorship, as in the attacks on Malawi's Hastings Banda or Kenya's Daniel Arap Moi. In the Kenyan case, Anglican archbishop David Gitari became the leading nemesis of the regime, prophetically denouncing every new tilt toward authoritarianism, at whatever risk to his life. Arguably still greater risks were run by Zimbabwean Catholic archbishop Pius Ncube, the most conspicuous public critic of that nation's dictator, Robert Mugabe. Ncube came close to calling for an uprising against Mugabe, and if that failed, he invited a British invasion of Zimbabwe. In the event, the regime did not need to resort to violence against Ncube, whose career was ruined by a 2007 sex scandal likely engineered by the government.[24]

The Roman Catholic Church was in demand as an honest broker even in countries that did not have a Christian majority. In Benin, Togo, and Congo/Brazzaville, senior clergy supervised transitions from dictatorship to democracy. And unlike in Latin America, Catholic activism in Africa did not run afoul of the Vatican, since local churches were evidently pushing for democratic constitutional reforms, rather than sweeping revolutionary change on a Marxist blueprint. Studying worldwide trends toward democratization in the 1980s, Samuel Huntington identified the Catholic Church as one of the principal engines for progress.[25]

Across Africa, senior clergy have become the focus of popular hopes and loyalties in a way in which the fragile nation-states of the continent cannot. We can see powerful analogies to the experience of European churches in the Middle Ages, and in both eras prelates are expected to run serious risks as a normal expectation of the job. To take an English example, between 1000 and 1650 no fewer than five archbishops of Canterbury died violently, whether by execution or assassination. Western European examples have been rarer in modern times, though struggles between Christianity and communism produced many modern-day clerical martyrs in the Soviet bloc, especially between the 1930s and the 1950s. The Russian church has canonized thousands of victims from this era as New Martyrs, *novomucheniki.*[26]

In terms of the scale of violence, though, there are few modern parallels to the dangers faced by African clergy, for whom cases of martyred prelates such as Thomas Beckett are not just matters of remote historical interest. To take an example that received next to no coverage in Western media, in 1996 Catholic archbishop Christophe Munzihirwa was murdered by Rwandan troops surging over his province in what was then eastern Zaire, and his body was left in the streets. Over the previous years, the archbishop had acquired a reputation for his impartial condemnation of violence and abuse in the region, no matter who the perpetrators were. He had repeatedly opposed and embarrassed the regime of dictator Mobutu Sese Seko, behavior that posed a grave threat to life and limb. When the Mobutu government collapsed, Archbishop Munzihirwa stood as the last hope that the hundreds of thousands of Rwandan refugees in his province might escape massacre. Reading the accounts of his last days, we recall the stories of bishops during the collapse of the Roman empire, trying to lead their flocks to safety from invading barbarians.[27] Then as now, the question was simple: if not the church, who else could the people turn to? Hoping to engineer a transition to democracy, the Congolese turned naturally to the Catholic archbishop of Kinshasa, Laurent Monsengwo Pasinya, who successively became president of the High Council of the Republic and speaker of a Transitional Parliament.

Heroic careers like those of archbishops Munzihirwa or Romero, or of Colombia's "Archbishop Isaías," have consequences that long outlast even the memories of those living individuals whom they have helped and defended. Deeply established in the Christian tradition is the idea of martyrdom and heroic sanctity, and it would be astonishing if these deaths were not soon commemorated through cults and shrines. Already, there is a groundswell for the canonization of Romero, but popular devotion has a habit of running far ahead of what the Vatican may decide. In future generations, the church will gain vastly enhanced strength from devotion to these new saints. In life, Romero, Luwum, Munzihirwa, Duarte, and their like were powerful nuisances to secular authority. In death, they became indomitable foes.

Reinforcing the medieval analogy has been the response of the embattled dictators. When a medieval king was denounced as an enemy of the church, he would commonly try to prove himself a paladin of piety, perhaps by launching a crusade or making a pilgrimage. In modern Africa, the situation is comparable. When Kenyan president Arap Moi came under attack from mainstream churches (Catholic, Anglican, and Presbyterian), his response was not to denounce the churches or to condemn religious intervention in politics, but rather to prove himself a fervently pious supporter of independent and Pentecostal churches. Making such alliances easier was the charismatic and sometimes authoritarian nature of leadership in some churches, which potentially makes these pastors important shapers of public opinion. Arap Moi's behavior illustrates the deeply religious and ecclesiastical nature of contemporary politics in Christian Africa. When Zairean Catholics criticized the abuses of the Mobutu government, the dictator launched an anti-Christian reaction, demanding that people abandon their Christian baptismal names. (He himself had been formerly Joseph Mobutu.) Even so, Mobutu also overtly favored rival Christian groups whom he saw as more docile and nationalist-minded than the Catholics, namely Protestants and Kimbanguists.[28]

Without understanding religious alignments, it is impossible to comprehend political life across most of Africa—all the more so as the religious institutions have so thoroughly mastered the means of communication and publicity. As a result, the most emotive issues in political life tend to be religious in character. Just to take one recent example, in 2010, Kenya suffered a constitutional crisis that was unusual in the violence of its outcome, but commonplace in the underlying issues involved. The government proposed a referendum on constitutional reforms that would allow limited abortion rights, while permitting Muslims to use *Shari'a* courts in matters involving marriage and landownership. Many churches opposed these laws, particularly energetic Pentecostal ministries like the Jesus Is Alive movement, led by the prophetic Bishop Margaret Wanjiru. Churches organized huge protest rallies, one of which culminated in a terrorist bomb attack that most observers blamed on government security forces. Ultimately, constitution supporters won, to the dismay of more conservative believers, but at every stage, the controversy focused on religious themes: religious toleration, the enforcement of morality, the toleration of minorities, and centrally, the concept of Kenya as a Christian nation. Campaigns were rooted in churches, and a government struck back against religious followers. That scenario allows precious little room for secular politics.[29]

ASIAN REGIMES

Clerical activism for human rights can give an enormous boost to church prestige, which in turn increases the church's political weight, and this cycle has occurred in Asia as well as Africa and Latin America. The Catholic

Church in the Philippines has a distinguished record of activism on social justice issues. Priests and ordinary clergy were prominent in anticolonial struggles against Spain and later the United States, even when higher church authorities were cool toward the resistance. One venerated national hero of the early twentieth century was former priest Gregorio Aglipay, who opposed Spanish prelates and tried to Filipinize the church. As "Spiritual Head of the Nation under Arms," he formed an independent Catholic Church that at its height attracted the loyalty of perhaps one-third of Filipinos. The Aglipayans today are only a small sect, largely because the mainstream Catholic Church has so firmly established its patriotic and activist credentials. By the 1970s Filipino clergy were influenced by liberation theology, and bishops such as Antonio Fortich, "Commander Tony," earned the same fiery reputation as Brazil's Helder Cámara. The Catholic Church dominated the revolutionary movement that led to the overthrow of dictator Ferdinand Marcos in 1986, and Cardinal Jaime Sin served as the symbolic focus of national resistance. When the Marcos regime ordered troops to move against its rivals, Sin summoned "all the children of God" to protect them, which they did, as protesters pleaded with troops to resist orders. For Sin, the whole popular movement was clearly a miracle, "scripted by God, directed by the Virgin Mary, and starring the Filipino people."[30]

Cardinal Sin played a similar role in the movement to impeach a subsequent Philippine leader, president Joseph Estrada, who was accused of receiving massive bribes. As the anti-Estrada campaign reached its climax in 2000, protests had a frankly ecclesiastical tone that would have been instantly understandable in medieval or early modern Europe. Services described as protest Eucharists were joined by members of Catholic social and labor groups and Catholic universities, and were led by Sin and other bishops. The Catholic Church was by no means alone in its campaign, which was supported by newer Protestant and charismatic groups, but there was no doubt about the potent religious content of the popular upsurge. As in the Kenyan conflict, the embattled president responded not by attacking religion, but by invoking his support of religious groups outside the mainstream. Through the controversy, one of his strongest supporters was Mike Velarde of the Catholic charismatic group El Shaddai.[31]

Korea has been a remarkable success story for the churches. Christian numbers have swelled since the 1970s, and the church's growing prestige and popularity has partly resulted from its willingness to stand up and suffer for democratic rights and for nationalist causes. Christian successes here also owe much to repeated official efforts to suppress the faith, a fact that would have been instantly understandable to the Christians of ancient times. If bishops are not actually executed, then jailing them can be almost as effective in promoting Christian solidarity, and in attracting recruits. The history of Korean Christianity since the seventeenth century has been turbulent. Under native Korean rule, the Christian rejection of ancestor cults repeatedly provoked massacres and persecutions, and thousands of Catholics perished in the 1860s and 1870s. Persecutions continued sporadically through the twentieth century, but in a dramatically different political context, as the occupying forces of imperial Japan tried to destroy Korean cultural identity. This repression put Christians in the position of patriotic martyrs. For ordinary Koreans, joining a Christian church was an effective symbolic means of declaring pride in Korea and opposition to the invaders. When Korean nationalists issued a symbolic Declaration of Independence in 1919, almost half the signatories were Christian, although Christians represented only 1 percent of the population at that time.[32]

Although persecutions in recent years have been nothing like as violent as those launched by the Japanese, we can see a continuation of older patterns. As popular opposition grew to South Korea's successive military regimes from the mid-1970s on, the churches emerged as forceful voices for reform. Protestants and Catholics allied to launch national protests, and bishops and laypeople became prominent as political prisoners. Korean churches evolved their *Minjung* theology, a local variant of liberationist thought. Dissident leader Kim Dae Jung has described his own Roman Catholic Church as "the centrifocal point of the spiritual struggle against the Park dictatorship." The opposition triumphed in 1992, when the country held free elections, and in 1997 Kim was elected president of the Republic of Korea. He has been described as Korea's Nelson Mandela. Vastly increasing Christian numbers reflect the prestige acquired by the churches through their sufferings.[33]

CHRISTIAN NATIONS

The modern story of Christian political activism is often an inspiring one, but history suggests that there are potentially disturbing sides of the story. To take an obvious problem, when a church helps establish a new government, religious leaders often expect some kind of recognition of their authority, perhaps even a share in government. In the Philippines, the president who replaced the controversial Estrada was mocked for her ostentatious displays of respect for the Catholic hierarchy. According to a journalistic critique, Gloria Macapagal-Arroyo was "busy polishing her Catholic credentials by adopting the bishops' line that cults are bad, and by handing down all sorts of pious edicts."[34] Such rhetorical displays may not pose any great threats to a nation's freedom, but far worse can occur in other settings.

It is not a vast leap from churches exercising political power to demanding an exclusive right to that power, perhaps within the confines of a theocratic Christian state. That assertion can offer a real provocation to non-Christian groups, to Muslims, traditional believers, and secularists, as well as to denominations that feel they are excluded from the new established order. Sometimes, the provocation is deliberate. In the Pacific nation of Fiji, native Fijians represent a majority of the population, closely followed by ethnic Indians, and for years the two communities have struggled for political and cultural dominance. Since the native community is heavily Christian, Fijian self-assertion takes the form of attempts to declare the nation a Christian state, as a snub to the Hindu minority.[35]

The complex religious makeup of most African nations ensures that political regimes have been cautious about speaking of themselves explicitly as Christian societies, but there are some exceptions. Zambia declared itself a Christian nation in 1991, and the nation's vice president urged citizens to "have a Christian orientation in all fields, at all levels." In the Ivory Coast too, recent regimes have been criticized for financially sponsoring Christian churches, organizations, and activities, in a land in which Muslims actually outnumber Christians. The trend found its most excessive manifestation in the astonishing basilica church of Our Lady of Peace, begun in the 1980s by then-president Félix Houphouët-Boigny in his hometown of Yamoussoukro at a cost of $300 million. This is claimed to be the world's largest Catholic church, larger than St. Peter's in Rome.[36]

Such grandiloquent ambitions seem so inappropriate to economic realities as to be mildly comic, but they do raise serious questions about the religious nature of Southern states. As we will see, one of the most divisive issues in modern Africa is the adoption of Islamic law in states such as Sudan and Nigeria, and predominantly Christian nations might retaliate by asserting their own religious beliefs through legislation. The separation of church and state is a wholly foreign idea in African nations, which follow the quite different models offered by former colonial powers such as Britain or Portugal. In these older views, church establishment was a perfectly familiar idea. We may yet see more Christian states, perhaps in which one denomination occupies the dominant role—what European scholars term a *Staatskirche*.

These newly defined Christian regimes would not necessarily share the passionate concern for democracy and constitutionalism that has so distinguished Southern churches in the age of Pius Ncube and Kim Dae Jung. Long before the recent rediscovery of the fiery prophetic tradition associated with liberation theology, church-state relations were commonly defined by doctrines of Christian acquiescence to political power. Christian political thought has long been influenced by the kind of submissive ideas represented in the thirteenth chapter of Paul's letter to the Romans ("Let every soul be subject to the governing authorities. For there is no authority except from God, and the authorities that exist are appointed by God"). Such ideas are generally held by independent and Pentecostal churches, who also have a deep devotion to the Old Testament, with all its accounts of kingdoms pledged to serving God's will. The idea of integralism is by no means confined to Catholics. We can imagine a future in which cooperative churches are enlisted into the service of government under the rhetoric of creating a Christian society, complete with appropriate moral legislation. Repressive regimes could benefit enormously from the support of these churches, which would provide a widespread propaganda network preaching the message of nonresistance to government, in exchange for their privileged status.[37]

Submission to a "Christian state" can easily turn into a willful refusal to acknowledge the flaws of that regime, and to connive at official corruption and violence. One of the rare independent African states to declare its Christian status from the outset was Liberia, in which religion was used to justify the gross corruption of the nation's political elite, and the oppression of the native country people. The Zambian president who proclaimed the nation's official Christianity, Frederick Chiluba, developed worrying tendencies to act unconstitutionally, and in the ensuing controversies, he could count on docile support from the Pentecostal churches that he ostentatiously favored. R. Drew Smith writes that "When opponents of the Chiluba government staged an unsuccessful coup...the general secretary of the Pentecostal Assemblies of God stated that 'God cannot allow Zambia to be disturbed by selfish individuals because he is in total control of the Christian nation.' He went on to say that 'thanks and praise should be given to God for enabling Zambian soldiers to crush the coup attempt.'" If there is one thing that struggling Third World states do not need, it is additional justifications to keep dictators in power.[38]

In addition, there is a real temptation for churches that have led or participated in revolutions to provide uncritical support for the new regimes, and to judge them by different standards from those applied to the old order. Acknowledging this temptation in the newly democratized South Africa, Archbishop Tutu shrewdly observed that "It is easy to be against. It is not nearly so easy to be clear about what we are *for*."[39] South African churches could easily have become pliant tools of the new government, the African National Congress at prayer. Accordingly, Tutu's Truth and Reconciliation effort examined the sins of the revolutionaries as searchingly as those of the government, and recognized both sides as requiring forgiveness. Other ecclesiastical radicals are not so perceptive.

FAILED STATES

Sometimes, religious activists campaign for greater powers that amount to theocracy. On occasion, however, they gain power by default, because they are the only plausible claimants. This theme may become more common in future decades as so much of the world's Christian population exists in what we despairingly term "failed states."

Every year, the Fund for Peace presents its list of the world's shakiest political entities. Entry qualifications for this undesirable club include such factors as demographic crisis, sharp economic decline, and bloody intergroup conflict. The state loses physical control of large parts of its territory and fails to provide rudimentary public services. In effect, state agencies become criminal organizations, allied with gangs and terrorist factions in bloody battles over state property and natural resources. Gradually, the accumulation of disasters leads to the utter collapse of state authority, and its replacement by private militias or warlords. In 2010, the roster of states viewed as either wholly failed or on the verge of collapse was led by Somalia, followed by Chad, Sudan, Zimbabwe, and Congo-Kinshasa, but other nations gave cause for acute concern.[40]

Already today, failed states provide troubled homes for some of the world's largest populations of both Christians and Muslims, and the concentration of both faiths in dysfunctional and violent countries will grow apace in the coming decades. Literally billions of people will have to cope with settings utterly lacking in the fundamental protections and services that modern Euro-Americans take for granted. African nations lead the way in state failure, with eleven of the top twenty examples in last year's listing; six more are in east and south Asia. The fact that most of the candidates cluster in the tropics will matter immensely if climate change develops as predicted in coming decades. These are the areas most likely to be hit by global warming, with all that implies for spreading desertification, and the limited access to water and food that follows.

State collapse will be a central theme in the future development of global religion, and the world's religious geography. By 2050, some six hundred million Muslims—around a quarter of the world's total—will live in just three of these endangered countries, namely Pakistan, Bangladesh, and Nigeria. The picture for Christians is almost as bleak. Of the nations that should by 2050 have the world's largest Christian communities, five are high on the critical list of current or potential state failure. Taken together, Nigeria, Ethiopia, Uganda, Kenya, and the Democratic Republic of the Congo could by that point have almost six hundred million Christians, more than in the whole of Europe. In 2009, the U.S. Joint Forces Command warned that even Mexico could collapse as a functioning state.[41]

The consequences of state failure are many and grievous. This matters, for instance, as a factor driving interfaith conflict. Failed states offer fertile environments for religious persecution: desperate people turn against minorities, while private armies offer the means to kill or expel large numbers. Sudan usually features high in catalogues of political failure. The anarchy prevailing in turbulent nonstates can also infect neighboring lands. Uganda, for instance, was one of the states sending forces to control the chaos in Somalia, and to limit the power of the terrifying al-Shabaab militia. That attempt led directly to lethal 2010 bombings that killed over seventy Ugandans. Al-Shabaab justified the attack as a strike against "a major infidel country supporting the so-called government of Somalia." Not surprisingly, the incident further escalated interfaith tensions in Uganda itself.

Factoring out the state also has a huge impact on the everyday religious experience and practice of the people who remain in those lands, whether these are Christians or Muslims. Of necessity, religious organizations have to take over most of the responsibilities and activities that a Westerner might expect to fall to government. But if the government simply is not there, then churches or mosques supply the social services. These are where people turn for any medical or educational services, and foreign governments and NGOs know that religious groups are the only effective conduits for aid or disaster relief.

In many instances too, religious groups take over legal and justice functions, ranging from arbitration to community policing. It is scarcely surprising that Islamic courts thrive in Somalia, Sudan, or parts of Pakistan where secular justice is only a vague rumor. Both Christians and Muslims dream, however fancifully, of full-fledged religious states that could suppress the anarchy and misery. Quite plausibly, a large share of the Christian world could by the middle of the present century be living under religious rule. Conceivably, armed force would be needed to enforce or defend that authority.

CHRISTIAN FIGHTS CHRISTIAN

In other ways too, Christian growth can on occasion lead to violence. We have already seen how commonplace messianic, prophetic, and apocalyptic groups have been in the Christianizing world. Usually, such groups tend to be peaceful, confining their threats of divine judgment to the other world; but a few movements, singularly fanatical, carry out actual violence in the present life. One notorious example occurred in 2000, when a Ugandan church with Catholic roots apparently launched a mass suicide that claimed the lives of over a thousand believers. Reportedly, the Movement for the Restoration of the Ten Commandments of God gathered at Kanungu to await a mystical vision of the Virgin Mary; followers then immolated themselves by fire, in what was described as an African Jonestown. Subsequent reporting raised serious doubts about this interpretation, and the believers are more likely to have been murdered in what was in reality an act of organized crime or terrorism. Still, the Kanungu disaster focused attention on other fringe African movements that indisputably have been involved in grossly violent acts.[42]

Often, such millenarian and messianic movements grow out of the many civil wars that have rent the continent in recent decades, producing social collapse and general despair. During the civil conflicts in Uganda over the past thirty years, one of the most ruthless guerrilla groups has been the Lord's Resistance Army, which became notorious for its mass abductions of children. The army grew out of a classic messianic anti-witchcraft movement called the Holy Spirit Mobile Force, founded by the prophet Alice Lakwena. Thousands of this group's followers perished when they went into battle believing that the magic oils smeared on their bodies would protect them from bullets.[43]

Religious rivalries are also problematic. Often, relations between expanding denominations are cordial or at least nonconfrontational, on the grounds that each church has plenty of room to grow, with ample likely converts. In much of Africa, different denominations have evolved good working relations in the form of conferences or federations of Christian churches. Serious conflicts appear, though, when a new denomination makes inroads into areas that another faith has traditionally regarded as its own distinctive territory. This kind of rivalry can be all the more deadly when religious loyalties coincide with national or tribal frontiers, so that religion provides yet another incentive for violence. Many of southern Africa's independent churches are closely linked to existing tribal leaderships, so that a religious challenge automatically becomes a political threat, demanding a forcible response.

A linkage between tribalism and religious zealotry has been alleged in several recent conflicts in Africa. One of the most alarming involved the genocidal violence in Rwanda in 1994, one of the worst single acts of carnage in the world since the end of World War II. The violence was overwhelmingly tribal in nature, with Hutus murdering members of the minority Tutsi tribe. Some of the activists in the slaughter were themselves Hutu Christian clergy, including both Catholic and Anglican bishops and clergy, and even nuns (though some Hutu clergy risked their lives to prevent murders). At the least, clerical involvement in mass murder raises questions about the nature of Christian conversion in a region that had been held up as a model of successful evangelization. More serious is the issue of whether denominational loyalties might actually have encouraged the violence. Reportedly, Hutus in the Catholic hierarchy used the massacres as an opportunity to purge Tutsi priests and laity. The only religious group that emerged from the affair with credit was Rwanda's small Muslim community, which courageously protected fugitives.[44]

Based on this experience, John Allen cites the alarming point made by a Burundian Catholic priest, Emmanuel Ntakarutimana. In terms of percentages of population, the four most heavily Christian nations in Africa are Burundi, Rwanda, the Democratic Republic of the Congo, and Congo-Brazzaville. Since the mid-1990s, these have also been the epicenters of dreadful carnage, including the Rwandan genocide and the ensuing Congo wars. Father Ntakarutimana concludes that, statistically, "the more Christian an African nation is, the higher the odds of being slaughtered there."[45]

In some circumstances, surging religious zeal can lead to instability and bloodshed, and often in countries that already have more than enough difficulties standing in the way of their development. In Europe, modernization and state-building could only advance once the wars of religion had been fought to a standstill, and the would-be messiahs driven out of mainstream political life. This was a piecemeal process taking centuries, and it is unlikely that a parallel change in Africa or Asia would be much more rapid.

BETTER THAN GUNSHIPS?

Latin America provides many cases in which religious change has led to political instability. As Protestant and Pentecostal numbers have soared over the last thirty years, Catholic authorities have become increasingly resentful. Backed by the Vatican, local bishops regularly condemn the growth of "sects," a term that in Romance languages usually signifies a dangerous fringe movement, rather like what the U.S. media would term a cult. In 1992 Pope John Paul II warned the Latin American Bishops Conference, CELAM, about these "ravenous wolves." He also said that evangelicals were spreading "like an oil stain" in the region, where they "threaten to pull down the structures of faith in numerous countries." Journalist Diego Cevallos has described the poisonous rhetoric that has become commonplace: "'You have to be shameless to be a Protestant,' declared the cardinal of Guadalajara, Mexico, Juan Sandoval Iñiguez, while the former papal nuncio to Mexico, Girolamo Prigione, commented that 'these sects are like flies that ought to be swatted with a newspaper.'" Even Honduran cardinal Oscar Rodríguez characterizes the new evangelical churches as "just one more industry.... It's enough to open a church, even in a garage. But there are two essential elements: be anti-Catholic, and demand tithes. That makes this a very attractive line of work. You don't need a degree in theology or any preparation. It's enough to pick up a Bible and say whatever you want, as long as you collect the tithes." Worse, the evangelicals are sometimes portrayed as a *gringo* export. One Brazilian study of the new churches is titled *Os Demônios Descem Do Norte,* "The Demons Come Down From the North."[46]

This is one of the few issues on which Catholic radicals see eye to eye with the conservative hierarchy, since liberationists are also very suspicious of Protestant advances. From their perspective, though, the chief sin of the *evangélicos* is that they preach political quietism, and damp down the flames of revolution. In Brazil, liberationist bishop Pedro Casaldáliga declared that "These sects create individuals who are mindless and alienated. They kill the soul of the people." As Andrew Chesnut remarks, "the Catholic Church has chosen the poor, but the poor chose the Pentecostals," and the choice rankles.[47]

Some of the weightiest charges about religious rivalries derive from Central America, which in the early 1980s seemed to be on the verge of a general popular revolution. In Guatemala and El Salvador, insurgencies were suppressed by extreme official violence, accompanied by massacre and torture, and it was in the midst of these dirty wars that Protestant and

Pentecostal churches made their greatest advances. According to common allegations made at the time, military authorities were exasperated with Catholic radicalism and explicitly decided to foster more amenable Pentecostal churches, which would preach unquestioning obedience to government. Pentecostal preachers were "better than gunships," not to mention cheaper.[48] Local governments were supposedly aided in this effort by U.S. agencies that were funded by conservative evangelical groups.

From this perspective, the Protestant/Pentecostal expansion of the 1980s was (at least in this region) little more than a cynical counterinsurgency tool, virtually a CIA plot to divide and rule. To quote Virginia Garrard-Burnett, one of the best-informed observers of the region, "To many, the proliferation of Protestantism in Latin America is proof of the complete U.S. cultural conquest of the region, a conquest bought—not won—by money, political influence and consumer goods." The linkage between Protestantism and repression was symbolized by Guatemala's born-again Protestant dictator Efraín Ríos Montt, who directed the armed forces during the most vicious antiguerrilla actions of the early 1980s. Many of those murdered as dissident leaders were Catholic lay activists and catechists. In terms of interdenominational bloodshed, Guatemala in the 1980s looked a little like France or Germany in the 1580s.[49]

Aggravating the conflicts was the special appeal of Protestantism to Native or indigenous groups. Since the Conquest, native peoples in Guatemala and elsewhere had largely relied on their traditional religion and customs in order to defend their cultural identity, but now the new churches threatened a fundamental shift to individualism. Worse, *evangélico* converts were encouraged to reject older beliefs as paganism or witchcraft. One Ecuadorian native leader presents evangelization as a weapon of aggressive globalization, the spiritual destruction of local communities and traditions: "There are a huge number of sects in Ecuador, I believe over three hundred, whose role is to pacify, divide and tame the people, subordinating them to the interests of the dominant powers or big corporations, like the oil companies."[50]

Many Westerners, somewhat simplistically, agree with the view of Latin American Protestantism as a conservative Trojan Horse, though of course it is far more than that. There is now a huge literature on the Pentecostal churches of the region, especially in Central America, and these studies show convincingly that *evangélicos* come in all political shades, including a minority of radicals, and even Sandinistas. Brazil in particular has a strong evangelical Left, which responded enthusiastically to the populist Lula administration (2003–2010), while some Venezuelan and Bolivian

Protestants have supported the leftist nationalist regimes of those countries. On matters of wages, pensions, and government intervention, evangelicals tend to express views that are strongly liberal by U.S. standards.

Even when not politically radical, Pentecostals are often heavily involved
in community organizing and social action, and it is misleading to see them
as necessarily quietist or submissive. Chile offers an interesting example of
this process. Pentecostal numbers boomed during the iron-heeled repression of the 1980s, when any secular political movement for the poor was
crushed without mercy, and it would be easy to see the churches as a refuge
from real-life struggles, a "haven of the masses." Yet Chilean Pentecostals
offered believers far more than pie in the sky, and worked enthusiastically
for social improvement. Although the armed forces might in some nations
have supported Pentecostals as a way of undermining radical Catholics,
that strategy rarely proved useful, since the new converts so enthusiastically adapted the faith to their own needs and interests. Far from manifest-
ing globalization at its most stereotypical and demonic, the new
Pentecostalism has flourished by channeling local interests and responding
to local grievances.[51]

Whatever its origins, Protestantism has indeed emerged as a distinctive
force in mass politics across Latin America, and has destabilized long-fa-
miliar social arrangements. Protestant and Pentecostal voting blocs have
emerged in several nations, with the churches serving as efficient electoral
machines and propaganda outlets. Often, believers are sincerely concerned
to elect leaders who will effect social improvements, but also at work is the
cozy principle of "Brother Votes for Brother." A political turning point
occurred in 1990, when a Peruvian *evangélico* bloc emerged in the contest
that elected president Alberto Fujimori: a number of Pentecostal legislators
were elected on his coattails. Some months later, Guatemala became the
first Latin American nation to choose a Protestant president through
democratic election. *Evangélico* politicians have since emerged at all levels
of government. A *Los Angeles Times* article noted that Protestant influence
"extends from that of small-town mayors in the Brazilian interior to the
governor of Mexico's Chiapas state. Colombian president Alvaro Uribe,
although a Catholic, meets regularly with an evangelical pastor to read the
Bible and pray." In coming years, Protestant and Catholic parties will probably struggle for power across the continent, an additional source of tension
in what is already a very divided region.[52]

Religious conflicts would be all the more dangerous if election battles
were to be accompanied by literal fights in the streets and villages, and
something like this has occurred in some areas. One uniquely troubled area

is the Mexican province of Chiapas, where tens of thousands of *evangéli-cos* and their families have been expelled by Catholic neighbors over the last thirty years, and many within the last two or three years. Pentecostals, in turn, have been among the government's most enthusiastic supporters in campaigns against local *Zapatista* rebels. And although the ongoing religious war in Chiapas is untypical in its length and brutality, this is not the only area where religious conflicts are fought out through night-riding and vigilantism. According to one 2005 account, "expulsion, impris-onment, physical beatings and the denial of educational and medical services are among the manifestations of the religious sectarianism that has emerged in recent years in large areas of the southern Mexican states of Chiapas, Oaxaca and Guerrero, where the majority of the population is indigenous."[53]

As in the time of the European Reformation, sectarian violence is often provoked by symbolic acts that seem petty to outsiders, such as insults to figures of the Virgin or saints. In a Latin context, such iconoclasm is a frontal assault not just on religion but on national and racial pride—espe-cially in societies in which the Virgin symbolizes indigenous traditions. In one incendiary incident, the head of the IURD in São Paulo was seen on television kicking an image of *Nossa Senhora Aparecida,* Brazil's patron saint: this desecration led to attacks on the church's buildings and bomb threats. In Ecuador, when Pentecostals taunted pilgrims visiting the Marian shrine of El Quinche, Catholics retaliated by burning down a local Protestant chapel. Isolated actions against Protestant churches are not new, but what has changed is that, increasingly, Protestants are now strong enough to defend themselves, and to counterattack.[54]

Projecting the future of these partisan feuds is all but impossible, but Great Britain might provide one useful historical analogy for understanding how religious rivalries evolve over time. After hopes for political revolution collapsed during the early nineteenth century, Britain's urban and industrial masses converted to rising sects such as Methodism, which is credited with saving Britain from anything like the regular armed risings of contempo-rary France. Yet by the end of the nineteenth century, these disciplined and motivated Methodist faithful were often the shock troops for effective trade unionism.[55] This might conceivably serve as a blueprint for future Pen-tecostal progress in the Americas. Also, political clashes between Protestants and Catholics in modern Latin America recall the battles in nineteenth-century England between the established church and the rising Protestant sects. The conflict eventually turned into the familiar duel between constitutional parliamentary parties, the Conservatives representing the church, while the sects dominated the Liberals, and later the Labour Party. It would be wonderful if Latin American struggles could have such a bloodless and well-organized outcome, but few expect this in the near future.

UNDER WESTERN EYES

If we look at the role of religion in politics worldwide, we can already see a clear global division. The politics of religion are very much alive in the South, as they are not, generally, in the North, and the difference is likely to continue and increase. Religious issues will form political loyalties, and churches and clergy will play a key role as political leaders. Across much of the South, politics will be Christian politics. (In this matter as in so much else, the United States occupies a role somewhere between Southern fervor and European torpor.)[56] As self-described Christian states face both internal crises and external conflicts with Christian neighbors, they might look to co-religionists to settle disputes. We may be entering the great age of Vatican diplomacy.

Political scenarios for the coming decades commonly assume a shift in political power and economic influence to nations of the global South. A few years ago, a South African journal published an article titled "Gondwanaland Revisited: Toward a South African Strategic Concept?" Gondwanaland was the ancient supercontinent that broke up to form the present continents of Africa, Latin America, and South Asia. Originally proposed as almost an academic joke, the Gondwana concept has since been much discussed in South African government and business circles, where it offers the basis of a kind of South–South dialogue, a natural global alliance led by South Africa, India, and Brazil. The idea has become ever more popular because of its overlap with other forecasts, which identify the nations that might within a few decades be challenging the United States economically. In 2003 Goldman Sachs coined the term BRICs for the four nations of Brazil, Russia, India, and China, all of which could by 2050 have Gross Domestic Products rivaling or surpassing those of the wealthiest Northern nations. Other observers focus on rising economic powers such as Indonesia and South Korea. Already, South–South alignments have appeared at global economic gatherings, to the consternation of North Americans and Europeans.[57]

But consider these overlapping lists of powers from a religious perspective. South Africa and Brazil are both overwhelmingly Christian, the homes of some of the world's fastest growing and most aggressively expansionist churches. Both also have rich traditions of church involvement in politics, and the politics of neither nation can be understood except in that context. Much the same is true of South Korea. China, India, and Indonesia all contain very substantial Christian minorities. Already, there are considerably more active Christians in China than in most nations of Western Europe. The prospects are that these numbers will grow substantially in years to come, so that quite feasibly, India and China between them could have 140 million Christians by 2050. Understanding the emerging new world order may require a good knowledge of the three great non-Western religions: Islam, Hinduism, and Christianity.

In addition, policymakers will have to understand relations between and among these faiths. As we will see in the next chapter, the international politics of the coming decades are likely to revolve around interreligious conflict, above all, the clash between Christianity and Islam. These divisions will be increasingly incomprehensible to the North, which in this sense could be confined to the sidelines of history. Northerners are going to find themselves ever more out of touch with the religious dimensions that shape the new world, and literally unable to communicate with the new people of faith.

Although I can make no worthwhile prediction about the power balances or issues of thirty or forty years hence, the dual religious and demographic trends are hard to ignore. We will be looking at a world with an ever-greater imbalance between where the people are and where the wealth is. It would not take a great speculative leap to see the North–South economic divide as the key issue of the coming years, and also (given the demographics) to see the clash being defined in religious terms. In the 1990s the global campaign to forgive Third World debt was led by such Southern religious figures as Cardinal Rodríguez of Honduras, and South African Anglican primate Njongonkulu Ndungane, Desmond Tutu's successor in the see of Cape Town. These moderate clerics might look very benevolent indeed when compared with the fierier religious leaders who could easily emerge in another decade or two. Just to take the Roman Catholic Church, the militant political conservatism of Pope John Paul II and Benedict XVI might represent a passing phase in the long history of the papacy, and we may yet see a revival of the radicalization of the 1970s.

And revolutionary forces may revive in the global South. When the U.S. intelligence community was projecting likely changes in the world political scene in the near future, religious activism occupied a prominent place, and not just the familiar theme of radical Islam. The report suggested that "Christianity and Islam, the two largest religious groupings, will have grown significantly.

Both are widely dispersed in several continents, already use information technologies to spread the faith, and draw on adherents to fund numerous nonprofit groups and political causes. Activist components of these and other religious groupings will emerge to contest such issues as genetic manipulation, women's rights, and the income gap between rich and poor." By far the most pressing of these would, of course, be the income gap and calls for a global redistribution of wealth.[58]

In one possible scenario of the world to come, an incredibly wealthy though numerically shrinking Northern population espouses the values of secular humanism, ornamented with the vestiges of liberal Christianity and Judaism. (And though the United States remains a far more religious nation than Europe, North American elites are almost as secular as their European counterparts.) Meanwhile, this future North confronts the poorer and vastly more numerous global masses who wave the flags not of red revolution but of ascendant Christianity and Islam. Although this sounds not unlike the racial nightmares of the Cold War years, one crucial difference is that the have-nots will be inspired by the scriptures and the language of apocalyptic, rather than by the texts of Marx and Mao. In this vision, the West could be the final Babylon.

This picture may simply be too far-reaching, but a secularized North could well be forced to deal with religious conflicts that it genuinely does not understand. One augur of this cultural divide is the dismal record of the United States and its allies in dealing with the growing Islamic fundamentalism that emerged in the 1970s. We recall the policy disasters that resulted in Iran, Lebanon, Iraq, and elsewhere from a basic failure to take seriously the concept of religious motivation. Western policymakers have never excelled at understanding Islam, but perhaps the great political unknown of the coming decades, the most powerful international wild card, will be that mysterious non-Western ideology called Christianity.

As Northern media come to recognize the growing importance of Southern states, and seek to explain their values, Southern world Christianity may be interpreted through the same kind of racial and cultural stereotypes that have so often been applied to fundamentalist or enthusiastic religion. Two related processes will interact here, namely a familiar kind of Orientalism, and a racially based concept of Third World primitivism. As emerging Christianity becomes ever stranger to Northern eyes, it will acquire the same kind of bleak stereotypes that were in bygone years applied to Muslims. The Christian faith of the rising states, we will probably hear, is fanatical, superstitious, demagogic: it is politically reactionary and sexually repressive.

Even today, on the rare occasions that the media report a religion-related story from the Third World, it is often associated with images of fanaticism, such as the Ugandan mass killings in 2000, or the more recent attempts in that country to pass stringent anti-gay legislation.[59] In the case of the mass killings, the media uncritically accepted the bizarre and ill-substantiated theory of mass suicide, because it so exactly meshed with stereotypes of primitive Africa. In 2008, African Christianity even featured as a theme in a U.S. election, when Sarah Palin was stigmatized by an apparent association with African witchcraft beliefs. As Christianity becomes ever more distinctively associated with Africa and the African diaspora, the religion as a whole may come to be dismissed as only what we might expect from the Heart of Darkness. (Although this term was originally applied to central Africa, the experiences of the twentieth century suggest that the label more justly belongs to Europe, to regions somewhere between Berlin and Moscow.)

Such stereotypes were abundantly on display during the British scandals about African and Afro-Caribbean churches involved in practices of spiritual warfare and exorcism that allegedly endangered children. Though initial charges concerned the exorcisms themselves, the media were soon suggesting that churches themselves were sacrificing or ritually abusing the young, as the tabloids declared that "Children Sacrificed in London Churches, Say Police."[60] In retrospect, the whole affair must be seen as a media-driven moral panic. The whole affair indicates staggering official ignorance of charismatic Christianity, as well as the distinctive religious practices of African and global South believers.

Modern Western media generally do an awful job of reporting on religious realities, even within their own societies. Despite its immense popularity in North America, evangelical and fundamentalist religion often tends to be dismissed as merely a kind of reactionary ignorance. It would be singularly dangerous if such uncomprehending attitudes were applied on a global scale and aggravated by racial stereotyping. As Christianity comes to be seen as, in effect, jungle religion, the faith of one-third of the human race would increasingly be seen as alien and dangerous, even a pressing social problem. The North, in turn, would define itself against this unfortunate presence: the North would be secular, rational, and tolerant, the South primitive and fundamentalist. The North would define itself against Christianity.

＋＋＋＋＋＋＋＋＋＋ EIGHT ＋＋＋＋＋＋＋＋＋＋

The Next Crusade

Narrated Abu Huraira: Allah's Apostle said "How will
you be when the son of Mary descends amongst
you, and he will judge people by the Law of the
Qur'an and not by the law of Gospel?"
—*The Hadith of the Prophet Muhammad,*
Fateh-ul Bari

Religion is the key to history.
—*Lord Acton*

Religious loyalties are at the root of many of the world's ongoing civil wars and political violence today, and in many cases, the division is the age-old battle between Christianity and Islam. However much this would have surprised political analysts a generation or two earlier, the critical political frontiers around the world are not decided by attitudes to class or dialectical materialism, but by rival concepts of God.[1] Across the regions that will be the most populous by the midcentury, vast religious contests are already in progress, although most of these impinge little on Western public opinion. For every one bumper sticker expressing concern about the fate of Christians in the Sudan or Indonesia, thousands cry out for a Free Tibet. Nor have the persecutions of Christians attracted any great attention on college campuses. Matters have changed somewhat as the U.S. government has paid more attention to religious freedom issues around the world, but persecutions still register little in the mass media.[2]

Demographic projections suggest that religious feuds will endure. The future centers of global population are chiefly in countries that are already divided between the two great religions, and where divisions are likely to intensify. Often, struggles become peculiarly intense when one religious tradition seeks to declare that nation X is or should be following its dictates, and attempts to enforce the appropriate legal and cultural values, with all the problems that implies for the minority faith. In present-day battles in Africa and Asia, we may today be seeing the political outlines of the next half-century, and even the roots of future great power alliances.

UNDERSTANDING NUMBERS

In trying to understand the global religious balance, we have to decide just what can and cannot be known with any accuracy. Projecting religious futures is just as difficult whether we are dealing with Christian or non-Christian communities. Just as Western societies with established or official churches tend to claim every citizen as a church member, so states in which Islam occupies a special constitutional role often exaggerate Muslim loyalties in their society.

Other factors can come into play in such a process of official definition. Take for instance the nation of Indonesia, purportedly the world's most populous Muslim country. While most people would agree that Islam is very strong in Indonesia, political factors partly explained the enormous growth of self-described Muslims in that nation from the mid-1960s on. At a time of homicidal anticommunism, failure to acknowledge any religion on identity papers immediately raised suspicions about a person's possible seditious attitudes, and as a result, millions declared themselves Muslim. Memories of this era may explain why Indonesia appears to have such a vast Muslim population, 85 percent of the whole, or some 200 million strong. Similar patterns apply with other religions also. In India, religious loyalties are defined by a "none of the above" test. Under Indian law, all citizens are formally presumed to be Hindus unless they are specifically identified either as a Christian, Parsi, or Jew. According to some interpretations, this reading explicitly includes as Hindu all Sikhs, Buddhists, and Jains, who are otherwise regarded as members of separate religions.[3]

Also, not all countries are as impartial as the United States or Europe in undertaking a census. Whenever we read religious estimates for a particular African or Asian nation, we should recall that minority citizens of that society are often scornful of any official data, and ask, suspiciously, what else would one expect a Muslim (or Christian) regime to say? Rightly or wrongly, the expectation is that governments massage statistics to make their own side look more powerful, especially in regions with deep political and cultural divisions. The widespread assumption is that Muslim governments such as Chad and Sudan vastly undercount the number of Christians, just as Christian-dominated Kenya or the Philippines simply make false statements about Muslim strength in those societies. Egyptian governments have long been accused of understating the numbers of Coptic Christians, partly to ensure the country's international status as a leader in the Muslim world. In a piece of statistical chicanery, the Indian national census only acknowledges that untouchables (Dalits) might belong to the Hindu, Sikh, or Buddhist faiths. In practice, this means ignoring the religious beliefs of at least 14 million Dalit Christians—the figure may well be much larger—not to mention tens of millions of Muslims.[4] Sometimes, too, mistakes can be made honestly, when minorities are concentrated in inaccessible or out-of-the-way regions that represent difficult territory for census takers. However impressive the statistics look, they can only be as accurate as the bureaucracies involved wish to make them.

ISLAM AND THE WORLD

With all these caveats, Muslims stand to benefit from exactly the same demographic trends that are producing the unimaginably rich harvest for Christians. Both religions have acquired vastly more adherents in the past century, but in some ways, Muslims have significantly outpaced Christians. When considered as a share of global population, Christian numbers have proved strikingly stable over the past century. In the year 1900, about one-third of the world's people were Christians, and that proportion remains more or less unchanged today. Moreover, if we project our estimate forward to the year 2050, that proportion should still be about one-third. But if we look at Muslim numbers in the same terms, as a share of the world's people, then that religion has enjoyed a far more impressive surge. In 1900, the 200–220 million Muslims then living comprised some 12 or 13 percent of humanity, compared to 22.5 percent of the world today, and a projected figure of 27 percent by 2050. Christians in 1900 outnumbered Muslims by 2.8 to 1. Today the figure is 1.5 to 1, and by 2050 it should be 1.3 to 1. Put another way, there are four times as many Christians alive today as there were in 1900; but over the same period, Muslims have grown at least seven-fold.

So how can Christian numbers be exploding, but still be left so far behind Muslims in the relative global rate of expansion? The answer lies in differential demographics, namely that some parts of the world are growing much faster than others. European numbers have been growing very slowly indeed in comparison with those of Africa, Asia, and Latin America, and that is very good news indeed for a faith based chiefly in Asia and Africa, as Islam was historically; it is bad news for creeds rooted in Europe. To appreciate how critical the southward shift of population is to understanding global religious change, just imagine what the picture of Christian expansion would look like if we left Europe out of the story. (I mean just the landmass of Europe, rather than people of European stock throughout the world.) Today, the number of *non-European* Christians stands at around 1.7 billion, compared to just 180 million in 1900. The figure has grown by a factor of 9.5 in just over a century, a growth rate even higher than that of Islam.

In large measure, then, Muslim growth occurred because Muslims were concentrated in regions that maintained very high fertility rates throughout the twentieth century. A rising tide lifts all religions as well as all churches. We can see the expansion in any part of the Islamic world. In 1900, Muslims made up perhaps 80 percent of Egypt's 10 million people. Today, the proportion of Muslims is certainly somewhat higher, but the overall population has swelled from 10 million to perhaps 80 million. Iran has experienced comparable overall growth, from 10 million in 1900 to 67 million today. As Muslims comprise the overwhelming mass of that nation, that represents a huge gain in Islamic numbers.

Indonesia presents a similar case. In 1900, the Dutch East Indies had a population of around 42 million, rising to 70 million by 1940. (From 1949, the country became known as Indonesia.) Today the total population is estimated at 240 million. Since 1900, reported Muslim numbers in that territory have grown accordingly, from around 34 million to 200 million. The number of Indonesian Muslims today is not far short of what the *global* total was back in 1900. The Indian subcontinent offers a similar story. In 1900, Muslims were a major component of the population of British India, concentrated in what would be the later nation-states of Pakistan and Bangladesh. This area contained at least 65 million Muslims, perhaps as many as 80 million. Today, however, the same regions have between 450 and 480 million Muslims, a rate of increase quite comparable to that in Indonesia.

These demographic trends are likely to continue, as the countries that presently have the highest fertility rates in the world are neatly divided between mainly Christian states like Uganda, and solidly Muslim nations such as Afghanistan. The number of Muslims will rise because of the growth of Bangladesh and Pakistan, and (as with Christians) from rising populations in Africa. In 1900, the lands that would comprise Nigeria had around 16 million people, but that population is now 158 million, and the effect on Islamic strength is apparent. Nigeria had 4 million Muslims in 1900, as against 72 million today. As a share of the whole Muslim world, that proportion grew from 2 percent in 1900 to almost 5 percent today. From being a thinly populated outlier on the edges of the Muslim world, Nigeria is increasingly a key player in that realm—just as it is in the emerging Christian world. Demography and conversions work together.[5]

Islam has other centers of growth. There are 300 million Arabs today, and they will be over half a billion strong by 2050. Islam is now booming across Central Asia, in young and growing countries that have classic Third World demographic profiles. The faith of Muhammad faces uncertain but intriguing prospects in China. Just as Chinese Christians are believed to be very numerous, so Muslims may run into the tens of millions in that vast country.

Growth in the Middle East and Central Asia is all the more important politically because of the continuing connection between Islam and oil wealth. The key factor is not so much where oil resources are located today but rather where they will continue to be found in fifty or a hundred years, the areas with the richest reserves and the deepest geological pockets. By this standard, Islam will have an enduring material foundation for its power, since the areas of key population growth are also those that will still be producing at a time when other historic oil-nations will be exhausting their reserves. This trend bodes very well for the nations of the Arabian peninsular as well as for nearby countries such as Iraq and Iran.

Possibly, too, this economic fact is bad news for global Christianity. When Muslims and Christians come to blows in a Third World nation, the United States and Europe might well find that helping the Muslim cause promotes good relations with Middle Eastern oil producers, and that helps keep the oil flowing to Western ports. Intervening on behalf of Christians, though, offers no advantage beyond the sentimental, and even that element will probably shrink as the West distances itself ever more from Christianity.

ISLAM'S DEMOGRAPHIC TRANSITION?

Throughout this book, I have emphasized the vital importance of demographics in shaping religious geography worldwide, and have remarked how often uncontrollable growth leads to instability and discord. This makes it all the more important to understand a global trend now well under way that could potentially have an enormous impact on interfaith relations, and even conceivably to defuse many sources of tension and strife in some parts of the world.

I have already described the extremely high fertility rates recorded in many Muslim nations. However, some nations of the Middle East and North Africa have experienced a precipitous plunge in fertility rates since the late 1980s, and that trend shows no sign of slowing. Iran offers a startling example. From the 1970s, many Iranians came to believe that women should be educated and allowed to enter the workforce, and this idea persisted even after the 1979 Islamic revolution. With growing numbers of women working (and, therefore, less available to parent a huge family), and with more financial options available to women outside of marriage, fertility rates inevitably dropped. From 1950 through 1980, Iran had extraordinarily high fertility rates, between 6.5 and 7 children per woman. During the 1990s, however, the rate tumbled from 5.6 to 2.5, and today, the rate is just 1.7. Iran's demographic profile has moved from the paradigmatic Third World model (high fertility rates, high growth) to the First World pattern.[6]

Nor is Iran unusual. European scholars observe that the closer a woman lives to Rome, the fewer children she has. Now, surprisingly, the same is true on the Muslim side of the Mediterranean. Just in the last twenty-five years, Algeria's fertility rate has plunged from 6.7 to 1.76, Tunisia's from 4.8 to 1.71. All these countries are now well below replacement level, and fertility continues to decline year by year. Soon, all should have profiles comparable to Germany or even Italy. And although other neighboring countries like Morocco and Turkey are still above replacement, their fertility rates have halved since the 1980s.

Almost certainly, this demographic change will have religious consequences. In the short term, religious fundamentalists might benefit from popular unease over the changing role of women, and the emergence of alternative family models. Over time, however, lower fertility promotes religious and political stability. At a minimum, a society in which women hold higher status has to change its religious practice to include and accommodate them, as we see, for instance, in the enhanced role of women within Moroccan Islam in recent years.

The Islamic world thus seems to be dividing into a two-tier model, a demographic schism between countries with low fertility rates, and those with rates at 5 or 6—countries such as Pakistan, Egypt, and Saudi Arabia. The highest birthrates of all are in such nightmare lands and failed or failing states as Iraq, Somalia, Sudan, Afghanistan, and Palestine/Gaza. Quite possibly, low-fertility countries will become more secular, more European in fact, while large-family nations remain religious. Algeria might have far more in common culturally and socially with France than with Egypt. In that case, concepts of Muslim identity would become ever more tenuous, and so would any prospects for a future clash of civilizations. Anything we say about the prospects for Muslim-Christian conflict must be taken in the context of this rapidly spreading demographic transition.

DIVIDED GIANTS

It will take some decades for the demographic stabilization to take full effect: even in Iran and Algeria, we still see the youth bulge that resulted from the baby boom of twenty years ago. In the immediate future, therefore, the prospect of religious rivalry has to be taken very seriously.

An earlier chapter projected the most populous countries of 2050, and we can look at these again in terms of their religious loyalties (see table 8.1). Of the world's twenty-five largest nations by 2050, at least nineteen will be predominantly or entirely either Christian or Muslim. If we imagine that the current religious balance will still continue at that point, then there should be a remarkably even balance between Muslim and Christian forces. Seven countries will be wholly or mainly Muslim, ten wholly or mainly

TABLE 8.1

The Religious Balance of Power among the Largest Nations of the Twenty-first Century

1. Overwhelmingly Muslim
Pakistan**   Bangladesh   Turkey*   Iran**

2. Mainly Muslim with significant Christian minorities
Indonesia*   Egypt*   Sudan**

3. Overwhelmingly Christian
USA   Brazil   Mexico

4. Mainly Christian with significant Muslim minorities
Philippines   D. R. Congo   Germany   Russia*   Uganda   France   United Kingdom

5. Christian and Muslim, with neither a strong majority
Nigeria**   Ethiopia

6. Other nations, dominated by neither Christianity nor Islam
India*   China*   Vietnam*   Thailand   Japan   Burma**

* denotes a country on the USCIRF's Watch List for violations of religious freedom. Bangladesh is "closely monitored."
** denotes a Country of Particular Concern, as identified in *Annual Report* 2010, USCIRF (United States Commission on International Religious Freedom) (Washington, D.C.: U.S. Commission on International Religious Freedom, 2010).

Christian, and two deeply divided between the two faiths. Muslims also represent a large minority within mainly Hindu India.

In terms of the potential for violence, we note the number of countries with divided populations, and thus a narrow gap between the two faiths in terms of numbers and power. Relatively homogeneous states are not likely to pose a major threat of religious antagonism. While there might be controversy about the practice of minority faiths in Saudi Arabia, non-Muslim dissidents are never going to pose a threat to the state. By far the greater danger will come from adherents of rival forms of Islam. Christians will never threaten Pakistani society, any more than Muslims will become a significant force in Mexico. The potential flashpoints are those states with minorities representing 10 or 20 percent of the population, amply sufficient to resist efforts at religious harmonization, and quite enough to sustain military struggles against an unpopular government. Of the divided states listed in this table, several have already experienced prolonged religious violence, with heavy loss of life.

No fewer than twelve of the world's twenty-five largest states in 2050 could be profoundly divided between Islam and Christianity, and conceivably, any or all of them could be the scene of serious interfaith combat. As we see, the U.S. government has already identified several as prone to outbreaks of religious violence and/or persecution. Six of the countries divided between Muslims and Christians (Sudan, D. R. Congo, Pakistan, Nigeria, Ethiopia, Uganda) are currently highly ranked among the world's top twenty failed or failing states.

Two factors threaten to create religious instability, and perhaps violence. One is that population growth does not observe national or religious boundaries. Matters would be less complicated in a fictitious world where countries were entirely made up of a given ethnic or religious group, so that it would matter little whether the country's population grew or shrank. In the real world, though, there are precious few such countries, since most nations have minorities of varying sizes, and population change aggravates existing tensions. Since poorer or immigrant groups have higher birth rates than the better-off, their religious and cultural traditions become more influential over time, a trend which in the worst case could lead to instability. An example of this process in miniature occurred in Lebanon, where a Shi'ite Muslim minority made up the traditional underclass. Over time, their high rate of population growth made Shi'ites a very potent force indeed, and much of that nation's civil war (1975–90) revolved around the issue of accommodating the poor masses. Most West European nations face huge disparities between fertile immigrant groups and relatively static old-stock populations, and religious instability could result. In the long run, immigrant communities come to share the social and demographic characteristics of the host societies, so their populations will stabilize over time, but that process can take several decades to accomplish. For the next three or four decades, therefore, the demographic gap will be a salient fact in European life.

Also threatening to cause antipathy is the issue of conversions. All the projections quoted here are based on the idea that Islam and Christianity will maintain roughly their present share of population in the respective countries, but that is a bold assumption. Both are successful missionary religions, and neither makes a secret of its aspiration to convert the entire globe. Both, too, have been advancing in very much the same parts of the world. Competition for converts is already acute in those regions of Africa that are currently blessed (or cursed) with the world's fastest rates of population growth. Rivalry is troublesome enough when both sides are competing for converts among followers of traditional indigenous religions, but in some situations Christians are seeking to convert Muslims, and vice versa. Buoyed by successes across the globe, Western evangelicals are talking seriously about spreading their faith within the 10–40 window, which includes the heartlands of Islam. To appreciate the sensitivity of such a movement, we have to remember that for a Muslim to abandon his or her faith is apostasy, an act punishable by death under Islamic law. As the maxim holds, "Islam is a one-way door. You can enter through it, but you cannot leave."

Indeed, the better we understand the relative success of Christian evangelism worldwide over the past century, the easier it is to comprehend what seems like wanton aggression on the part of Muslim communities. This is not for a second to justify acts of violence and persecution by either side, but it does provide an important context, namely that the Muslim reaction has a strongly defensive quality. To understand the religious changes of recent years, we can look for instance at the figures for Africa, as reported by the *World Christian Encyclopedia* (see table 8.2). This table indicates the two basic realities of modern African religion, namely the steep decline of older animist traditions ("ethno-religionists"), and the concomitant rise of the two monotheist faiths, especially Christianity. Between 1900 and 2000, around 40 percent of the continental population transferred their allegiance away from native religions or animism to different shades of Christianity. The change shocked Muslims, who had always regarded Africa as part of their natural sphere of cultural influence, and whose power had been consolidated under colonial regimes. At some point in the 1960s,

Christians first outnumbered Muslims on the whole continent, and that preponderance has grown since that date.

The strength of Christianity is all the more striking in view of its relative novelty. In the early nineteenth century, the area that we now call Nigeria was home to vibrant and powerful Muslim regimes, living alongside the animist believers of the South. The Christian presence developed during the early twentieth century, most successfully among the Igbos of the southeast, but the religion soon spread farther afield. Between 1900 and 1970, the Christian share of the population grew from roughly 1 percent to around 40 percent, while Muslim growth rates were far slower (see table 8.3). Today, the largest Christian denominations are the Anglicans and Roman Catholics, each with 21 million followers. These two groupings between them account for almost 60 percent of Nigerian Christians.

Observing these trends, Muslims could be forgiven for asking just how much farther Christian advances might proceed, especially when they were backed by Western money and techniques of mass evangelism. For many African Muslims, the awful question undoubtedly presented itself: would their children or grandchildren be Christian?

TABLE 8.2
Adherents of Major Religions on the African Continent
(Numbers are given in millions, followed by percentages in parentheses)

Adherents (%)	1900	1970	2000	2025 (projection)
Christians	9.9 (9.2)	144 (40.3)	360 (46.0)	634 (48.8)
Muslims	34.5 (32.0)	143 (40.1)	317 (40.5)	519 (40.0)
Ethno-religionists	62.7 (58.2)	67.4 (18.9)	96.8 (12.3)	126 (9.7)

Source: David B. Barrett, George T. Kurian, and Todd M. Johnson, *World Christian Encyclopedia*, 2nd ed. (New York: Oxford University Press, 2001).

TABLE 8.3
Religious Change in Nigeria
(Numbers are given in millions, followed by percentages in parentheses)

	1900	1970	2010	2025 (projected)
Muslims	4.2 (26)	23 (41)	72 (46)	99 (47)
Christians	0.2 (1)	23 (40)	72 (46)	99 (47)
Native religions	12.0 (73)	10 (18)	14 (9)	11 (5)

Source: World Christian Database

CROSS AND CRESCENT

The fundamental question is whether Islam and Christianity can coexist. The question may seem idle, since for centuries, the two faiths have existed side by side, often for long periods. Islam is after all the only one of the major religions that enshrines in its scriptures an injunction to tolerate other religions, other "peoples of the book."

Muslims and Christians have so very much in common. Scarcely known to most Christians, the Muslim scriptures are almost entirely focused on the same characters who feature in the Christian Bible. The Qur'an has far more to say about the Virgin Mary than does the New Testament, and Jesus is, apart from Muhammad, the greatest prophet of Islam. It is Jesus, not Muhammad, whose appearance will usher in the Day of Judgment. Moreover, Jesus was the primary inspiration for Islamic mysticism, the beloved model and mentor of the Sufis. In the 1980s, Western Christians protested the portrayal of Jesus in the film *The Last Temptation of Christ*, but only Muslim states actually banned the work. In parts of the Muslim world, the 2004 film *The Passion of the Christ* was warmly received, and Muslim clerics encouraged their flocks to see it. Other clergy were hostile, but not out of hostility to the memory of Jesus: rather, they viewed any such cinematic portrayal as blasphemous.[7]

In practice, both Christians and Muslims have often enjoyed good relations. For most of the Middle Ages, Jews and Christians survived in Muslim states, at a time when Muslims or Jews were massacred or expelled by their Christian neighbors. Even today, with all the well-publicized horrors of inter-religious violence in the Middle East, there are powerful demonstrations of harmony. Most Muslim states tolerate Christian worship, even Gulf nations such as Oman and the United Arab Emirates, provided there are no attempts to convert Muslims. Ironically, in view of other religious divisions, modern Palestine was long a model of Muslim–Christian coexistence. When Pope John Paul II visited Egypt and Syria, he was greeted enthusiastically by crowds of ordinary Muslims, as well as by senior Muslim clerics. In most of Africa, too, Muslim–Christian relations at local level have often (at least until recently) been characterized by a live-and-let-live attitude. Partly, this reflects the strong affinity between the daily practice of the two great African religions, both of which have drawn on older animist traditions. Across East and Southeast Asia, the Western-style Christmas has become a widespread secular holiday, marked enthusiastically even by many Indonesian Muslims.[8]

Having said all this, the long-term prognosis for interfaith relations is not good. This does not mean that either religion is of itself violent or intolerant, but both have potent traditions of seeking to implement their views through political action: the two sisters are simply too much alike to live side by side. Both Christian and Muslim states can exist for decades or centuries without seeking to persecute minorities. All too often, though, persecution erupts, perhaps in response to some natural cataclysm, or to the rise of a particularly zealous regime. The minority community is reduced or scattered, and even after the hard times end, matters can never be quite the same again. Peace then resumes until the next cycle of intolerance begins, but the ratchet turns yet another notch, and life becomes correspondingly more difficult for the survivors of the shrinking minority. It is much the same story as that of the Jews in medieval or early modern Europe.[9]

Even if the dominant religion is generally tolerant, it only takes an outbreak of fanaticism every half-century or so to devastate or uproot a minority, and that has been the fate of religious minorities across the Middle East in recent years. Although Christian communities survive across the region, their numbers are a pathetic shadow of what they were even in 1850, and whole peoples have been obliterated since that time. The Armenian genocide of 1915 is well known, but quite as devastating were the massacres of tens of thousands of Lebanese and Syrian Christians in 1860, by both Muslims and Druzes. In 1915 the Turks slaughtered and expelled hundreds of thousands of Christians of all sects. A famine deliberately induced by the Turkish military claimed the lives of 100,000 Lebanese Maronite Christians. Across the Middle East, it was above all the bloodshed of 1915 that destroyed ancient Christian cultures that had lasted successfully since Roman times, groups such as the Jacobites, Nestorians, and Chaldaeans. And the carnage continued after the war ended. Between 1919 and 1925, Greek Christians were expelled en masse from the new Kemalist state of Turkey. In 1923 Istanbul's Greek Christian population was around 400,000: today, it may at most be 4,000.[10]

These experiences remind us of the sad historical lesson that persecution can indeed be very effective, if carried out with enough ruthlessness. Perhaps one cannot kill an idea, but it is not too hard to massacre or convert everyone who holds or expresses it. We ignore this unpalatable fact because so few scholars ever write about the end of a church or religious movement, preferring to tell stories of ascent and growth. Once, the Nestorian church was one of the largest and most widespread institutions in the world: by 1500 it had almost ceased to exist. Once, Turkey had large Christian minorities, but these were squeezed out of existence in a decade or two. These events provide a bleak precedent for modern minority populations. Conceivably, the religious violence in Iraq over the past decade might succeed in eliminating that nation's ancient Christian minority just as thoroughly as occurred in Turkey.

Undeniably, modern Christians have committed their share of atrocities. The Serbian massacre of 8,000 Bosnian Muslims at Srebrnica in 1995 remains the largest single crime of its kind in post-1945 Europe.[11] In recent years, though, the pattern of religious conflict has shifted decisively. In the world as a whole, there is no question that the threat of intolerance and persecution chiefly comes from the Islamic side of the equation. Around the world, Muslim states are passing through one of these historic phases of zeal and persecution of the sort just mentioned.

We can discuss at length why this extremism should be occurring. Over the last twenty years, the Muslim world has been caught up in a massive religious revival, and this movement has expressed itself in calls for pure religious states upheld by the full apparatus of Islamic law. Perhaps this idea appeals to people afraid of losing their cultural identity in the face of globalization, or else it might seem to offer a solution for the desperately poor in a world dominated by the wealthy and callous West. For whatever reason, Middle Eastern nations have coped very badly with the challenges of modernity and globalization, and have fallen ever farther behind in terms of technological innovation and commercial development—behind the West, of course, but also behind Japan and the Pacific Rim nations, and now both China and India. Although populous, Muslim nations supply only a minuscule fraction of the world's scientific research, as measured by patents and articles in major journals. It would be surprising if these cumulative failures did *not* produce a search for scapegoats, and the kind of demonization offered by fundamentalist Islam. At the same time, Christian missionaries exploit Western political and media influence in order to make inroads into Dar al-Islam, representing what even moderate Muslims viewed as intolerable aggression.[12]

If these explanations are correct, then Islamic extremism will be with us for many years to come. Looking at matters in social and economic terms does not mean that we should not take the demand for Islamic rule at face value, and accept that people genuinely believe that their faith really does require such a political expression. But whatever the reasons, interreligious violence in recent years tends to be initiated by Muslims against Christians, and that trend is unlikely to change.[13]

BATTLE FRONTS

To illustrate the dynamics of violence, we can consider some of the main fronts of religious warfare today, all of which occur in countries that will soon be among the world's largest, countries like Sudan and Egypt, Pakistan and Nigeria. Significantly, these are also the countries that appear most immune from the demographic transition that is likely to reduce religious zeal in lands such as Iran and Algeria.

One brutal conflict has occurred in the Sudan, where religious and racial boundaries coincide. The country is dominated by a northern Muslim population, which speaks Arabic, while the south is black African, Christian, and animist. According to official statistics, the Sudan has around 28 million Muslims, 2 million Christians, and 10 million animists (by 2050, though, the overall population could be as high as 97 million). Despite this ethnic and cultural balance, the Sudanese government introduced Islam as the official religion for the whole country, declared Arabic the national language, and established Friday rather than Sunday as the day of rest. Southerners naturally resisted Muslim control. One bloody rebellion raged from 1963 through 1972, and the insurgency re-erupted in the 1980s when the government officially applied Muslim religious law, the *Shari'a*, to the whole country. Peace was notionally restored in 2005, but few observers would be surprised if violence flared anew. In 2011, the nation officially fragmented into two regions, north and south.

This has been one of Africa's bloodiest struggles, costing two million lives to date. The U.S. State Department described systematic atrocities against the non-Muslim population, including "indiscriminate bombings, the burning and looting of villages, and the killings, abductions, rapes, and arbitrary arrests and detentions of civilians."[14] Many regions of the Third World have experienced brutal wars of this kind, but what distinguishes the conflict in Sudan is its explicitly religious nature, as Muslim governments have increasingly accepted fundamentalist notions of the religious role of the state. Sudan is also one of the very few countries that still avowedly practices slavery, the other being the Muslim African nation of Mauretania. In both cases, the normal pattern involves lighter-skinned Arabic slave-owners, and black slaves. Often, too, Sudanese slaves are Christian.

We can debate how far the Sudanese experience reflects the inevitable nature of Islamic rule, and the Muslim treatment of minorities. Of course, we might argue, backward nations such as Sudan and Yemen are far more intolerant than wealthy and advanced France or Sweden, but that is a consequence of poverty and backwardness, not of religious traditions. We should not compare apples with oranges. Yet having said this, equally poor Christian-dominated states have not acted anything like as severely toward their religious minorities. At the same time, we find severe intolerance and persecution in much wealthier and more advanced Muslim states, which officially tolerate the existence of minorities, but rigidly control the exercise of those faiths. Saudi Arabia strictly prohibits Christian worship or practice of any kind.

The Sudanese experience shows how, in the new religious climate, existing non-Muslim minorities can be reduced or even eliminated. The same bitter lesson may be in progress in Sudan's far more important neighbor, Egypt, the home of the ancient community of Coptic Christians. The position of the Copts has deteriorated steadily in recent decades, although conditions are nothing like as bad as in the Sudan. During the 1990s, well-armed Islamic guerrillas attacked Coptic villages, provoking intercommunal riots.[15]

Muslim–Christian conflicts have not abated, with recurring pogroms and religious attacks. Often, Copts protested as much against the systematic official bias that they encountered following such outbreaks as against the attacks themselves. Repeatedly, Copts have been convicted of trumped-up criminal charges, or have suffered severe prison sentences for uttering words supposedly critical of Islam. When Copts suffer acts of mob violence, police regularly ignore the perpetrators, while using the investigation as an excuse to inflict further persecutions on the Christian victims themselves. Such episodes raise the long-term question of whether Christians can survive under Islam, even as despised minorities.[16]

NIGERIAN COLLISIONS

The twin experiences of Sudan and Egypt explain why African Christians, so uncomfortably close to the scene of action, should be nervous about any extension of Islamic law and political culture. If Muslims insist that their faith demands the establishment of Islamic states, regardless of the existence of religious minorities, then violence is assuredly going to occur.[17]

This issue becomes acute in the very important nation of Nigeria, which is today about equally divided between Christians and Muslims—although estimates of the exact balance vary. Complicating this picture is that the religious groups are not equally distributed: the north of the country is chiefly Muslim, the east largely Christian, so each group can aspire to impose its standards in the respective areas. This distribution also means that, as in Sudan, religious allegiances coincide with ethnic, tribal, and geographical loyalties. Of the three major ethnic groupings, the northern Hausa are solidly Muslim, the eastern Igbo are Christian, and the Yoruba are equally divided between the two faiths.[18]

Muslim–Christian rivalries have often led to violence. In 1966 tens of thousands of Christian Igbos were massacred in the north, forcing survivors to flee to safe areas. These events strengthened Muslim hegemony in the north and reduced the remaining Christians to a clear minority status. Between 1967 and 1970, the Christian east tried unsuccessfully to secede from Nigeria, leading to a bloody civil war that claimed close to a million lives. Although religion played an important part in detonating the war, the conflict was not a pure Muslim–Christian affair. Christians made up perhaps half of the federal Nigerian army, and the federal leader was a distinguished lay Christian. But the destruction visited upon the secessionist east, in so-called Biafra, was a catastrophe for the country's Christian population.

Tensions grew during the 1980s, as Muslim forces became determined not just to halt Christian advances but to press for a full-scale evangelization of Africa, a project backed by the mighty financial resources of Middle Eastern oil states. In 1989 the Nigerian federal capital of Abuja hosted an "Islam in Africa" conference. The exact conclusions of this gathering are controversial, and some conspiracy theories have published what purport to be secret plans for the violent Islamization of the continent, culminating in the subjugation and forced conversion of all nonbelievers. However we treat such materials, there is no question that the Abuja gathering coincided with a vociferous campaign for the application of *Shari'a* law wherever feasible.

The plight of Nigeria's Christian minorities under Muslim rule, never easy, has deteriorated since the early 1990s, when Muslim-dominated states began imposing *Shari'a*. Local authorities in these areas hinder the building or repair of churches, while actively sponsoring Islamic causes, paying for pilgrimages and mosque-building. National events encouraged Muslim intransigence. From 1979 through 1999, Nigeria was ruled by a series of cosmically corrupt federal regimes, in which military influence was always key. With one brief exception, all these regimes were headed by Muslims. In 1999, however, the new president was Olusegun Obasanjo, a Yoruba Christian who claimed to have experienced a life-transforming evangelical rebirth. Particularly at a time of intense Christian evangelism, Obasanjo's ascendancy stirred fears among Muslim authorities. By 2003 twelve of

Nigeria's thirty-six states had imposed *Shari'a* in whole or in part, and others were discussing the idea, so that *Shari'a* prevailed in all the states along the nation's northern border. The spread of *Shari'a* owed something to growing religious zeal, but can also be seen as a symbolic statement of Muslim identity and Hausa tribal pride. And throughout the debate over Islamic law, we repeatedly see the perceived need to reassert threatened gender roles and family structures, which are so threatened by economic change. In this context, Christianity provides an ideal symbol at once of Westernization, globalization, and sexual upheaval.[19]

Nigerian Christians understandably fear the prospect of living under *Shari'a*. This reform has many practical consequences for non-Muslim minorities, from the irritating (such as the elimination of alcohol) to the severely oppressive. In extreme cases, non-Muslims might be subjected to the whole battery of Islamic civil, criminal, and family law, so that Christians could suffer any of the physical punishments, floggings, and mutilations ordained by that tradition. Under *Shari'a* law, the religious activities of non-Muslims are severely constrained. Any kinds of evangelism are strictly prohibited, while apostasy from Islam leads to the death penalty.

The effects on gender relations are far-reaching, since women can face restrictions on their ability to move and work freely. In the Muslim stronghold of Kano, a police purge in 2000 resulted in the arrest of several hundred people who had been seen talking to members of the opposite sex in public, leading to investigations for adultery or prostitution. An interfaith crisis developed when a Kano man converted to Islam and insisted that his daughters accept arranged marriages with Muslim husbands. The daughters, both Christian, sought refuge with local Anglican clergy and lay families. The police then intervened, arresting the Christian helpers for kidnapping and further provoking a worsening political crisis.[20]

Since the late 1990s, successive waves of communal riots and massacres have recalled the bloodbath of the 1960s, and tension escalated further when *Shari'a* was imposed. In a few weeks in 2000, some two thousand people were killed in intercommunal rioting in the Muslim-dominated state of Kaduna; in retaliation, several hundred Muslims were killed in eastern Christian towns. In a sequence of events reminiscent of the dreadful 1960s, the remaining Muslims began an exodus from Christian states to return to their home regions, while Christians fled the north.[21]

Other notorious events stirred new violence, especially in divided cities such as Jos. In 2001, news of the September 11 attacks in the United States aroused Muslim militancy and attacks on Christians. Rival mobs dragged motorists from cars, and determined their loyalties by demanding them to recite key scriptures. Muslims proved their religious identity by repeating the Shahada, the proclamation of faith; Christian mobs wanted to know whether their captives could recite John 3:16. Those who gave the wrong answers—members of rival religions, or simply the theologically ill-informed—were slaughtered and mutilated. When a Danish newspaper published offensive cartoons of Muhammad, worldwide protests by enraged Muslims naturally spilled over into Nigeria. Between 2000 and 2005, just in the single state of Plateau, interfaith riots killed or displaced some fifty thousand, and new outbreaks have occurred regularly since that point. Prominent Christian clergy, including the Anglican bishop of Jos, have been attacked and been the targets of assassination attempts. Nigerian religious clashes spread over the borders into neighboring countries such as Niger, which over the last few years have for the first time ever experienced religious-based rioting.[22]

The importance of these events can hardly be exaggerated. Nigeria might have 260 million people by 2050, perhaps 400 million by the end of the century, and it is a huge oil-producer. Provided the state holds together, and that is an open question, a country of this size and wealth will assuredly be a major regional state, and possibly a global power. Depending on the course of religious conflicts, Nigeria could become a Muslim super-state, or it could fragment into two or three smaller entities, neatly defined by both religious and tribal identity. The U.S. intelligence community has for years viewed the possible explosion of religious and ethnic tensions in Nigeria as major threat to international security. Depending on international alignments, the religious fate of Nigeria could be a political fact of immense importance for generations to come.[23]

ASIAN THEATERS

In Asia too, religious divisions and persecutions threaten to initiate future struggles. The progressive hardening of attitudes in recent years is evident from Pakistan, which despite its overwhelmingly Muslim character has a small Christian minority. Christians constitute around 2 percent of Pakistanis, some three million people, usually drawn from the humblest classes. While notionally tolerated, Christians and other minorities regularly fall prey to legal penalties under provisions theoretically directed against blasphemy and apostasy. Under a 1986 law, anyone who "directly or indirectly by word, gesture, innuendo, or otherwise defiles the name of the Holy Prophet Muhammad will be punished with death or life imprisonment." These laws offer a potential death sentence for anyone evangelizing Muslims, or even considering conversion, and several Christians have been condemned to death for related offenses. Ordinary Christians are subjected to mob violence, murder, and rape.[24]

Nobody doubts that Pakistan in practice will continue to be a solidly Islamic country, but in other states, religious identity is bitterly contested. Another very populous state is Indonesia, and as in Nigeria, ethnic divisions aggravate religious battles. Also as in Nigeria, struggles under way today may be defining the nation's religious politics for years to come. Though overwhelmingly Muslim, Indonesia has substantial minorities, most significant among which is a Christian community of 23 million: Christians make up 9 or 10 percent of the whole population. Christians are concentrated in particular regions and ethnic groups. In the cities, Christianity has made inroads among the ethnic Chinese communities who play such a key role in the nation's commercial life. In addition, Christian regions are scattered across the eastern half of the island nation, in areas that, like the Philippines, traditionally looked to Spanish and Portuguese power, or which claimed a strong Dutch heritage. Major Christian centers include Timor, the islands of Sulawesi and Lombok, and Maluku (the Moluccas or Spice Islands).[25]

Since the late 1990s, violence between Christians and Muslims has raged through all the eastern regions. Particularly savage was the repression against the Catholic territory of East Timor, which Indonesia invaded and occupied in 1975. The Indonesian campaign, in which 150,000 Timorese perished, is among the forgotten genocides of the modern era. This was by no means an exclusively interreligious struggle, but when the region voted on its independence in 1999, government militias targeted Catholic clergy and faithful for massacre.

The worst recent violence occurred in Maluku, where the government lost control of the area in 1999 and 2000 while a civil war killed five thousand, the number equally divided between the two communities.[26] Usually, it is Christians who have been massacred and expelled, as militant political Islam has spread through the region. By the end of 2000, half a million Maluku Christians had been expelled, mainly by Muslim paramilitaries of the *Laskar Jihad*, operating with the tacit support of Indonesian armed forces. Thousands of North Maluku Christians were forced to convert to Islam in public ceremonies, some of which included circumcision for both men and women. Hundreds of Christians were killed for refusing to convert. Large numbers of churches were also destroyed in a successful act of ethnic/religious cleansing that was largely ignored by Western governments and media. Besides Maluku, another battlefront was Central Sulawesi, where Islamists tried to drive Christians from the region by overt terror. These events raised fears that Christianity would be extirpated across much of eastern Indonesia over the next decade or two.[27]

Episodes of mass disorder have become less common in recent years, but mainly because of the success of the ethnic cleansing: in many areas, few minority Christians remained to be persecuted. But extreme Islamist militancy survived, and became far better coordinated, as Muslim militias were armed and trained by fanatical groups linked to the *Jemaah Islamiyah*. The *Jemaah* seeks a *Daulah Islam Nusantara*, a Southeast Asian Muslim Emirate under *Shari'a* rule that would incorporate all the lands currently occupied by the states of Indonesia, the Philippines, and Malaysia. The group has even been implicated in plots in Thailand and Cambodia. The *Jemaah* has been described as a component of the al-Qaeda network, although it is unclear whether this represents anything more than a tactical alliance between like-minded groups. Islamist terrorists were responsible for some notorious anti-Western attacks, such as the 2002 Bali bombings that killed two hundred. More recently, jihadis have operated through the *Jamaah Ansharut Tauhid*, or JAT.[28]

Below the level of the well-known terror groups, a network of smaller militant networks undertakes local massacres and anti-Christian purges. In a horrible incident in 2005, three teenage girls were beheaded in Central Sulawesi, solely for the crime of being Christian. Jihadis left the head of one of the girls outside her Pentecostal church in what one murderer later claimed was a special *Eid al-Fitr* gift to the nation's Muslims. *Eid al-Fitr* is a cherished Muslim holiday, and his statement is roughly equivalent to a Christian terrorist boasting of launching a Christmas massacre of civilians.

One activist group is the Islamic Defenders Front, which demands the imposition of *Shari'a* law across Indonesia. According to one 2010 news report from the city of Bekasi,

> The front, known for smashing bars, attacking transvestites and going after minority sects with bamboo clubs and stones, is now leading a charge against Christians in the area. A spate of attacks has rocked Bekasi: Mobs have forced shut two churches this year. Last month, a statue of three women was torn down by authorities after hundreds of hard-liners wearing skull-caps and white robes took to the streets, claiming the monument symbolized the Holy Trinity.

Militants find potent ammunition in charges that Christians are attempting to proselytize, to draw Muslims away from their faith, and such claims win support even in traditionally tolerant regions. The movement protested furiously against a Christian group that was allegedly planning a mass baptism—the claim was allegedly based on the group having acquired a pool. The local militant leader urged the execution of the Christian pastor concerned.[29]

Anti-Christian violence has many sources. Partly, the motives are explicitly religious, and groups such as the *Jemaah* indicate the rise of a Wahhabistyle fundamentalist Islam quite new to Indonesia. Islamist extremism has found expression in organized political groups, including vigilantes who destroy bars and supposedly immoral establishments. The hatred also has a nationalist component, since Christianity is strong in areas such as Irian Jaya that have powerful secessionist movements. To kill a Christian is to destroy a potential traitor, and to reassert national unity. In a bizarre juxtaposition, Islamists target both nightclubs *and* churches, which they see as twin symbols of foreign infiltration and moral decadence.

But religious bigotry has a strong economic component. In Indonesia, urban Christianity is associated with the Chinese mercantile community, and when the economy went into a tailspin in 1997, Muslim mobs targeted Chinese Christians. As in Malaysia, the more Christianity wins support among ethnic Chinese, the easier it is for agitators to portray the religion as a symbol of the foreign exploiters who keep the nation in poverty. Combining these elements, anti-Christianity looks as varied and as potent an ideology as the populist anti-Semitism that swept Europe in the late nineteenth century, and which would have such parlous consequences in the twentieth. As in Nigeria, the question for Indonesia is whether this vast emerging regional power is to continue as a multiethnic, multireligious nation, or if it is to become a purely Muslim state.

Like Indonesia, the Philippines will soon be one of the Pacific Rim's most populous states, and here too, recent events raise doubts about the possibility of coexistence. Although the Philippines is traditionally a strongly Catholic society, a strong Muslim presence exists in the southern island of Mindanao, which culturally looks to its neighbors in Indonesia. Since the 1970s the Muslim Moro ("Moor") peoples of the southern Philippines have been engaged in a prolonged struggle for autonomy, which culminated in 1996 when the government reached a limited settlement with the largest guerrilla group.

Other paramilitary forces, however, kept the struggle alive. In 2000 the long-running revolt suddenly revived, and several hundred soldiers and civilians were killed: today, some eighty thousand Philippine troops operate in Mindanao, with the support of U.S. Special Forces. This campaign brought to the fore the terrorist Abu Sayyaf group, which is as much an organized crime network as a terrorist movement, but its rhetoric meshes closely with that of other Islamist extremists, and it seeks a pure Muslim state in Mindanao. The movement has engaged in explicitly anti-Christian actions, including the murder of a Catholic bishop outside his cathedral in 1997, and the subsequent kidnapping of Christian Filipinos and American missionaries. In 2009, the Moro Islamic Liberation Front detonated a bomb outside the Catholic cathedral in Cotabato City, killing five. As in Indonesia, Christmas usually proves a popular time for anti-Christian bombings and pogroms.[30]

Not even Malaysia has escaped the trend toward religious confrontation. Thirty years ago, commentators on Islam would have singled out Malaysia as a model of tolerance and peaceful interaction with other faiths. Just 9 percent of Malaysians are Christian, often of Chinese stock, and therein lies a problem. Malaysian nationalists commonly identify their own cause with Islam while Christianity is presented as an imported creed, associated with foreign exploitation. In 2009, a Malaysian court prohibited non-Muslims from using the word Allah to refer to God (a usage that is standard in the Muslim lands of the Middle East). Christians were thus to be prevented from blasphemously appropriating the divine name, but in practice, this meant ordering the suppression of much Christian literature. Thousands of Malay-language Bibles now became contraband. Churches were firebombed, as popular Islamic militancy surged. To quote one analyst, "Islam is becoming the defining force in politics in Malaysia and in Indonesia.... The pluralistic days are over in Southeast Asia."[31]

CYCLES OF VIOLENCE

The most disturbing feature of contemporary Christian/Muslim strife is how very commonplace it has become, how unremarkable. The bloodshed in Nigeria and Indonesia does receive some coverage in the West, yet violence of this sort has become almost too widespread to report, even in Egypt, which long operated on the principle of live-and-let-live. Over the past decade, Muslim–Christian violence has occurred in places that have long been held up as models of friendship and toleration, including among the Palestinian Arabs, and in traditionally peaceful Malaysia. In bygone years, one of the areas most frequently cited as a model of tolerance was the Indonesian territory of Maluku, where elaborate social customs were designed to encourage respect between the faiths. It was long customary to visit members of the other religion during their respective holiday seasons:

Muslims would visit Christian neighbors over Christmas, the visits being repaid over Ramadan. After all the slaughter of the last few years, such relationships lie in ruins.

Similar breakdowns have occurred across Africa, often in places where ten or twenty years ago no observer would have foreseen religious strife—in Kenya, even in long peaceable Côte d'Ivoire. Clearly, issues of group conflict and minority rights are going to remain central to African politics for decades to come, and the opportunities for international meddling and destabilization are rampant. These are all the more dangerous given the growing importance of Africa as a source of U.S. oil. Africa already provides 20 percent of U.S. crude oil imports, and a much larger proportion of Chinese oil supplies. The religious fault line across Africa often follows the oil deposits, and stirring religious violence would prove an effective way of striking at U.S. interests.[32]

Another example of such unexpectedly confessional violence occurred in Europe itself. The savagery that erupted in the former Yugoslavia in the 1990s occurred among communities hitherto famous for their relaxed attitude toward religion. Interfaith marriages and friendships were common among Catholics, Orthodox Christians, and Muslims. When the violence began, however, religious identities reasserted themselves forcefully. The respective groups began to fight and kill on behalf of their faiths, destroying the religious symbols of their enemies in addition to eliminating populations. As a worrying omen of the future direction of other such struggles, international groups took such religious claims very seriously, so that the wars in Bosnia and Kosovo genuinely did turn into international crusades and jihads.[33]

Once it has started, communal violence tends to become self-sustaining. Where communities have historically existed side by side, potential insults and provocations are usually treated with restraint, but once fighting has occurred, the threshold for violence is lowered. When civil disorders displace minority communities, these refugees in turn become detonators for further violence, since they advocate harder line policies in future conflicts.

Once peoples are primed to believe in the rightness of religious warfare, it becomes easier for outside groups to manipulate public sentiment for their own ends. While we are rightly suspicious of conspiracy theories that imagine sinister clandestine agents trying to stir communal violence, some conspiracies are genuine, and some intelligence agencies do carry out seemingly random attacks as part of a strategy of tension. Actions of this kind are well documented in the South Africa of the 1980s. More recently, such disruptive strategies have generally been aimed at inciting religious violence, with the goal of discrediting democratic regimes. A common interpretation of the upsurge of violence across Indonesia in 2000–2001 is that it was ignited by agents of that nation's former dictatorship, in order to discredit its democratic successor. Whatever the truth, it is depressing that the provocateurs found such dry tinder for their efforts, and that once the cycle of violence had begun, it continued with little further encouragement.

EUROPE

Just how inevitable Muslim–Christian conflict is becoming is now a serious question in much of Europe, and not only in the Balkans. Religious rivalries have for some time played at least a marginal role in social tensions in several Western European nations. In France, North Africans make up a large proportion of the underclass youth who have so often clashed with police in urban rioting since the 1980s.

At that stage, hostility was chiefly ethnic in nature, but specifically religious grievances became more obvious in 1989 when the Iranian regime issued its death sentence, a *fatwa*, against British writer Salman Rushdie. This campaign against supposed blasphemy mobilized many thousands of Muslim demonstrators in Britain, France, Germany, Belgium, and the Netherlands. The Rushdie affair marked a new stage of Muslim political organization and radicalization, and the affair has had later echoes across Europe, as in the furor over the Danish cartoons of the prophet Muhammad in 2005–2006. Such controversies raise troubling contradictions for liberal Europeans, whose fundamental belief in free speech and artistic expression runs up against values of multiculturalism and the respect for minority sensibilities. Even politically moderate Europeans began to take seriously the prospect of Islamization. In 2009, Elena Tchoudinova's nightmare vision of an Islamized France, *The Mosque of Notre Dame,* became a French best seller. The book opens with a description of a public stoning on the Place de l'Arc de Triomphe in the year 2048.[34]

Signs of active insurgency have accelerated over the past decade, with a series of terrorist outrages, and increasing evidence of extensive clandestine organization by Muslim extremists, centered in radical mosques and pseudo-charities. Among the most notorious incidents were the 2004 bombings in Madrid and the subway attacks in London the following year, which together left some 250 dead; another was the assassination of Dutch filmmaker Theo van Gogh. The London bombings were all the more frightening because they drew attention to a whole subculture of supposedly integrated second-generation Muslims.

With these precedents in mind, many fear that interreligious violence could erupt in Europe itself, with Muslim paramilitary groups waging jihad on French or German soil. We have to be cautious about painting future confrontations in strictly religious terms, since much unrest—such as the French urban riots of 2005—seem to be motivated more by class grievances and anti-police sentiment, rather than religious extremism. Yet the potential for Muslim militancy is present. Even if actual violence is avoided, then future governments will have to strive to avoid inciting religious conflict, and this should have a dramatic effect on European attitudes to external politics, above all in the Middle East. This is all the more likely since European nations rely heavily on oil supplies from Muslim Middle Eastern nations. Such considerations will also make European nations tread very carefully when tempted to criticize the repression of religious minorities in Muslim nations.

Interfaith controversies have subtly changed the shape of European debates over immigration, which traditionally were presented in simple racial terms. Now, though, religion is entering the picture. Some conservative Europeans have argued that governments should deliberately promote Christian immigration, as a means of reducing Islamic influence. In Italy, Bologna's cardinal Giacomo Biffi made the controversial suggestion that while immigrants were definitely needed, preference should be given to people of Catholic background. "And there are many," he said, "Latin Americans, Filipinos and Eritreans." Though Biffi's ideas reflect familiar concerns about defending traditional notions of European culture, they are far removed from any standard racist rhetoric.[35] Issues of cross and crescent will in future become ever more important in European political discourse.

CHRISTIAN, MUSLIM, JEW

The question of Christian–Muslim relations becomes very sensitive because of the place of Judaism in such a dialog. In both Europe and the United States, Jews have long been regarded as the chief, almost the sole, religious Other, and the main subject of interfaith dialogue. This raises difficulties when good relations with Jews domestically also require a distinctive foreign policy stance. American Christians have usually followed their government in expressing an absolute and generally uncritical support for the state of Israel. This fact infuriates not just the bulk of the world's Muslims but also many Third World Christians (not to mention the millions of Arab Christians). Islamic fundamentalism would probably not have enjoyed the success it has over the last thirty years had it not been for the continuing provocation of the existence of Israel. The reasons for the West's pro-Israel policy are not hard to seek, grounded as they are in Western guilt over the Holocaust and the failure to rescue Europe's Jews in the 1940s.

But the consequences are alarming. Put in the crudest numerical terms, there are rather fewer than 15 million Jews in the world, compared to over a billion Muslims, and the disparity is going to grow sharply in coming decades. By 2050 Muslims worldwide should outnumber Jews by more than a hundred to one. It has to be asked whether relations between Muslims and Christians can possibly improve as long as the West, and particularly the United States, maintains a Middle East policy that is seen, rightly or wrongly, as virulently anti-Muslim.

Looking to the future, a number of different scenarios suggest themselves. In one, the issue of Israel serves to divide Northern Christians not just from Muslims but also from the rising churches of the South. Lacking the heritage of guilt that underlies Western attitudes toward Judaism, Christians in Africa and Asia might identify far more with the oppressed Palestinian people than with the Israeli nation, so that in this one area, Southern Christians might align themselves with Muslims. This raises questions about the whole future of Christian–Jewish relations.

Quite apart from active anti-Semitism, Christian theology has for most of its history been founded on the idea of supersession, the theory that Christianity perfected and replaced Judaism, which was therefore obsolete: the Church is the new Israel. This replacement theology became controversial following the Holocaust, and it has become a minority view in Western and particularly North American thought. The idea could well revive in a Southern-dominated church, in areas where actual Jewish communities are quite rare, and in a religious culture founded upon biblical literalism. African and Asian Christians do not necessarily share Northern qualms about blaming the Jews for the death of Jesus, or believing that this guilt should fall upon the whole race. We may once more see the familiar medieval symbols of the vibrant Church trying to enlighten her stubborn sister Synagogue. Outside art and theology, it would not be impossible to see a revival of religious anti-Judaism, directed against the state of Israel.

Alternatively, Christians could find their practical interests in close harmony with those of the Jewish state. Israel has a long record of allying with

Christian groups at odds with Muslim rivals, in order to keep its own Muslim enemies off balance. As far back as the 1960s, Israeli advisers were supporting Christian rebels in Sudan.[36] With all its military abilities and intelligence capacity, so out of proportion for such a tiny nation, Israel could be a potent ally for African or Asian Christians confronting Muslim neighbors. In that scenario, Israel's continuing struggles with its Arab and Muslim enemies could actually aggravate Christian–Muslim relations well beyond the immediate Middle Eastern theater of conflict.

In either case, though, interactions between not just the two but the three religions are going to be critical for the foreseeable future. It would be disastrous if American or European policymakers were fully conversant with the ideas and attitudes of Judaism, yet relied on discredited stereotypes to interpret Islam.

NOT JUST ISLAM

Although news reports of religious violence generally focus on Muslim–Christian tensions, this is not the only possible axis of conflict. Christian expansion also threatens to provoke violent reactions from the two other largest world religions, namely Hinduism and Buddhism, and the issues at stake closely resemble those dividing Christian and Muslim.

The case of Hinduism is critical since India, still home to most members of that faith, will soon surpass China in population, and could reach 1.5 billion by 2040 or so. By 2050 there will be around 1.2 billion Hindus. In recent years, reports of violence against Christian clergy and missionaries have occasionally attracted attention in the Western media, but usually with little background or explanation. In contrast to their suspicious stereotype of Islam, many Westerners have a benevolent image of Hinduism, which is associated with dreamy mysticism, Gandhian nonviolence, and limitless tolerance. In theory, Hinduism should be sufficiently expansive to include almost any theological idea. Why should Jesus not be seen as simply another avatar or manifestation of the divine? Gandhi himself loved the New Testament. Hindu violence against Christianity seems puzzling, especially since the St. Thomas Christians have been a familiar part of the Indian landscape for over eighteen hundred years. Christian schools are popular with the families of Indian elites, including some of the most reactionary Hindu fundamentalists. The present leader of India's mighty Congress Party, Sonia Gandhi, is a Roman Catholic. Why, then, should Christianity be a source of tension or hatred?

Despite its positive image, Hinduism within India suffers from massive internal tensions, which could conceivably threaten the future of the religion. By far the most sensitive concerns the so-called untouchables, the Dalits, a vast community that today comprises anywhere from 150 to 250 million people. To put it in perspective, even the lower estimate for Dalit numbers is comparable to the combined populations of Britain, France, and Italy. Although legal discrimination against these people has been outlawed since 1950, Dalits still suffer from appalling persecution and violence, and there are regular stories of murder, torture, and rape. It is baffling why a Western world that committed itself so utterly to the plight of black South Africans under apartheid is so ignorant of the comparable maltreatment of India's far more numerous Dalits. This is, simply, the largest single case of continuing institutional injustice in the world today.[37]

The Dalit issue is also a religious struggle. Successive movements for Dalit rights have threatened to detach the community from the oppressive Hindu system altogether, by converting en masse to some other religion free of the blight of caste, whether that be Islam, Buddhism, or Christianity. There is, however, a massive catch. Modern Indian governments have tried to assist Dalits by a kind of affirmative action program, setting aside government jobs and contracts for people from disadvantaged castes. But such blessings only apply provided the peoples in question remain within the Hindu system, and do not defect to other religions, and government agencies exercise intrusive surveillance to ensure that Dalits are not drifting away to—for instance—Christian churches. Dalits who do convert often condemn themselves to penury as well as persecution. Lower-class Christian converts can expect a persistent pattern of low-level bullying and violence. Dalit "converts can point to the wounds they have received, or those who died, in order to establish the right to worship on a Sunday."[38]

Yet despite these massive structural burdens, Christian missionaries have for decades enjoyed success among the poorest, often people of the lowest castes, or Dalits: many other converts are "tribal" people, who likewise stand on the fringes of Hindu society. In the nation as a whole, only 2 percent of the present population is officially reportedly to be Christian, but as we noted earlier, that might be an underestimate. Many of the 40 million or so Indian Christians are Dalits. Dalits represent 90 percent of the membership of the Protestant Church of North India, about half that of the Church of South India, as well as 60 percent of India's 19 million Roman Catholics. This success has occurred although the churches themselves are by no means free of caste prejudice. Of the 156 Catholic bishops in India, 150 are of the higher castes, as are the vast majority of Catholic priests.[39]

Carried to a logical conclusion, Christian evangelism of the lowest castes would constitute a radical overturning of Hindu society, and even Gandhi was sternly opposed to Christians seeking converts in India. Fears that Christians might make still deeper inroads among the poorest go far toward explaining the recurrent persecutions and mob violence directed against the churches across India, actions that often occur with the tacit acquiescence of local police and government. Matters have deteriorated sharply since 1997, when Hindu nationalists enjoyed an electoral upsurge. In one incident, Australian missionary Graham Staines and his two young sons were burned to death by a mob in Orissa. The specific grievance causing this crime was Christian successes in converting tribal peoples.[40]

Such well-publicized outbreaks represent only a tiny proportion of actual incidents, of attacks on churches, clergy, and ordinary believers. The movement International Christian Concern "receives more persecution reports from India than from any other country." The state of Gujarat has been the scene of some of the worst violence, in which dozens of churches have been destroyed there. In one incident, a mob took over an evangelical church, and turned the building into a Hindu temple. Following devastating earthquakes in the same state, Hindu fundamentalists intercepted relief supplies from Christian activist groups, relabeling them as their own before distributing them to disaster victims. Survivors were required to declare loyalty to Hindu causes before receiving food.[41]

Another storm center is the eastern state of Orissa, where Christians find themselves trapped between two warring movements, namely Hindu fundamentalists and fanatical Maoist rebels. Although little noticed in Western media, the Maoists, the so-called Naxalites, constitute a vast challenge to modern India, running an armed insurgency that now affects some 40 percent of the nation's territory. In Orissa and elsewhere, they target Hindu extremists and religious leaders, whom they regard, plausibly enough, as fascist enemies. Commonly though, such attacks provoke Hindu retaliation against the resented Christian minorities, who are much easier and safer to victimize than are the well-armed Naxalites. In 2007–2008, such scapegoating drove savage persecutions against Orissa Christians. Following the Naxalite assassination of a charismatic Hindu religious leader "a retaliatory wave of murder, arson and rape forced 50,000 Christians to abandon their homes. As many as 200 people were killed, according to church groups. The bleakly beautiful countryside of Kandhamal, the district of Orissa that suffered the worst unrest, remains dotted with ruined Christian villages and charred churches." For some Christians, the only route to safety lay in accepting forced conversions: "They were ordered to get on their knees and bow before the portrait of a Hindu preacher. They were told to turn over their Bibles, hymnals and the two brightly colored calendar images of Christ that hung on their wall. Then, Mr. Digal, 45, a Christian since childhood, was forced to watch his Hindu neighbors set the items on fire."[42]

In addition to ad hoc local vigilantism, there have been repeated calls for official discrimination against Christianity, and such measures are a common platform for fundamentalist Hindu political groups such as the powerful Bharatiya Janata Party, the BJP. The BJP teaches the ultranationalist ideology of Hindutva, which presents India as under siege from foreign invaders, and makes (Hindu) religion inseparable from national identity and culture. Under the influence of Hindutva, individual cities and states have banned conversions or raised legal obstacles for potential converts, including the requirement that changes of religion be registered with local authorities. Typically, such laws prohibit "conversion from one religion to another by use of force or allurement or by fraudulent means"—however one might interpret the word "fraudulent." The main target of such measures is evangelism or conversion, even as a result of interfaith marriage.

According to Hindu critics, converts are seduced by money payments from Western missionaries. Such an allegation is rhetorically necessary, as it explains why so many Indians would wish to leave the Hindu fold. In 2001, even the Dalai Lama signed a Hindu-inspired declaration opposing "conversions by any religious tradition using various methods of enticement."[43] As we have seen, it is difficult for many liberal Westerners to become too exercised about a ban on conversions or evangelism, since they agree with the basic point that religion is purely a cultural matter. They also agree that it is scarcely proper to visit a clearly extraneous Western religion upon an authentic Third World culture, especially one as idealized as Hinduism.

The fourth of the world's largest religions is Buddhism, which is today rarely cited as a political force, but this will soon change. Viewed over the long span of human history, Buddhism today is at a very atypically low ebb. As recently as 1900, Buddhists claimed the loyalty of 15 or 20 percent of the world's people, though that figure now stands closer to 5 percent. The reasons for that decline are not hard to seek, in that the centers of Buddhist faith happened, disastrously, to be at the vortices of antireligious revolution, in China, Tibet, Mongolia, Vietnam, and Cambodia. The worst era of repression and massacre seems to be ended, and over the next thirty years, Buddhism will be struggling to revert to its historic position as the religion of East and Southeast Asia. The main foci of growth would be in some of the very populous nations, including China, Vietnam, and Thailand. In China particularly, the government is investing heavily in promoting a revival of Buddhism, in large measure as a counter to surging Christianity. The revival finds a surprising face in a 300-foot-high statue of the bodhisattva Guan Yin on the island of Hainan, a sacred Buddhist image sponsored and paid for by a supposedly atheist communist regime.[44]

Across east and southeast Asia, reviving Buddhism will find itself in competition with other expanding religions, above all, Christianity and Islam. That competition certainly need not involve open conflict, and Asian Christians have worked hard to maintain channels of communication and dialogue with Buddhist thinkers. It would also be tempting to think that Buddhism, a religion founded upon peace and self-sacrifice, would not provide an ideological justification for the violence of states and mobs, but the same can also be said of Christianity. Resurgent Buddhism will add another irritant to the religious politics of the coming decades.[45]

CROSSING BORDERS

As populations grow in the regions of most intense religious struggle, issues of faith will increasingly shape secular politics, domestic and international. Now, the role of religion in international affairs is open to some debate, and clear-cut faith-based alliances are usually more a matter of rhetoric than reality. Even in early modern Europe, when governments were supposedly motivated by faith, religious boundaries often failed to overcome cynical political calculations. In the sixteenth and seventeenth centuries, when the Ottoman Turks were threatening to absorb most of eastern and central Europe, they often acted in close alliance with the Most Christian King of France, who saw the Muslim empire as a necessary counterweight to his fellow Catholics, the Habsburg rulers. When the French king allied with the Ottomans in 1544, he helpfully transformed Toulon Cathedral into a temporary mosque for the benefit of the tens of thousands of Turkish servicemen stationed in his country. Even popes allied with the Sultan when they saw fit. In modern times, some of the world's bloodiest wars have occurred within or between Muslim states. Such was the extraordinarily bloody civil war that split Bangladesh from Pakistan in 1971, and killed upward of a million people, mainly civilians; while the long struggle between Iran and Iraq during the 1980s claimed another million lives. Such also is the bloody persecution of the Muslim people of Darfur by their Sudanese rulers.

More recently, Western powers have indicated that they make no pretence of respecting confessional ties. During the Yugoslav crisis of the 1990s, the United States and Western Europe sided consistently with Muslim interests against the Christian Serbs, to the point of intervening militarily in Kosovo. Although Western media generally depicted the war in very one-sided terms, equating Serbs with German Nazis, such an image could only be sustained by ignoring a great deal of aggression and brutality by Muslim forces, including well-armed international brigades of fundamentalists. At the same time, the oppressed Christians of the Sudan were receiving no support either from NATO, or from any Western or Christian entity. Mainstream Western churches were unwilling to be too forthright in denouncing persecution. For Konrad Raiser, head of the World Council of Churches, massacres in Indonesia and Nigeria should teach Christians to reassess their missionary endeavors, to avoid causing offense to other cultures. After the September 11 terrorist attacks, moreover, the U.S. administration made extraordinary efforts to avoid depicting the struggle against Islamist extremism as in any sense a confrontation with Islam as such. All subsequent administrations have struggled mightily to avoid presenting Islam as the enemy, whether in the wars in Iraq and Afghanistan, or indeed in the continuing campaign against al-Qaeda. For the West at least, the age of the Crusades is long past.[46]

But having said this, we can easily imagine scenarios in which religion will indeed decide political action. Even without existing religious tensions, demographic change itself will provoke more aggressive international policies, as countries with swollen populations try to expand to acquire living space or natural resources. These actions could be undertaken by governments, or by the kind of ruthless private armies that marauded over Liberia and Sierra Leone during the 1990s. These extremely destructive wars were fought by militias made up of uneducated fourteen-year-old boys, armed to the teeth and ready to kill or die for whatever warlord directed them. Border tensions will be very high in regions in which young and expanding populations confront older stagnant nations inhabiting vast geographical spaces. Additionally, growing states with severe domestic tensions might try to unify their discontented peoples by diverting them into foreign adventures. Religious rivalries would provide an obvious justification for external interventions.[47]

Several areas of the globe offer possible settings for future wars of this kind. Australian governments have long been nervously aware of the booming Indonesian population just to their north: by 2050 Indonesians will outnumber Australians by around eleven to one. In this region especially, militant religion might aggravate demographic and economic pressures. We can also look at the former Soviet Union, which often faced serious difficulties over how to accommodate its restive Muslim minority. The breakup of the USSR provided a temporary solution by spinning off the Central Asian republics, but in the long term, this separation also created new political regimes capable of independent action. Sparsely inhabited Russian territory (with its oil wealth) will offer a tempting prize for overpopulated Muslim neighbors to the south and east. If we take the five Central Asian republics together, their current combined population of 61 million should grow to 70 million by midcentury, a worrying contrast to declining Russia.[48] A similar point could also be made about the growth of the former Soviet republics in the Caucasus.

Demography promises to shift the religious balance within these new nation-states. Since Russian and European populations within these countries have far lower birthrates than their Asian Muslim neighbors, Russians could find themselves in the position of Christian minorities within strict Muslim states. In the ex-Soviet successor-state of Kazakhstan, the population is presently divided roughly fifty-fifty Christian–Muslim, but long-term trends assure a substantial Muslim majority. Muslims outnumber Christians by four to one in Kyrgyzstan, nine to one in Uzbekistan, and the disparities are growing steadily. Currently, most of these governments are suspicious of Muslim political activism, but that could change. If Christians in any of these regions complained of religious persecution, the odds of Russia intervening militarily would be high, and the disastrous example of the tiny region of Chechnya suggests how bloody such a religious and national war might be. Religious and racial warfare in the former Soviet Union would be aggravated by the struggle for natural resources—above all oil. Not surprisingly, the U.S. intelligence community has listed Central Asia as a "regional hot spot" in the next decade or two.[49]

If we look at the most populous and fastest growing states across the global South, then we often find Christian and Muslim states standing next to each other, and close to other countries sharply split between the two faiths. Curiously, too, religious minorities are disproportionately likely to reside in areas of rich natural resources, raising the likelihood that religious battles might be economically profitable. The fact that minorities are so preferentially located may seem like an odd manifestation of God's sense of humor, but the phenomenon has a sound historical basis. In bygone centuries, religious dissidents were commonly forced to live far removed from the centers of political power, which were located in the more fertile agricultural areas. In order to survive, minorities resorted to remote and marginal lands, which were relatively poor according to the standards of traditional economies. As oil exploration and other extractive industries developed in modern times, these marginal lands often proved to be immensely rich, leaving the minorities in a position of unprecedented influence. This history explains why, for instance, Shi'ite Muslim minorities in the Arab world are so regularly found in oil-rich regions. It also suggests why, religious zeal apart, it is so tempting for a nation to intervene on the behalf of co-religionists who represent a persecuted minority in some neighboring country.

Currently, most of the rising states of Africa and Asia are strictly limited in their capacity to undertake international military operations: witness the disastrous failure of regional African coalitions seeking to end the civil wars in Liberia and Sierra Leone. But this weakness will not continue indefinitely, and African and Asian countries will develop significant military capacities, perhaps based on chemical or biological weapons. If that ever occurred, then regional powers would be under heavy pressure not to stand idly by if co-religionists in nearby countries were threatened with persecution and massacre.

THE WAR OF THE END OF THE WORLD

We can imagine a future in which Muslim and Christian alliances blunder into conflict, rather as the dual networks of European states reached the point of war in 1914. Several plausible African scenarios should cause strategic planners sleepless nights. Few sub-Saharan states have boundaries that coincide neatly with either ethnic or natural realities. Many ethnic and tribal groupings are scattered over two or more states, although they retain close cultural and religious links, and an insult against one faction can have international ramifications. The Rwandan massacres in 1994 detonated a series of wars and interventions that spilled over into the huge territory of the Congo, what was then Zaire. Angola, Zimbabwe, Namibia, Uganda, and Rwanda all became directly involved in what was described as Africa's equivalent of the First World War, and several other nations watched nervously.[50] By the time the carnage ended in 2004, perhaps five million Congolese had died. Even so, few Westerners know or care about the slaughter, because it occurred so far from centers of media activity, and because there was little risk of superpower involvement, no danger that weapons of mass destruction would be employed. Nor is there any guarantee how long the restored peace will endure. The Congo might still become a perpetual war zone reminiscent of Germany during the Thirty Years War.

And that analogy should give us pause, because we know in hindsight that Germany would not remain a hapless victim forever, and neither will African states. Perhaps some will fail and crumble, but others might yet reorganize into more formidable entities, perhaps allied with Asian or European powers. China has already developed a very strong commercial and political presence in Africa, which may well become a significant sphere of influence.

Let us imagine a near future in which (say) Nigeria, Uganda, and the Congo are all well-armed regional powers. When Muslims and Christians begin killing each other in another smaller state—in Cameroon, perhaps—tribal and religious allies in neighboring lands are swiftly drawn in. Muslim Nigeria demands a cessation of hostilities and threatens to send in forces. Christian powers respond with their own threats, and the situation escalates as other major states intervene. Muslim and Christian alliances face off in a model example of cultural and religious confrontation, a fault-line war. Meanwhile, each power tries to destabilize its rivals by stirring up sympathetic minorities within enemy states—Ugandan agents provoke religious rioting across eastern Nigeria, Nigerians reciprocate with terrorist attacks against their rivals. Matters are complicated by the presence of refugees expelled from the zone of conflict, who tell atrocity stories and demand vengeance. As the situation becomes more overtly religious, fundamentalists on each side advocate harder line positions. Mosques and churches pour forth intemperate propaganda, warning against compromise with the forces of evil.

Worse, religious fundamentalism is sometimes associated with theocratic and authoritarian forms of government, exactly the sort of regime one does not want to be handling delicate international crises. Perhaps the main protagonist nations will themselves be led by religious authorities, by sheikhs or pastors. Some of the likely winners in the religious economy of the next forty years are precisely those groups who have a strongly apocalyptic mind-set, in which the triumph of righteousness is associated with the vision of a world devastated by fire and plague. This could be a perilously convenient ideology for a new international order dominated by countries armed to the teeth with nuclear and biological arsenals. The situation could become so sensitive that a global catastrophe could be provoked by the slightest misjudgment: just like 1914.

A similar conflagration might evolve from an Asian struggle between (say) a vigorously Christian Philippines and a resolutely Muslim Indonesia, especially if each nation offered clandestine support to secessionist groups in its neighbor's territory. Open warfare could develop along this eastern fault line, and could draw in allied religious powers. Even without the religious factor, this part of the Pacific Rim is going to be one of the major areas of strategic confrontation over the next twenty or thirty years. Again, the growth of China is a critical factor. As the country grows militarily, it projects its power in the South China Sea, the vital maritime region bounded by Taiwan, the Philippines, Malaysia, and Vietnam. Some Chinese maps claim this area as that nation's territorial waters, which is worrying because the South China Sea is the primary route for oil supplies to East Asia's leading industrial nations. Religious-based instability vastly aggravates the potential for great power clashes, especially when (as in Indonesia or Malaysia) anti-Christian violence is directed against ethnic Chinese. The People's Republic might assume a role as the outraged protector of Chinese people everywhere, intervening to save kith and kin from slaughter by Muslim militias. The natural protector and patron of Asia's Christian communities in years to come might not be the United States, Britain, or Australia, but antireligious China. It would be a curious irony if, in this eventuality, the Anglo-Saxon powers found themselves on the other side, fighting to defend Muslim states against a pro-Christian intervention.[51]

The scenarios described here are pure fantasy, but the background is anything but speculative. The countries mentioned will all be significant political players, and they will be at the forefront of growth among both Christians and Muslims. It is conceivable that within a few decades, the two faiths will have agreed on amicable terms of coexistence, and growing demographic stability might defuse religious zeal. Looking at matters as they stand today, though, that happy consummation seems unlikely. Issues of theocracy and religious law, toleration and minority rights, conversion and apostasy, should be among the most divisive in domestic and international politics for decades to come. It is quite possible to imagine a future Christendom not too different from the old, defined less by any ideological harmony than by its unity against a common outside threat. We must hope that the new *Res Publica Christiana* does not confront an equally militant Muslim world, *Dar al-Islam*, or else we really will have gone full circle back to the worst features of the thirteenth century.

NINE

Coming Home

Be nice to whites, they need you to rediscover their
humanity.

—Archbishop Desmond Tutu

In 1933, Evelyn Waugh's short story "Out of Depth" told how a magi-
cian sent a modern-day Londoner forward in time to the England of the
twenty-fifth century. This future England is a primitive peasant society
colonized by advanced African nations. At the climax of the story, "in a
log-built church at the coast town he was squatting among a native congregation.... All around him, dishevelled white men were staring ahead with
vague, uncomprehending eyes, to the end of the room where two candles
burned. The priest turned toward them his bland, black face. '*Ite, missa
est*'"—the Mass is ended.[1] At the time Waugh wrote, the notion that
Africans might someday be re-Christianizing Europe would have seemed
bizarre, but as the years have gone by, the image seems ever less startling.
And however fantastic the setting, the story raises a fundamental issue.
How will the global North—and especially Europe—change in response to
the rise of a new global Christianity? Will its religious character remain
Christian, perhaps with a powerful Southern cast? Or will it entirely lose
its Christian character?

Repeatedly throughout church history, observers have noted missionary
successes in heavily populated parts of the globe and speculated that the future
of Christianity might lie in these mission fields. As Europe was tearing itself
apart during the Thirty Years War, St. Vincent de Paul recalled Jesus's promise

that his church would continue until the end of days—but he also noted that Jesus had said nothing about the faith necessarily surviving in Europe.[2] The Christian future might well lie in Africa or South America, in China or Japan. Such an insight became all the more probable when set against the religion's long history: the "Christian heartland" has repeatedly shifted as time went on. Syrians and Mesopotamians had once believed that their lands would always be solidly Christian, just as modern Europeans imagine that Christianity will survive on their continent. In 1850 Lord Macaulay warned the then-triumphant British Empire that religion was not the prerogative of any single region, still less a political entity: churches often outlive states and even world empires. In a much-quoted passage, he wrote that the Roman Catholic Church "may still exist in undiminished vigor, when some traveler from New Zealand shall, in the midst of a vast solitude, take his stand on a broken arch of London Bridge to sketch the ruins of St. Paul's."

More recent critics have agreed that Christianity's days might be numbered in Europe. Waugh's story was written during the Great Depression, when Western civilization seemed to be on the verge of collapse. Also in 1933, Charles Williams published his fantasy novel *Shadows of Ecstasy*, in which the peoples of Africa are inspired to invade a spiritually desolate Europe. As their manifesto declares, "The prophets of Africa have seen that mankind must advance in the future by paths which the white people have neglected and to ends which they have not understood."[3]

No serious observer today expects a literal Southern invasion of Europe or North America. In religious terms, though, the apocalyptic-sounding visions of St. Vincent, Charles Williams, and the others are sounding ever more credible. Not only is traditional Christianity weakening in Europe, but it is indeed being reinforced and reinvigorated by Southern churches by means of immigration and evangelization. And the Christianity spread by such means has a predictably Southern cast, conservative and charismatic. How this process develops over the coming century is enormously significant, not just for the future shape of religious alignments but also for political history. The success of the "prophets of Africa"—and of Asia and Latin America—will determine exactly what kind of North will be confronting a rising South.

FEAR OF A BLACK PLANET

Europeans and North Americans have often felt nervous about population trends that leave whites such a conspicuous global minority. During the colonial years, writers agonized that Southern forces might be mobilized by a messianic religious movement that would smash imperial domination and overwhelm Europe and America. Shades of Muhammad's career and the early history of Islam usually lay behind such visions, which seemed more plausible following the rise of native prophets such as William Wadé Harris and John Chilembwe. In 1922 Lothrop Stoddard published his epic account of *The Rising Tide of Color Against White World Supremacy*, in which he envisaged the Southern races joining together in a massive anti-white jihad, perhaps led by Islam. The Chilembwe revolt was an early warning sign of this "peculiarly fanatical form of Ethiopianism." A character in John Buchan's 1910 novel *Prester John* remarks, "He did not see why a kind of bastard Christianity should not be the motive of a rising. The Kaffir finds it an easy job to mix up Christian emotion and pagan practice. Look at Haiti and some of the performances in the Southern States."[4]

The vision of global racial and religious war continues to galvanize the racist right. A cult classic in these circles is Jean Raspail's 1973 novel *The Camp of the Saints*, a fantasy of the near future, which describes how the Third World's black and brown people invade and overwhelm the white North. The Roman Catholic Church is at the forefront of Raspail's indictment of gutless Western liberalism, because the church preaches subversive messages of racial equality and the evils of imperialism. The familiar nightmare reflected here is that the colonialist trend might be reversed: if there was once a Belgian Congo, could there not someday be a Congolese Belgium? And just as Christianity had spread with the European expansion, so it would collapse with the Fall of the West. The Asian masses of *Camp of the Saints* are explicitly fighting to erase Europe's failed God, and passages from the biblical book of Revelation are scattered throughout the work. The book has been quoted ever more widely over the past few years, as Europe's growing Muslim populations have become more visible, and more restive.[5]

In a perverse way, Raspail really was reflecting political perceptions of his day, in the sense that liberals and radicals did indeed place their hopes in the southward shift of Christian populations. We have already seen the high hopes that Western Christians placed in the emerging nations of Africa and Asia, and their wholehearted commitment to political liberation movements. On the other side, conservatives loathed the World Council of Churches, never more than when WCC money armed African liberation movements. (The Council is one of Raspail's special banes.) In view of this heritage of hostility, it is striking how favorably many religious conservatives today view the "browning" of world Christianity. In recent debates, it has been the traditionalists who have looked south for allies, in a few cases to the extent of placing themselves under African or Asian ecclesiastical jurisdictions. They almost seem to be awaiting a benevolent *Camp of the Saints* scenario, in which quite genuine saints from Africa or Asia would pour north, not seeking racial revenge, but rather trying to reestablish a proper moral order.

These ideological reversals make better sense if we think of them in terms of political alignments in the contemporary United States. Conservatives generally dislike immigration and the browning of America, and fear the loss of cultural homogeneity. At the same time, though, this process might promote other issues that conservatives do favor. Many of the new immigrants are Christians of a traditionalist bent, with conservative attitudes toward faith and family. They have few qualms about public displays of religion, and show little sympathy for the rigid American separation of church and state. For exactly the same reasons, liberals who generally favor racial diversity will discover that a rainbow America also espouses an uncomfortably traditional kind of religion. Traditional mappings of left and right are ill fitted to comprehend present and future religious changes.

CATHOLICS

The North–South cultural schism is a familiar story within the largest single religious structure on the planet, namely the billion-strong Roman Catholic Church. Although we are not here describing anything like a re-evangelization of the North, the Catholic example does show how Southern pressures are transforming religion around the world. The conservatism of that church, so often denounced and derided, must partly be seen as a response to the changing demographics of world religion.

The Catholic church has long had to deal with trends that other religious communities are only now beginning to face. Back in 1920, Hilaire Belloc not only proclaimed that "Europe is the Faith" but made his boast specifically Catholic: "The Church is Europe; and Europe is The Church."[6] If this was ever true, it has not been so for a good many years. Euro-American Catholics ceased to enjoy majority status a generation ago, and the bulk of the world's Catholics now live in the global South (see table 9.1). The geographical balance is certain to shift more heavily in coming years.

One suggestive statistic involves baptisms, since regions with the largest number of baptisms are also the centers of the most dynamic growth. Of 18 million Catholic baptisms recorded in 1999, 8 million took place in

TABLE 9.1
Catholics Worldwide 2025: A Projection

	Number of Catholics (millions)	
Continent	2000	2025
Latin America	461	606
Europe	286	276
Africa	120	228
Asia	110	160
North America	71	81
Oceania	8	11
TOTAL	1,056	1,362

Source: David B. Barrett, George T. Kurian, and Todd M. Johnson, eds., *World Christian Encyclopedia*, 2nd ed. (New York: Oxford University Press, 2001), 12.

Central and South America, and no less than 3 million in Africa. Today, the annual baptismal totals for Nigeria and the Democratic Republic of the Congo are each higher than those for such familiar Catholic lands as Italy, France, Spain, and Poland, which are today the major centers of Catholic population in Europe. As John Allen points out, 37 percent of all baptisms in Africa today are of adults. Observers consider this figure an important gauge of evangelistic efforts, because it means that people are making a deliberate decision to convert from some other faith tradition.[7]

By 2025 Africans and Latin Americans combined will make up about 60 percent of Catholics, and that number should reach 66 percent before 2050. European and Euro-American Catholics will by that point be a small fragment of a church dominated by Filipinos and Mexicans, Vietnamese and Congolese (though of course, the North still provides a hugely disproportionate share of church finances). According to sociologist Rogelio Saenz, "From 2004 to 2050, Catholic populations are projected to increase by 146 percent in Africa, 63 percent in Asia, 42 percent in Latin America and the Caribbean, and 38 percent in North America. Meanwhile, Europe will experience a 6 percent decline in its Catholic population between 2004 and 2050." The number of Catholics in Africa will exceed that in Europe around 2030, and by 2050, Asia's Catholic population will approach Europe's.[8] The twentieth century was the last in which whites dominated the Catholic church: Europe simply is *not* The Church. Latin America may be.

The shift in numbers is increasingly acknowledged at the highest ranks of the church, among its princes, the cardinals. It is not long since the

College of Cardinals was almost wholly European; now its composition has changed substantially. Only in 1960 did the College of Cardinals acquire its first African member, Tanzanian Laurian Rugambwa. In 2001, though, when Pope John Paul II elevated forty-four new cardinals, no fewer than eleven were from Latin America, and two each from India and Africa (see table 9.2).[9]

Northern Catholics still hold influence disproportionate to their numbers. The United States, for instance, currently has the world's fourth largest Catholic population, following Mexico, Brazil, and the Philippines; but during the 2005 conclave that elected Pope Benedict XVI, eleven cardinals represented the United States, more than for those three other nations combined. But the world is clearly changing. Over 40 percent of the cardinals eligible to vote in 2005 came from Third World nations, leading commentators to note that the church's center was moving away from Europe. The changes are evident throughout other Church institutions. Although the United States long possessed the largest component of the Society of Jesus, that honor has now passed to the Indian province.

Understanding these numbers goes far toward explaining the Catholic politics of the last forty years or so. Even the election of Pope John Paul II in 1978 owed much to the geographical shift, since global South cardinals were adamantly opposed to another incumbent from western Europe, and at least the Polish candidate represented a decisive break with tradition. When John Paul died in 2005, there was intense media speculation that he would be followed by a man from the global South—perhaps Francis Arinze from Nigeria, Brazil's Claudio Hummes, or Honduran Oscar Rodríguez Maradiaga. In the event, the new pope was of course the German,

TABLE 9.2
Roman Catholic Cardinals as of 2009

	Number of Cardinals	
	Total	Eligible to vote
Africa	14	9
Asia	19	10
Central and South America	24	15
Europe	100	57
Oceania	4	2
North America	24	20
TOTAL	185	113

Source: Catholic Almanac

Joseph Ratzinger, who became Benedict XVI. In the aftermath of that conclave, it is all the more likely that not long after Benedict's time, the church will be led by a global South pontiff. In fact, the choice of Ratzinger itself raises interesting questions about the strength of Catholicism in various regions of the world. Although Benedict is an impressive figure in his own right, much of his appeal at this particular moment was the sense that the church urgently needed to stage a last-ditch defense in Western Europe, where organized Christianity was so conspicuously waning. And that, of course, was before the recent abuse crisis shook Catholic confidence so badly in many European nations, discrediting some once powerful leaders. It cannot be too long before Africa produces its first pope in many centuries, and pundits are already quietly ranking their candidates—Kinshasa's archbishop Laurent Monsengwo Pasinya, Ghana's Peter Turkson, or Johannesburg's Buti Tlhagale.[10]

The growing Southern emphasis has also shaped the politics of morality within the Catholic church. Repeatedly in recent years, the Catholic hierarchy has become associated with positions that appear conservative or reactionary, to the despair of most Western commentators. For many, both John Paul II and Benedict symbolized obscurantism on issues of gender, morality, and sexual orientation, to the extent that some Catholics see an inevitable schism between the churches of the liberal West and the irredeemably reactionary papacy. The ordination of women to the priesthood is a crucial point of disagreement here, as are matters such as contraception and homosexuality. In all these matters, liberal and feminist pressure groups are convinced that their views must triumph in time, once the gerontocracy in the Vatican has faded into history. Undoubtedly, the abuse crisis has advanced reformist views, if only because of the widespread impression that clerical celibacy contributed substantially to the widespread abuse of children. (The lack of any comparative data for other professions or churches makes it impossible to test this interpretation, but it has certainly had its impact.) In Europe and North America at least, liberalism seems to be in the ascendant.

A global view suggests a different interpretation of Catholic behavior, and which part of the church might plausibly claim to speak for the future. The hierarchy knows that many liberal issues dear to American or West European Catholics are unpalatable to many socially traditional societies of the South. When John Allen imagines the Catholic Church of midcentury, he lists ten megatrends, some of which raise issues quite unpalatable for old-line Northern believers. These trends include globalization and demographic change, the challenge of Islam, evangelical

Catholicism, and Pentecostalism. Throughout his work, Allen stresses the rise of charismatic and Pentecostal belief and worship within Catholicism: "As Roman Catholicism in the future speaks with an African and Hispanic accent, it will also speak in tongues." While the church has always regarded itself as "One, Holy, Catholic, and Apostolic," Allen sees the coming Southward-weighted institution as "Global, Uncompromising, Pentecostal, and Extroverted."[11]

Distinctive theological perspectives have moral implications. While the ordination of women may seem an essential point of justice to Westerners, it is anathema for much of Africa and Asia, and homosexual issues are still more sensitive. Now, as noted earlier, church leaders do not necessarily follow the familiar American patterns of conservative or liberal, so that a Latin American cardinal might be progressive on social issues, while traditional on matters of theology and sexual discipline. But on these latter areas, the newer Catholic churches tend to be conservative. If, again, a church has to be highly conscious of its relationship with Islam, that must constrain its attitudes on sexual issues.[12]

This fact is neatly symbolized by Nigeria's cardinal Francis Arinze, who was long touted as a possible future pope. The prospect of a black African pope understandably excites Christians of all political persuasions, and not just Catholics, but in terms of ideology, an Arinze papacy would have been a very conservative era. Arinze himself is an Igbo, a people whose Christian roots now run deep. He is firmly in the mold of popes John Paul II and Benedict, and it has been said that "His theology has always been: 'Where does Rome stand? There I stand.'" This conservatism emerges in issues of academic freedom, where Arinze's views seem repressive and restrictive by Western liberal standards. (To the relief of liberals everywhere, the cardinal is now retired.) African Catholicism is far more comfortable with notions of authority and charisma than with newer ideas of consultation and democracy.[13]

The question of religious toleration also looks quite different when viewed from the South. In 2000 the Vatican issued another encyclical seemingly designed for the sole purpose of enraging American liberals, when in *Dominus Jesus* it reasserted the exclusive role of Christ and Catholic Christianity as vehicles of salvation. The Vatican warned that "The Church's constant missionary proclamation is endangered today by relativistic theories which seek to justify religious pluralism." Against this position, the document scorned any idea that the Christian message needed to be supplemented from any other faith tradition. "The theory of the limited, incomplete, or imperfect character of the revelation of Jesus Christ, which would be complementary to that found in other religions, is contrary to the Church's faith." All religions simply are not equal.[14]

For the United States or Europe, this material seemed offensive, to Jews in particular. It sabotaged decades of attempts at dialogue with other faiths, and was uncomfortably reminiscent of ancient statements that there was no salvation outside the church. How could the church issue such a reactionary rant? In Western parlance, pluralism is always a good thing. At least for some Asian Catholic leaders too, the statements undermined efforts at dialogue with the continent's ancient faiths. But from other perspectives—especially in Africa—*Dominus Jesus* addressed crucial issues of daily significance, by warning clergy and believers to observe strict limits in their relations with the other faiths they lived among. It was directed to the faithful in the intense religious atmospheres of Nigeria and Tanzania, of Korea and India, where the terms of interaction with rival religions have to be hammered out afresh each day.[15] In such cases, the Vatican was warning, friendly relations were one thing, but syncretism was quite another. The encyclical was not addressed to Northern liberals practicing cafeteria religion, but to fast-growing Southern churches anxious for practical rules to ensure their authenticity. What North Americans did not realize was that the Vatican just was not speaking to them.

The conservative tone of much African and Latin American Catholicism suggests why Catholic leaders are less than concerned when Catholics in Boston or Munich threaten schism. In the traditionalist view, adapting to become relevant or sensitive to the needs of Western elites would be suicidal for the long-term prospects of the church. Liberal criticism derives especially from only selected regions of the world, and moreover, the very regions in which Catholic numbers are stagnant, or worse. The relative importance of Northern and Southern interests within Roman Catholicism can be illustrated by the experience of the Netherlands. The Dutch church is one of the most liberal branches of Catholicism, and since the 1960s it has regularly been a thorn in the side of the Vatican. But for all its wealth and activism, the numerical strength of the Dutch church is tiny. The population of the Netherlands is virtually stable: in 2050, like today, the country will have around 16 or 17 million inhabitants. Church membership, however, is plummeting. About 5 million Dutch people consider themselves Roman Catholics, though only half of these demonstrate any serious commitment to the church. To put these numbers in context, there are about half as many Catholics in the whole of the Netherlands as in (say) just the Manila metropolitan area. And as Christian strength has withered in Europe, so other religions have grown. The Netherlands currently has a Muslim population of 1 million, some 6 percent of the whole, but the proportion by 2050 could be 15 or 20 percent.

Similar stories would emerge if we look at other lands that were once Catholic strongholds in Europe, but where Catholic loyalties are now fading fast. If the church had to choose whether to appeal to the Catholics of Brazil or Belgium, of the Congo or France, then on every occasion, simple self-interest would persuade them to favor the burgeoning Southern community. Of course the leaders of the Roman Catholic Church are conservative: they can count.

GENDER AND SEXUALITY

Not just within the Roman Catholic Church, religious conservatives are looking southward with happy expectation. Most of the reasons for this involve disputes over gender and sexuality. Over the last thirty years, religious attitudes in North America and Europe have shifted beyond recognition, with the advance of feminist and progressive causes, and the growth of sexual liberalism. The change is symbolized by the general acceptance of women's ordination, and by the free discussion of gay causes within the mainline Protestant churches. These have proved the defining issues that separate progressives and conservatives, ecclesiastical Left and Right. They are simply not matters on which it is possible to imagine a church member having no opinion. Although conservatives have suffered repeated defeats, they have been heartened by new support from the global South. Contrary to liberal expectations, churches in Africa and Asia have been strictly conservative on moral and sexual issues. As New Left activists of the 1960s often remarked, in a different context, causes that have been lost in Europe or North America might still be won in Africa or Asia.

Just why we are seeing a hemispheric gulf over issues of sexuality needs some explanation. Generally, the newer churches are more conservative and even reactionary than the Northern mainstream. This may sound curious, since as we have already seen, women are critical to the growth of new churches across the global South. This is evident in Latin American Pentecostalism, and in many of the African Independent churches, some of which owe their foundation to female prophets. In some instances, respect for women's spiritual gifts has led to formal leadership positions: Brazil's controversial IURD has long ordained women. In some regions, women clergy are also appearing in mainstream churches such as the Anglicans and Presbyterians. In 2004 Archbishop Desmond Tutu ordained his

daughter Mpho to the Anglican priesthood. Also, activist women's cau-
cuses have appeared in some regions, and believing women are evolving a
creative Christian theology that is both feminist and distinctively African
(or Asian). In the long term, such thinkers may herald an authentic social
and structural revolution within global South Christianities and across the
region.[16]

Despite these examples, at present Southern churches are by and large
more comfortable than their Northern neighbors in preaching a traditional
role for women. This is especially true in much of Africa, where Muslim
notions exercise a powerful cultural influence. Although Christians do not
accept the whole Islamic package of mores on this or any issue, they do
imbibe a conservatism general to the whole community. Though it is hard
to generalize about such diverse cultures, Southern nations tend to be more
patriarchal than Europe or North America. To take a crude guide to social
attitudes, abortion is strictly prohibited in almost all African nations,
though some nations grant exceptions where the life of the mother is
endangered, or where a fetus is severely deformed. (Abortions occur in
millions each year across Africa, but the great majority are criminal acts.)
A lively debate over abortion law reform rages across the continent, but the
state of the law is roughly where it was in Europe or North America in the
1950s. Only politically progressive South Africa permits abortion on
request. In Latin America too, the powerful Catholic cultural inheritance
means that abortion is commonly prohibited, or permitted only to save the
life of the mother. Only Cuba and Guyana permit abortion on demand,
and nations such as Chile prohibit abortion in all circumstances.[17] Again
with the exception of South Africa, organized women's politics are nothing
like as developed in most of Africa as in Europe or North America, and
that kind of gender balance is inevitably reflected in ecclesiastical life.

GAY DEBATES

On issues of homosexuality too, a chasm divides the world's religious
communities, nowhere more visibly than in contemporary Africa. Viewed
over the span of history, African cultures are no more homogeneous in
these matters than those of Europe. Same-sex relationships have often
been recorded among different peoples, and the degree of social approval
has varied enormously according to time and place. As in traditional
Europe, most African societies lacked any notion of a homosexual as a
distinct type, as opposed to an individual who happened to be sexually

active with members of the same gender. In recent years though, the revolutionary change in social attitudes to homosexuality in Europe and North America has created a social gulf with many Third World societies. As many Northern countries regard gay rights as a fundamental component of human liberty, so homosexuality as such has come to be portrayed as a distinctly Western phenomenon, irrelevant or worse to African or Asian societies.[18]

The anti-homosexual reaction has been virulent, such that Zimbabwe president Robert Mugabe has declared homosexuals worse than pigs and dogs. Other African leaders condemned his antigay tirades. Some of the harshest responses came from South Africa, where the constitution guarantees freedom of sexual expression, and where in 2005, the highest court declared that sexual rights extended to the legalization of gay marriage. Former South African Anglican primate Ndungane called homosexuality at worst a "pastoral, secondary problem." Nevertheless, Mugabe was giving voice to a widespread populist opinion, and his views were widely echoed. Former Kenyan leader Daniel Arap Moi called homosexuals a "scourge," while the president of Namibia agreed that homosexuality was an "alien practice...most of the ardent supporters of these perverts are Europeans, who imagine themselves to be the bulwark of civilization and enlightenment." Nigerian president Olusegun Obasanjo described homosexuality as "clearly unbiblical, unnatural, and definitely un-African. Surely the good Lord who created us male and female knew exactly what he was doing. To my understanding of the Scripture, any other form of sexual relationship is a perversion of the divine order, and a sin." The presidents of Namibia and Uganda put their rhetoric into practice by ordering severe police crackdowns on gays, to "arrest, deport and imprison" homosexuals. Gambian dictator Yahya Jammeh publicly fantasizes about beheading homosexuals.[19] Antigay rhetoric combines with anti-Western and anti-imperialist activism.

Recent controversies also raise the issue of the relationship between Northern world conservatives and global South churches. Since the late 1990s, Christian activists in Uganda have focused intensely on the evils of homosexuality, which (among other evils) they associate with the molestation of children. The most visible activist was Martin Ssempa, the well connected founder of the Makerere Community Church, who believes that "In Africa, sodomy is an abomination" (Makerere is so important to public opinion because it is the nation's leading university). In 2009, parliamentarian David Bahati introduced an Anti-Homosexuality Bill "to establish a comprehensive consolidated legislation to protect the traditional family by prohibiting any form of sexual relations between persons of the same sex." The law would have imposed draconian penalties. The death penalty could be imposed on "serial offenders," or for those committing homosexual sex acts with minors or the disabled, or homosexual sex while being HIV-positive.[20]

This proposed measure attracted widespread protest from Europe and North America, including from many churches. Apart from the specific law itself, opponents also focused on the forces driving Uganda's antigay activism. According to critics, the impetus began with hard-core American conservatives who had visited Uganda since the 1990s, and who had in effect imported extreme right-wing U.S. beliefs into African Christianity. In the words of one commentary, "Just as the United States and other northern societies routinely dump our outlawed or expired chemicals, pharmaceuticals, machinery, and cultural detritus on African and other Third World countries, we now export a political discourse and public policies our own society has discarded as outdated and dangerous, Africa's antigay campaigns are to a substantial degree made in the U.S.A." Ssempa himself was an important link with U.S. evangelicals such as Rick Warren.[21]

Beyond question, American conservatives were active in the Ugandan movement, although all criticized the capital punishment clause (Warren was outspoken in his denunciation). The American activists helped draw attention to antigay sentiment in Uganda, and that their visibility on the global stage gave the movement credibility, making the gay issue much more central than it had been hitherto. But that does not mean that the Americans imported an idea wholesale, and imposed it on a gullible or passive population, or that Ugandan campaigners like Martin Ssempa were the puppets of these outside manipulators.

The suggestion that these campaigns are "Made in the USA" is condescending and dated. Much current African legislation on sexuality is an inheritance from the British colonial regimes, recalling a time—quite recent in the span of history—when Western nations certainly did not regard homosexual behavior as any kind of legal right. Western campaigners are basically demanding that Africans and Asians should automatically follow the Euro-American lead in moral issues, and it is scarcely surprising that the citizens of now independent nations should resent those assumptions. Homosexuality was already a highly sensitive theme across Africa in the 1990s, and Christian opposition intensified as gay causes advanced in Euro-American mainline churches. It is a long time since African or Asian churches uncritically followed the lead of Northern world mentors. If they do follow Euro-American leadership on a given issue, it is because it resonates with local perceptions and interests.

We are not dealing with any kind of ethnic determinism, in the sense that African or Asian societies are intrinsically more hostile either to women's rights, or to alternative expressions of sexuality. Indeed, the outburst of antigay sentiment in Namibia, Uganda, and elsewhere have actually inspired minor gay rights movements, which achieved some public visibility. The main difference is that these communities have not yet experienced the kind of secularizing and modernizing trends that have transformed the West in the last century or so. Southern churches are unlikely to respond to Northern calls to accept general secular trends toward liberalization in these matters, to "join the modern world." They are doubly unlikely to do so, since these same trends are associated with Western cultural imperialism. Why should Southerners wish to join this world if they have any chance of remaining separate? If Northerners worry that Southern churches have compromised with traditional paganism, then Southerners accuse Americans and Europeans of selling out Christianity to neo-paganism, in the form of secular liberalism.

Approaches to both feminism and gay issues also raise the critical issue of authority, of just how different factions justify their opinions. Northern liberals demand that church texts and traditions be viewed in the context of the cultures that produced them, so that it is legitimate and necessary for churches to change in accordance with secular progress. Just because St. Paul seemed to defend slavery does not justify the practice in the modern world. Southerners, however, demand that all churches respect traditional moral values and gender roles, all the more emphatically when these standards are clearly prescribed in scripture. Liberals judge scripture by the standards of the world; conservatives claim to set an absolute value on scripture and religious sources of authority. For the foreseeable future, the newer churches will remain bastions of conservatism on key issues of women's equality and gay rights. It remains to be seen whether the Southern churches will remain so staunch about these social issues as they evolve and diversify.

SCHISM?

During the past decade, debates over gender and sexuality have become so intense in some denominations as actually to threaten global schisms, which would roughly follow North–South lines. The question must now arise whether any church aspiring to universality can contain within itself the very diverse attitudes to sexual morality prevailing in different parts of the world.

Best publicized have been the clashes within the Anglican Communion. During the 1990s, the traditionally dominant provinces of the global North—Britain, the United States, and Canada—came under increasing pressure to adopt more liberal attitudes toward the ordination of women, and subsequently to enact more gay-friendly policies. In the U.S. Episcopal Church (ECUSA) particularly, openly gay clergy had been ordained for some years, and church leaders were debating forms of blessing for gay unions or marriages. In 2003, ECUSA approved the consecration of Gene Robinson—a noncelibate homosexual—as bishop of New Hampshire, and the Church of England proposed gay canon, Jeffrey John, as bishop of Reading.[22]

Northern proposals met fierce opposition from Southern church leaders. The collision first achieved wide publicity with the 1998 Lambeth Conference of the global Communion, in which Southern bishops formed a solid bloc to defeat liberal motions on gay rights. The Anglican episcopate worldwide now contains a majority of African and Asian clerics. Of 736 bishops registered at Lambeth in 1998, only 316 were from the United States, Canada, and Europe combined, while Africa sent 224 and Asia 95. This body easily passed a statement describing homosexual practice as "incompatible with scripture," so that homosexual conduct could not be reconciled with Christian ministry. Western responses to the homosexuality statement can best be described as incomprehension mingled with sputtering rage. Yet the geographical balance within the Anglican Communion tilts ever more heavily to the South. Outside Africa, moral traditionalism was supported by figures such as Moses Tay, the Singapore-based archbishop of Southeast Asia. Archbishop Tay refused to attend international Anglican meetings called by clergy who favor gay rights, on the grounds that the liberals were not just ill-advised, but heretical. His successor, Datuk Yong Ping Chung, was an equally determined conservative.[23]

By 2003, Southern opposition found a visible face in Peter Jasper Akinola, the primate of the powerful Church of Nigeria, who expressed implacable opposition to Anglo-American sexual liberalism. He complained of a Northern betrayal of the most basic tenets of Christianity, a literally diabolical lurch into non-Christian heresy. Akinola described the proposed elevation of Jeffrey John as "a Satanic attack on God's Church." To the prospect of gay unions, he warned that "If England adopts a new faith, alien to what has been handed to us together, they can walk apart....No Church can ignore the teaching of the Bible with impunity, and no Church is beyond discipline." Giving weight to his statements, his Nigerian church was both numerous and growing rapidly, from 5 million members in the 1970s to around 21 million today, and a projected 35 million by 2025 or so. Statistically, the Nigerian church should properly be counted as the heart of Anglican Christianity. In 1979 this church had sixteen dioceses, organized in a single province; today it has over 120 dioceses, organized in ten provinces. In 1979 Nigeria had a single archbishop; today it has ten, overseeing a whole national hierarchy.[24]

As in 1998, Northern-world Anglicans reacted bitterly to African and Asian attacks, which were attributed variously to invincible African ignorance and Akinola's personal ambition. But the opposition went far beyond Akinola. The conservative movement mobilized such distinguished African leaders as Kenya's David Gitari, a heroic opponent of that nation's dictatorial regime, as well as Rwandan archbishop Emmanuel Kolini, and Henry Orombi, primate of the 12-million strong Ugandan church. As Orombi said, "There is a tradition on human sexuality that was passed to us by the apostles, and if we're an apostolic church, how come the Episcopal Church claims they are better than St. Paul? Why do they turn their back on the faith their grandparents brought to us?"[25]

Over the past decade, Anglican leaders have been involved in a desperate attempt to avoid a total North–South schism. In 2004 the Eames Commission produced the so-called Windsor Report, which tried to forge some kind of reconciliation, though facing the dilemma that little compromise is possible between the two positions of consecrating or not consecrating overtly gay bishops. In calling for North–South toleration and reciprocal apologies, the Commissioners missed the point that African leaders saw the recent decisions of the North Atlantic churches as going far beyond merely controversial or ill-advised. If implemented (in their view) these decisions would literally end the fully Christian status of the Anglican churches of Britain and North America. On the other side of the debate, supporters of full gay inclusion in the churches felt just as strongly that any form of exclusion or limitation was itself a denial of Christian principles of equality and liberation. Absolutes collided.[26]

Factions grew farther apart, until by 2005 Akinola was presiding over a convention of global South Anglicans that represented some two-thirds of the planetary total. Meeting in Egypt, they consciously invoked the ancient African heritage of Christian learning and activism associated with that land. Such precedents gave special force to the group's resolution of hemispheric solidarity and orthodoxy:

We reject the expectation that our lives in Christ should conform to the misguided theological, cultural and sociological norms associated with sections of the West.... The unscriptural innovations of North American and some western provinces on issues of human sexuality undermine the basic message of redemption and the power of the Cross to transform lives. These departures are a symptom of a deeper problem, which is the diminution of the authority of Holy Scripture.

As North–South debates intensified, Akinola pronounced an obituary: "Let there be no illusions. The Communion is broken and fragmented. The Communion will break."[27] When the worldwide Anglican Communion met for its 2008 Lambeth conference, at least 200 of the 880 bishops boycotted the event because the church had not sufficiently condemned ECUSA. Conservatives gathered for a Global Anglican Future Conference (GAFCON), which looked uncomfortably like an alternative Lambeth. The diplomacy of archbishop of Canterbury Rowan Williams prevented Lambeth 2008 from degenerating into an open global fracture, but time was against him.

In the United States itself, the two moral positions clashed repeatedly at the Episcopal church's triennial conventions. The 2006 gathering voted to accept the Windsor Report in principle, encouraging leaders to "exercise restraint" before approving openly gay bishops. However, liberal U.S. dioceses made it clear that they would resist or ignore the nonbinding recommendation, which was in any case meant only as a stopgap, rather than a repudiation of past policies. Aggravating tensions, the U.S. church chose as its new presiding bishop a woman, Katharine Jefferts Schori, at a time when few global South churches acknowledge female bishops. When ECUSA gathered anew for its 2009 convention, it ended the moratorium on gay ordinations. In 2010, the diocese of Los Angeles consecrated openly lesbian Mary Glasspool as suffragan bishop.[28]

Schism now seems all but certain. Rowan Williams shocked American liberals when he suggested creating a two-tier system within the Anglican Communion, in which churches like ECUSA that followed practices rejected by the wider Communion would possess only "associate" rather than full membership. Following the Glasspool affair, Williams suspended the U.S. church from participating in ecumenical negotiations. Yet even this response to ECUSA was not enough for the Nigerians, who had long argued that "A cancerous lump in the body should be excised if it has defied every known cure."[29]

One ironic moment in the saga came when U.S. presiding bishop Katharine Jefferts Schori invoked the C-word: colonialism. Rejecting attempts by the wider communion to impose their solutions on her church, she protested that such efforts threatened to repeat the "spiritual violence" of colonial missionaries at the height of British imperialism. "We live in great concern that colonial attitudes continue, particularly in attempts to impose a single understanding across widely varying contexts and cultures." On this occasion of course, the alleged colonialism was directed from Africa toward North America.[30]

When the world's Anglican prelates gather at the next Lambeth conference in 2018, it is far from certain who will participate. Quite conceivably, by that point, the rest of the Anglican world will no longer recognize ECUSA's credentials. Such an open schism would represent the first such break between Northern and Southern components of a major denomination; but quite possibly, not the last. If these disputes roiled only the Anglican Communion, that would be a matter of limited interest, but as we will see, similar issues of gender and sexuality have also surfaced in other churches, among Lutherans, Methodists, and Presbyterians. In years to come, similar feuds might conceivably arise among Roman Catholics, and at some point, perhaps it will be liberals who will secede from a conservative-dominated global church.

SOUTHERN ALLIES

The moral and sexual conservatism of Southern believers is music to the ears of North Americans or Europeans who find themselves at odds with the progressive leaderships of their own churches. When they suffer an ideological defeat at home—when for instance a new denomination approves same-sex marriages—conservatives are tempted to look South and to say, in effect, "Just you wait." History is on the side of the Southern churches, which will not tolerate this nonsense. These observers echo the hopes of George Canning, the British statesman who looked at the newly independent Latin America of the 1820s and declared that "I called the New World into existence to redress the balance of the old." Finding Southern allies is doubly precious for traditionalists, since conservative positions stand a much better chance of gaining a hearing in the mainstream media when they are presented by African or Asian religious leaders rather than the familiar roster of white conservatives. Also, Northern traditionalists are tempted to believe that the tides of history are clearly running their way. As old liberal mainline churches lose their influence in the face of changing world demographics, so their progressive ideas are expected to fade along with them.

But Northern-world conservatives have not been content to wait for the currents of history, and some have sought to use like-minded Southern churches for their own purposes. In 2000 some conservative Episcopalians took a step that was remarkable enough at the time, and would have been shocking only a few years earlier. Two (white) American clergy traveled to Singapore where they were ordained as bishops by conservative archbishops Tay and Kolini, assisted by several other African and American clerics. By ancient tradition, an archbishop is free to ordain whoever he pleases within his province, so that one of the U.S. dissidents legally became a bishop within the province of Rwanda. In addition, though, these Americans assumed a controversial new role within North America. They effectively became missionary bishops charged to minister to conservative congregations, where they would support a dissident "virtual province" within the church. They, and their conservative colleagues, became part of the Anglican Mission in America (AMIA). This grouping aspired to help "lead the Episcopal Church back to its biblical foundations," to restore traditional teachings on issues such as the ordination of gay clergy, and blessing same-sex marriages: in short, to combat the "manifest heresy" of the ECUSA leadership.[31]

The established hierarchies of North America were predictably hostile, but the AMIA strategy gathered momentum as other disaffected conservatives found themselves much closer politically to the upstart churches of Africa and Asia than to their own church elites. Conservative Anglicans have placed themselves under global South prelates, as they look to Singapore and Rwanda, Nigeria or Uganda, to defend themselves against New York and Ottawa. Others turn to the Province of the Latin American Southern Cone, as priests resident in Baltimore or Philadelphia notionally serve the Anglican Church of Chile or Bolivia. African and Asian prelates are now a familiar sight at U.S. Anglican gatherings, as conservatives seek alliances with orthodox and traditional believers across the ecclesiastical spectrum. As the use of the Anglican term suggests, conservatives seek to place their own views in the global context, rather than merely using the local American term "Episcopal."

Since 2003 the conservative wing of the Episcopal church has been in ferment, with an upsurge of new networks and pressure groups. In 2009, most of the breakaway groups came together in a new Anglican Church in North America (ACNA), which sought to displace ECUSA as the globally recognized manifestation of Anglicanism in the United States. ACNA won recognition from the Anglican primates of such key global South jurisdictions as Nigeria, Rwanda, Uganda, and Kenya. The Episcopal church mainstream now has around two million members in the United States, down significantly from a peak of 3.5 million in the 1960s, while the dissident Anglicans attract about a hundred thousand followers.[32]

Dissidents face major obstacles in their attempts to detach a substantial number of believers from ECUSA. Partly, this is a matter of legality. People are free to join or leave any religious denomination, but in most cases, Episcopal dioceses ensure that the church facilities are the property of the diocese and cannot be separated from that jurisdiction, even if the entire body of clergy and faithful in a particular parish fervently wish to do so. Some dissident parishes have been able to get around these restrictions and are able to take buildings and assets with them when they secede, and courts occasionally support them. In most instances, though, the property stays with ECUSA. This poses an agonizing choice for conservative believers, especially those in older parishes, where families might have several generations of ancestors buried in a churchyard. However much they may dislike the directions taken by ECUSA, it takes enormous willpower to abandon a cherished and stately church building to begin a new congregation worshipping in a high school gymnasium. Furthermore, new Anglican groupings often have an evangelical or charismatic tone, which is uncongenial for traditionalists of liturgical leanings. For many reasons then, the widespread unhappiness of many Episcopalians with the ultraliberalism of their leadership is unlikely to translate into a large-scale schism within North America.

Even so, the existence of AMIA, ACNA, and other conservative breakaways is in itself a remarkable statement of changing perceptions of Christian orthodoxy and the geographical bases of authority within the church. For many conservative American believers, orthodoxy travels from the South to the North. After a visit to his distant archdiocesan home in Africa, one AMIA cleric asked wonderingly, "Who should be missionaries to whom?"[33] For many, that question is now thoroughly settled.

Nor, as noted earlier, are the Anglicans unique in seeking to turn the ecclesiastical world upside down. The United Methodist church for instance has around eleven million members, and until recently it was clearly based in North America. In the last twenty years, though, the African share of membership has grown from a tiny fraction to a sizable minority, with expansion in Nigeria, the Congo, and Liberia, and by the 2020s Africans may constitute a majority. That change has its political impact. In 2004, overseas members made up 20 percent of the United Methodist General Conference, and that number should swell to 40 percent by 2012.

Overwhelmingly, these overseas delegates are far more conservative than Americans on morality issues, and that attitude acts as a brake on liberal tendencies within the church.[34]

The closest present-day analogy to Anglican circumstances occurs among the world's Lutherans, another church that originated in Northern Europe, but which now finds its chief centers of growth in Africa and Asia. Although Lutherans claim 70 million members worldwide, a large proportion of these are at best nominal adherents of the historic state churches of Scandinavia, Germany, and the Baltic states, and these bodies are stagnant or declining. In contrast, membership is soaring in the upstart African churches, which together account for some 14 million Lutherans. One example of such growth is the Ethiopian Evangelical Church Mekane Yesus (EECMY), formed in 1959 with twenty thousand members. The church grew to over a million members by 1991, topped 5 million by 2008, and continues to boom. As a Lutheran church report notes, in a surprisingly matter of fact tone, the EECMY "has experienced a 15 percent per year growth rate for many years."[35]

As in the Anglican case, the Northern branches of the Lutheran denomination are very liberal and seek to enforce progressive views on conservative clergy. Those clergy in turn sought the help and protection of traditional-minded African prelates, such as Walter Obare Omwanza, presiding bishop of Kenya's Evangelical Lutheran Church. Bishop Obare denounced the Swedish church for practicing "a secular, intolerant, bureaucratic fundamentalism inimical to the word of God and familiar from various church struggles against totalitarian ideologies during the twentieth century." He attacked the ordination of women as "a Gnostic novelty," which "cannot tolerate even minimal co-existence with classical Christianity."[36]

In 2010, the Lutheran church of Tanzania made the wrenching decision to refuse all financial aid, financial and otherwise, from north European churches that allowed same-sex marriages. Given the extreme poverty of these East African churches, their decision indicates the extraordinary importance that they attach to these theological wars. As the Tanzanian church declared, "The ELCT accepts that moral values may change among people as their situations change; however, ELCT believers know and believe that there are some things that cannot change, such as people having noses, ears and mouths.... based on the teaching of the Word of God, there are values that cannot be adjusted even under the pressure of changing conditions and locations. One of these unwavering values concerns the issue of marriage and its meaning."[37]

YOUR BELIEFS ARE TOO YOUNG

We have heard much in the past few years about strife between the emerging churches of the South and the older established counterparts of the West, and the threat of schism. To illustrate the nature of this encounter, I will describe an actual conversation between a representative of a solid mainstream denomination and an upstart church from the newly evangelized world; although I admit that I am doctoring the quote by altering a couple of key words.

The mainstream cleric complains that "your beliefs are too young," suggesting that the new churches simply do not have the intellectual capacity to understand the sophisticated theological debates then roiling the advanced world. But the man from the emerging church stands his ground. He retorts that "all heresies have emanated from you, have flourished among you; by us, that is by the Southern nations, they have been here strangled, here put an end to." The new churches are the defenders of orthodoxy. The upstart cleric concedes the charge of youth and inexperience, which he holds out as a virtue. An ancient church, he replies, is a weary and decadent one, and has compromised with worldly wisdom. "Since you declare the faith of the Africans to be young, I quite agree with you; for always the faith of Christ is young.... Where faith is not accompanied by works, then faith is not young but old, and people make fun of it for its age, like an old worn-out garment."[38]

This dialogue occurred in Constantinople around 970 between a leading cleric of the Orthodox church, and the Western visitor, Liutprand of Cremona. In reality, Liutprand was defending Western nations, not Southern; and he boasted of the faith of the Germans, not the Africans. But the accusations between the two sides seem familiar today. The overly sophisticated Byzantines produced heresies, Western popes suppressed them: new churches are the defenders of orthodoxy. Liutprand also declared that "The race of the Saxons, from the time when it received the holy baptism and the knowledge of God, has been spotted by no heresy which would have rendered a synod necessary of an error which did not exist." Do I draw too improbable an analogy by applying this passage today, substituting for the defiant Liutprand an African or Chinese bishop; for the arrogant Byzantines an American or European?

As a coda to that story, we recall the decisive break between the churches, the still unhealed schism of 1054. Remarkably for such a vast event, its causes lay less in great issues of theology than in matters that seem culturally driven, more symbolic than substantial: the use of unleavened bread in the Eucharist, and whether priests should be clean shaven. In retrospect, most appear on a par with Gulliver's discovery of two nations divided over the proper way to open an egg—the big end or the small? But while priests' beards scarcely seem sufficient a cause to divide Christ's church, the incident reminds us of a powerful fact. Divisions that are "just cultural" are often the most deeply felt, especially when one party feels such a sense of grievance and historic exploitation.[39]

EVANGELIZING THE NORTH

In numerical terms, the schisms within the global denominations are still very much a fringe phenomenon, but might they be an early sign of a much larger trend? Are we likely to see global South Christians actually converting or re-Christianizing the North—again, particularly in Europe? Even today, some denominations draw upon the burgeoning spiritual resources of the South. Within the Roman Catholic Church, Northern dioceses are increasingly likely to use priests from lands in Africa, Asia, or Latin America, which are still fertile ground for vocations. About one-sixth of the priests currently serving in American parishes, some 7,600 men, are foreign born, with roots in Mexico, Nigeria, India, Vietnam, and the Philippines, as well as Poland. One-third of U.S. seminarians studying for the priesthood are foreign born. The Los Angeles diocese alone has almost four hundred foreign-born priests, New York and Newark combined have five hundred. African priests are appearing across Europe, including—of all places—Ireland, that ancient nursery of Catholic devotion. Remarking on this phenomenon, an Irish friend recalled how as a child she had collected pennies to "save black babies in Africa." She wondered whether some of these babies might have grown up to save Irish souls in recompense.

Immigrant communities in Northern lands themselves are also becoming important resources. Although Asians and Pacific Islanders make up only 2 percent of U.S. Catholics, they now provide more than 12 percent of the men currently studying for the priesthood, and a sizable majority of these are Vietnamese. At St. Patrick's Seminary in northern California, Asians make up 43 percent of the candidates for priesthood. One Vietnamese American priest evokes an earlier age of Catholic enthusiasm when he notes that "If you go to a Vietnamese parish and ask people, would they prefer that their son be the president, a doctor or a priest, they would say, 'A priest.' It is seen as a blessing from God for the family." Of the seminarians ordained in the United States in 2001, 28 percent were born outside the country, 5 percent in Mexico, 5 percent more in Vietnam.[40]

In Protestant denominations too, Southerners are increasingly visible as clergy and as actual missionaries. We have already noted the elevation of Ugandan John Sentamu to the historic Anglican see of York, while other Africans and Asians are deeply committed to evangelizing the global North. Archbishop Akinola observes that "If a fire is not burning, then it is no longer fire. If the Church is not evangelizing, then it is like a dead fire." Great Britain today plays host to some fifteen hundred missionaries from fifty nations, and many express disbelief at the spiritual desert they encounter in this "green and pagan land." To quote Stephen Tirwomwe, a Ugandan missionary active in the rust-belt north of England: "It was so depressing when I first arrived to find churches empty, and being sold, when in Uganda there is not enough room in our churches for the people. There is a great need for revival in Britain—it has become so secular and people are so inward-looking and individualistic. The country needs reconverting." Announcing a new missionary endeavor, the Anglican primate of Brazil declared that "London is today's field of mission. It's so secular we have to send people for their salvation."[41]

These particular clerics come from the Anglican tradition, but the independent churches are now beginning to take the lead in evangelism across Europe. Reading their New Testaments, African and Asian Christians encounter the Great Commission that instructs followers to go and make disciples of all nations. They take their claims to catholicity seriously. One active missionary body is the Nigerian-based Redeemed Christian Church of God (RCCG), founded in 1952: its prophetic founder was a veteran of the Cherubim and Seraphim church, part of the Aladura movement. Its core beliefs include "biblical inerrancy, the power of the Holy Spirit, divine healing and prophecy." The RCCG has a strong missionary outreach: its statement of beliefs declares that

> It is our goal to make heaven. It is our goal to take as many people as possible with us....In order to take as many people with us as possible, we will plant churches within five minutes walking distance in every city and town of developing countries; and within five minutes driving distance in every city and town of developed countries.[42]

Since 1981, the RCCG boasts that

> an open explosion began with the number of parishes growing in leaps and bounds. At the last count, there are at least about four thousand

parishes of the Redeemed Christian Church of God in Nigeria. On the international scene, the church is present in other African nations including Côte D'Ivoire, Ghana, Zambia, Malawi, Zaire, Tanzania, Kenya, Uganda, Gambia, Cameroon, and South Africa. In Europe the church is spread in England, Germany, and France.

It is also active in the United States, Haiti, and Jamaica. It aspires "to have home cells in all countries in the northern part (Islamic) of Africa." As the church proclaims, this global presence "is obviously in fulfillment of the vision that had been given to the founder Papa Akindayomi, that this church would spread to cover the whole earth, and that it would be a viable part of the body of Christ that the Savior would meet here when He returns."[43]

Usually, such independents attract little attention from the media unless they become the focus of scandal, which they do periodically. The Brazilian IURD is one of many bodies expanding its influence into Europe and North America, where it has purchased radio stations and real estate. Like the RCCG, this church too sees a rich potential harvest in the lands of the African diaspora, and the IURD operates missions in southern Africa. Similarly, the EJCSK, the Kimbanguist church, is active in Republic of Congo (Brazzaville), Congo Democratic (Kinshasa), Angola, Gabon, Central African Republic, Zambia, Zimbabwe, Rwanda, Burundi, South Africa, Nigeria, Madagascar, Spain, Portugal, France, Belgium, Switzerland, and England. "Many Kimbanguist faithful are over the world, in USA, in Canada and other countries." The Brazilian-based *Sal da Terra* (Salt of the Earth) church has missionaries in Britain, Ireland, Portugal, India, and Japan. Such internationally oriented churches use the Internet as a global recruiting tool. The pious surfer can investigate online the IURD, *Sal de Terra*, the RCCG, EJCSK, the Church of the Lord (Aladura), Celestial Church of Christ, Harrists, and dozens of other like bodies. Some, of course, are on Facebook.[44]

The IURD's notoriety distracts attention from the substantial achievements of independent churches on European soil, and from the strong likelihood that they will enjoy major growth. Conditions are ideal, in that most such churches suffer from no substantial language barrier, and they encounter very little competition or resistance from established bodies such as the Church of England. The language issue is important: unlike in North America, where the new churches will be overwhelmingly Spanish-speaking, their counterparts in Europe speak the languages of the old colonial powers, English in Britain, French in France and Belgium. Yoweri Museveni, long-serving president of Uganda, offers a nice image. He told a British conference that "When we were fighting in the bush, the regime in power got arms from abroad. Our job as guerrillas was simply to wait and grab those arms. You came to our countries and we captured your language. Here I am speaking to you in your own tribal language."[45] Independent churches use these captured languages as the basic tools of evangelism.

Immigrant churches are also crucial, and we have already seen how such congregations make up an ever larger proportion of Christian activity across Europe and Canada. Some are already contemplating outreach to host communities, as black and brown Christians evangelize whites. One successful evangelist is Sunday Adelaja, who in 1987 left his native Nigeria to travel to the USSR, part of the Soviet attempt to recruit bright Third World students to their cause. After the USSR collapsed, Adelaja settled in the Ukraine, where in 1992 he began a Pentecostal church that would become known as the Embassy of the Blessed Kingdom of God. Today, that church has perhaps thirty thousand followers, overwhelmingly Ukrainian or Russian, and represents a significant political force in the Ukraine. The church offers a charismatic and supernatural-oriented message, as followers claim to have been cured of cancer, AIDS, and to have been raised from the dead.[46]

Another Nigerian founded one of Britain's most successful black congregations, London's Kingsway International Christian Centre. Its chief pastor, Matthew Ashimolowo, launched a Breaking Barriers Crusade, with the specific goal of recruiting white members. As he remarked, white converts would feel restive among what he frankly described as "a sea of black faces," and he was anxious to create a hospitable environment. Initially, white recruits are uncomfortable with the worship style of an African or West Indian church, particularly since British culture is traditionally suspicious of public displays of religious enthusiasm. Echoing older missionary debates about cultural relevance, Pastor Ashimolowo complains that "The trouble is we are seen as a Black thing and not a God thing." New churches such as the KICC have to treat white habits and worldviews with due respect and sensitivity: to practice inculturation, in fact.[47]

How feasible is it that this church, or any of its counterparts, might succeed in "breaking barriers," in drawing large numbers of white Europeans into the world of African Christianity, as Sunday Adelaja has already done? Clearly, this question is enormously significant for the future direction of Christianity, at least in Europe. If they do not succeed, then the religion will increasingly be defined as something alien, suspicious, and even hostile.

As time goes by, moreover, Southern-style churches may well make inroads beyond the immigrant population, and into the white community. Particularly important as intermediaries are the steadily growing number of mixed-race people, who can be expected to draw friends and relatives into the churches. Latin American theologians are exactly right in seeing a pivotal role for such *mestizo* Christians. Just what these new Euro-African and Euro-Asian churches will look like in terms of liturgy and worship style is anybody's guess, but the process of interaction will be fascinating to watch.[48]

Matters should proceed very differently in the United States, since the country has never experienced the same kind of general secularization as Europe, and despite all its critics, American Christianity is very much alive and well. Even so, the country has been designated as mission territory by some Southern churches, which presently evangelize migrant populations. Both the Brazilian Assemblies of God and the IURD have missions in Los Angeles, and El Shaddai works among Filipino Americans. Boston offers a neatly symbolic juxtaposition, since an IURD storefront church stands just around the corner from the venerable Episcopalian cathedral.

Another recent example of missionary work involves the churches of the Argentine Revival, a Pentecostal movement that emerged during the social and political disasters that nation experienced during the early 1980s. The Argentine movement believes firmly in concepts of spiritual warfare against the demonic forces that pervade society, and its Lighthouses of Prayer are networks of believers who pray systematically for their neighbors. The Argentine Revival has also sought to evangelize in North America. In 1999 revivalist Carlos Annacondia preached to some twelve thousand Philadelphians in the city's first Latino-driven mass crusade.[49]

African churches have also targeted the United States and now have been spreading networks of congregations. The Church of the Pentecost, a major Ghanaian denomination, has fifty-seven churches in the United States, including five in New York City, where it serves "Francophone Africans, from Togo, Benin and Ivory Coast, as well as a smattering of Latinos and African-Americans."[50]

Particularly active have been Nigerian churches such as the Deeper Life Bible Fellowship, and with its eighty thousand Nigerian residents, the city of Houston plays a pivotal role in these schemes. The RCCG now has two hundred parishes in the United States, including operations in "Dallas, Tallahassee, Houston, New York, Washington, and Chicago, Atlanta, Detroit, Maryland, etc." One congregation, in Bowie, Maryland, claims two thousand members. The RCCG is currently building a splendid new

North American headquarters near Greenville, Texas, a town that in the early twentieth century boasted the motto of "The blackest land and the whitest people." In a facsimile of its Nigerian center, the proposed Texas complex would include "a large dormitory, a 10,000-seat sanctuary, an amphitheater, an artificial lake and perhaps even a modest water park."[51]

Another growing denomination is Christ Apostolic Church (CAC) that, like the RCCG, is rooted in the Aladura movement. According to the group's official history, its international outreach began in Ibadan, Nigeria, in 1979 when Prophet T. O. Obadare decided "to hold three days of fasting and prayer concerning the situation of Nigerians abroad. After the three-day revival, a lady prophesied for almost an hour concerning the same issue of Nigerians abroad. The prophet then went into an additional seven days of prayer and fasting concerning the issue." After forming a CAC church in London, Prophet Obadare moved to Houston in 1981, and then developed a network of congregations across the United States. Christ Apostolic Church of America has now developed congregations in New York, New Jersey, Baltimore, Washington, D.C., Birmingham (Alabama), Chicago, Houston, Dallas, Oklahoma City, and Los Angeles. These are distinct from a number of rival denominations that also claim to be the rightful inheritors of the true CAC tradition, such as Christ Apostolic Church Babalola.[52]

Although these newer churches might have a major impact on the United States, and particularly on urban communities, the many cultural differences make it unlikely that they will have anything like the transforming effect that we will likely see in Europe. Yet in the United States too, the coming decades should witness a wholly new phase of religious synthesis and hybridization, as immigrant communities Americanize. To take only one ethnic force, a United States with 100 million Latinos is very likely to have a far more Southern religious complexion than anything we can imagine at present.

SOUTHERN MIRRORS

Time and again, when European and American Christians look south, they see what they want to see. A generation ago, liberals saw their own views reflected by the rising masses of the Third World, marching toward socialism and liberation. Today, conservatives have the rosier view. On the basis of population alone, the Southern churches are indeed going to matter far more than they do now, but whether they will continue to have the same political and cultural tone is far from certain. As we have seen, it is likely that as the rising churches mature, their social positions will become quite as diverse as those of their Northern counterparts. Who knows, as Southern societies change, perhaps some of their churches too will someday favor ordaining women and even blessing gay marriages. If a single lesson emerges from all the recent scholarship on the rising churches, it is that they define themselves according to their own standards, despite all the eager efforts to shape them in the mold of the Old Christendom.

TEN

Seeing Christianity Again for the First Time

> One of the games to which [the human race] is most
> attached is called "Keep tomorrow dark," and which is
> also named... "Cheat the prophet." The players listen
> very carefully and respectfully to all that clever men
> have to say about what is to happen in the next
> generation. The players then wait until all the clever
> men are dead, and bury them nicely. They then go and
> do something else. That is all. For a race of simple
> tastes, however, it is great fun.
>
> —*G. K. Chesterton*, The Napoleon of Notting Hill

If only we had known.... Attempts to forecast the future usually derive
from more than just intellectual curiosity. Ideally, knowing what is
going to happen should better equip us to deal with it, to prevent
things we dread. The problem with this approach is that sometimes things
that are predicted just do not occur; more frequently they do indeed happen but in forms quite different from what anyone expected. In the case of
the southward movement of Christianity, we can be quite sure that the
event will occur, but interpreting it or preparing for it is quite a different
matter. Does our knowledge of future trends allow us to form any appropriate responses? Although precious little can perhaps be done in terms of
practical policy, looking at the ways Christianity is now developing tells us
a great deal about the essence of the religion. Considering possible futures
is so valuable because it can tell us so much about the realities of the present day.

Let us for a moment assume the impossible, that a wormhole in time
opened long enough to give us access to something like the *World Christian
Encyclopedia* for the year 2050, complete with detailed population tables
of Christian communities worldwide at that future date. Logically, such a
treasure would be of huge value for Christian churches in knowing where
to allocate resources, how to invest people and funds in particular cities or

regions, with the goal of getting in on the ground floor of future population growth. If we knew that a given Asian city that currently had just 500,000 people was going to swell to 20 million by midcentury, that would present a wonderful opportunity to serve the needy.

In worldly terms, too, such an investment would pay rich returns. If churches established themselves there now, established the kernel of future social services and community networks, then they would be ideally placed to dominate the religious economy of that burgeoning region. People who turned to that church for food and help would be likely to be loyal members of its congregation, and would build the denomination. In an age of competition between faiths, such a farsighted policy would be an enormous advantage. In an ideal world, Christians and Muslims, Catholics and Pentecostals would be engaged in a friendly rivalry as to who could best help the poor, without thought of who was gaining the greatest numbers and influence. This is, however, not an ideal world.

Wormholes may or may not exist, but we do already have much of the information that we would hope to garner from an encyclopedia visited on us from the future. Take the example of the cities that will be growing rapidly; we know today where many of these places are going to be, and where an investment of resources could pay off spectacularly. Barring catastrophe, nothing is going to stop African cities such as Nairobi, Dar es Salaam, Kinshasa, and Kampala from becoming even larger goliaths than they are presently or from absorbing millions more uprooted rural people. All exist in countries with minimal social service networks, and each stands in a region of lively religious competition. The faith or denomination that builds there today is very likely to be profiting richly in a decade or two. Generally, though, they are not doing this building, nor to anything like the degree we might expect. Why would anyone fail to respond to such obvious future trends?

Of course, some groups are indeed developing a presence across the future centers of growth, but equally striking are the ones that are not. For all their vast wealth, many churches in North America and Europe have far less interest or commitment in the global South than they once had. American mainline churches have dramatically cut back on their budgets for missions. In large measure, this represents a response to charges of cultural imperialism in bygone years, and a guilty sense that there was much justice to the conventional stereotypes of missionary work. Also, Western congregations feel reluctant to interfere in the domains of new native churches, which, they believe, should be allowed to stand on their own feet. For whatever reason, Western investment in missions has been cut back dramatically at just the point it is most desperately needed, at the peak of the current surge in Christian numbers.

Some Western churches do not wish to respond to the new global challenges. Others, though, are simply unable, because churches face rival demands on scarce resources. This is well illustrated by the Roman Catholic Church, which globally faces severe challenges from other denominations, and other faiths. Logically, the church should be responding by reallocating clergy to the regions of greatest need. In practice, the Catholic tradition is highly dependent on its clergy, and the church is strongest where its priests and religious are ablest and most numerous. Unfortunately, though, the church faces a massive and growing imbalance between the Catholic faithful and their pastors. Though we can understand the historical circumstances that have led to this situation, it almost seems as if the church has scientifically allocated its available resources to create the minimum possible correlation between priests and the communities that need them most. The Devil himself could scarcely have planned it better. The Catholic example illustrates how badly the North is failing to respond to changing global realities and to the structural reasons why the situation is unlikely to change.

In this matter, as in so many others, the North–South imbalance is quite stark. The Northern world, Europe and North America, presently accounts for 35 percent of Catholic believers and 68 percent of priests; Latin America has 42 percent of believers but only 20 percent of the priests. In terms of the ratio of priests to faithful, the Northern world is four times better supplied with clergy than the global South. To understand what these figures mean, we should recall the endless complaints about priest shortages in Europe and the United States, and the dreadful consequences for parish life. Now imagine conditions elsewhere in the world, where priests are in far shorter supply. While the ratio of priests to faithful is about one to 1,600 in the United States, the corresponding figure for Mexico is one to 6,400; in Brazil and the Philippines, it is 1 to 8,400. If the North American priest shortage really is such a disaster as many argue, how can we begin to describe the situation in the South? It is scarcely surprising that the Vatican is so alarmed by evangelical inroads into the ill-shepherded Catholic faithful, or that they see Protestant conversions in terms of sectarian wolves preying on vulnerable believers.

The lack of priests is enormously damaging for Catholicism across Latin America. In Brazil, Protestant pastors already outnumbered priests by the mid-1980s, and today they outnumber priests two to one. Some Brazilian Catholic parishes notionally have fifty thousand members. Among Mexican

Protestants, meanwhile, the customary ratio of pastors to believers is 1 to 250, making them far more accessible than Catholic clergy, some of whom might notionally have fifty villages under their care. In practice, the Latin American churches would collapse without its devoted network of lay catechists, who so rarely receive the praise they deserve.[1]

In Africa, too, the church has over the last fifty years enjoyed probably the most rapid numerical expansion in its whole history, but the clergy shortage raises questions about how long this boom can be sustained. Some Nigerian dioceses have only one priest for every eight thousand Catholics. The scale of the problem becomes obvious when we compare the European situation. Europe as a whole has one priest for every 1,450 Catholics; the African ratio is 1:4,700. To put the issue in sharper focus, compare the ancient Catholic land of Italy with the rising church of the Congo. Italy's 57 million Catholics are served by 26,000 parishes, giving an average of 2,200 of the faithful for each parish. With 33 million believers, the Congo has just 1,300 parishes, an average of 25,000 Catholics per parish. For the church hierarchy, this issue of resource distribution is far more immediately pressing than any social or theological controversies.

It is widely recognized that a severe problem exists, solutions, however, are by no means obvious. It is inconceivable that Northern bishops might seek global equity by shipping half their priests off to the Third World—though the prospect has probably crossed the mind of many a prelate troubled by an obstreperous cleric under his authority. Amazingly enough, the main steps taken so far to remedy priest shortages have been entirely in the opposite direction, namely in importing Third World priests in order to meet shortfalls in North America and Europe. Viewed in a global perspective, such a policy can be described at best as painfully shortsighted, at worst as suicidal for Catholic fortunes. If even an organization as centralized and as globally minded as the Catholic church cannot mobilize its resources to meet the emerging challenges and opportunities of the global South, what hope is there for any other body?

SEEING CHRISTIANITY AGAIN

Even if we are exactly right in all our predictions, knowing something about the future of Christianity may or may not help any particular church or group to do anything practical to prepare for that future. Still, it might do a great deal in understanding the present and acting accordingly. If there is one thing we can reliably predict about the next half-century, it is that an increasing share of the world's people is going to identify with one of two religions, either Christianity or Islam, and the two have a long and disastrous record of conflict and mutual incomprehension. For the sake of both religion and politics, and perhaps of simple planetary survival, it is vitally necessary for Christian and Jewish Northerners to gain a better understanding of Islam. But odd as it may sound, perhaps the more pressing need is to appreciate that other religious giant, the strangely unfamiliar world of the new Christianities of the global South. The Third Church is not just a transplanted version of the familiar religion of the older Christian states; the New Christendom is no mirror image of the Old. It is a truly new and developing entity—just how different from its predecessor remains to be seen.

Studying Christianity in a predominantly Christian society can pose surprising difficulties. I teach in a religious studies program, which like most of its counterparts in universities across the United States, introduces students to the global dimensions of religious experience. In practice, that means providing a wide range of courses on the World Religions, such as Islam, Buddhism, and so on. The main religion that tends to suffer in this package is Christianity, which receives nothing like the attention it merits in terms of its numbers and global scale. Whatever the value of Christian claims to truth, it cannot be considered as just one religion out of many; it is, and will continue to be, by far the largest in existence. A generation ago, the neglect of Christianity in academic teaching made more sense than it does today, in that students could be expected to absorb information about the faith from churches, families, or from society at large. Today, though, that is often not a realistic expectation, and one encounters dazzling levels of ignorance about the basic facts of the religion.

If Christianity as such receives short shrift, the situation is still worse when it comes to the religion outside the West. Until just a few years ago, textbooks discussed the faith in Africa and Asia chiefly in negative ways, in the context of genocide, slavery, and imperialism, and autonomous Southern Christian voices were rarely heard. Fortunately, this situation is now changing, with the appearance of solid textbooks that seek to provide truly global coverage, but much still remains to be done. Given the present and future distribution of Christians worldwide, a case can be made that understanding the religion in its non-Western context is a prime necessity for anyone seeking to understand the emerging world. American universities prize the goal of diversity in their teaching, introducing students to the thought-ways of Africa, Asia, and Latin America, often by using texts from non-Western cultures. However strange this may sound in terms of conventional stereotypes, teaching about Christianity would be a wonderful way to teach diversity, all the more so now that non-Western religion is returning to its roots. Imagine teaching a course on globalization based wholly on Christian sources from around the global South, on novels and memoirs, feature films and documentaries.

But such a project would face real obstacles, because of the kind of religious life to be explored. Significantly, few religious studies departments in public universities offer courses in Pentecostalism, as compared with the substantial numbers teaching on Buddhism or Islam. Partly, this reflects political prejudices. At least in the humanities, most academics are strongly liberal and take a dim view of Pentecostalism and fundamentalism. And while colleges do discuss Catholicism, the issues involved in these courses are very much those of interest in the West, rather than the lived realities of Catholic practice in Latin America or Africa.

Considering Christianity as a global reality can make us see the whole religion in a radically new perspective, which is both startling and, often, uncomfortable. In fact, to adapt a phrase coined by theologian Marcus Borg, it is as if we are seeing Christianity again for the first time.[2] In this encounter, we are forced to see the religion not just for what it is but what it was in its origins—and what it is going to be in future. To take one aspect of these startling rediscoveries, consider Christianity's deep association with poverty. Contrary to myth, the typical Christian is not a white fat cat in the United States or western Europe, but rather a poor person, often unimaginably poor by Western standards.

The grim fact of Christian impoverishment becomes all the more true as Africa assumes its place as the religion's principal center. We are dealing with a continent that has endured countless disasters since independence, measured by statistics that become wearying by their unrelieved horror, whether we are looking at life expectancy, child mortality, or deaths from AIDS. Africa contributes less than 2 percent of the world's total GDP, though it is home to 13 percent of world population, and the GDP for the whole of sub-Saharan Africa is equivalent to that of the Netherlands. Overall, "the continent is slipping out of the Third World into its own bleak category of the nth World." Matters are made infinitely worse by the unraveling of several African states, a process attended by severe bloodshed. The U.S. intelligence community sees no chance of improvement in the foreseeable future: "In Sub-Saharan Africa, persistent conflicts and instability, autocratic and corrupt governments, overdependence on commodities with declining real prices, low levels of education, and widespread infectious diseases will combine to prevent most countries from experiencing rapid economic growth."[3] That is the underlying reality for the Christian masses of the present and near-future.

Of course, by no means all Christians in the global South fall into the category of the poor, and enthusiastic kinds of Christianity are succeeding among professional and technologically oriented groups, notably around the Pacific Rim, and in the United States itself. But for the foreseeable future, deep poverty does characterize the lives of many millions of Christians in Africa, Asia, and Latin America. These are people for whom the New Testament Beatitudes have a direct relevance inconceivable for most Christians in Northern societies. When Jesus told the "poor" they were blessed, the word used does not imply relative deprivation, it means total poverty, or destitution. A majority of global South Christians (and increasingly, of all Christians) really are the poor, the hungry, the persecuted, even the dehumanized. India has a perfect translation for Jesus's word in the term *Dalit*, literally "crushed" or "oppressed." This is how that country's so-called Untouchables now choose to describe themselves: as we might translate the biblical phrase, blessed are the untouchables.

Knowing all this should ideally have policy consequences, which are at least as urgent as redistributing church resources to meet the needs of shifting populations. Above all, the disastrous lot of so many Christians worldwide places urgent pressure on the wealthy societies to assist the poor. Thirty years ago, Ronald J. Sider published the influential book *Rich Christians in an Age of Hunger*, which attacked First World hypocrisy in the face of the grinding poverty of the global South. The book could easily be republished today with the still more pointed title *Rich Christians in an Age of Hungry Christians*, and the fact of religious kinship adds enormously to Sider's indictment.[4] When American Christians see the images of starvation from Africa, like the hellish visions from Ethiopia in the 1980s, or the Congo at the start of this century, few realize that the victims involved share not just a common humanity but in many cases the same religion. Those are Christians starving to death.

THE BIBLE IN THE SOUTH

Looking at Southern Christianities gives a surprising new perspective on some other things that might seem to be very familiar. Perhaps the most striking example is how the newer churches can read the Bible in a way that makes that Christianity look like a wholly different religion from the faith of prosperous advanced societies of Europe or North America. We have already seen that many global South churches are quite at home with biblical notions of the supernatural, with ideas such as dreams and prophecy. Just as relevant in their eyes are that book's core social and political themes, themes of martyrdom, oppression, and exile. In the present day, it may be that it is only in the newer churches that the Bible can be read with any authenticity and immediacy, and that the Old Christendom should listen attentively to Southern voices.[5]

When we read the New Testament, so many of the basic assumptions seem just as alien in the global North as they do normal and familiar in the South. When Jesus was not talking about exorcism and healing, his recorded words devoted what today seems like an inordinate amount of attention to issues of persecution and martyrdom. He talked about what believers should do when on trial for the faith, how to respond when they are expelled and condemned by families, by villages, and by Jewish religious authorities. A large proportion of the Bible, both Old and New Testaments, addresses the sufferings of God's people in the face of evil secular authorities.

As an intellectual exercise, modern Westerners can understand the historical circumstances that led to this emphasis on bloodshed and confrontation, but the passages concerned have little current relevance. Nor, for many, do the apocalyptic writings that are so closely linked to the theme of persecution and martyrdom, the visions of a coming world in which God will rule, persecutors will perish, and the righteous be vindicated. In recent decades, some New Testament scholars have tried to undermine the emphasis on martyrdom and apocalyptic in the New Testament by suggesting that these ideas did not come from Jesus's mouth, but were rather attributed to him by later generations. The real Jesus, in this view, was a rational Wisdom teacher much more akin to modern Western tastes, a kind of academic gadfly, rather than the ferocious Doomsday Jesus of the Synoptic Gospels. From this perspective, Jesus's authentic views are reflected in mystical texts such as the *Gospel of Thomas*. For radical critics, *Thomas* has a much better claim to be included in a revised New Testament than the book of Revelation, which is seen as a pernicious distortion of Christian truth.

For the average Western audience, New Testament passages about standing firm in the face of pagan persecution have little immediate relevance, about as much perhaps as farmyard images of threshing or vine-grafting. Some fundamentalists imagine that the persecutions described might have some future reality, perhaps during the End Times. But for many Southern Christians, there is no such need to dig for arcane meanings.

We're not exposed to brokenness that is called in the Gospel.

274   THE NEXT CHRISTENDOM

Millions of Christians around the world do in fact live in constant danger of persecution or forced conversion, either from governments or local vigilantes. For modern Christians in Nigeria, Egypt, India, or Indonesia, it is quite conceivable that they might someday find themselves before a tribunal that would demand that they renounce their faith upon pain of death.[6]

Q why me? In these varied situations, ordinary believers are forced to understand why they are facing these sufferings, and repeatedly they do so in the familiar language of the Bible and of the earliest Christianity. To quote one Christian in Maluku, massacres and expulsions in that region are "according to God's plan. Christians are under purification from the Lord." The church in Sudan, surviving in spite of savage religious repression, integrated its sufferings into its liturgy and daily practice, and produced some moving literature in the process ("Death has come to reveal the faith / It has begun with us and it will end with us").[7] Churches everywhere preach death and resurrection, but nowhere else are these realities such an immediate prospect. As in several other crisis regions, the oppressors in Sudan were Muslim, but elsewhere they might be Christians of other denominations. In Guatemala or Rwanda, as in the Sudan, martyrdom is not merely a subject for historical research, it is a real prospect, and the situation is likely to get worse rather than better.

Persecution is not confined to nations in such a state of extreme violence. Even in situations when actual violence might not have occurred for months or years, there is a pervasive sense of threat, a need to be alert and avoid provocations. Hundreds of millions of Christians live in deeply divided societies, constantly needing to be acutely aware of their relationships with Muslim or Hindu neighbors. Unlike the West, difficulties in interfaith relations in these settings do not just raise the danger of some angry letters to local newspapers but might well lead to bloodshed and massacre. In these societies, New Testament warnings about humility and discretion are not just laudable Christian virtues; they can make the difference between life and death.

Just as relevant to current concerns is exile, forcible removal from one's homeland, which forms the subject of so much of the Hebrew Bible. About half the refugees in the world today are in Africa, and millions of these are Christian. The wars that swept over the Congo and central Africa from the mid-1990s were devastating in uprooting communities. Often it is the churches that provide the refugees with cohesion and community, and offers them hope, so that exile and return acquire powerfully religious symbolism. Themes of exile and return also exercise a powerful appeal for those removed voluntarily from their homelands, the tens of millions of migrant workers who have sought better lives in the richer lands.[8]

Read against the background of martyrdom and exile, it is not surprising that so many Christians look for promises that their sufferings are only temporary, and that God will intervene directly to save the situation. In this context, the book of Revelation looks like true prophecy on an epic scale, however unpopular or discredited it may be for most Americans or Europeans. In the South, Revelation simply makes sense, in its description of a world ruled by monstrous demonic powers. These forces might be literal servants of Satan or symbols for evil social forces, but in either case, they are indisputably real. To quote one Latin American liberation theologian, Néstor Míguez, "The repulsive spirits of violence, racial hatred, mutilation, and exploitation roam the streets of our Babylons in Latin America (and the globe); their presence is clear once one looks behind the glimmering lights of the neon signs."[9]

Making the biblical text sound even more relevant to modern Third World Christians, the evils described in Revelation are distinctively urban. Then as now, evil sets up its throne in cities. Brazilian scholar Gilberto da Silva Gorgulho remarks that "The Book of Revelation is the favorite book of our popular communities. Here they find the encouragement they need in their struggle and a criterion for the interpretation of official persecution in our society....The meaning of the church in history is rooted in the witness of the gospel before the state imperialism that destroys the people's life, looming as an idol and caricature of the Holy Trinity."[10] To a Christian living in a Third World dictatorship, the image of the government as Antichrist is not a bizarre religious fantasy but a convincing piece of political analysis. Looking at Christianity as a planetary phenomenon, not merely a Western one, makes it impossible to read the New Testament in quite the same way ever again. And the Christianity we see through this exercise looks like a very exotic beast indeed, intriguing, exciting, and a little frightening.

Christianity is flourishing wonderfully among the poor and persecuted, while it atrophies among the rich and secure. Using the traditional Marxist view of religion as the opium of the masses, it would be tempting to draw the conclusion that the religion actually does have a connection to underdevelopment and premodern cultural ways, and will disappear as society progresses. That conclusion would be fatuous, though, given the continuing appeal of Christianity to upwardly mobile groups around the world. Yet the distribution of modern Christians might well show that the religion does succeed best when it takes very seriously the profound pessimism about the secular world that characterizes the New Testament. If it is not exactly a faith based on the experience of poverty and persecution, then at least it regards these things as normal and expected elements of life. That view is not derived from complex theological reasoning but is rather a lesson drawn from lived experience. Christianity certainly can succeed in other settings, even amid peace and prosperity, but perhaps it does become harder, as hard as passing through the eye of a needle.[11]

A healthy distrust of worldly power and success is all the more necessary given the remarkable reversals of Christian fortunes over the ages, and the number of times that the faith seemed on the verge of destruction. In the year 500, Christianity was the religion of empire and domination; in 1000, it was the stubborn faith of exploited subject peoples, or of barbarians on the irrelevant fringes of the great civilizations; while in 1900, Christian powers ruled the world. Knowing what the situation will be in 2100 or 2500 would take a truly inspired prophet. But if there is one overarching lesson from this record of changing fortunes, it is that (to adapt the famous adage about Russia), Christianity is never as weak as it appears, nor as strong as it appears.[12] And whether we look backward or forward in history, we can see that time and again, Christianity demonstrates a breathtaking ability to transform weakness into strength.

NOTES

ABBREVIATIONS

CC	*Christian Century*
CT	*Christianity Today*
FEER	*Far Eastern Economic Review*
IBMR	*International Bulletin of Missionary Research*
IRM	*International Review of Mission*
LAT	*Los Angeles Times*
NCR	*National Catholic Reporter*
NYT	*New York Times*
USCIRF	*US Commission on International Religious Freedom*
WP	*Washington Post*
WSJ	*Wall Street Journal*

CHAPTER 1

1. John Mbiti is quoted in Kwame Bediako, *Christianity in Africa* (Edinburgh: Edinburgh University Press, 1995), 154.

2. *Status of Global Mission,* 2005, at http://www.globalchristianity.org/resources.htm. For future projections, see David B. Barrett, George T. Kurian, and Todd M. Johnson, *World Christian Encyclopedia,* 2nd ed. (New York: Oxford University Press, 2001), 12–15. I use these related sources extensively, though in several instances, my numbers differ from theirs. Large disparities separate estimates about the size of Christian populations, especially in countries in which the religion is subject to official disapproval. In both India or China, the *World Christian Encyclopedia* gives strikingly high figures. If current estimates are too high, then any projections of future numbers are necessarily exaggerated. In its projections for the year 2025, for instance, this work suggests Christian populations of 135 million for China, 98 million for India, and the figures for 2050 would be correspondingly higher. These statistics might be accurate, but they are far out of line with other estimates, and therefore I am not using them here. I may well be overly cautious in this. Where such conflicts of evidence occur, I have erred on the side of conservatism, taking an average of available estimates: this means that my

statistics often differ from those of the Center for the Study of Global Christianity and the *World Christian Encyclopedia*.

3. Barrett et al., *World Christian Encyclopedia*; Todd M. Johnson and Kenneth R. Ross, eds., *Atlas of Global Christianity* (Edinburgh University Press, 2009). My demographic projections are drawn from two sources, respectively the U.S. Census Bureau and the United Nations. U.S. government figures can be found through the U.S. Department of Commerce, Bureau of the Census, International Database, online at http://www.census.gov/ipc/www/idbrank.html. UN figures are online at http://www.popin.org/.

4. *North-South: A Programme for Survival* (Cambridge, Mass.: MIT Press, 1980).

5. Peter I. Hajnal, *The G8 System and the G20* (Aldershot, UK: Ashgate, 2007).

6. Walbert Buhlmann, *The Coming of the Third Church* (Slough, UK: St. Paul, 1976); Sergio Torres and Virginia Fabella, eds., *The Emergent Gospel* (Maryknoll, N.Y.: Orbis, 1978); Edward R. Norman, *Christianity and the World Order* (Oxford: Oxford University Press, 1979); idem, *Christianity in the Southern Hemisphere* (Oxford: Oxford University Press, 1981); Andrew F. Walls, *The Missionary Movement in Christian History* (Maryknoll, N.Y.: Orbis, 1996); idem, *The Cross-Cultural Process in Christian History* (Maryknoll, N.Y.: Orbis, 2001). The Walls quote about "the standard Christianity" is from Christopher Fyfe and Andrew Walls, eds., *Christianity in Africa in the 1990s* (Edinburgh: Centre of African Studies, University of Edinburgh, 1996), 3; "anyone who…" is from Andrew Walls, "Eusebius Tries Again," *IBMR* 24, no. 3 (2000): 105–11; Kosuke Koyama, *Water Buffalo Theology* (Maryknoll, N.Y.: Orbis, 1974); John S. Pobee, *Toward an African Theology* (Nashville, Tenn.: Abingdon, 1979).

7. Mbiti is quoted in Bediako, *Christianity in Africa*, 154. See also John S. Mbiti, *Bible and Theology in African Christianity* (Nairobi, Kenya: Oxford University Press, 1986); Harvey Cox, *Fire from Heaven* (Reading, Mass.: Addison-Wesley, 1995).

8. For some global surveys of Christian history, see Adrian Hastings, ed., *A World History of Christianity* (Grand Rapids, Mich.: Eerdmans, 1999); David Chidester, *Christianity* (San Francisco: Harper San Francisco, 2000); Paul R. Spickard and Kevin M. Cragg, *A Global History of Christians* (Grand Rapids, Mich.: Baker Book House, 2001); Dale T. Irvin and Scott W. Sunquist, *History of the World Christian Movement* (Maryknoll, N.Y.: Orbis Books, 2001); Donald M. Lewis, ed., *Christianity Reborn* (Grand Rapids, Mich.: Eerdmans, 2004); John W. Coakley and Andrea Sterk, eds., *Readings in World Christian History* (Maryknoll, N.Y.: Orbis Books, 2004); Klaus Koschorke, Frieder Ludwig, and Marian Delgado, eds., *History of Christianity in Asia, Africa, and Latin America, 1450–1990* (Grand Rapids, Mich.: Eerdmans, 2007); Lamin O. Sanneh, *Disciples of All Nations* (New York: Oxford University Press, 2007); Martin E. Marty, *The Christian World* (New York: Modern Library, 2008); Robert Bruce Mullin, *A Short World History of Christianity*

(Louisville, Ky.: Westminster John Knox, 2008); Diarmaid MacCulloch, *Christianity: The First Three Thousand Years* (New York: Viking, 2010).

Although scholars may disagree about the significance of the global shift in Christianity, few actually question that it is occurring, and that it represents a critical historic transformation: one rare dissenter is Robert Wuthnow, in his *Boundless Faith* (Berkeley: University of California Press, 2009).

9. Samuel P. Huntington, *The Clash of Civilizations and the Remaking of World Order* (New York: Simon & Schuster, 1996), 65.

10. Huntington, *Clash of Civilizations*, 64–66, 116–19 (the quote is from 65); Stig Jarle Hansen, Atle Mesøy, and Tuncay Kardas, eds., *The Borders of Islam* (New York: Columbia University Press, 2009).

11. James C. Russell, *The Germanization of Early Medieval Christianity* (New York: Oxford University Press, 1996); Thomas F. X. Noble and Julia M. H. Smith, eds., *Early Medieval Christianities, c.600–c.1100, Cambridge History of Christianity*, vol. 3 (Cambridge: Cambridge University Press, 2008); Daniel E. Bornstein, ed., *Medieval Christianity* (Minneapolis, Minn.: Fortress Press, 2009).

12. Norman, *Christianity and the World Order*; and idem, *Christianity in the Southern Hemisphere*; Philip Jenkins, *The New Faces of Christianity* (New York: Oxford University Press, 2006).

13. Lamin O. Sanneh, *Whose Religion Is Christianity?* (Grand Rapids, Mich.: Eerdmans, 2003); Frans Wijsen and Robert Schreiter, eds., *Global Christianity* (Amsterdam, Netherlands: Rodopi, 2007); Sebastian Kim and Kirsteen Kim, *Christianity As a World Religion* (New York: Continuum, 2008); Mary Farrell Bednarowski, ed., *Twentieth-Century Global Christianity* (Minneapolis, Minn.: Fortress, 2008).

14. Teresa Okure, Jon Sobrino, and Felix Wilfred, eds., "Rethinking Martyrdom," in *Concilium* 1(2003) (London: SCM, 2003).

15. Barrett et al., *World Christian Encyclopedia*, 4; compare Pew Forum, *Spirit and Power: A 10-Country Survey of Pentecostals*. Poll, October 5, 2006, at http://pewforum.org/Christian/Evangelical-Protestant-Churches/Spirit-and-Power.aspx; Amos Yong, *The Spirit Poured Out on All Flesh* (Grand Rapids, Mich.: Baker, 2005); David Maxwell, *African Gifts of the Spirit* (Athens: Ohio University Press, 2007); Donald E. Miller and Tetsunao Yamamori, *Global Pentecostalism* (Berkeley: University of California Press, 2007); Allan Anderson, *Spreading Fires* (Maryknoll, N.Y.: Orbis Books, 2007); Michael Bergunder, *The South Indian Pentecostal Movement in the Twentieth Century* (Grand Rapids, Mich.: Eerdmans, 2008); Veli-Matti Kärkkäinen, ed. *The Spirit in the World* (Grand Rapids, Mich.: Eerdmans, 2009); Ruth Marshall, *Political Spiritualities* (Chicago: University of Chicago Press, 2009).

16. For the impact of emerging global Christianity on theology, see Craig Ott and Harold A. Netland, eds., *Globalizing Theology* (Grand Rapids, Mich.: Baker Academic, 2006); Timothy C. Tennent, *Theology in the Context of World Christianity* (Grand Rapids, Mich.: Zondervan, 2007).

17. Obituary for Paul Abrecht, *NYT*, June 19, 2005; Paul Abrecht and Ninan Koshy, eds., *Before It's Too Late* (Geneva: World Council of Churches, 1983).

18. John Spong, *Why Christianity Must Change or Die* (San Francisco: Harper San Francisco, 1998), and see also idem, *A New Christianity for a New World: Why Traditional Faith Is Dying and How a New Faith Is Being Born* (San Francisco: Harper San Francisco, 2002); John Wilson, "Examining Peacocke's Plumage," *CT*, posted to website March 12, 2001.

19. Stewart J. Brown and Timothy Tackett, *Cambridge History of Christianity: Enlightenment, Reawakening and Revolution* 1660–1815 (Cambridge: Cambridge University Press, 2006); Sheridan Gilley and Brian Stanley, eds., *Cambridge History of Christianity: World Christianities* 1815–1914 (Cambridge: Cambridge University Press, 2005).

20. G. K. Chesterton, "The Catholic Church and Conversion," in *The Collected Works of G.K. Chesterton*, vol. 3 (Ignatius Press, 1990), 102.

21. Judith Herrin, *The Formation of Christendom* (Princeton, N.J.: Princeton University Press, 1987); Adriaan Hendrik Bredero, *Christendom and Christianity in the Middle Ages* (Grand Rapids, Mich.: Eerdmans, 1994); Peter Brown, *The Rise of Western Christendom*, rev. ed. (Oxford: Blackwell, 2003).

22. For "post-Christendom," see for instance Stanley Hauerwas, *After Christendom?* (Nashville, Tenn.: Abingdon Press, 1991); Thomas J. Curry, *Farewell to Christendom* (New York: Oxford University Press, 2001); Hugh McLeod and Werner Ustorf, eds., *The Decline of Christendom in Western Europe, 1750–2000* (New York: Cambridge University Press, 2003). Stuart Murray, *Post-Christendom* (Paternoster, 2004); Stuart Murray, *Church after Christendom* (Paternoster, 2005).

23. "Governments will have less and less control" is from *Global Trends* 2015, http://www.dni.gov/nic/NIC_globaltrend2015.html. "In areas of Africa and Asia" is from *Global Trends 2025: A Transformed World*, National Intelligence Council's 2025 Project, http://www.dni.gov/nic/NIC_2025_project.html at p.1; "Although states will not disappear" is at p. 81.

24. Benedict Anderson, *Imagined Communities*, rev. ed. (London: Verso, 1991); the remark about quasi states is from Paul Gifford, *African Christianity* (Bloomington: Indiana University Press, 1998), 9.

25. Hedley Bull, *The Anarchical Society* (New York: Columbia University Press, 1977), 254; compare Stephen J. Kobrin, "Back to the Future," *Journal of International Affairs* 51 (1998): 361–86. The speculation that environmentalism might be the future global ideology is from Paul Lewis, "As Nations Shed Roles, Is Medieval the Future?" *NYT*, January 2, 1999.

26. For the reshaping of mission in the face of the new global Christianity, see Samuel Escobar, *The New Global Mission* (Downers Grove, Ill.: InterVarsity Press, 2003); Andrew F. Walls and Cathy Ross, eds., *Mission in the Twenty-First Century* (Maryknoll, N.Y.: Orbis Books, 2008); Soong-Chan Rah, *The Next Evangelicalism* (Downers Grove, Ill.: InterVarsity Press, 2009); Ogbu U. Kalu, Peter Vethanayagamony, and Edmund Kee-Fook Chia, eds., *Mission After Christendom*

(Louisville, Ky.: Westminster John Knox Press, 2010); Afe Adogame and James V. Spickard, eds., *Religion Crossing Boundaries* (Boston, Mass.: Brill, 2010).

27. Christopher Tyerman, *Fighting for Christendom* (New York: Oxford University Press, 2004).

28. *Global Trends 2025: A Transformed World.*

29. John Micklethwait and Adrian Wooldridge, *God Is Back* (London: Allen Lane, 2009).

CHAPTER 2

1. Kwame Bediako, *Christianity in Africa* (Edinburgh: Edinburgh University Press/Orbis, 1995). Dyron B. Daughrity, *The Changing World of Christianity* (New York: Peter Lang, 2010). Throughout this chapter, I have used Dana L. Robert, *Christian Mission* (Wiley-Blackwell, 2009).

2. Edward W. Blyden, *Christianity, Islam and the Negro Race* (Edinburgh University Press, 1967); Ronald Segal, *Islam's Black Slaves* (New York: Farrar, Straus and Giroux, 2001); Bernard Lewis, *Race and Slavery in the Middle East* (New York: Oxford University Press, 1990).

3. Andrew F. Walls, "Eusebius Tries Again," *IBMR* 24, no. 3 (2000): 105–11; Philip Jenkins, *The Lost History of Christianity* (San Francisco: HarperOne, 2008).

4. Elizabeth Isichei, *A History of Christianity in Africa* (Grand Rapids, Mich.: Eerdmans, 1995); Bengt Sundkler and Christopher Steed, *A History of the Church in Africa* (Cambridge: Cambridge University Press, 2000); Thomas C. Oden, *How Africa Shaped the Christian Mind* (Downers Grove, Ill.: InterVarsity Press, 2008); Margaret M. Mitchell and Frances M. Young, eds., *Origins to Constantine, Cambridge History of Christianity*, vol. 4 (Cambridge: Cambridge University Press, 2006). For Hadrian, see Bede, *Ecclesiastical History*, IV, i, at http://www.ccel.org/ccel/bede/history.v.iv.i.html.

5. Philip Jenkins, *Jesus Wars* (San Francisco: HarperOne, 2010).

6. Richard Hovannisian, ed., *The Armenian People from Ancient to Modern Times* (New York: St. Martin's, 1997).

7. The phrase about the Ark of the Covenant is from Adrian Hastings, *The Church in Africa, 1450–1950* (Oxford: Clarendon Press, 1996), 4; Taddesse Tamrat, *Church and State in Ethiopia, 1270–1527* (Oxford: Clarendon Press, 1972); Marilyn Eiseman Heldman, *African Zion* (New Haven: Yale University Press, 1993).

8. Hastings, *Church in Africa, 1450–1950*, 3–45; Ethiopian royal origins are recounted in the book known as the *Kebra Nagast*; Sir E. A. Wallis Budge, *The Queen of Sheba and Her Only Son Menyelek*, 2nd ed. (London: Oxford University Press, 1932).

9. Sundkler and Steed, *History of the Church in Africa*, 928; David B. Barrett, George T. Kurian, Todd M. Johnson, *World Christian Encyclopedia*, 2nd ed. (New York: Oxford University Press, 2001), 265–69.

10. Jenkins, *Lost History of Christianity*.

11. The quote about the Alexandrian primates is from Kenneth Baxter Wolf, *Christian Martyrs in Muslim Spain* (Cambridge: Cambridge University Press, 1988). Emmanouela Grypeou, Mark Swanson, and David Thomas, eds., *The Encounter of Eastern Christianity With Early Islam* (Leiden, Netherlands: E. J. Brill, 2006); Sidney H. Griffith, *The Church in the Shadow of the Mosque* (Princeton, N.J.: Princeton University Press, 2007); Jenkins, *Lost History of Christianity*.

12. John H. Watson, *Among the Copts* (Eastbourne, UK: Sussex Academic Press, 2000); Michael Angold, ed., *The Cambridge History of Christianity, Volume 5: Eastern Christianity* (Cambridge: Cambridge University Press 2006). For the Coptic language, see Hastings, *Church in Africa, 1450–1950*, 7; Leonard Ralph Holme, *The Extinction of the Christian Churches in North Africa* (New York: B. Franklin, 1969: repr. of the 1898 edition).

13. Ian Gillman and Hans-Joachim Klimkeit, *Christians in Asia before 1500* (Ann Arbor: University of Michigan Press, 1999); Samuel H. Moffett, *A History of Christianity in Asia*, 2nd rev. ed. (Maryknoll, N.Y.: Orbis, 1998); Jenkins, *Lost History of Christianity*. The text of the Nestorian Tablet can be found at www.fordham.edu/halsall/eastasia/781nestorian.html.

14. Stephen Neill, *A History of Christianity in India* (Cambridge: Cambridge University Press, 1984); Leonard Fernando and George Gispert-Sauch, *Christianity in India* (New Delhi: Penguin India, 2004); Robert Eric Frykenberg, *Christianity in India* (New York: Oxford University Press, 2008).

For Prester John, see Elaine Sanceau, *The Land of Prester John* (New York: Knopf, 1944); undoubtedly, tales of the Ethiopian state also contributed to the legend.

15. For the Jacobites, see Gillman and Klimkeit, *Christians in Asia before 1500*, 71.

16. David B. Barrett, *World Christian Encyclopedia*, 1st ed. (Nairobi, Kenya: Oxford University Press, 1982), 796.

17. Dalrymple, *From the Holy Mountain*; Betty Jane Bailey and J. Martin Bailey, *Who Are the Christians in the Middle East?* 2nd ed. (Grand Rapids, Mich.: W.B. Eerdmans, 2010). The *World Christian Encyclopedia* gives Syria's present Christian population as 7.8 percent of the whole (719).

18. Dalrymple, *From the Holy Mountain*, 154; Angold, ed., *The Cambridge History of Christianity, Volume 5: Eastern Christianity*.

19. Laurence Edward Browne, *The Eclipse of Christianity in Asia* (Cambridge: Cambridge University Press, 1933); Jenkins, *Lost History of Christianity*. For the 'Ayn Jalut campaign, see Peter Thorau, *The Lion of Egypt* (London: Longman, 1992).

20. The quote about genocide is from Hastings, *Church in Africa, 1450–1950*, 137; compare 62–70; Sundkler and Steed, *History of the Church in Africa*, 73–75.

21. Giles Milton, *White Gold* (New York: Farrar, Straus and Giroux, 2005); Robert C. Davis, *Christian Slaves, Muslim Masters* (New York: Palgrave Macmillan,

2004); Linda Colley, *Captives* (New York: Anchor, 2004); Luther is quoted from the "Appeal to the German Nobility," which can be found at http://history.hanover.edu/texts/luthad.html.

22. Stephen C. Neill, *A History of Christian Missions* (London: Penguin, 1964); Robert, *Christian Mission*.

23. Neill, *History of Christian Missions*, 170; David Chidester, *Christianity* (San Francisco: Harper San Francisco, 2000), 365; Nicholas Griffiths, *The Cross and the Serpent* (Norman: University of Oklahoma Press, 1996).

24. David P. Henige, *Numbers from Nowhere* (Norman: University of Oklahoma Press, 1998); Nicholas Griffiths and Fernando Cervantes, eds., *Spiritual Encounters* (Lincoln: University of Nebraska Press, 1999).

25. Neill, *History of Christian Missions*; Erick Langer and Robert H. Jackson, eds., *The New Latin American Mission History* (Lincoln: University of Nebraska Press, 1995); John Frederick Schwaller, *The History of the Catholic Church in Latin America* (New York: New York University Press, 2011).

26. Neill, *History of Christian Missions*, 168–76. For Catholic responses to Native religion and cultural syntheses, see John D. Early, *The Maya and Catholicism* (Gainesville: University Press of Florida, 2006); Martin Austin Nesvig, ed., *Local Religion in Colonial Mexico* (Albuquerque: University of New Mexico Press, 2006); Yanna Yannakakis, *The Art of Being In-Between* (Durham, N.C.: Duke University Press, 2008). Compare Carolyn Brewer, *Shamanism, Catholicism and Gender Relations in Colonial Philippines* 1521-1685 (Burlington, Vt.: Ashgate, 2004).

27. For the prolonged process of conversion and cultural interaction in Mexico, see Osvaldo F. Pardo, *The Origins of Mexican Catholicism* (Ann Arbor: University of Michigan Press, 2004); Viviana Díaz Balsera, *The Pyramid under the Cross* (Tucson: University of Arizona Press, 2005); Jaime Lara, *Christian Texts for Aztecs* (South Bend, In.: University of Notre Dame Press, 2008); Guy Stresser-Péan, *The Sun God and the Savior* (Boulder: University Press of Colorado, 2009); William F. Hanks, *Converting Words* (Berkeley: University of California Press, 2010); Edward W. Osowski, *Indigenous Miracles* (University of Arizona Press, 2010).

For developments in the Andean region, see Alan Durston, *Pastoral Quechua* (South Bend, In.: University of Notre Dame Press, 2007) and John Charles, *Allies at Odds* (Albuquerque: University of New Mexico Press, 2010).

For Philippine parallels, see Vicente L. Rafael, *Contracting Colonialism* (Ithaca, N.Y.: Cornell University Press, 1988).

28. The remark about Mvemba Nzinga is from Sundkler and Steed, *History of the Church in Africa*, 51; the Portuguese priest is quoted from Hastings, *Church in Africa, 1450–1950*, 83.

29. "A literate elite": John K. Thornton, *The Kongolese Saint Anthony* (Cambridge: Cambridge University Press, 1998), 2. For the Virginia colony, see Lisa Rein, "Mystery of Va.'s First Slaves Is Unlocked 400 Years Later," *Washington Post*, September 3, 2006.

30. Neill, *History of Christianity in India*; Frykenberg, *Christianity in India*. For Akbar, see William Dalrymple, "NS Christmas Essay," *New Statesman*, December 19, 2005.

31. R. Po-chia Hsia, ed., *Cambridge History of Christianity: Reform and Expansion* 1500–1660 (Cambridge: Cambridge University Press, 2006); Samuel Hugh Moffett, *History of Christianity in Asia: 1500 to 1900*, vol. 2 (Maryknoll, N.Y.: Orbis, 2005); Ines G. Zupanov, *Missionary Tropics* (Ann Arbor: University of Michigan Press, 2005); Luke Clossey, *Salvation and Globalization in the Early Jesuit Missions* (New York: Cambridge University Press, 2008).

For Japan, see Ikuo Higashibaba, *Christianity in Early Modern Japan* (Leiden, Netherlands: Brill, 2001); Robert Lee, *The Clash of Civilizations* (Harrisburg, Penn.: Trinity Press International, 1999); Andrew C. Ross, *A Vision Betrayed* (Maryknoll, N.Y.: Orbis, 1994).

32. Jonathan D. Spence, *The Memory Palace of Matteo Ricci* (New York: Viking, 1984); Liam Matthew Brockey, *Journey to the East* (Cambridge, Mass.: Harvard University Press, 2007); Jean Charbonnier, *Christians in China* (San Francisco: Ignatius Press, 2007); Florence C. Hsia, *Sojourners in a Strange Land* (Chicago: University of Chicago Press, 2009); R. Po-chia Hsia, *A Jesuit in the Forbidden City* (New York: Oxford University Press, 2010).

For missions in Tibet, see Trent Pomplun, *Jesuit on the Roof of the World* (New York: Oxford University Press, 2009).

33. The *Propaganda* is quoted in Neill, *History of Christian Missions*, 179; Ralph Covell, *Confucius, the Buddha, and Christ* (Maryknoll, N.Y.: Orbis, 1986); Gianni Criveller, *Preaching Christ in Late Ming China* (Taipei/Brescia: Taipei Ricci Institute, 1997).

34. "I know that at the present time" is quoted in Lamin O. Sanneh, *West African Christianity* (Maryknoll, N.Y.: Orbis, 1983), 35; George Minamiki, *The Chinese Rites Controversy* (Chicago: Loyola University Press, 1985); Ross, *Vision Betrayed*; the edict banning Christianity is quoted from http://www.yutopian.com/religion/christian/Kangxi.html.

35. For the Protestant missionary movement, see Neill, *History of Christian Missions*, 261–321; Michele Gillespie, *Pious Pursuits* (New York: Berghahn Books, 2007); Rachel Wheeler, *To Live upon Hope* (Ithaca, N.Y.: Cornell University Press, 2008).

36. Kevin Ward, Brian Stanley, and Diana K. Witts, eds., *The Church Mission Society and World Christianity, 1799–1999* (Grand Rapids, Mich.: Eerdmans, 1999); John de Gruchy, ed., *The London Missionary Society in Southern Africa, 1799–1999* (Athens: Ohio University Press, 2000); Tom Hiney, *On the Missionary Trail* (New York: Atlantic Monthly Press, 2000); Dana L. Robert, ed., *Converting Colonialism* (Grand Rapids, Mich.: Eerdmans, 2008); Robert, *Christian Mission*.

For the boom in missionary activity within the emerging cultural sphere of the Black Atlantic, see Jon Sensbach, *Rebecca's Revival* (Cambridge, Mass.: Harvard University Press, 2006); Colin Kidd, *The Forging of Races* (Cambridge: Cambridge

University Press, 2006); Chima J. Korieh, ed., *Olaudah Equiano and the Igbo World* (Trenton, N.J.: Africa World Press, 2009); Carla Gardina Pestana, *Protestant Empire* (Philadelphia: University of Pennsylvania Press, 2009).

37. Throughout this section, I have used Sundkler and Steed, *History of the Church in Africa*, and Hastings, *Church in Africa, 1450–1950*. For Christianity in West Africa, see Lamin O. Sanneh, *Abolitionists Abroad* (Cambridge, Mass.: Harvard University Press, 2000), and idem, *West African Christianity*.

For the missionary experience in China, see Joseph Tse-Hei Lee, *The Bible and the Gun* (New York: Routledge, 2003); David Cheung, *Christianity in Modern China* (Leiden, Netherlands: Brill, 2004); Eric Reinders, *Borrowed Gods and Foreign Bodies* (Berkeley: University of California Press, 2004).

For India, see Jeffrey Cox, *Imperial Fault Lines* (Stanford, Calif.: Stanford University Press, 2002); Robert Eric Frykenberg and Alaine M. Low, eds., *Christians and Missionaries in India* (Grand Rapids, Mich.: Eerdmans, 2003); Chad Bauman, *Christian Identity and Dalit Religion in Hindu India, 1868–1947* (Grand Rapids, Mich.: Eerdmans, 2008).

38. Hastings, *Church in Africa, 1450–1950*, 385–87.

39. Elizabeth Isichei, *A History of Christianity in Africa* (Grand Rapids, Mich.: Eerdmans, 1995), 92. Andrew Porter, ed., *The Imperial Horizons of British Protestant Missions, 1880–1914* (Grand Rapids, Mich.: Eerdmans, 2003); Norman Etherington, *Missions and Empire* (New York: Oxford University Press, 2005); Rowan Strong, *Anglicanism and the British Empire, c.1700–1850* (New York: Oxford University Press, 2007); Chima J. Korieh, *Missions, States, and European Expansion in Africa* (New York: Routledge, 2007); John H. Darch, *Missionary Imperialists?* (London: Paternoster, 2009); Catherine Coquery-Vidrovitch, *Africa and the Africans in the Nineteenth Century* (Armonk, N.Y.: M.E. Sharpe, 2009).

40. Sundkler and Steed, *History of the Church in Africa*.

41. Joseph Dean O'Donnell, *Lavigerie in Tunisia* (Athens: University of Georgia Press, 1979).

42. Stephen C. Neill, *A History of Christian Missions*, rev. ed. (London: Penguin, 1990), 421; Alvyn Austin, *China's Millions* (Grand Rapids, Mich.: Eerdmans, 2007).

43. F. M. P. Libermann, quoted in Sundkler and Steed, *History of the Church in Africa*, 103; Kevin Ward, *A History of Global Anglicanism* (Cambridge: Cambridge University Press, 2006); Pamela Welch, *Church and Settler in Colonial Zimbabwe* (Leiden, Netherlands: Brill, 2008).

44. Frederick Howard Taylor, *Hudson Taylor and the China Inland Mission* (Philadelphia: China Inland Mission, 1934).

45. Hastings, *Church in Africa, 1450–1950*, 294; Jeffrey Cox, *The British Missionary Enterprise since 1700* (New York: Routledge, 2008), 14.

46. Andrew Porter, *Religion versus Empire?* (Manchester, UK: Manchester University Press, 2004); Brian Stanley, *Missions, Nationalism, and the End of Empire* (Grand Rapids, Mich.: Eerdmans, 2003).

47. Vincent Carretta and Ty M. Reese, eds., *The Life and Letters of Philip Quaque* (Athens: University of Georgia Press, 2010); Hastings, *Church in Africa, 1450–1950*, 178–79; Crowther is discussed in Neill, *History of Christian Missions*, 377–79; Sanneh, *West African Christianity*, 168–73; Hastings, *Church in Africa, 1450–1950*, 338–93. For numbers of native clergy, see Sundkler and Steed, *History of the Church in Africa*, 627.

48. Sundkler and Steed, *History of the Church in Africa*, 627, 906.

49. Brian Stanley, *The World Missionary Conference, Edinburgh* 1910 (Grand Rapids, Mich.: Eerdmans, 2009). "Medical work" is from J. R. Mott, *The Evangelization of the World in This Generation* (New York: Student Volunteer Movement for Christian Missions, 1905), 13; Charles Good, *The Steamer Parish* (Chicago: University of Chicago Press, 2004); H. J. A. Bellenoit, *Missionary Education and Empire in Late Colonial India, 1860–1920* (London: Pickering & Chatto, 2007).

50. Neill, *History of Christian Missions*, rev. ed., 473.

CHAPTER 3

1. Robert W. Hefner, ed., *Conversion to Christianity* (Berkeley: University of California Press, 1993); Lewis R. Rambo, *Understanding Religious Conversion* (New Haven: Yale University Press, 1993).

2. *Christianity—The Second Millennium*, broadcast on Arts and Entertainment Network, December 17–18, 2000.

3. The Gikuyu quote is from Adrian Hastings, *The Church in Africa, 1450–1950* (Oxford: Clarendon, 1996), 485; Ngugi wa Thiong'o, *I Will Marry When I Want* (London: Heinemann, 1982), 56–57.

4. Chinua Achebe, *Arrow of God* (London: Heinemann, 1964), 105; the "leper" quote is from J. N. Kanyua Mugambi, ed., *Critiques of Christianity in African Literature* (Nairobi, Kenya: East African Educational Publishers, 1992), 51; Dana L. Robert, *Christian Mission* (Wiley-Blackwell, 2009).

5. Mongo Beti, *The Poor Christ of Bomba* (London: Heinemann, 1971), 189; Leslie Marmon Silko, *Almanac of the Dead* (New York: Simon & Schuster, 1991), 416–17; Nicholas Kristof, "God on Their Side," *NYT*, September 27, 2003.

6. See for example Christopher Hitchens, *The Missionary Position* (New York: Verso Books, 1997), a hostile biography of Mother Teresa.

7. Barbara Kingsolver, *The Poisonwood Bible* (New York: HarperFlamingo, 1998), 13. Peter Mathiessen, *At Play in the Fields of the Lord* (1965; New York: Bantam, 1976); James A. Michener, *Hawaii* (New York: Random House, 1959); Brian Moore, *Black Robe* (New York: Dutton, 1985).

8. Kingsolver, *The Poisonwood Bible*, 25–27.

9. Nick Holdstock, "Burning Books," *London Review of Books*, July 22, 2010; Nick Holdstock, *The Tree That Bleeds* (Edinburgh, Scotland: Luath Press, 2010).

10. Thomas C. Reeves, *The Empty Church* (New York: Free Press, 1996), 13; Adrian Hastings, *A History of African Christianity,* 1950–1975 (Cambridge: Cambridge University Press, 1979). For Fuller Seminary, see Brad A. Greenberg, "How Missionaries Lost Their Chariots of Fire," *WSJ,* July 2, 2010.

11. Sathianathan Clarke, *Dalits and Christianity* (Delhi: Oxford India Paperbacks, 1999), 37–38; Robert Eric Frykenberg, *Christianity in India* (New York: Oxford University Press, 2008).

12. Chinua Achebe, *Things Fall Apart* (1959; repr. New York: Fawcett, 1969), 133.

For the African experience, see especially the essays of Ogbu Kalu collected in Wilhelmina J. Kalu, Nimi Wariboko, and Toyin Falola, eds., *Christian Missions in Africa* (Trenton, N.J.: Africa World Press, 2010). Cyril C. Okorocha, *The Meaning of Religious Conversion in Africa* (London: Avebury, 1987); Ogbu Kalu, *The Embattled Gods* (Lagos, Nigeria: Minaj, 1996); Nkem Hyginus M. V. Chigere, *Foreign Missionary Background and Indigenous Evangelization in Igboland* (Münster, Germany: Verlag Lit, 2001); Paul V. Kollman, *The Evangelization of Slaves and Catholic Origins in Eastern Africa* (Maryknoll, N.Y.: Orbis Books, 2005).

13. Sundkler and Steed, *History of the Church in Africa,* 470, 88–89.

14. Robert, *Christian Mission,* 142–2.

15. Dana L. Robert, "World Christianity as a Women's Movement," *IBMR* 30(4)(2006) 180–88.

For mission as a gendered enterprise, see Dorothy L. Hodgson, *The Church of Women* (Bloomington: Indiana University Press, 2005); Hyaeweol Choi, *Gender and Mission Encounters in Korea* (Berkeley: University of California Press, 2009); Robert, *Christian Mission* 114–41; Elizabeth E. Prevost, *The Communion of Women* (New York: Oxford University Press, 2010); Jessie G. Lutz, ed., *Pioneer Chinese Christian Women* (Bethlehem, Penn.: Lehigh University Press, 2010).

For the role of women in modern-day churches, see Frances S. Adeney, *Christian Women in Indonesia* (Syracuse, N.Y.: Syracuse University Press, 2003); Eliza F. Kent, *Converting Women* (New York: Oxford University Press, 2004); R. Marie Griffith and Barbara Dianne Savage, eds., *Women and Religion in the African Diaspora* (Baltimore: Johns Hopkins University Press, 2006); Jane E. Soothill, *Gender, Social Change and Spiritual Power* (Leiden, Netherlands: Brill, 2007); Deidre Helen Crumbley, *Spirit, Structure, and Flesh* (Madison: University of Wisconsin Press, 2008); Cordelia Moyse, *A History of the Mothers' Union* (Rochester, N.Y.: Boydell Press, 2009); Juliana Flinn, *Mary, the Devil, and Taro* (Honolulu: University of Hawai'i Press, 2010); Maria Frahm-Arp, *Professional Women in South African Pentecostal Charismatic Churches* (Leiden: Brill, 2010).

For Agnes Okoh, see Thomas Oduro, *Christ Holy Church International* (Minneapolis, Minn.: Lutheran University Press, 2007).

For hymn-writers, see Roberta King, Jean Ngoya Kidula, James R. Krabill, and Thomas A. Oduro, *Music in the Life of the African Church* (Waco, Tex.: Baylor University Press, 2008).

16. Achebe, *Things Fall Apart*, 137.

For Christian conversion in a Pacific context, see Joel Robbins, *Becoming Sinners* (Berkeley: University of California Press, 2004); Webb Keane, *Christian Moderns* (Berkeley: University of California Press, 2007).

17. For Madagascar, see Sundkler and Steed, *History of the Church in Africa*, 491.

18. Sundkler and Steed, *History of the Church in Africa*, 562–93; Hastings, *Church in Africa, 1450–1950*, 371–85, 464–75.

19. Neill, *History of Christian Missions*, 415–18. Jacob Ramsay, *Mandarins and Martyrs* (Palo Alto, Calif.: Stanford University Press, 2008).

20. Ngugi wa Thiong'o, *The River Between* (London: Heinemann, 1965), 147; Elizabeth Isichei, *A History of Christianity in Africa* (Grand Rapids, Mich.: Eerdmans, 1995), 244–46.

21. Jonathan D. Spence, *God's Chinese Son* (New York: Norton, 1996), 57; Thomas P. Reilly, *The Taiping Heavenly Kingdom* (Seattle: University of Washington Press, 2004).

China produced many other native Christian movements, often prophetic in nature, but none as lethal as the Taiping. See for instance, Lars P. Laamann, *Christian Heretics in Late Imperial China* (New York: Routledge, 2006); Eugenio Menegon, *Ancestors, Virgins, and Friars* (Cambridge, Mass.: Harvard University Press, 2009); Lian Xi, *Redeemed by Fire* (New Haven: Yale University Press, 2010).

22. Victoria Reifler Bricker, *The Indian Christ, the Indian King* (Austin: University of Texas Press, 1981); Michael Adas, *Prophets of Rebellion* (Chapel Hill: University of North Carolina Press, 1979); Robert W. Patch, *Maya Revolt and Revolution in the Eighteenth Century* (Armonk, N.Y.: M. E. Sharpe, 2002). For medieval European parallels, see Norman Cohn, *Pursuit of the Millennium*, 3rd ed. (London: Paladin, 1970).

23. Norman, *Christianity in the Southern Hemisphere*, 48–70. For the idea of a messianic role for the Latin American continent, see Thomas M. Cohen, *The Fire of Tongues* (Palo Alto, Calif.: Stanford University Press, 1998); Frank Graziano, *The Millennial New World* (New York: Oxford University Press, 1999); Euclides Da Cunha, *Rebellion in the Backlands* (Chicago: University of Chicago Press, 1944); "a multitude of extravagant superstitions" is from 111; "his teachings were no more than," 136; Mario Vargas Llosa, *The War of the End of the World* (New York: Farrar, Straus and Giroux, 1984). A new translation of Da Cunha's work is available as *Backlands*, translated by Elizabeth Lowe (New York: Penguin Classics, 2010).

24. Da Cunha, *Rebellion in the Backlands*, 133.

25. Quoted at http://www.sandino.org/failed.htm.

26. Sundkler and Steed, *History of the Church in Africa*, 59. The following account is mainly drawn from John K. Thornton, *The Kongolese Saint Anthony* (New York: Cambridge University Press, 1998).

27. Da Cunha, *Rebellion in the Backlands*, 153.

28. Deji Ayegboyin and S. Ademola Ishola, *African Indigenous Churches* (Lagos, Nigeria: Greater Heights Publications, 1997); James Amanze, *African Christianity in Botswana* (Gweru, Zimbabwe: Mambo Press, 1998); Da Cunha, *Rebellion in the Backlands*, 136.

29. Sanneh, *West African Christianity*, 123; Sundkler and Steed, *History of the Church in Africa*, 198–99; Hastings, *Church in Africa, 1450–1950*, 443–45, 505–7; Gordon M. Haliburton, *The Prophet Harris* (London: Longman, 1971); Sheila S. Walker, *The Religious Revolution in the Ivory Coast* (Chapel Hill: University of North Carolina Press, 1983).

30. "Let My People Go," television documentary in the *Sword and Spirit* series, BBC, 1989.

31. George Shepperson and Thomas Price, *Independent African*, 2nd ed. (Edinburgh: Edinburgh University Press, 1987).

32. Hastings, *Church in Africa, 1450–1950*, 508–35; the prayer is quoted from Sanneh, *West African Christianity*, 207; the Kimbanguist church has an Internet presence at http://www.kimbanguisme.net/.

33. Sundkler and Steed, *History of the Church in Africa*, 98; Hastings, *Church in Africa, 1450–1950*, 513–18; Isichei, *History of Christianity in Africa*, 279–83; Sanneh, *West African Christianity*, 168–209; Afe Adogame and Akin Omyajowo, "Anglicanism and the Aladura Churches in Nigeria," in Andrew Wingate, Kevin Ward, Carrie Pemberton, and Wilson Sitshebo, eds., *Anglicanism* (New York: Church Publishing, 1998), 90–97; J. D. Y. Peel, *Aladura* (Oxford: Oxford University Press, 1968).

For case studies of these churches, see Harold W. Turner, *History of an African Independent Church* (Oxford: Clarendon Press, 1967); J. Akinyele Omoyajowo, *Cherubim and Seraphim* (New York: NOK Publishers International, 1982); Afeosemime U. Adogame, *Celestial Church of Christ* (New York: Peter Lang, 1999).

34. Hastings, *Church in Africa, 1450–1950*, 524–25. Her title is more fully Alice Lenshina Mulenga Mubisha. Isaac Phiri, "Why African Churches Preach Politics," *Journal of Church and State* 41 (1999): 323–47.

35. Harvey Cox, *Fire from Heaven* (Reading, Mass.: Addison-Wesley, 1995), 243–62; Andrew F. Walls, *The Missionary Movement in Christian History* (Maryknoll, N.Y.: Orbis, 1996), 3–15.

36. Denis Basil M'Passou, *History of African Independent Churches in Southern Africa, 1892–1992* (Mulanje, Malawi: Spot, 1994); Lamin O. Sanneh, *Abolitionists Abroad* (Cambridge, Mass.: Harvard University Press, 2000), and idem, *West African Christianity*, 174; Ogbu U. Kalu, "Ethiopianism and the Roots of Modern African Christianity," in Sheridan Gilley and Brian Stanley, eds., *Cambridge History of Christianity: World Christianities c.1815–c.1914* (Cambridge: Cambridge University Press, 2005), 576–92.

37. Statement by Bishop B. E. Lekganyane at http://www.uct.ac.za/depts/ricsa/commiss/trc/zcc_stat.htm. For the independent churches, see Gerhardus

C. Oosthuizen, *Afro-Christian Religions* (Leiden, Netherlands: Brill, 1979); Marthinus L. Daneel, *Quest for Belonging* (Gweru, Zimbabwe: Mambo, 1987); Harvey J. Sindima, *Drums of Redemption* (Westport, Conn.: Greenwood, 1994); Ane Marie Bak Rasmussen, *Modern African Spirituality* (London: British Academic Press, 1996); Amanze, *African Christianity in Botswana*; Thomas T. Spear and Isaria N. Kimambo, eds., *East African Expressions of Christianity* (Athens: Ohio University Press, 1999).

CHAPTER 4

1. Dana L. Robert; "Shifting Southward," *IBMR* 24, no. 2 (2000): 50–58.
2. The quote about "organs and sinew" is from Robert, "Shifting Southward." Adrian Hastings, *A History of African Christianity, 1950–1975* (Cambridge: Cambridge University Press, 1979). The quote about "Black Africa today" is from Adrian Hastings, "Christianity in Africa," in Ursula King, ed., *Turning Points in Religious Studies* (Edinburgh: T & T Clark, 1990), 208; David B. Barrett, George T. Kurian, and Todd M. Johnson, *World Christian Encyclopedia*, 2nd ed. (New York: Oxford University Press, 2001), 5; see also Bengt Sundkler and Christopher Steed, *A History of the Church in Africa* (Cambridge: Cambridge University Press, 2000), 906; David Maxwell, "Post-Colonial Christianity in Africa," in Hugh McLeod, ed., *Cambridge History of Christianity: World Christianities c.1914–c.2000* (Cambridge: Cambridge University Press, 2006), 401–21. For the contemporary religious situation in individual countries, I have used the U.S. government's *Annual Reports on International Religious Freedom*, online at http://www.state.gov/g/drl/irf/. The *Dictionary of African Christian Biography* is accessible at http://www.dacb.org/.
3. Kenneth Woodward, "The Changing Face of the Church," *Newsweek*, April 16, 2001.
4. Thomas Hobbes, *Leviathan* (1651), chap. 47; David Martin, *Tongues of Fire* (Oxford: Blackwell, 1990), 4.
5. John L. Allen, "Global South Will Shape the Future Catholic Church," *National Catholic Reporter*, October 7, 2005; John L. Allen Jr., *The Future Church* (New York: Doubleday, 2009). Bryan T. Froehle and Mary Gautier, *Global Catholicism* (Maryknoll, N.Y.: Orbis Books, 2003); Ian Linden, *Global Catholicism* (New York: Columbia University Press, 2009).
6. Rodney Stark and Buster Smith, *Faith on Earth* (forthcoming).
7. "Global View of the Catholic Church over the Past 25 Years," *L'Osservatore Romano* (2005) at http://www.ewtn.com/library/CHISTORY/annu2003.htm. For Nigeria, Robyn Dixon, "African Catholics Seek a Voice to Match Their Growing Strength," *LAT*, April 16, 2005. The reference to Bigard Memorial Seminary is from Andrew Maykuth, "Africa's Star Rising," *Philadelphia Inquirer*, June 8, 2006. For Nairobi, see John L Allen, "A Kenyan Lesson in Faith, Politics, and the Christian Future," *NCR*, July 30, 2010, at http://ncronline.org/blogs/all-things-catholic/kenyan-lesson-faith-politics-and-christian-future.

8. Frieder Ludwig, *Church and State in Tanzania* (Leiden, Netherlands: Brill, 1999), 177–79; Thomas D. Blakely, Dennis L. Thomson, and Walter E. Van Beek, eds., *Religion in Africa* (London: Heinemann, 1994); Barrett et al., *World Christian Encyclopedia*, 12, 729; Adrian Hastings, *African Catholicism* (London: SCM, 1989).

9. Woodward, "The Changing Face of the Church."

10. Adrian Hastings, *African Christianity* (New York: Seabury, 1976); Andrew Wingate, Kevin Ward, Carrie Pemberton, and Wilson Sitshebo, eds., *Anglicanism* (New York: Church, 1998); Ian T. Douglas and Pui-Lan Kwok, eds., *Beyond Colonial Anglicanism* (New York: Church, 2001); Kevin Ward, *A History of Global Anglicanism* (Cambridge: Cambridge University Press, 2006).

For three British-derived faiths in one country, see Akinyele Omoyajowo, ed., *The Anglican Church in Nigeria (1842–1992)* (Lagos, Nigeria: Macmillan Nigeria, 1994); Ogbu U. Kalu, ed., *A Century and a Half of Presbyterian Witness in Nigeria, 1846–1996* (Lagos, Nigeria: Ida-Ivory, 1996); M. M. Familusi, *Methodism in Nigeria, 1842–1992* (Ibadan, Nigeria: NPS Educational Publishers, 1992); Elizabeth Isichei, ed., *Varieties of Christian Experience in Nigeria* (London: Macmillan, 1982).

11. Paul Gifford, *African Christianity* (Bloomington: Indiana University Press, 1998), 112–80.

12. Sentamu is quoted from Stephen Bates, "A Cleric's Journey," *Guardian*, June 18, 2005.

13. For the *balokole*, see Hastings, *Church in Africa, 1450–1950*, 596–600, 608; Elizabeth Isichei, *A History of Christianity in Africa* (Grand Rapids, Mich.: Eerdmans, 1995), 241–44; Amos Kasibante, "Beyond Revival," in Wingate et al., eds., *Anglicanism: A Global Communion*, 363–68; Allan Anderson, "African Anglicans and/or Pentecostals" in ibid., 34–40; Frieder, *Church and State in Tanzania*, 181–91.

14. Mark Shaw, *Global Awakening* (Downers Grove, Ill.: InterVarsity Press, 2010).

15. Interview with Mark Noll, "Does Global Christianity Equal American Christianity?" *Christianity Today*, July 8, 2009, http://www.christianitytoday.com/ct/2009/july/19.38.html; Mark A. Noll, *The New Shape of World Christianity* (Downers Grove, Ill.: InterVarsity Press, 2009).

16. For the size of the evangelical population in different countries, see Edward L. Cleary and Juan Sepúlveda, "Chilean Pentecostalism," in Cleary and Stewart-Gambino, eds., *Power, Politics, and Pentecostals*, 106; Anne Motley Hallum, *Beyond Missionaries* (Lanham, Md.: Rowman & Littlefield, 1996). Justo L. González and Ondina E. González, *Christianity in Latin America* (Cambridge: Cambridge University Press, 2007); Timothy J. Steigenga and Edward L. Cleary, eds., *Conversion of a Continent* (New Brunswick, N.J.: Rutgers University Press, 2008); Lee M. Penyak and Walter J. Petry, ed., *Religion and Society in Latin America* (Maryknoll, N.Y.: Orbis Books, 2009).

17. For Guatemala, see Virginia Garrard-Burnett, *Protestantism in Guatemala* (Austin: University of Texas Press, 1998); Amy L. Sherman, *The Soul of Development* (New York: Oxford University Press, 1997); Everett Wilson, "Guatemalan Pentecostals," in Edward L. Cleary and Hannah W. Stewart-Gambino, eds., *Power, Politics, and Pentecostals in Latin America* (Boulder, Colo.: Westview, 1997), 139–62. R. Andrew Chesnut, *Competitive Spirits* (New York: Oxford University Press, 2003). For Pentecostalism elsewhere in Latin America, see Daniel Míguez, *To Help You Find God* (Amsterdam, Netherlands: Free University of Amsterdam, 1997); Cornelia Butler Flora, *Pentecostalism in Colombia* (Madison, N.J.: Fairleigh Dickinson University Press, 1976).

18. Martin, *Tongues of Fire*, 93–98; Kurt Derek Bowen, *Evangelism and Apostasy* (Montreal: McGill-Queen's University Press, 1996); James W. Dow and Alan R. Sandstrom, eds., *Holy Saints and Fiery Preachers* (Westport, Conn.: Praeger, 2001); Peter S. Cahn, *All Religions Are Good in Tzintzuntzan* (Austin: University of Texas Press, 2003); Todd Hartch, *Missionaries of the State* (Tuscaloosa: University of Alabama Press, 2006); Martin Nesvig, ed. *Religious Culture in Modern Mexico* (Lanham, Md.: Rowman & Littlefield, 2007). For Oaxaca, see Toomas Gross, "Protestantism and Modernity," *Sociology of Religion* 64 (2003): 479–505.

19. David Stoll, *Is Latin America Turning Protestant?* (Berkeley: University of California Press, 1990); Martin, *Tongues of Fire;* Virginia Garrard-Burnett and David Stoll, eds., *Rethinking Protestantism in Latin America* (Philadelphia: Temple University Press, 1993); Guillermo Cook, ed., *New Face of the Church in Latin America (*Maryknoll, N.Y.: Orbis, 1994); Barbara Boudewijnse et al., eds., *More Than Opium* (Lanham, Md.: Scarecrow, 1998); Karl-Wilhelm Westmeier, *Protestant Pentecostalism in Latin America* (Madison, N.J.: Fairleigh Dickinson University Press/Associated University Presses, 1999).

20. For the debate on Latin American religious statistics, see Virginia Garrard-Burnett and David Smilde, "Trustworthy Statistics?" at http://www.providence.edu/las/Trustworthy%Statistics.htm#Virginia.

21. Karla Poewe, ed., *Charismatic Christianity as a Global Culture* (Columbia: University of South Carolina Press, 1994); Harvey Cox, *Fire From Heaven* (Reading, Mass.: Addison-Wesley, 1995), 161–84; Steve Brouwer, Paul Gifford, and Susan D. Rose, *Exporting the American Gospel* (New York: Routledge, 1996); Ian Cotton, *The Hallelujah Revolution* (Amherst, N.Y.: Prometheus Books, 1996); Allan H. Anderson and Walter J. Hollenweger, eds., *Pentecostals after a Century* (Sheffield: Sheffield Academic, 1999); Richard Shaull and Waldo A. Cesar, *Pentecostalism and the Future of the Christian Churches* (Grand Rapids, Mich.: Eerdmans, 2000); Simon Coleman, *The Globalisation of Charismatic Christianity* (Cambridge: Cambridge University Press, 2000); André Corten and Ruth Marshall-Fratani, eds., *Between Babel and Pentecost* (Bloomington: Indiana University Press, 2001); David Martin, *Pentecostalism* (Oxford: Blackwell, 2002); Allan Anderson, *An Introduction to Pentecostalism* (Cambridge: Cambridge University Press, 2004);

Donald E. Miller and Tetsunao Yamamori, *Global Pentecostalism* (Berkeley: University of California Press, 2007).

22. Edward L. Cleary, in Cleary and Stewart-Gambino, eds., *Power, Politics, and Pentecostals*, 4; Martin, *Tongues of Fire*, 143; Edith L. Blumhofer, *Restoring the Faith* (Urbana: University of Illinois Press, 1993). For the appeal of Pentecostalism, see Diane J. Austin-Broos and Raymond T. Smith, *Jamaica Genesis* (Chicago: University of Chicago Press, 1997). For the Jotabeche Methodist Pentecostal church, see http://www.jotabeche.cl/.

23. For Brazil, see R. Andrew Chesnut, *Born Again in Brazil* (New Brunswick, N.J.: Rutgers University Press, 1997); David Lehmann, *Struggle for the Spirit* (London: Polity Press/Blackwell, 1996); Paul Freston, "Brother Votes for Brother," in Garrard-Burnett and Stoll, eds., *Rethinking Protestantism in Latin America*, 68; André Corten, *Pentecostalism in Brazil* (New York: St. Martin's, 1999). For the *Igreja do Evangelho Quadrangular*, see http://www.quadrangularbrasil.com.br/.

24. For the "fifty-two largest denominations," Freston, "Evangelicalism and Politics," 23; Cox, *Fire From Heaven*, 167.

25. Chesnut, *Born Again in Brazil*, 45–48; Stephen Buckley, "'Prosperity Theology' Pulls on Purse Strings," *WP*, February 13, 2001; http://www.arcauniversal.com/iurd/.

26. Maria Alvarez, Laura Italiano, and Luiz C. Ribeiro, "Holy-Roller Church Cashes in on Faithful," *New York Post*, July 23, 2000.

27. Byron Rempel-Burkholder, "Ethiopian Church Strives to Keep Spiritual Fires Alive," at http://www.mennoweekly.org/2004/10/18/ethiopian-church-strives-keep-spiritual-fires-aliv/.

28. Tibebe Eshete, *The Evangelical Movement in Ethiopia* (Waco, Tex.: Baylor University Press, 2009).

29. Richard N. Ostling and Joan K. Ostling, *Mormon America* 2nd ed. (San Francisco: Harper San Francisco, 2007).

30. Penny Lernoux, *Cry of the People* (New York: Penguin, 1982); Warren E. Hewitt, *Base Christian Communities and Social Change in Brazil* (Lincoln: University of Nebraska Press, 1991); Cecilia Loreto Mariz, *Coping with Poverty* (Philadelphia: Temple University Press, 1994); Madeleine Adriance, *Promised Land* (Albany, N.Y.: SUNY Press, 1995).

Africa too has its charismatic Catholics: Ludovic Lado, *Catholic Pentecostalism and the Paradoxes of Africanization* (Leiden, Netherlands: Brill, 2009).

31. For Brazil, see David O'Reilly and Jennifer Moroz, "Fight of Its Life," *Philadelphia Inquirer*, June 6, 2006; http://www.padremarcelorossi.org.br/.

32. For the Philippines, see http://www.chanrobles.com/elshaddai.htm; Katharine L. Wiegele, *Investing in Miracles* (Honolulu: University of Hawai'i Press, 2004).

33. For Tanzania, see Ludwig, *Church and State in Tanzania*, 182. For African charismatics, see Cox, *Fire From Heaven*, 249, 246; Paul Gifford, *African Christianity* (Bloomington: Indiana University Press, 1998), 33–39; Allan Anderson

and Sam Otwang, *Tumelo* (Pretoria, South Africa: UNISA Press); Allan H. Anderson, *African Reformation* (Trenton, N.J.: Africa World Press, 2001); Ogbu U. Kalu, ed., *African Christianity* (Pretoria, South Africa: University of Pretoria, 2005); Matthews A. Ojo, *The End-Time Army* (Africa World Press, 2006); Cephas Omenyo, *Pentecost Outside Pentecostalism* (Zoetermeer, Netherlands: Boekenzentrum, 2006); Jane E. Soothill, *Gender, Social Change and Spiritual Power* (Leiden, Netherlands: Brill, 2007); Robert Mbe Akoko, *"Ask and You Shall Be Given"* (Leiden, Netherlands: African Studies Centre, 2007); Ogbu Kalu, *African Pentecostalism* (New York: Oxford University Press, 2008).

34. Paul Gifford, *Ghana's New Christianity* (Bloomington: Indiana University Press, 2004); J. Kwabena Asamoah-Gyadu, *African Charismatics* (Leiden, Netherlands: Brill, 2005); David Maxwell, *African Gifts of the Spirit* (Athens: Ohio University Press, 2007).

35. Richard Elphick and Rodney Davenport, eds., *Christianity in South Africa* (Berkeley: University of California Press, 1998); Martin Prozesky and John De Gruchy, eds., *Living Faiths in South Africa* (New York: Palgrave, 1995); for the emergence of new sects, see David B. Barrett, *Schism and Renewal in Africa* (Nairobi, Kenya: Oxford University Press, 1968).

36. Bill Keller, "A Surprising Silent Majority in South Africa," *NYT Magazine*, April 17, 1994; *Man, God, and Africa*, television documentary made by Channel 4 (UK), 1994; Tangeni Amupadhi, "At Zion City, You Pray—and Pay," *Electronic Mail and Guardian* (South Africa), April 8, 1997; Thokozani Mtshali, "Shembe— The Incredible Whiteness of Being," *Electronic Mail and Guardian*, August 11, 1999.

37. James Amanze, *African Christianity in Botswana* (Gweru, Zimbabwe: Mambo, 1998). For Zimbabwe, see David Maxwell, *African Gifts of the Spirit* (Athens: Ohio University Press, 2007); Matthew Engelke, *A Problem of Presence* (Berkeley: University of California Press, 2007).

38. Dickson Kazuo Yagi, "Christ for Asia," *Review and Expositor* 88, no. 4 (1991): 375.

39. Interview with Mark Noll, "Does Global Christianity Equal American Christianity?"; Daniel H. Bays, ed., *Christianity in China from the Eighteenth Century to the Present* (Palo Alto, Calif.: Stanford University Press, 1996); Richard Madsen, *China's Catholics* (Berkeley: University of California Press, 1998); Stephen Uhalley and Xiaoxin Wu, eds., *China and Christianity* (Armonk, N.Y.: M. E. Sharpe, 2000); David Cheung, *Christianity in Modern China* (Leiden, Netherlands: Brill, 2004).

For Catholics, see Louisa Lim, "China's Divided Catholics Seek Reconciliation," National Public Radio, July 20, 2010, at http://www.npr.org/templates/story/story.php?storyId=128548164.

40. F. Carson Mencken, "Empirical Study of Religion in China," unpublished paper. Louisa Lim, "Chinese Turn to Religion to Fill a Spiritual Vacuum," National Public Radio, July 18, 2010, http://www.npr.org/templates/story/story.php?storyId=

128544048; and "In the Land of Mao, a Rising Tide of Christianity," July 19, 2010, http://www.npr.org/templates/story/story.php?storyId=128546334&ft=1&f=1016.

41. David Jeffrey is quoted from Nicholas D. Kristof, "Where Faith Thrives," *NYT*, March 26, 2005; Arthur Waldron, "Religion and the Chinese State," in Mark Silk, ed., *Religion on the International News Agenda* (Hartford, Conn.: Leonard F. Greenberg Center for the Study of Religion in Public Life, 2000), 19–36, at 30; for the Tienanmen protesters, see Richard Spencer, "Converts Inspired by Democracy Protests and Western Values," *Daily Telegraph* (London), July 30, 2005.

42. David Aikman, *Jesus in Beijing* (Chicago: Regnery, 2003); Francesco Sisci, "China's Catholic Moment," *First Things*, June–July 2009; Lian Xi, *Redeemed by Fire* (New Haven: Yale University Press, 2010). For Christianity as a modernizing ideology, see Nanlai Cao, *Constructing China's Jerusalem* (Stanford, Calif.: Stanford University Press, 2011).

43. Charles E. Farhadian, *Christianity, Islam and Nationalism in Indonesia* (New York: Routledge, 2005); May Ling Tan-Chow, *Pentecostal Theology for the Twenty-first Century* (Aldershot, UK: Ashgate, 2007); Jan Sihar Aritonang and Karel Steenbrink, eds., *A History of Christianity in Indonesia* (Leiden, Netherlands: Brill, 2008); Peter C. Phan, ed., *Christianity in Asia* (New York: Wiley-Blackwell, 2010). For the role of different forms of "charismatic technology" in spreading Christianity in this region, see Francis Khek Gee Lim, ed., *Mediating Piety* (Leiden, Netherlands: Brill, 2009).

44. Wi Jo Kang, *Christ and Caesar in Modern Korea* (Albany: SUNY Press, 1997); David Chung, *Syncretism* (Albany: SUNY Press, 2001); Robert E. Buswell Jr. and Timothy S. Lee, eds., *Christianity in Korea* (Honolulu: University of Hawai'i Press, 2005); Timothy S. Lee, *Born Again* (Honolulu: University of Hawai'i Press, 2010).

45. H. Vinson Synan, "The Yoido Full Gospel Church," *Cyberjournal for Pentecostal-Charismatic Research* 2 (1997) at http://www.pctii.org/cyberj/cyberj2/synan.html.

46. *USCIRF Annual Report* 2010 (Washington, D.C.: U.S. Commission on International Religious Freedom, 2010), 184–203; Julius Bautista and Francis Khek Gee Lim, eds., *Christianity and the State in Asia* (New York: Routledge, 2009).

47. Robert Eric Frykenberg, *Christianity in India* (New York: Oxford University Press, 2008).

48. The phrase "post-industrial wanderers" is from Cox, *Fire From Heaven*, 107. For the modern diasporic worlds of international migrants, refugees, and nomads, see Mark Fritz, *Lost on Earth* (New York: Routledge, 2000); Robert Neuwirth, *Shadow Cities* (New York: Routledge, 2004); Emma Wild-Wood, *Migration and Christian Identity in Congo* (Leiden, Netherlands: Brill, 2008); Robin Cohen, *Global Diasporas* 2nd ed. (London: Routledge, 2008); Ben Jones,

Beyond the State in Rural Uganda (Edinburgh: Edinburgh University Press, 2009).

49. The Agua Branca story is quoted from Monte Reel, "Brazil's Priests Use Song and Dance to Stem Catholic Church's Decline," *WP*, April 14, 2005; Phillip Berryman, *Religion in the Megacity* (Maryknoll, N.Y.: Orbis, 1996).

50. "Come and Receive Your Miracle," *CT*, posted February 2, 2001; Bonnke ministries has a website at http://www.cfan.org/. For Nigerian Pentecostals, see Richard Burgess, *Nigeria's Christian Revolution* (Eugene, Ore.: Wipf & Stock, 2008); Ruth Marshall, *Political Spiritualities* (Chicago: University of Chicago Press, 2009).

51. Cox, *Fire From Heaven*, 15; the study of Bogotá is from Rebecca Pierce Bomann, *Faith in the Barrios* (Boulder, Colo.: L. Rienner Publishers, 1999), 32. For the complex reasons driving conversion, see David Smilde, *Reason to Believe* (Berkeley: University of California Press, 2007).

52. Martin is quoted from *Tongues of Fire*, 230.

53. Hannah W. Stewart-Gambino and Everett Wilson, "Latin American Pentecostals," in Cleary and Stewart-Gambino, eds., *Power, Politics, and Pentecostals*, 227–46; Chesnut, *Born Again in Brazil*, 104; Elizabeth W. Kiddy, *Blacks of the Rosary* (University Park: Pennsylvania State University Press, 2005); Peggy Brock, ed., *Indigenous Peoples and Religious Change* (Leiden, Netherlands: Brill, 2005); C. Mathews Samson, *Re-Enchanting the World* (Tuscaloosa: University of Alabama Press, 2007); Aparecida Vilaça and Robin M. Wright, eds., *Native Christians* (Farnham, England: Ashgate, 2009).

54. John Burdick, *Blessed Anastácia* (New York: Routledge, 1998).

55. Joseph M. Murphy, *Working the Spirit* (Boston: Beacon, 1994); "This is the time of the African" is quoted from Robyn Dixon, "African Catholics Seek a Voice to Match Their Growing Strength," *LAT*, April 16, 2005; Toyin Falola and Matt D. Childs, eds., *The Yoruba Diaspora in the Atlantic World* (Bloomington: Indiana University Press, 2005).

56. Carol Ann Drogus, "Private Power or Public Power," in Cleary and Stewart-Gambino, eds., *Power, Politics, and Pentecostals*, 55–75, quotes are from 55, 57; Martin, *Tongues of Fire*, 181–84; Chesnut, *Born Again in Brazil*; Carol Ann Drogus and Hannah Stewart-Gambino, *Activist Faith* (University Park: Pennsylvania State University Press, 2005); Dana L. Robert, "World Christianity as a Women's Movement," *IBMR* 30(4)(2006) 180–188; Harold J. Recinos and Hugo Magallanes, eds., *Jesus in the Hispanic Community* (Louisville, Ky.: Westminster John Knox Press, 2010).

57. Elizabeth E. Brusco, *The Reformation of Machismo* (Austin: University of Texas Press, 1995). Some scholars take a less optimistic view of impact of the new churches on women's lives. See Cecilia Loreto Mariz and Maria das Dores Campos Machado, "Pentecostalism and Women in Brazil," in Cleary and Stewart-Gambino, eds., *Power, Politics, and Pentecostals*, 41–54.

58. Drogus, "Private Power or Public Power," 62; compare Carol Ann Drogus, *Women, Religion and Social Change in Brazil's Popular Church* (South Bend, Ind.: University of Notre Dame Press, 1997).

59. Peter Brown, *The World of Late Antiquity* (London: Thames and Hudson, 1971), 67–68.

60. See for instance, E. P. Thompson, *The Making of the English Working Class* (New York: Vintage Books, 1963); David Hempton, *Methodism* (New Haven: Yale University Press, 2005). In a different economic setting, there are obvious American parallels: see Christine Leigh Heyrman, *Southern Cross* (New York: Knopf, 1997).

61. Bomann, *Faith in the Barrios*, 40–41.

62. "Their main appeal": quoted in Ed Gitre, "Pie-in-the-Sky Now," *CT*, posted to website November 27, 2000; MacHarg, "Brazil's Surging Spirituality"; the Pentecostal pastor is quoted from John Burdick, "Struggling against the Devil" in Garrard-Burnett and Stoll, eds., *Rethinking Protestantism in Latin America*, 23.

63. Gifford, *Ghana's New Christianity*.

64. Chesnut, *Born Again in Brazil*, 51; see chap. 6 notes. For the pervasive violence, see Janice Perlman, *Favela* (New York: Oxford University Press, 2010).

65. Wole Soyinka, *Three Short Plays* (Oxford: Oxford University Press, 1974); Simon Coleman, *The Globalisation of Charismatic Christianity* (Cambridge: Cambridge University Press, 2000).

CHAPTER 5

1. *The World at Six Billion* (Population Division, Department of Economic and Social Affairs, United Nations, 1999); John Bongaarts and Rodolfo A. Bulatao, eds., *Beyond Six Billion* (Washington, D.C.: National Academy Press, 2000). As noted earlier, U.S. government figures on individual countries are drawn from Bureau of the Census, International Database, online at http://sasweb.ssd.census. gov/idb/ranks.html. These are somewhat different from the projections employed by the United Nations, though the rank-orderings are roughly the same: see http://www.un.org/popin/.

2. W. W. Rostow, *The Great Population Spike and After* (New York: Oxford University Press, 1998).

3. Michael S. Teitelbaum and Jay Winter, *A Question of Numbers* (New York: Hill and Wang, 1998). Philip Longman, *The Empty Cradle* (New York: Basic, 2004).

4. George Magnus, *The Age of Aging* (Singapore: John Wiley & Sons (Asia), 2009); Eric Kaufmann, *Shall the Religious Inherit the Earth?* (London: Profile Books, 2010).

5. Michael J. Mazarr, *Global Trends 2005* (New York: St. Martin's Press, 1999), 25.

6. Information about the demographics of individual countries can be found in the *CIA World Fact Book*, online at https://www.cia.gov/library/publications/the-world-factbook/index.html.

The names of some African nations have changed in recent decades, causing confusion to outside observers. For present purposes, the most important case is the

Democratic Republic of the Congo, a populous and potentially important nation with a large Christian population. From 1908 to 1960 this territory was the Belgian Congo, and after independence it changed its name on a number of occasions. It was renamed Zaire from 1971 to 1997, at which point it received its present "Democratic Republic" name. Adding to an already complex situation is the presence of a neighboring and far smaller country known as the Republic of Congo, with its capital at Brazzaville. This nation is made up of former French territories, and the territory has variously been known as the French Congo and Congo-Brazzaville.

7. Richard N. Ostling and Joan K. Ostling, *Mormon America* 2nd ed. (San Francisco: Harper San Francisco, 2007).

8. Quoted in Richard Rodriguez, "A Continental Shift," *LAT*, August 13, 1989. John L. Allen Jr., *The Future Church* (New York: Doubleday, 2009).

9. The numbers offered here are lower than those found in the *World Christian Encyclopedia*, in some cases substantially so; see chap. 1 notes.

10. David B. Barrett, George T. Kurian, and Todd M. Johnson, *World Christian Encyclopedia*, 2nd ed. (New York: Oxford University Press, 2001), 762.

11. Barrett et al., *World Christian Encyclopedia*, 594–601.

12. For the thorough permeation of Filipino life and culture by vernacular Christianity, see Fenella Cannell, *Power and Intimacy in the Christian Philippines* (Cambridge: Cambridge University Press, 1999); Jose Mario C. Francisco, "Christianity as Church and Story and the Birth of the Filipino Nation in the Nineteenth Century," in Sheridan Gilley and Brian Stanley, eds., *Cambridge History of Christianity: World Christianities c.1815–c.1914* (Cambridge: Cambridge University Press, 2005); Francisco F. Claver, *The Making of a Local Church* (Maryknoll, N.Y.: Orbis Books, 2008).

13. Of course, much of the world's urban growth will also occur in medium and smaller cities: David Satterthwaite, *The Transition to a Predominantly Urban World and Its Underpinnings* (London: International Institute for Environment and Development, 2007); Hernando De Soto, *The Mystery of Capital* (New York: Basic Books, 2000).

14. Hugh McLeod and Werner Ustorf, eds., *The Decline of Christendom in Western Europe, 1750–2000* (New York: Cambridge University Press, 2003); Philip Jenkins, *God's Continent* (New York: Oxford University Press, 2007); Callum G. Brown and Michael Snape, eds., *Secularisation in the Christian World* (Aldershot, UK: Ashgate, 2010).

15. Theo Hobson, "Absent Anglicans" *TLS*, July 2, 2010; Adrian Hastings, *A History of English Christianity, 1920–1990*, 3rd ed. (London: SCM, 1991); Grace Davie, *Religion in Britain Since 1945* (Oxford: Blackwell, 1994); Callum G. Brown, *The Death of Christian Britain* (London: Routledge, 2001); Callum G. Brown, *Religion and Society in Twentieth-Century Britain* (London: Longman, 2006); Cole Moreton, *Is God Still an Englishman?* (London: Little, Brown, 2010).

16. For the current state of the Evangelical Church, and its views on contemporary issues, see its website, http://www.ekd.de/. For the much more advanced

secularization of Scandinavian Protestant lands, see Phil Zuckerman, *Society Without God* (New York University Press, 2008).

17. Grace Davie, *Religion in Britain Since* 1945; idem, *Religion in Modern Europe* (New York: Oxford University Press, 2000); idem, *Europe: The Exceptional Case* (London: Darton, Longman and Todd, 2002); Grace Davie, Paul Heelas, and Linda Woodhead, eds., *Predicting Religion* (Burlington, Vt.: Ashgate, 2003); George Weigel, *The Cube and the Cathedral* (New York: Basic, 2005); Jenkins, *God's Continent*; but see Andrew Greeley, *Religion in Europe at the End of the Second Millennium* (New Brunswick, N.J.: Transaction, 2003). Peter Berger, Grace Davie, Effie Fokas, *Religious America, Secular Europe?* (Burlington, Vt.: Ashgate, 2008). For pilgrimage, see Anna-Karina Hermkens, Willy Jansen, and Catrien Notermans, eds., *Moved by Mary* (Burlington, Vt.: Ashgate 2009).

18. Barrett et al., *World Christian Encyclopedia*, 4. Benjamin Forest, Juliet Johnson, and Marietta T. Stepaniants, eds., *Religion and Identity in Modern Russia* (Burlington, Vt.: Ashgate, 2005).

19. Ian Black, "Europe 'Should Accept' 75m New Migrants," *Guardian*, July 28, 2000.

20. *Mapping the Global Future*, at http://www.dni.gov/nic/NIC_globaltrend 2020_s2.html.

21. *Global Trends 2025: A Transformed World*, National Intelligence Council's 2025 Project, http://www.dni.gov/nic/NIC_2025_project.html, viii.

22. Jenkins, *God's Continent*; Anna Triandafyllidou, ed., *Muslims in 21st-century Europe* (New York: Routledge, 2010).

23. Gerrie ter Haar, *African Christians in Europe* (Nairobi, Kenya: Acton, 2001); and idem, ed., *Religious Communities in the Diaspora* (Nairobi, Kenya: Acton, 2001); Afe Adogame and Cordula Weisskoeppel, eds., *Religion in the Context of African Migration* (Bayreuth, Germany: Bayreuth African Studies Series, 2005); Afe Adogame and James V. Spickard, eds., *Religion Crossing Boundaries* (Boston, Mass.: Brill, 2010). For the Netherlands, see Mechteld Jansen and Hijme Stoffels, eds., *A Moving God* (Berlin: Lit Verlag, 2008).

24. Leo Benedictus, "From the Day We're Born Till the Day We Die, It's the Church," *Guardian*, January 21, 2005, my emphasis. Afe Adogame and Cordula Weisskoeppel, eds., *Religion in the Context of African Migration* (Bayreuth: Bayreuth African Studies Series, 2005); Jehu Hanciles, *Beyond Christendom* (Maryknoll, N.Y.: Orbis Books, 2008); Afe Adogame, Roswith Gerloff and Klaus Hock, eds., *Christianity in Africa and the African Diaspora* (New York: Continuum, 2009). For Asian migrants, see Knut A. Jacobsen and Selva J. Raj, eds., *South Asian Christian Diaspora* (Burlington, Vt.: Ashgate, 2008).

25. Jenkins, *God's Continent*; Richard Hoskins, *Sacrifice* (London: Little, Brown, 2006); Jean La Fontaine, ed., *The Devil's Children* (Burlington, Vt.: Ashgate 2009).

26. Emily Buchanan, "Black Church Celebrates Growth," BBC World Service, July 6, 2000; for the Kingsway Centre, see Victoria Combe, "Black Church in

Crusade to Woo Whites," *Electronic Telegraph*, February 16, 2001; Sarah Hall, "Praise Be, It's the Superchurch," *Guardian*, August 24, 1998; the Centre is online at http://www.kicc.org.uk/.

27. Richard Foot, "Anglican Ranks on Road to Extinction," *Vancouver Sun*, December 1, 2005. For a more optimistic view of the Canadian situation, see Reginald W. Bibby, *Restless Gods* (Kenilworth, South Africa: Novalis Press, 2004). For newer ethnic currents, see Terence Fay, *New Faces of Canadian Catholics* (Ottawa: Editions Novalis, 2009); Michael Wilkinson, ed., *Canadian Pentecostalism* (Montreal: McGill-Queen's University Press, 2009).

28. Joel Kotkin, *The Next Hundred Million* (New York: Penguin, 2010).

29. Helen R. F. Ebaugh and Janet Saltzman Chafetz, eds., *Religion and the New Immigrants* (Walnut Creek, Calif.: Altamira, 2000), 29; Mike Davis, *Magical Urbanism* (London: Verso, 2000).

30. Oscar Handlin, *The Uprooted*, 2nd ed. (Boston: Little, Brown, 1990). Diego Ribadeneira, "The Changing Face of Worship," *Boston Globe*, March 22, 1998. For the kaleidoscopic religious diversity of New York City, see Tony Carnes and Anna Karpathakis, eds., *New York Glory* (New York: New York University Press, 2001); compare Gerardo Marti, *A Mosaic of Believers* (Bloomington: Indiana University Press, 2004); Karen I. Leonard, Alex Stepick, Manuel A. Vásquez, and Jennifer Holdaway, eds., *Immigrant Faiths* (Lanham, Md.: AltaMira Press, 2005); Stephen Prothero, ed., *A Nation of Religions* (Chapel Hill: University of North Carolina Press, 2006); Soong-Chan Rah, *The Next Evangelicalism* (Downers Grove, Ill.: InterVarsity Press, 2009); Paul D. Numrich, *The Faith Next Door* (New York: Oxford University Press, 2009). For Ghanaian immigrant religion, see Moses Biney, *From Africa to America* (New York University Press, 2011).

31. For Rockland County, see Jennifer Medina, "If a Diverse Congregation Were Cash, This Church Would Be Rich," *NYT*, March 28, 2005.

32. Sam Quinones, "St. Cecilia's Revived By the Hands of Its Parishioners," *LAT*, February 10, 2008; Esmeralda Bermudez, "Expatriate Oaxacans Find a Home for Their Saints in Santa Monica," *LAT*, July 29, 2010.

33. "Changing Faiths," at http://pewforum.org/Changing-Faiths-Latinos-and-the-Transformation-of-American-Religion.aspx; Ebaugh and Chafetz, eds., *Religion and the New Immigrants*, 14; http://www.usccb.org/hispanicaffairs/demo.shtml. For New York figures, see Tatsha Robertson, "Pentecostalism Luring Away Latino Catholics," *Boston Globe*, April 15, 2005.

For the Latino church, see Timothy Matovina and Gerald Eugene Poyo, eds., *Presente!* (Maryknoll, N.Y.: Orbis, 2000); Timothy Matovina, *Guadalupe and Her Faithful* (Baltimore: Johns Hopkins University Press, 2005); Gastón Espinosa, Virgilio Elizondo, and Jesse Miranda, eds., *Latino Religions and Civic Activism in the United States* (New York: Oxford University Press, 2005); Gerald E. Poyo, *Cuban Catholics in the United States, 1960–1980* (South Bend, Ind.: University of Notre Dame Press, 2007); Gastón Espinosa and Mario T. García eds., *Mexican American Religions* (Durham, N.C.: Duke University Press, 2008); Mario T. García, *Católicos*

(Austin: University of Texas Press, 2008); Catherine E. Wilson, *The Politics of Latino Faith* (New York: New York University Press, 2008); Alyshia Galvez, *Guadalupe in New York* (New York: New York University Press, 2009).

34. Cruz is quoted from Robertson, "Pentecostalism Luring Away Latino Catholics"; Arlene Sanchez Walsh, *Latino Pentecostal Identity* (New York: Columbia University Press, 2003).

35. "An Evangelical zeal filled the air" is from Teresa Watanabe and Susana Enriquez, "Church Redefined," *LAT* April 24, 2005; "God made the salsa" is from Mary Otto, "Hispanic Catholics Celebrate Faith in Harmony," *WP*, March 19, 2006; compare David Cho, "Hispanic Priest Builds a Spirited Following," *WP*, June 28, 2001; Anna Adams, "*Bricando el Charco*," in Edward L. Cleary and Hannah W. Stewart-Gambino, eds., *Power, Politics, and Pentecostals in Latin America* (Boulder, Colo.: Westview, 1997), 163–78; R. Stephen Warner and Judith G. Wittner, eds., *Gatherings in Diaspora* (Philadelphia: Temple University Press, 1998); Manuel A. Vasquez and Marie F. Marquardt, *Globalizing the Sacred* (New Brunswick, N.J.: Rutgers University Press, 2003); Roberto R. Trevino, *The Church in the Barrio* (Chapel Hill: University of North Carolina Press, 2006).

36. Jeffrey M. Burns, Ellen Skerrett, Joseph M. White, eds., *Keeping Faith* (Maryknoll, N.Y.: Orbis, 2000); Ebaugh and Chafetz, eds., *Religion and the New Immigrants*; Jame Iwamura and Paul Spickard, eds., *Revealing the Sacred in Asian and Pacific America* (New York: Routledge, 2003); Fumitaka Matsuoka and Eleazar S. Fernandez, eds., *Realizing the America of Our Hearts* (St. Louis, Mo.: Chalice, 2003); Tony Carnes and Fenggang Yang, eds., *Asian American Religions* (New York: New York University Press, 2004); Lois Ann Lorentzen, ed., *Religion at the Corner of Bliss and Nirvana* (Durham, N.C.: Duke University Press, 2009).

37. Fenggang Yang, *Chinese Christians in America* (University Park: Pennsylvania State University Press, 1999); Russell Jeung, *Faithful Generations* (New Brunswick, N.J.: Rutgers University Press, 2004). For transnational networks, see Helen Rose Ebaugh and Janet Saltzman Chafetz, eds., *Religion Across Borders* (Walnut Creek, Calif.: AltaMira, 2002); Erika A. Muse, *The Evangelical Church in Boston's Chinatown* (New York: Routledge, 2005).

38. Ho Youn Kwon, Kwang Chung Kim, and R. Stephen Warner, eds., *Korean Americans and Their Religions* (University Park: Pennsylvania State University Press, 2001); Su Yon Pak, Unzu Lee, Jung Ha Kim, and Myungji Cho, *Singing the Lord's Song in a New Land* (Louisville, Ky.: Westminster John Knox Press, 2005); Elaine Howard Ecklund, *Korean American Evangelicals* (New York: Oxford University Press, 2006); Rebecca Y. Kim, *God's New Whiz Kids?* (New York University Press, 2006); David K. Yoo and Ruth H. Chung, eds., *Religion and Spirituality in Korean America* (Urbana: University of Illinois Press, 2008); David K. Yoo, *Contentious Spirits* (Stanford, Calif: Stanford University Press, 2010).

39. Diana L. Eck, *A New Religious America* (San Francisco: Harper San Francisco, 2001).

CHAPTER 6

1. Diego Irarrazaval, *Inculturation* (Maryknoll, N.Y.: Orbis, 2000); Andrew F. Walls, *The Cross-Cultural Process in Christian History* (Maryknoll, N.Y.: Orbis, 2001); Laurenti Magesa, *Anatomy of Inculturation* (Maryknoll, N.Y.: Orbis Books, 2004); Paul M. Collins, *Christian Inculturation in India* (Aldershot, UK: Ashgate, 2007).

2. "In Black Africa, rhythm is supreme and is everywhere": François Kabasele Lumbala, *Celebrating Jesus Christ in Africa* (Maryknoll, N.Y.: Orbis, 1998), 24. Louis Chauvet and François Kabasele Lumbala, eds., *Liturgy and the Body* (Maryknoll, N.Y.: Orbis Books, 1995).

3. Adrian Hastings, *The Church in Africa, 1450–1950* (Oxford: Clarendon, 1996), 318–25; Jeff Guy, *The Heretic* (Pietermaritzburg, South Africa: University of Natal Press, 1983).

4. Kang Xi is quoted from R. S. Sugirtharajah, *The Bible and the Third World* (Cambridge: Cambridge University Press, 2001), 13; the Walls quote is from G. C. Waldrep, "The Expansion of Christianity," CC, August 2–9, 2000, 792–95; Andrew F. Walls, *The Missionary Movement in Christian History* (Maryknoll, N.Y.: Orbis, 1996); 102–10.

5. Peter Brown, *The Rise of Western Christendom*, rev. ed. (Oxford: Blackwell, 2003); Philip Jenkins, *Jesus Wars* (San Francisco: HarperOne, 2010).

6. Bede, *History of the English Church and People*, I, 30; Richard Fletcher, *The Barbarian Conversion* (Berkeley: University of California Press, 1999); James C. Russell, *The Germanization of Early Medieval Christianity* (Oxford: Oxford University Press, 1996); R. A. Markus, *The End of Ancient Christianity* (Cambridge: Cambridge University Press, 1991).

7. Jaime Lara, *Christian Texts for Aztecs* (South Bend, Ind.: University of Notre Dame Press, 2008).

8. Ana Castillo, *Goddess of the Americas* (New York: Riverhead, 1996); David Brading, *Mexican Phoenix* (Cambridge: Cambridge University Press, 2001); Gastón Espinosa and Mario T. García eds., *Mexican American Religions* (Durham, N.C.: Duke University Press, 2008). For the context of Marian devotion in Mexican society, see Matthew D. O'Hara, *A Flock Divided* (Durham, NC: Duke University Press, 2010).

9. Gary H. Gossen and Miguel Leon-Portilla, eds., *South and Meso-American Native Spirituality* (New York: Crossroad, 1993); Manuel M. Marzal et al., *The Indian Face of God in Latin America* (Maryknoll, N.Y.: Orbis, 1996); Guillermo Cook, *Crosscurrents in Indigenous Spirituality* (Leiden, Netherlands: Brill, 1997); Allan Greer and Jodi Bilinkoff, eds., *Colonial Saints* (New York: Routledge, 2003); Edward L. Cleary and Timothy J. Steigenga, eds., *Resurgent Voices in Latin America* (New Brunswick, N.J.: Rutgers University Press, 2004). For Cuba, see Thomas A. Tweed, *Our Lady of the Exile* (New York: Oxford University Press, 1997).

10. Peter Phan, "Christianity in Indochina," in Sheridan Gilley and Brian Stanley, eds., *Cambridge History of Christianity: World Christianities c.1815–c.1914* (Cambridge: Cambridge University Press, 2005), 513–27; Salvador Martinez, "Jesus Christ in Popular Piety in the Philippines," in R. S. Sugirtharajah, ed., *Asian Faces of Jesus* (Maryknoll, N.Y.: Orbis, 1993), 247–58. For Vailankanni, see http://www.annaivailankanni.org/annaivailankanni/index.html.

11. Daniel Johnson Fleming, *Each with His Own Brush* (New York: Friendship, 1938); William A. Dyrness, *Christian Art in Asia* (Amsterdam, Netherlands: Rodopi, 1979); *Christian Imagery in African Art* (Notre Dame, Ind.: University of Notre Dame, The Museum, 1980); Volker Küster, *The Many Faces of Jesus Christ* (Maryknoll, N.Y.: Orbis, 2001).

12. Lamin Sanneh, "Pluralism and Christian Commitment," *Theology Today* 45/1 (1988): 27; Lamin O. Sanneh, *Disciples of All Nations* (New York: Oxford University Press, 2007).

13. Lumbala, *Celebrating Jesus Christ in Africa*, 113.

14. http://www.nestorian.org/east_asian_history_sourcebook_.html; Philip Jenkins, *The Lost History of Christianity* (San Francisco: HarperOne, 2008).

15. Quoted in Kwame Bediako, *Christianity in Africa* (Edinburgh: Edinburgh University Press/Orbis, 1995), 59.

16. Quoted in Elizabeth Isichei, *A History of Christianity in Africa* (Grand Rapids, Mich.: Eerdmans, 1995), 315; Hastings, *Church in Africa, 1450–1950*, 502–3; G. C. Oosthuizen, *The Theology of a South African Messiah* (Leiden, Netherlands: Brill, 1967); Irving Hexham and G. O. Oosthuizen, eds., *The Story of Isaiah Shembe* (Lewiston, N.Y.: Edwin Mellen Press, 1997). For the Ekuphakameni pilgrimage, see Thokozani Mtshali, "Shembe—The Incredible Whiteness of Being," *Electronic Mail and Guardian*, August 11, 1999. Anna-Karina Hermkens, Willy Jansen, and Catrien Notermans, eds., *Moved by Mary* (Burlington, Vt.: Ashgate, 2009).

For hymns and sacred music, see Roberta King, Jean Ngoya Kidula, James R. Krabill, and Thomas A. Oduro, *Music in the Life of the African Church* (Waco, Tex.: Baylor University Press, 2008).

17. Andrew Wingate, Kevin Ward, Carrie Pemberton, and Wilson Sitshebo, eds., *Anglicanism* (New York: Church, 1998), 68.

18. Sundkler and Steed, *History of the Church in Africa*, 1022–23; Lumbala, *Celebrating Jesus Christ in Africa*, 55–57; Thomas Bamat, and Jean-Paul Wiest, eds., *Popular Catholicism in a World Church* (Maryknoll, N.Y.: Orbis, 1999); Charles E. Farhadian, ed., *Christian Worship Worldwide* (Grand Rapids, Mich.: Eerdmans, 2007).

19. The speaker was Namibia's Bonifatius Haushiku, quoted in Alan Cowell, "Africa's Bishops Bring Harsh Realities to Vatican," *NYT*, May 1, 1994. There is now a flourishing literature on global South theologies: see for instance, John C. England, Jose Kuttianimattathil, John Mansford Prior, Lily A. Quintos, David Suh Kwang-Sun, and Janice Wickeri, eds., *Asian Christian Theologies*, 3 vols.

(Maryknoll, N.Y.: Orbis Books, 2002–2004); Timothy C. Tennent, *Theology in the Context of World Christianity* (Grand Rapids, Mich.: Zondervan, 2007); William A. Dyrness and Veli-Matti Karkkainen, eds., *Global Dictionary of Theology* (Downers Grove, Ill.: InterVarsity Press, 2008); Sebastian C. H. Kim, ed., *Christian Theology in Asia* (New York: Cambridge University Press, 2008).

20. For the idea of Jesus as Ancestor, see Bediako, *Christianity in Africa*, 84–85; Kwame Bediako, *Jesus and the Gospel in Africa* (Maryknoll, N.Y.: Orbis, 2004); Diane B. Stinton, *Jesus of Africa* (Maryknoll, N.Y.: Orbis, 2004); Victor I. Ezigbo, *Re-imagining African Christologies* (Eugene, Or.: Pickwick, 2010). The extracts from eucharistic prayers are selected from Lumbala, *Celebrating Jesus Christ in Africa*, 36–37; the first two are Gikuyu, the third is Igbo. For Jesus as physician, see James Amanze, *African Christianity in Botswana* (Gweru, Zimbabwe: Mambo, 1998).

For the rise of a distinctive African theology, see S. E. M. Pheko, *Christianity Through African Eyes* (Lusaka, Zambia: Daystar, 1969); J. N. Kanyua Mugambi, *African Christian Theology* (Nairobi, Kenya: Heinemann, 1989); John Parratt, *Reinventing Christianity* (Grand Rapids, Mich.: Eerdmans, 1995); John Parratt, ed., *Introduction to Third World Theologies* (Cambridge: Cambridge University Press, 2004); A. E. Orobator, *Theology Brewed in an African Pot* (Maryknoll, N.Y.: Orbis Books, 2008); Martien E. Brinkman, *The Non-Western Jesus* (Oakville, Conn: Equinox, 2009). For the idea of earth-keeping, see Marthinus L. Daneel, *African Earthkeepers* (Maryknoll, N.Y.: Orbis, 2001).

21. For Latino theology, see Luis G. Pedraja, *Teologia* (Nashville, Tenn.: Abingdon, 2004); Ada Maria Isasi-Diaz and Fernando F. Segovia, eds., *Hispanic/ Latino Theology* (Minneapolis, Minn.: Fortress, 1996). "The mestizo affirms…" is from Virgilio P. Elizondo, *The Future Is Mestizo*, rev. ed. (Boulder: University Press of Colorado, 2000), 84. See also Arturo J. Banuelas ed., *Mestizo Christianity* (Maryknoll, N.Y.: Orbis, 1995); Timothy Matovina, ed., *Beyond Borders* (Maryknoll, N.Y.: Orbis, 2000). For "roots" and "routes," see Paul Gilroy, *The Black Atlantic* (Cambridge, Mass.: Harvard University Press, 1993). For the new diasporas, see Manuel A. Vasquez and Marie F. Marquardt, *Globalizing the Sacred* (New Brunswick, N.J.: Rutgers University Press, 2003).

22. Virgilio P. Elizondo, *Galilean Journey* (Maryknoll, N.Y.: Orbis, 2000), 91.

23. Elizondo, *Galilean Journey*, 133; Edward L. Cleary and Timothy J. Steigenga, eds., *Resurgent Voices in Latin America* (New Brunswick, N.J.: Rutgers University Press, 2004).

24. Elizondo, *Galilean Journey*, 11;. Roberto S. Goizueta, "Why Are You Frightened?" in Peter Casarella and Raul Gomez, eds., *El Cuerpo de Cristo* (New York: Crossroad, 1998), 59; Timothy M. Matovina, *Mestizo Worship* (Collegeville, Minn.: Liturgical; 1998); Alyshia Galvez, *Guadalupe in New York* (New York: New York University Press, 2009). For messianic ideas surrounding *La Caridad*, see Tweed, *Our Lady of the Exile*.

25. Brading, *Mexican Phoenix*.

26. Sundkler and Steed, *History of the Church in Africa*, 970–71, and 924–25 for Zaytoun; Isichei, *History of Christianity in Africa*, 328; Ferdinand Nwaigbo, *Mary—Mother of the African Church* (New York: Peter Lang, 2001).

27. Joel A. Carpenter, "The Christian Scholar in an Age of Global Christianity," at http://www.calvin.edu/minds/volume01/issue02/global-christianity.php. Brian Stanley, *The World Missionary Conference, Edinburgh* 1910 (Grand Rapids, Mich.: Eerdmans, 2009).

28. Bengt Sundkler, *Zulu Zion and Some Swazi Zionists* (Oxford: Oxford University Press, 1976); Bengt Sundkler, *Bantu Prophets in South Africa*, 2nd ed. (New York: Oxford University Press, 1964); Gerhardus C. Oosthuizen, *The Healer-Prophet in Afro-Christian Churches* (Leiden, Netherlands: Brill, 1992); Oosthuizen, *Theology of a South African Messiah*; Hexham and Oosthuizen, eds., *Story of Isaiah Shembe*.

29. Kenneth Woodward, "The Changing Face of the Church," *Newsweek*, April 16, 2001.

30. "Bishop Spong Delivers a Fiery Farewell," *CC*, February 17, 1999.

31. Bregje De Kok, *Christianity and African Traditional Religion* (Lansing: Michigan State University Press, 2005); Gerrie ter Haar, *How God Became African* (Philadelphia: University of Pennsylvania Press, 2009).

32. Quoted in Sundkler and Steed, *History of the Church in Africa*, 633; compare Diedrich Westermann, *Africa and Christianity* (New York: Oxford University Press, 1937).

33. Quoted in David Martin, *Tongues of Fire* (Oxford: Blackwell, 1990), 140; David Chung, *Syncretism* (Albany: SUNY Press, 2001); Andrew E. Kim, "Korean Religious Culture and Its Affinity to Christianity," *Sociology of Religion* 61 (2000): 117–33.

34. Walls is quoted from Waldrep, "The Expansion of Christianity." Ter Haar, *How God Became African*.

35. The story is quoted in Bediako, *Christianity in Africa*, 155–56.

36. "Their very life and worship" is quoted from Patrick Chapita and Luka Mwale, "African Churches Heal War Trauma," *Africanews*, May 1996. The quote about the Cherubim and Seraphim movement is from Deji Ayegboyin and S. Ademola Ishola, *African Indigenous Churches* (Lagos, Nigeria: Greater Heights, 1997), 88; compare J. Akinyele Omoyajowo, *Cherubim and Seraphim* (New York: NOK Publishers International, 1982); Allan Anderson, "Prophetic Healing and the Growth of the Zion Christian Church in South Africa," at http://artsweb.bham.ac.uk/aanderson /Publications/prophetic_healing_and_the_growth.htm. Stephen Ellis and Gerrie ter Haar, *Worlds of Power* (New York: Oxford University Press, 2004).

37. Philip Jenkins, "Nigeria's Christian Videos," *CC*, November 4, 2008: 45.

38. "Pastor Muthee and Mayor Palin," September 25, 2008, at http://blogs. abcnews.com/politicalpunch/2008/09/pastor-muthee-a.html.

39. Shorter is quoted from Sunday Agang, "Who's Afraid of Witches?" September 16, 2009, http://www.christianitytoday.com/ct/2009/septemberweb-only/

1372–1.0.html; Peter Geschiere, *The Modernity of Witchcraft* (Charlottesville: University of Virginia Press, 1997); Adam Ashforth, *Madumo* (Chicago: University of Chicago Press, 2000); and idem, *Witchcraft, Violence, and Democracy in South Africa* (Chicago: University of Chicago Press, 2005); Isak A. Niehaus, Eliazaar Mohlala, and Kally Shokane, *Witchcraft, Power and Politics* (London: Pluto, 2001); Todd Vanden Berg, "Culture, Christianity and Witchcraft in a West African Context," in Lamin O. Sanneh and Joel A. Carpenter, eds., *The Changing Face of Christianity* (New York: Oxford University Press, 2005), 45–62.

40. "Saving Africa's Witch Children," Channel 4 documentary (UK), November 12, 2008.

41. John Thavis, "Pope Tells Africans Faith Can Liberate Them From Superstition, Fear," March 22, 2009, at http://www.catholicnews.com/data/stories/cns/0901329.htm.

42. Ephesians 6:12; Peter Brown, *The World of Late Antiquity* (London: Thames and Hudson, 1971), 55.

43. Stourton, *Absolute Truth*, 183–91; Niels Christian Hvidt, "Interview with Archbishop Immanuel Milingo," February 14, 1998, online at http://www.archbishopmilingo.org/interview-21-49-8.htm.

44. Ferdy Baglo, "Canadian Bishop Blocks Asian Church Leader from Visiting His Diocese," *CT*, November 29, 1999.

45. Andrew F. Walls, in Christopher Fyfe and Andrew Walls, eds., *Christianity in Africa in the* 1990s (Edinburgh: Centre of African Studies, University of Edinburgh, 1996), 13; Edward Stourton, *Absolute Truth* (London: Penguin, 1999), 183–91. Ellis and ter Haar, *Worlds of Power.*

46. Alvyn Austin, "Missions Dream Team," in *Christian History* 52 (1996).

47. Lamin O. Sanneh, *West African Christianity* (Maryknoll, N.Y.: Orbis, 1983), 184, links the epidemics of these years to the upsurge of healing churches. For the Church of the Lord (Aladura), see Ayegboyin and Ishola, *African Indigenous Churches*, 73, 95; Gerhardus C. Oosthuizen and Irving Hexham, eds., *Afro-Christian Religion and Healing in Southern Africa* (Lewiston, N.Y.: Edwin Mellen Press, 1991); Stephen Owoahene-Acheampong, *Inculturation and African Religion* (New York: Peter Lang, 1998). For the Lutheran example, see Frieder Ludwig, *Church and State in Tanzania* (Leiden, Netherlands: Brill, 1999), 184.

48. R. Andrew Chesnut, *Born Again in Brazil* (New Brunswick, N.J.: Rutgers University Press, 1997), 58, 81; Jill Dubisch and Michael Winkelman, eds., *Pilgrimage and Healing* (Tucson: University of Arizona Press, 2005).

49. Cox, *Fire from Heaven*, 226; Kim, "Korean Religious Culture and its Affinity to Christianity." For Umbanda, see Lindsay Hale, *Hearing the Mermaid's Song* (Albuquerque: University of New Mexico Press, 2009). For Macedo, see Ken Serbin, "Brazilian Church Builds an International Empire," *CC*, April 10, 1996; H. Vinson Synan, "The Yoido Full Gospel Church," *Cyberjournal for Pentecostal-Charismatic Research*, at http://www.pctii.org/cyberj/cyberj2/synan.html. For shamanic survivals,

see Frédéric B. Laugrand and Jarich G. Oosten, *Inuit Shamanism and Christianity* (Montreal: McGill-Queen's University Press, 2010).

50. Sundkler and Steed, *History of the Church in Africa*; Timothy C. Morgan, "Have We Become Too Busy with Death?" *CT*, February 7, 2000, 36–44.

51. Wingate et al., *Anglicanism: A Global Communion*, 59; Robert C. Garner, "Safe Sects?" *Journal of Modern African Studies* 38 (2000): 41–69; Isabel Apawo Phiri, Beverley Haddad, and Madipoane Masenya, eds., *African Women, HIV/ AIDS, and Faith Communities* (Pietermaritzburg, South Africa: Cluster, 2003); Musa W. Dube and Musimbi Kanyoro, eds., *Grant Me Justice!* (Maryknoll, N.Y.: Orbis, 2006); Helen Epstein, *The Invisible Cure* (New York: Viking, 2008); Felicitas Becker and P. Wenzel Geissler, eds., *AIDS and Religious Practice in Africa* (Leiden, Netherlands: Brill, 2009).

52. Martin, *Tongues of Fire*, 147; Philip Jenkins, *The New Faces of Christianity* (New York: Oxford University Press, 2006). "Go back" is from Matthew 11:2–5; the Macedonian story is from Acts 16:9.

53. Martin, *Tongues of Fire*, 146. For Shaull, see Ed Gitre, "Pie-in-the-Sky Now," *CT*, posted to website November 27, 2000. For the relationship between biblical and charismatic authority, see Matthew Engelke, *A Problem of Presence* (Berkeley: University of California Press, 2007); Thomas G. Kirsch, *Spirits and Letters* (New York: Berghahn Books, 2008).

54. David A. Shank, quoted in Bediako, *Christianity in Africa*, 104.

55. Quoted in Isichei, *History of Christianity in Africa*, 256. For the followers of Johane Masowe, see David Maxwell, *African Gifts of the Spirit* (Athens: Ohio University Press, 2007); Engelke, *A Problem of Presence*. The Old Testament passage is from 1 Samuel 3:1. Bilinda Straight, *Miracles and Extraordinary Experience in Northern Kenya* (Philadelphia: University of Pennsylvania Press, 2006).

56. Ayegboyin and Ishola, *African Indigenous Churches*, 142.

57. Ayegboyin and Ishola, *African Indigenous Churches*, 114–24; Knut Holter, *Yahweh in Africa* (New York: Peter Lang, 2000); Isichei, *A History of Christianity in Africa*, 289–90.

58. Cedric Pulford, "Debate Continues on Incorporating Animal Sacrifices in Worship," *CT*, October 25, 2000; Lumbala, *Celebrating Jesus Christ in Africa*, 96–98.

59. Thomas E. Sheridan, "The Rarámuri and the Leadville Trail 100," in Thomas E. Sheridan and Nancy J. Parezo, eds., *Paths of Life* (Tucson: University of Arizona Press, 1996), 144–58. Compare Guy Stresser-Péan, *The Sun God and the Savior* (Boulder: University Press of Colorado, 2009).

60. Amanze, *African Christianity in Botswana*, 125. "Agnes Okoh," at http://www.dacb.org/stories/nigeria/okoh_agnes.html.

61. Amanze, *African Christianity in Botswana*, 125.

62. The vase ritual described here is taken from Lumbala, *Celebrating Jesus Christ in Africa*; compare Allan Anderson, "African Pentecostalism and the

Ancestors," *Missionalia* 21 (1993): 26–39; Nicholas M. Creary, "African Inculturation of the Catholic Church in Zimbabwe, 1958–1977," *Historian* 61 (1999): 765–81.

63. Sundkler and Steed, *History of the Church in Africa*, 90–91; George Nnaemeka Oranekwu, *The Significant Role of Initiation in the Traditional Igbo Culture and Religion* (Frankfurt am Main: Verlag für Interkulturelle Kommunikation, 2004).

64. Lumbala, *Celebrating Jesus Christ in Africa*, 12–18.

65. The quote is from G. C. Waldrep, "The Expansion of Christianity"; Andrew F. Walls, "Eusebius Tries Again," *IBMR* 24, no. 3 (2000): 105–11.

66. Jane Lampman, "Targeting Cities with 'Spiritual Mapping' Prayer," *Christian Science Monitor*, September 23, 1999. Michael W. Cuneo, *American Exorcism* (New York: Doubleday, 2001).

67. These arguments are summarized in Philip Jenkins, *Mystics and Messiahs* (New York: Oxford University Press, 2000).

68. David Hempton, *Methodism* (New Haven: Yale University Press, 2005).

69. Keith Thomas, *Religion and the Decline of Magic* (New York: Scribner, 1971); Martin, *Tongues of Fire*; Euan Cameron, *Enchanted Europe* (New York: Oxford University Press, 2010).

CHAPTER 7

1. Jeffrey Haynes, *Religion in Third World Politics* (Boulder, Colo.: Lynne Rienner Publishers, 1994); Pippa Norris and Ronald Inglehart, *Sacred and Secular* (Cambridge: Cambridge University Press, 2004); John Micklethwait and Adrian Wooldridge, *God Is Back* (London: Allen Lane, 2009).

2. Eric Patterson, *Latin America's Neo-Reformation* (New York: Routledge, 2005); Paul Freston, ed., *Evangelical Christianity and Democracy in Latin America* (New York: Oxford University Press, 2008).

3. Michael A. Burdick, *For God and Fatherland* (Albany, N.Y.: SUNY Press, 1995); Anthony James Gill, *Rendering Unto Caesar* (Chicago: University of Chicago Press, 1999).

4. Owen Chadwick, *The Christian Church in the Cold War* (London: Allen Lane, 1992); Edward R. Norman, *Christianity and the World Order* (Oxford: Oxford University Press, 1979).

5. Penny Lernoux, *Cry of the People* (New York: Penguin, 1982); Robert McAfee Brown, *Unexpected News* (Philadelphia: Westminster Press, 1984); Penny Lernoux, *People of God* (New York: Penguin, 1989).

6. *USCIRF Annual Report* 2010 (Washington, D.C.: U.S. Commission on International Religious Freedom, 2010), 40–46.

7. Anna L. Peterson, *Martyrdom and the Politics of Religion* (Albany, N.Y.: SUNY Press, 1997); Jon Sobrino, *Witnesses to the Kingdom* (Maryknoll, N.Y.: Orbis, 2003); Francisco Goldman, *The Art of Political Murder* (New York: Grove Press, 2007).

8. CELAM is the *Consejo Episcopal Latino-Americano.* For Medellín, see Edward Stourton, *Absolute Truth* (London: Penguin, 1999), 113. Gustavo Gutiérrez, *A Theology of Liberation* (Maryknoll, N.Y.: Orbis, 1973); Alain Gheerbrant, *The Rebel Church in Latin America* (London: Penguin, 1974); Edward R. Norman, *Christianity and the World Order* (Oxford: Oxford University Press, 1979), 24; Richard Shaull, *Heralds of a New Reformation* (Maryknoll, N.Y.: Orbis, 1984); Angel D. Santiago-Vendrell, *Contextual Theology and Revolutionary Transformation in Latin America* (Eugene, Ore.: Pickwick, 2010).

9. Warren E. Hewitt, *Base Christian Communities and Social Change in Brazil* (Lincoln: University of Nebraska Press, 1991); Rowan Ireland, *Kingdoms Come* (Pittsburgh: University of Pittsburgh Press, 1991); John Burdick, *Looking for God in Brazil* (Berkeley: University of California Press, 1993); Cecília Loreto Mariz, *Coping with Poverty* (Philadelphia: Temple University Press, 1994); Madeleine Adriance, *Promised Land* (Albany, N.Y.: SUNY Press, 1995); Manuel A. Vasquez, *The Brazilian Popular Church and the Crisis of Modernity* (Cambridge: Cambridge University Press, 1998).

10. German Guzman Campos, *Camilo Torres* (New York: Sheed and Ward, 1969); see also http://www.angelfire.com/md/TobyTerrar/Colombia.html.

11. James R. Brockman, *The Word Remains* (Maryknoll, N.Y.: Orbis, 1982); Hannah Stewart-Gambino, *The Church and Politics in the Chilean Countryside* (Boulder, Colo.: Westview, 1992).

For the progressive church at its height, see Scott Mainwaring and Alexander Wilde, eds., *The Progressive Church in Latin America* (South Bend, Ind.: University of Notre Dame Press, 1989). Edward L. Cleary, ed., *Born of the Poor* (South Bend, Ind.: University of Notre Dame Press, 1990); Paul E. Sigmund, *Liberation Theology at the Crossroads* (New York: Oxford University Press, 1992); Michael Lowy, *The War of Gods* (London: Verso, 1996); Robin Nagle and Jill Nagle, *Claiming the Virgin* (New York: Routledge, 1997); Virginia Garrard-Burnett, ed., *On Earth as It Is in Heaven* (Wilmington, Del.: Scholarly Resources, 2000).

For the crackdown under Pope John Paul II, see Harvey Cox, *The Silencing of Leonardo Boff* (Oak Park, Ill.: Meyer-Stone Books, 1988); Edward Stourton, *Absolute Truth* (London: Penguin, 1999), 107–49.

12. Barbara J. Fraser, "Peru's New Cardinal Known for Standing with the Powerful," *NCR*, March 23, 2001.

13. For Mexico, see Roderic Ai Camp, *Crossing Swords* (New York: Oxford University Press, 1996). For Maciel, see Jason Berry and Gerald Renner, *Vows of Silence* (New York: Free Press, 2004).

14. Kenneth Serbin, "The Catholic Church, Religious Pluralism, and Democracy in Brazil," in Peter Kingstone and Timothy Power, eds., *Democratic Brazil* (Pittsburgh: University of Pittsburgh Press, 2000).

For the continuing tradition of liberation theology, see John Burdick, *Legacies of Liberation* (Burlington Vt.: Ashgate, 2004); and Carol Ann Drogus and Hannah Stewart-Gambino, *Activist Faith* (University Park: Pennsylvania State University

Press, 2005). For Church involvement in indigenous issues, Edward L. Cleary and Timothy J. Steigenga, eds., *Resurgent Voices in Latin America* (New Brunswick, N.J.: Rutgers University Press, 2004); Christine Kovic, *Mayan Voices for Human Rights* (Austin: University of Texas Press, 2005).

15. Enzo Romeo, *L'Oscar Color Porpora* (Rome: Ancora, 2006); John L. Allen, "New Cardinal Symbolizes Direction of Global Catholicism," *NCR*, March 9, 2001. See also http://www.natcath.com/NCR_Online/documents/Rodriguez.htm. "Neoliberal capitalism carries injustice" is from John L. Allen, "The Word From Rome," *NCR*, March 5, 2004, at http://www.nationalcatholicreporter.org/word/word030504.htm.

16. Gregory Wilpert, *Changing Venezuela* (London: Verso, 2007); Hugh O'Shaughnessy, *The Priest of Paraguay* (London: Zed Books, 2009); Christine Hunefeldt and Misha Kokotovic, *Power, Culture, and Violence in the Andes* (Portland, Ore.: Sussex Academic Press, 2009); Jeffery R. Webber, *From Rebellion to Reform in Bolivia* (London: Haymarket Books, 2011).

17. "Bolivian President Attacks Bishops," *Catholic Herald*, July 31, 2009, http://archive.catholicherald.co.uk/articles/a0000607.shtml. For Venezuela, see *USCIRF Annual Report 2010* (Washington, D.C.: U.S. Commission on International Religious Freedom, 2010), 318–23.

18. "Archbishop Isaias Duarte Cancino," *Guardian*, March 18, 2002, at http://www.guardian.co.uk/colombia/story/0,11502,669181,00.html.

19. Paul Freston, ed., *Evangelical Christianity and Democracy in Latin America* (New York: Oxford University Press, 2008); Jason Pierceson, Adriana Piatti-Crocker, and Shawn Schulenberg, eds., *Same-Sex Marriage in the Americas* (Lanham, Md.: Lexington Books, 2010).

20. For Brazil, see Henry Chu, "Moved by the Spirit to Govern," *LAT*, June 7, 2004. Lorraine Orlandi, "Mexico's Catholic Church Raises Voice in 2006 Race," Reuters, October 18, 2005; Paul Freston, *Protestant Political Parties* (Aldershot, UK: Ashgate, 2004).

21. Frieder Ludwig, *Church and State in Tanzania* (Leiden, Netherlands: Brill, 1999), 104, 107; Dana L. Robert, "Shifting Southward," *IBMR* 24, no. 2 (2000): 50–58; Holger Bernt Hansen and Michael Twaddle, eds., *Religion and Politics in East Africa* (Athens: Ohio University Press, 1995).

22. Tristan Anne Borer, *Challenging the State* (South Bend, Ind.: University of Notre Dame Press, 1998); James Cochrane, John W. De Gruchy, and Stephen Martin, eds., *Facing the Truth* (Athens: Ohio University Press, 1999).

23. Bengt Sundkler and Christopher Steed, *A History of the Church in Africa* (Cambridge: Cambridge University Press, 2000), 904. For Ugandan affairs, see Paul Gifford, *African Christianity* (Bloomington: Indiana University Press, 1998), 112–80. For Congo/Brazzaville, see Abraham Okoko-Esseau, "The Christian Churches and Democratization in the Congo," in Paul Gifford, ed., *The Christian Churches and the Democratisation of Africa* (Leiden, Netherlands: Brill, 1995), 148–67; Margaret Ford, *Janani* (London: Marshall, Morgan and Scott, 1979).

24. Philip Jenkins, *The New Faces of Christianity* (New York: Oxford University Press, 2006). See also Gifford, *African Christianity*; Jeffrey Haynes, *Religion and Politics in Africa* (London: Zed Books 1996); Isaac Phiri, *Proclaiming Political Pluralism* (Westport, Conn.: Praeger, 2001); Galia Sabar, *Church, State and Society in Kenya* (London: Frank Cass, 2002).

25. Samuel P. Huntington, *The Third Wave* (Norman: University of Oklahoma Press, 1991); Patrick Claffey, *Christian Churches in Dahomey-Benin* (Leiden, Netherlands: Brill, 2007).

26. Paul Froese, *The Plot to Kill God* (Berkeley: University of California Press, 2009); John Garrard and Carol Garrard, *Russian Orthodoxy Resurgent* (Princeton, N.J.: Princeton University Press, 2010).

27. John L. Allen, "Faith, Hope and Heroes," *NCR*, February 23, 2001. For parallels with ancient bishops, see the account of the collapse of Roman rule along the frontier in what is now Austria, in Eugippius, *The Life of Saint Severin* (Washington, D.C.: Catholic University of America Press, 1965).

28. Sundkler and Steed, *History of the Church in Africa*, 966; Gifford, ed., *Christian Churches and the Democratisation of Africa*, 5; Michael G. Schatzberg, *The Dialectics of Oppression in Zaire* (Bloomington: Indiana University Press, 1988); Michela Wrong, *In the Footsteps of Mr. Kurtz* (New York: HarperCollins, 2001).

29. "Slain by the Spirit," *The Economist*, July 1 2010; Terence O. Ranger, ed., *Evangelical Christianity and Democracy in Africa* (New York: Oxford University Press, 2008).

30. "Scripted by God" is from the obituary of Cardinal Sin, *Daily Telegraph* (London), June 22, 2005. For the religious and anticlerical roots of the nationalist movement, see Jose P. Rizal, *Noli Me Tangere* (Honolulu: University of Hawai'i Press, 1997); John N. Schumacher, *Revolutionary Clergy* (Quezon City, Philippines: Ateneo de Manila University Press, 1981); Wilfredo Fabros, *The Church and Its Social Involvement in the Philippines, 1930–1972* (Quezon City, Philippines: Ateneo de Manila University Press, 1988); Kathleen M. Nadeau, *Liberation Theology in the Philippines* (Westport, Conn.: Praeger, 2002); Jose Mario C. Francisco, "Christianity as Church and Story and the Birth of the Filipino Nation in the Nineteenth Century," in Sheridan Gilley and Brian Stanley, eds., *Cambridge History of Christianity: World Christianities c.1815–c.1914* (Cambridge: Cambridge University Press, 2005), 528–41.

31. John N. Schumacher, *Revolutionary Clergy*; Benjamin Pimentel, "Battle of Prayers," *San Francisco Chronicle*, December 5, 2000; Sophie Lizares-Bodegon, "Thousands of Filipino Christians Pray for Estrada's Swift Resignation," *CT*, posted to website December 11, 2000.

32. Robert, "Shifting Southward"; Wi Jo Kang, *Christ and Caesar in Modern Korea* (Albany, N.Y.: SUNY Press, 1997); Timothy S. Lee, *Born Again* (Honolulu: University of Hawai'i Press, 2010).

33. David Martin, *Tongues of Fire* (Oxford: Blackwell, 1990), 141; Sang-T'aek Yi, *Religion and Social Formation in Korea* (New York: Mouton de Gruyter, 1996);

Paul S. Chung, *Constructing Irregular Theology* (Leiden, Netherlands: Brill, 2009). The quote from Kim Dae Jung is taken from "Nobel Winner Has Credited Catholic Faith with Helping Him Survive Torture," *Tidings*, Los Angeles, October 20, 2000, 26. David Halloran Lumsdaine, ed., *Evangelical Christianity and Democracy in Asia* (New York: Oxford University Press, 2009).

34. Mark Mitchell, "The Philippines," *FEER*, April 19, 2001.

35. Ralph R. Premdas, *Ethnic Conflict and Development* (Brookfield, Vt.: Avebury, 1995); Matt Tomlinson, *In God's Image* (Berkeley: University of California Press, 2009).

36. Isaac Phiri, "Why African Churches Preach Politics," *Journal of Church and State* 41 (1999): 323–47.

37. The Pauline text is Romans 13:1.

38. R. Drew Smith, "Missionaries, Church Movements, and the Shifting Religious Significance of the State in Zambia," *Journal of Church and State* 41 (1999): 525–50. For the abuse of church authority in the service of government, see Paul Gifford, *Christianity and Politics in Doe's Liberia* (Cambridge: Cambridge University Press, 1993). For Zambia, see Isaac Phiri, "Why African Churches Preach Politics"; Odhiambo Okite, "Church Leaders Publicly Oppose Term for Christian President," *CT*, April 23, 2001; Ranger, ed., *Evangelical Christianity and Democracy in Africa*.

39. Desmond Tutu, "Identity Crisis," in Gifford, ed., *Christian Churches and the Democratisation of Africa*, 97.

40. "The Failed States Index 2010," http://www.foreignpolicy.com/articles/2010/06/21/2010_failed_states_index_interactive_map_and_rankings.

41. *The Joint Operating Environment* 2008 (U.S. Joint Forces Command, 2008), http://www.jfcom.mil/newslink/storyarchive/2008/JOE2008.pdf.

42. CESNUR, the Center for the Study of New Religions, offers a large collection of texts and documents about this incident online at: http://www.cesnur.org/testi/uganda_updates.htm.

43. Stephen Ellis and Gerrie ter Haar, *Worlds of Power* (New York: Oxford University Press, 2004); Niels Kastfelt, ed., *The Role of Religion in African Civil Wars* (London: C. Hurst, 2001); Heike Behrend, *Alice Lakwena and the Holy Spirits* (Athens: Ohio University Press, 2000); Stephen Ellis, *The Mask of Anarchy* (New York: New York University Press, 1999); Stephen L. Weigert, *Traditional Religion and Guerrilla Warfare in Modern Africa* (London: Macmillan, 1995).

44. Emmanuel M. Katongole and Jonathan Wilson-Hartgrove, *Mirror to the Church* (Grand Rapids, Mich.: Zondervan, 2009); Timothy Longman, *Christianity and Genocide in Rwanda* (New York: Cambridge University Press, 2009).

45. John L. Allen, "Synod for Africa opens to high hopes, but realism," October 2009, http://ncronline.org/news/vatican/synod-africa-opens-high-hopes-realism.

46. The pope is quoted in Hannah W. Stewart-Gambino and Everett Wilson, "Latin American Pentecostals," in Edward L. Cleary and Hannah W. Stewart-Gambino,

eds., *Power, Politics, and Pentecostals in Latin America* (Boulder, Colo.: Westview, 1997), 228. For the "oil stain," see Kenneth D. MacHarg, "Healing the Violence," *CT*, posted to website July 25, 2000. Prigione is quoted from Diego Cevallos, "Indigenous Peoples Divided by Faith," Inter Press, Service News Agency, September 5, 2005, at http://www.ipsnews.net/news.asp?idnews=28583. Rodríguez is quoted in Barbara Fraser and Paul Jeffrey, "Latin America: Search for a Future," *NCR*, May 14, 2004, at http://ncronline.org/NCR_Online/archives2/2004b/051404/051404a.php.

47. Casaldáliga is quoted from Cevallos, "Indigenous Peoples Divided by Faith." Chesnut is quoted from Elma Lia Nascimento, "Praise the Lord and Pass the Catch-Up," *Brazzil* magazine, November 1995, at http://www.brazzil.com/cvrnov95.htm.

48. Virginia Garrard-Burnett, *Protestantism in Guatemala* (Austin: University of Texas Press, 1998), 21.

49. "The proliferation of Protestantism..." is from Virginia Garrard-Burnett, in Virginia Garrard-Burnett and David Stoll, eds., *Rethinking Protestantism in Latin America* (Philadelphia: Temple University Press, 1993), 199; Philip Berryman, *The Religious Roots of Rebellion* (London: SCM, 1984); Mark Danner, *The Massacre at El Mozote* (New York: Vintage, 1994); Brian H. Smith, *Religious Politics in Latin America* (South Bend, Ind.: University of Notre Dame Press, 1998); Paul Freston, *Evangelicals and Politics in Asia, Africa and Latin America* (Cambridge: Cambridge University Press, 2001); Virginia Garrard-Burnett, *Terror in the Land of the Holy Spirit* (New York: Oxford University Press, 2010).

50. Quoted in Diego Cevallos, "Indigenous Peoples Divided by Faith."

51. Christian Lalive d'Epinay, *Haven of the Masses* (London: Lutterworth, 1969); Frans Kamsteeg, *Prophetic Pentecostalism in Chile* (Lanham, Md.: Scarecrow, 1998); Philip J. Williams, "The Sound of Tambourines," in Cleary and Stewart-Gambino, eds., *Power, Politics, and Pentecostals*, 179–200; Hannah W. Stewart-Gambino and Everett Wilson, "Latin American Pentecostals"; John Burdick, "Struggling against the Devil," in Garrard-Burnett and Stoll, eds., *Rethinking Protestantism in Latin America*, 20–44; Ireland, *Kingdoms Come*; Freston, *Evangelicals and Politics in Asia, Africa and Latin America*; Timothy J. Steigenga, *Politics of the Spirit* (Lanham, Md.: Lexington Books, 2001); Freston, ed., *Evangelical Christianity and Democracy in Latin America*; Kevin O'Neill, *City of God* (Berkeley: University of California Press, 2009).

52. Paul Freston, "Brother Votes for Brother" in Garrard-Burnett and Stoll, eds., *Rethinking Protestantism in Latin America*, 66–110; Thomas W. Walker and Ariel C. Armony, eds., *Repression, Resistance, and Democratic Transition in Central America* (Wilmington, Del.: Scholarly Resources, 2000). The quote about Protestant influence is from Henry Chu, "Moved by the Spirit to Govern," *LAT*, June 7, 2004; Freston, *Protestant Political Parties*.

53. The quote is from Cevallos, "Indigenous Peoples Divided by Faith"; MacHarg, "Healing the Violence"; Ginger Thompson, "In a Warring Mexican

Town, God's Will Is the Issue," *NYT*, August 13, 2000; Christine Kovic, *Mayan Voices for Human Rights* (Austin: University of Texas Press, 2005).

54. Nascimento, "Praise the Lord and Pass the Catch-Up"; McDonnell, "Pentecostals and Catholics on Evangelism and Sheep-Stealing."

55. David Hempton, *Methodism* (New Haven: Yale University Press, 2005).

56. Ian Buruma, *Taming the Gods* (Princeton, N.J.: Princeton University Press, 2010).

57. Francis Kornegay, "Afro-Asian Entente Key to Gondwanaland Axis," *Business Day* (Johannesburg), October 13, 2003; "Dreaming with BRICs," available at http://www2.goldmansachs.com/ideas/index.html. BRICs are a central theme of *A Transformed World*, National Intelligence Council's 2025 Project, http://www.dni.gov/nic/NIC_2025_project.html.

58. "Global Trends 2015," online at http://www.dni.gov/nic/NIC_global-trend2015.html.

59. Rosalind I. J. Hackett, "Religious Freedom and Religious Conflict in Africa," in Mark Silk, ed., *Religion on the International News Agenda* (Hartford, Conn.: Leonard F. Greenberg Center for the Study of Religion in Public Life, 2000), 102–14; Claire Hoertz Badaracco, ed., *Quoting God* (Waco, Tex.: Baylor University Press, 2005).

60. Richard Hoskins, *Sacrifice* (London: Little, Brown, 2006); Jean La Fontaine, ed., *The Devil's Children* (Burlington, Vt.: Ashgate 2009).

CHAPTER 8

1. Samuel P. Huntington, *The Clash of Civilizations and the Remaking of World Order* (New York: Simon & Schuster, 1996); Peter L. Berger, Jonathan Sacks, David Martin, and Grace Davie, eds., *The Desecularization of the World* (Grand Rapids, Mich.: Eerdmans, 1999); Karen Armstrong, *The Battle for God* (New York: Knopf, 2000); Mark Juergensmeyer, *Terror in the Mind of God*, 3rd ed. (Berkeley: University of California Press, 2003); Mark Juergensmeyer, *Global Rebellion* (Berkeley: University of California Press, 2008); Charles Selengut, *Sacred Fury* (Lanham, Md.: Rowman & Littlefield, 2008); John Micklethwait and Adrian Wooldridge, *God Is Back* (London: Allen Lane, 2009).

2. Allen D. Hertzke, *Freeing God's Children* (Lanham, Md.: Rowman & Littlefield, 2004). Throughout this chapter, I have made extensive use of the detailed reports in the *USCIRF Annual Report* 2010 (Washington, D.C.: U.S. Commission on International Religious Freedom, 2010).

3. Arvind Sharma, ed., *Our Religions* (San Francisco: Harper San Francisco, 1993).

4. Anto Akkara, "Churches Angry that Indian Census Ignores Fourteen Million Christian Dalits," *CT*, March 2, 2001.

5. Bengt Sundkler and Christopher Steed, *A History of the Church in Africa* (Cambridge: Cambridge University Press, 2000), 646–49; Nehemia Levtzion and

Randall L. Pouwels, eds., *The History of Islam in Africa* (Athens: Ohio State University, Center for International Studies, 2000); Charlotte A. Quinn and Frederick Quinn, *Pride, Faith, and Fear* (New York: Oxford University Press, 2003).

6. Philip Longman, *The Empty Cradle* (New York: Basic, 2004); Eric Kaufmann, *Shall the Religious Inherit the Earth?* (London: Profile Books, 2010).

7. Tarif Khalidi, *The Muslim Jesus* (Cambridge, Mass.: Harvard University Press, 2001); Philip Jenkins, *The Lost History of Christianity* (San Francisco: HarperOne, 2008).

8. For Africa, see Adeline Masquelier, *Prayer Has Spoiled Everything* (Durham, N.C.: Duke University Press, 2001); Mark Faulkner, *Overtly Muslim, Covertly Boni* (Leiden, Netherlands: Brill, 2006).

9. Jenkins, *Lost History of Christianity*.

10. From a vast literature on the Armenian massacres, see Peter Balakian, *The Burning Tigris* (New York: HarperCollins, 2003). Bruce Clark, *Twice a Stranger* (Cambridge, Mass.: Harvard University Press, 2006).

11. David Rohde, *Endgame* (New York: Farrar, Straus and Giroux, 1997).

12. Eliza Griswold, *The Tenth Parallel* (New York: Farrar, Straus and Giroux, 2010); Francois Burgat, *The Islamic Movement in North Africa* (Austin: University of Texas Press, 1997); Beverley Milton-Edwards, *Islamic Fundamentalism since 1945* (New York: Routledge, 2005). For the attitudes of Muslims and Christians in Africa, see Pew Forum, *Tolerance and Tension,* 2010, at http://pewforum.org/executive-summary-islam-and-christianity-in-sub-saharan-africa.aspx.

13. Stig Jarle Hansen, Atle Mesøy, and Tuncay Kardas, eds., *The Borders of Islam* (New York: Columbia University Press, 2009); *Global Trends 2025: A Transformed World*, http://www.dni.gov/nic/NIC_2025_project.html.

14. *USCIRF Annual Report* 2010 (Washington, D.C.: U.S. Commission on International Religious Freedom, 2010), 139–57; John O. Hunwick, *Religion and National Integration in Africa* (Evanston, Ill.: Northwestern University Press, 1992); Marc Nikkel, *Why Haven't You Left?* Grant LeMarquand, ed. (London: Church Publishing, 2005); Richard Cockett, *Sudan* (New Haven, Conn.: Yale University Press, 2010); Griswold, *The Tenth Parallel*.

15. Sana Hassan, *Christians versus Muslims in Modern Egypt* (New York: Oxford University Press, 2003); Jenkins, *Lost History of Christianity*; Rachel M. Scott, *The Challenge of Political Islam* (Stanford, Calif.: Stanford University Press, 2010).

16. *USCIRF Annual Report* 2010, 227–240.

17. For relations between the two faiths in Africa, see Benjamin F. Soares, ed., *Muslim-Christian Encounters in Africa* (Leiden, Netherlands: Brill, 2006); Lamin O. Sanneh, *The Crown and the Turban* (Boulder, Colo.: Westview, 1996); idem, *Piety and Power* (Maryknoll, N.Y.: Orbis, 1996); Lissi Rasmussen, *Christian-Muslim Relations in Africa* (London: British Academic Press, 1993); Noel Quinton King, *Christian and Muslim in Africa* (New York: Harper and Row, 1971).

18. Hunwick, *Religion and National Integration in Africa*; Niels Kastfelt, *Religion and Politics in Nigeria* (London: British Academic Press, 1994); Toyin Falola, *Violence in Nigeria* (Rochester, N.Y.: University of Rochester Press, 1998); Karl Meier, *This House Has Fallen* (London: Allen Lane, 2001); Niels Kastfelt, ed., *The Role of Religion in African Civil Wars* (London: C. Hurst, 2001); Patrick Lambert Udoma, *The Cross and the Crescent* (London: Saint Austin Press, 2002); Andrew E. Barnes, *Making Headway* (Rochester, N.Y.: University of Rochester Press, 2009); Julius O. Adekunle, ed., *Religion in Politics* (Trenton, N.J.: Africa World Press, 2009).

19. Ustaz Yoonus Abdullah, *Sharia in Africa* (Ijebu-Ode, Nigeria: Shebiotimo Publications, 1998); Paul Marshall, ed., *Radical Islam's Rules* (Lanham, Md.: Rowman & Littlefield, 2005); Richard Burgess, *Nigeria's Christian Revolution* (Eugene, Ore.: Wipf & Stock 2008); Ruth Marshall, *Political Spiritualities* (Chicago: University of Chicago Press, 2009); Adekunle, ed., *Religion in Politics*; Griswold, *The Tenth Parallel*.

20. *USCIRF Annual Report* 2010, 80–90.

21. Norimitsu Onishi, "Deep Political and Religious Rifts Disrupt Harmony of Nigerian Towns," *NYT*, March 26, 2000; idem, "Winds of Militant Islam Disrupt Fragile Frontiers," *NYT*, February 2, 2001.

22. For neighboring countries, see Barbara M. Cooper, *Evangelical Christians in the Muslim Sahel* (Bloomington: Indiana University Press, 2006).

23. "Global Trends 2015."

24. Mano Ramalshah, "Living as a Minority in Pakistan," in Andrew Wingate, Kevin Ward, Carrie Pemberton, and Wilson Sitshebo, eds., *Anglicanism* (New York: Church, 1998), 264–70; Hassan Abbas, *Pakistan's Drift into Extremism* (Armonk, N.Y.: M. E. Sharpe, 2005); *USCIRF Annual Report* 2010, 94–102.

25. Robert W. Hefner, *Civil Islam* (Princeton, N.J.: Princeton University Press, 2000); Donald K. Emmerson, ed., *Indonesia Beyond Suharto* (Armonk, N.Y.: M. E. Sharpe, 1999); Jan Sihar Aritonang and Karel Steenbrink, eds., *A History of Christianity in Indonesia* (Leiden, Netherlands: Brill, 2008). For the older Islam of the region, see Ronald Lukens-Bull, *A Peaceful Jihad* (New York: Palgrave Macmillan, 2005).

26. John T. Sidel, *Riots, Pogroms, Jihad* (Ithaca, N.Y.: Cornell University Press, 2006); Julius Bautista and Francis Khek Gee Lim, eds., *Christianity and the State in Asia* (New York: Routledge, 2009).

27. Alex Spillius, "Indonesian Christians Forced into Islamic Faith," *Daily Telegraph*, February 5, 2001. Incidents of persecution are tabulated at http://www.persecution.org/Countries/indonesia.html; Richard Lloyd Parry, *In the Time of Madness* (London: Jonathan Cape, 2005); Maribeth Erb, Priyambudi Sulistiyanto, and Carole Faucher, eds., *Regionalism in Post-Suharto Indonesia* (New York: Routledge, 2005); Sidel, *Riots, Pogroms, Jihad*; Griswold, *The Tenth Parallel*.

28. Mike Millard, *Jihad in Paradise* (Armonk, N.Y.: M. E. Sharpe, 2004); *USCIRF Annual Report* 2010, 255–66.

29. Niniek Karmini, "Indonesian Islamists Open Front Against Christians," Associated Press, July 4, 2010.

30. Zachary Abuza, *Balik-Terrorism* (Carlisle, Penn.: Strategic Studies Institute, U.S. Army War College, 2005), online at http://purl.access.gpo.gov/GPO/LPS64419.

31. Rajiv Chandrasekaran, "Southeast Asia Shaken by Rise of Strict Islam," *WP*, November 5, 2000; Simon Elegant, "Bound by Tradition," *FEER*, July 27, 2000; Robert W. Hefner and Patricia Horvatich, ed., *Islam in an Era of Nation-States* (Honolulu: University of Hawai'i Press, 1997); John L. Esposito, John O. Voll, and Osman Bakar, eds., *Asian Islam in the Twenty-first Century* (New York: Oxford University Press, 2008).

32. John Ghazvinian, *Untapped* (London: Houghton Mifflin Harcourt, 2007); Frans Wijsen and Bernardin Mfumbusa, *Seeds of Conflict* (Nairobi, Kenya: Paulines Publications Africa, 2004).

33. Paul Mojzes, ed., *Religion and the War in Bosnia* (Atlanta: Scholars Press, American Academy of Religion, 1998).

34. For Rushdie, see Malise Ruthven, *A Satanic Affair* (London: Chatto and Windus, 1990) and Kenan Malik, *From Fatwa to Jihad* (New York: Atlantic Books, 2009).

For contemporary Europe, see Philip Jenkins, *God's Continent* (New York: Oxford University Press, 2007); Michael Burleigh, *Sacred Causes* (New York: HarperCollins, 2007); Alison Pargeter, *The New Frontiers of Jihad* (Philadelphia: University of Pennsylvania Press, 2008); Jytte Klausen, *The Cartoons That Shook the World* (New Haven, Conn.: Yale University Press, 2009); Elena Tchoudinova, *La Mosquée Notre-Dame de Paris* (Paris: Tatamis, 2009); Christopher Caldwell, *Reflections on the Revolution in Europe* (New York: Doubleday, 2009); Ian Buruma, *Taming the Gods* (Princeton, N.J.: Princeton University Press, 2010), 83–125.

35. "Anti-Muslim Remarks Create a Furor," *San Francisco Chronicle*, September 15, 2000; "Cardinal Asks Italy to Favor Catholic Immigrants," *America*, September 30, 2000, 5.

36. Joel Peters, *Israel and Africa* (London: British Academic Press, 1992).

37. J. Aruldoss, "Dalits and Salvation," in Wingate et al., *Anglicanism*, 294–300; Leonard Fernando and George Gispert-Sauch, *Christianity in India* (New Delhi: Penguin India, 2004); Robert Eric Frykenberg, *Christianity in India* (New York: Oxford University Press, 2008). For the National Campaign on Dalit Human Rights, see http://www.ncdhr.org.in/.

38. Aruldoss, "Dalits and Salvation," 295. Peniel Rajkumar, *Dalit Theology and Dalit Liberation* (Burlington, Vt: Ashgate, 2010).

39. Sathianathan Clarke, *Dalits and Christianity* (Delhi: Oxford India Paperbacks, 1999); T. K. Oommen and Hunter P. Mabry, *The Christian Clergy in India* (Thousand Oaks, Calif.: Sage 2000); Anto Akkara, "Study of Indian Clergy Exposes Inequalities in Church Leadership," *CT*, October 9, 2000; Thomas C. Fox, "Intolerance in India," *NCR*, May 4, 2001; Rowena Robinson

and Joseph Marianus Kujur, eds., *Margins of Faith* (Thousand Oaks, Calif.: Sage Publications, 2010).

40. Michael Fischer, "The Fiery Rise of Hindu Fundamentalism," *CT*, March 1, 1999.

41. Anti-Christian violence in India has become so commonplace as to be rarely noted with any prominence in the media, although the magazine *Christianity Today* provides excellent coverage in the West.

42. *USCIRF Annual Report* 2010, 241–254; Robinson and Kujur, eds., *Margins of Faith*.

43. "Dalai Lama Condemns Christian, Muslim Practice of Seeking Converts," BBC World Service, January 26, 2001; Jason Overdorf, "Criminal Conversions," *FEER*, September 18, 2003. Bautista and Lim, eds., *Christianity and the State in Asia*.

44. Yoshiko Ashiwa and David L. Wank, eds., *Making Religion, Making the State* (Palo Alto, Calif.: Stanford University Press, 2009); Louisa Lim, "Beijing Finds Common Cause with Chinese Buddhists," National Public Radio, July 22, 2010, http://www.npr.org/templates/story/story.php?storyId=128691021.

45. For dialogue between the two faiths, see Aloysius Pieris, *Fire and Water* (Maryknoll, N.Y.: Orbis, 1996); Kenneth Fleming, *Asian Christian Theologians in Dialogue with Buddhism* (New York: Peter Lang, 2002); Thomas C. Fox, *Pentecost in Asia* (Maryknoll, N.Y.: Orbis, 2002); Peter C. Phan, *Being Religious Inter-religiously* (Maryknoll, N.Y.: Orbis, 2004).

46. Gill Donovan, "Leader Says Churches Need to Rethink Missionary Work," *NCR*, May 11, 2001.

47. Robert D. Kaplan, *The Coming Anarchy* (New York: Random House, 2000); Jon Abbink and Ineke van Kessel, eds. *Vanguard or Vandals* (Leiden, Netherlands: Brill, 2005).

48. Hilary Pilkington and Galina Yemelianova, eds., *Islam in Post-Soviet Russia* (New York: Routledge Curzon, 2003). The five Central Asian republics are Uzbekistan, Kazakhstan, Turkmenistan, Kyrgyzstan, and Tajikistan. For religious conflicts in these regions, see *USCIRF Annual Report* 2010, 158—83, 297–302; A. Christian van Gorder, *Muslim-Christian Relations in Central Asia* (New York: Routledge, 2008).

49. Vitaly V. Naumkin, *Radical Islam in Central Asia* (Lanham, Md.: Rowman & Littlefield, 2005); Galina Yemelianova, ed., *Radical Islam in the Former Soviet Union* (New York: Routledge, 2010).

50. Thomas Turner, *The Congo Wars* (London: Zed Books, 2007); Gérard Prunier, *Africa's World War* (New York: Oxford University Press, 2008); Rene Lemarchand, *The Dynamics of Violence in Central Africa* (Philadelphia: University of Pennsylvania Press, 2009).

51. Michael Pillsbury, ed., *Chinese Views of Future Warfare*, rev. ed. (Washington, D.C.: National Defense University Press, 1998); Michael Pillsbury, *China Debates the Future Security Environment* (Washington, D.C.: National

Defense University Press, 2000); Ishtiaq Ahmed, ed., *The Politics of Religion in South and Southeast Asia* (London: Routledge, 2011).

CHAPTER 9

1. *Complete Stories of Evelyn Waugh* (Boston: Little, Brown, 1999), 144: thanks to Chilton Williamson Jr. for drawing my attention to this story.

2. H. Daniel-Rops, *The Church in the Seventeenth Century* (London: Dent, 1963), 46.

3. Charles Williams, *Shadows of Ecstasy* (London: Faber and Faber, 1965), 40.

4. Lothrop T. Stoddard, *The Rising Tide of Color Against White World Supremacy* (New York: C. Scribner's Sons, 1920); John Buchan, *Prester John* (New York: T. Nelson and Sons, 1910); Edward W. Blyden, *Christianity, Islam and the Negro Race* (Edinburgh: Edinburgh University Press, 1967).

5. Jean Raspail, *The Camp of the Saints* (New York: Scribner, 1975). In *Almanac of the Dead* (New York: Simon & Schuster, 1991), Leslie Marmon Silko offers a left-wing counterpart to *Camp of the Saints*, depicting the Native masses of Central and South America pouring north into the ruins of the United States, to overwhelm white civilization and Christianity. Unlike Raspail, Silko clearly sympathizes with the invaders.

6. Hilaire Belloc, *Europe and the Faith* (New York: Paulist Press, 1920), ix.

7. All figures are drawn from *The Official Catholic Directory*; John L. Allen, "Faith, Hope and Heroes," *NCR*, February 23, 2001; John L. Allen Jr., *The Future Church* (New York: Doubleday, 2009); Ian Linden, *Global Catholicism* (New York: Columbia University Press, 2009).

8. Rogelio Saenz, "The Changing Demographics of Roman Catholics," (2005) at http://www.prb.org/Template.cfm?Section=PRB&template=/ContentManagement /ContentDisplay.cfm&ContentID=12740.

9. For Cardinal Rugambwa, see Frieder Ludwig, *Church and State in Tanzania* (Leiden, Netherlands: Brill, 1999); John L. Allen, "Global South Will Shape the Future Catholic Church," *NCR*, October 7, 2005.

10. Edward Stourton, *Absolute Truth* (London: Penguin, 1999), 66, for the election of Pope John Paul II; John L. Allen, *The Rise of Benedict XVI* (New York: Doubleday, 2005).

11. For the movement FutureChurch, see http://www.futurechurch.org/.

12. Allen, "Global South Will Shape the Future Catholic Church." Allen, *The Future Church*.

13. Ann M. Simmons, "A Potentially Historic Choice," *LAT*, March 17, 2001; Francis Cardinal Arinze, with Gerard O'Connell, *God's Invisible Hand* (San Francisco: Ignatius Press, 2006).

14. *Dominus Jesus*, online at http://www.vatican.va/roman_curia/congregations/ cfaith/documents/rc_con_cfaith_doc_20000806_dominus-iesus_en.html.

15. David Chung, *Syncretism* (Albany, N.Y.: SUNY Press, 2001).

16. Philip Jenkins, *The New Faces of Christianity* (New York: Oxford University Press, 2006).

17. Lynn Thomas, *Politics of the Womb* (Berkeley: University of California Press, 2003); Lara M. Knudsen, *Reproductive Rights in a Global Context* (Nashville, Tenn.: Vanderbilt University Press, 2006).

18. Stephen O. Murray and Will Roscoe, eds., *Boy-Wives and Female-Husbands* (New York: St. Martin's Press, 1998); Marc Epprecht, *Hungochani* (Montreal: McGill-Queen's University Press, 2004); Neville Hoad, *African Intimacies* (Minneapolis: University of Minnesota Press, 2007).

19. Chris McGreal, "Debt? War? Gays Are the Real Evil, Say African Leaders," *Guardian*, October 2, 1999. The Obasanjo quote is from http://www.christianitytoday.com/ct/2004/143/32.0.html. For Ndungane, see Jason Kane, "Archbishop Challenges the Church," *WP*, May 13, 2006.

20. The Ugandan affair was widely covered in U.S. media. See for instance, Sarah Pulliam Bailey, "Anti-Homosexuality Bill Divides Ugandan and American Christians," *Christianity Today*, December 17, 2009, at http://www.christianityto-day.com/ct/2009/decemberweb-only/151–41.0.html.

21. "Just as the United States" is from the introduction to Kapya Kaoma, *Globalizing the Culture Wars* (Somerville, Mass.: Political Research Associates, 2009), iv; Miranda K. Hassett, *Anglican Communion in Crisis* (Princeton, N.J.: Princeton University Press, 2007).

22. Stephen Bates, *A Church at War* (New York: I. B. Tauris, 2004); William L. Sachs, *Homosexuality and the Crisis of Anglicanism* (Cambridge: Cambridge University Press 2009).

23. Ferdy Baglo, "Canadian Bishop Blocks Asian Church Leader from Visiting His Diocese," *CT*, November 29, 1999.

24. Philip Jenkins, "Defender of the Faith," *Atlantic Monthly*, November 2003: 46–49; "If England adopts a new faith" is quoted in Pat Ashworth, "Global South Won't Split Communion, Says Venables," *Church Times* (UK), September 16, 2005.

25. Orombi is quoted by Larry B. Stammer, "A Prelate of Evangelical Intensity," *LAT*, September 5, 2004.

26. *The Lambeth Commission on Communion: The Windsor Report* 2004 (London: Anglican Communion Office, 2004), at http://www.anglicancommunion.org/windsor2004/downloads/index.cfm; Ian Douglas and Paul Zahl, *Understanding the Windsor Report* (New York: Church, 2005); Andrew Linzey and Richard Kirker, eds., *Gays and the Future of Anglicanism* (Winchester, UK: O Books, 2005); Ephraim Radner and Philip Turner, *The Fate of Communion* (Grand Rapids, Mich.: Eerdmans, 2006); Hassett, *Anglican Communion in Crisis*; Frank G. Kirkpatrick, *The Episcopal Church in Crisis* (Westport, Conn.: Praeger, 2008).

27. "We reject the expectation" is from *A Third Trumpet from the South*, at http://www.globalsouthanglican.org/index.php/blog/comments/third_trumpet_communique_from_3rd_south_to_south_encounter. Akinola is quoted from Ashworth, "Global South Won't Split Communion, Says Venables."

28. Ruth Gledhill, "Dr. Rowan Williams Criticises Election of Lesbian Bishop," *Times*, March 19, 2010; Hassett, *Anglican Communion in Crisis*.

29. The Nigerian response is from http://www.anglican-nig.org/response_abc_june06.htm.

30. Daniel Burke, "Episcopal Head Lashes Out at Anglican 'Colonial' Uniformity," Religion News Service, June 7, 2010.

31. Bates, *A Church at War*.

32. Websites of some of the main organizations involved can be found at http://www.americananglican.org/ and http://www.theamia.org/.

33. Gustav Niebuhr, "Episcopal Dissidents Find African Inspiration," *NYT*, March 6, 2001.

34. Although it is a strongly partisan source, the Institute on Religion and Democracy provides detailed coverage of divisions within the Methodist church and other mainline denominations: http://www.theird.org/.

35. http://www.lutheranworld.org/News/LWI/EN/1404.EN.html; http://www.elca.org/country ackets/ethiopia/church.html. For the EECMY church, see Oeyvind Eide, *Revolution and Religion in Ethiopia* 2nd edition (Oxford, UK: James Currey, 2000).

36. "African, European Lutherans Go on Distance," at http://www.afrol.com/articles/15708.

37. "ELCT Takes A Bold Stand on Sexuality Issue," at http://www.africa-lutheran.org/index.php?option=com_content&view=article&id=323%3Aelct-takes-a-bold-stand-on-sexuality-issue&catid=1&lang=en&showall=1.

38. Liutprand of Cremona, "Report of His Mission to Constantinople," at http://medieval.ucdavis.edu/20A/Luitprand.html.

39. Henry Chadwick, *East and West* (Oxford: Oxford University Press, 2003); and Henry Chadwick, *The Early Church* (London: Penguin, 2005).

40. The Vietnamese priest is quoted in Neela Banerjee, "Clergy's Call Still Strong for Young Vietnamese," *NYT*, December 9, 2005. Peter C. Phan, *Vietnamese-American Catholics* (New York: Paulist Press, 2005).

41. Akinola is quoted from Jenkins, "Defender of the Faith"; Victoria Combe, "Missionaries Flock to Britain to Revive Passion for Church," *Daily Telegraph*, January 18, 2001. For the Anglican primate of Brazil, Glauco Soares de Lima, see "Green and Pagan Land," *Economist*, June 21, 2001; "Missionaries to Spread Word in 'Heathen' Britain," *Sunday Times* (London), July 1, 2001; Mechteld Jansen and Hijme Stoffels, eds., *A Moving God* (Berlin: Lit Verlag, 2008).

42. http://www.rccg.org/Church_Ministry/Mission_Statement/mission_statement.htm. The quote about biblical inerrancy is from Ayuk A. Ayuk, "Portrait of a Nigerian Pentecostal Missionary," *Asian Journal of Pentecostal Studies* 8:1 (2005): 117–41. Asonzeh Ukah, *A New Paradigm of Pentecostal Power* (Trenton, N.J.: Africa World Press, 2008).

43. "An open explosion" is from http://www.facebook.com/rccg.org. The second quote ("obviously in fulfillment") is from http://www.rccgschiedam.org/

ministers.htm. For the church's presence in Muslim Africa, see http://mission.rccg. org/rccg_missions_policy.htm.

44. The note about the Kimbanguist international presence is taken from the church's website at http://www.kimbanguisme.com/e-option2.htm. The RCCG has a website at http://www.rccg.org/. For the IURD, see http://www.igrejauniversal.org.br/; Paul Freston, "The Universal Church of the Kingdom of God—A Brazilian Church Finds Success in Southern Africa," *Journal of Religion in Africa* 35, no. 1 (2005): 33–65. The Church of the Lord (Aladura) can be found at http://www.aladura.de/. The Nigerian-founded Celestial Church of Christ is at http://www.celestialchurch.com/.

45. Andrew Wingate, Kevin Ward, Carrie Pemberton, and Wilson Sitshebo, eds., *Anglicanism* (New York: Church, 1998), 13.

46. http://www.it-is-easy.org/contact/friends/sunday.php; Dawn Herzog Jewell, "From Africa to Ukraine," (2005), at http://www.christianitytoday.com/tc/2005/006/4. 42.html. Catherine Wanner, *Communities of the Converted* (Ithaca, N.Y.: Cornell University Press, 2007); Afe Adogame and James V. Spickard, eds., *Religion Crossing Boundaries* (Boston, Mass.: Brill, 2010).

47. Victoria Combe, "Black Church in Crusade to Woo Whites," *Electronic Telegraph*, February 16, 2001. Refugee communities are also significant; see for example, Kevin Ward, "Ugandan Christian Communities in Britain," *IRM* 89 (2000): 320–28.

48. Soong-Chan Rah, *The Next Evangelicalism* (Downers Grove, Ill.: InterVarsity Press, 2009).

49. R. Andrew Chesnut, *Born Again in Brazil* (New Brunswick, N.J.: Rutgers University Press, 1997), 7; Marc Schogol, "Argentinians Pray for a Phila. Revival," *Philadelphia Inquirer*, February 11, 2001; Daniel Míguez, *To Help You Find God* (Amsterdam, Netherlands: Free University of Amsterdam, 1997); idem, *Spiritual Bonfire in Argentina* (Amsterdam, Netherlands: Center for Latin American Studies, 1998); Carlos Annacondia, *Listen to Me, Satan!* (Lake Mary, Fla.: Creation House, 1998).

50. "Francophone Africans" is from Daniel J. Wakin, "Missionaries Reverse a Path Taken for Generations," *NYT*, July 11, 2004. Afe Adogame and Cordula Weisskoeppel, eds., *Religion in the Context of African Migration* (Bayreuth, Germany: Bayreuth African Studies Series, 2005); Jacob Olupona and Regina Gemignani, eds, *African Immigrant Religions in America* (New York: New York University Press, 2007); Jehu Hanciles, *Beyond Christendom* (Maryknoll, N.Y.: Orbis Books, 2008); Afe Adogame, Roswith Gerloff, and Klaus Hock, eds., *Christianity in Africa and the African Diaspora* (New York: Continuum, 2009); Ira Berlin, *The Making of African America* (New York: Viking, 2010); Moses Biney, *From Africa to America* (New York: New York University Press, 2011).

51. The list of RCCG congregations is from http://www.rccg.org/Church_ Ministry/Trustees/history.htm and http://www.rccgna.org/. Andrew Rice, "Mission

From Africa," *New York Times Magazine*, April 12, 2009. For Bowie, see http://rccgvictorytemple.org/.

52. For the development of the Christ Apostolic Church in North America, see the group's websites at http://www.christapostolicchurch.org/; and http://www.firstcac.org/bio.html. The list of CAC churches is from http://www.christapostolicchurch.org/national.html. Compare Maura Kelly, "Praising Lord in So Many Ways," *Chicago Tribune*, March 10, 2000.

CHAPTER 10

1. David Martin, *Tongues of Fire* (Oxford: Blackwell, 1990); Edward Cleary, *How Latin America Saved the Soul of the Catholic Church* (Mahwah, N.J.: Paulist Press, 2009); Ruth J. Chojnacki, *Indigenous Apostles* (New York: Rodopi, 2010).

2. Marcus J. Borg, *Meeting Jesus Again for the First Time* (San Francisco: Harper San Francisco, 1995); idem, *Reading the Bible Again for the First Time* (San Francisco: Harper San Francisco, 2001). For an anthropological attempt to treat Christianity as seriously or sympathetically as other global religions, see Fenella Cannell, ed., *The Anthropology of Christianity* (Durham, N.C.: Duke University Press, 2006).

3. The quote about the "*n*th World" is from Paul Gifford, *African Christianity* (Bloomington: Indiana University Press, 1998), 15; "In Sub-Saharan Africa," is from "Global Trends 2015," online at http://www.dni.gov/nic/NIC_globaltrend2015.html; Ogbu Kalu, *Power, Poverty and Prayer* (New York: Peter Lang, 2000).

4. Ronald J. Sider, *Rich Christians in an Age of Hunger* (Downers Grove, Ill.: InterVarsity Press, 1977).

5. I discuss these issues at length in Philip Jenkins, *The New Faces of Christianity* (New York: Oxford University Press, 2006). From a large recent literature on different ways of Bible reading, see for example, Gerald O. West, ed., *Reading Other-Wise* (Atlanta: Society of Biblical Literature, 2007); Hans de Wit and Gerald O. West, eds., *African and European Readers of the Bible in Dialogue* (Leiden, Netherlands: Brill, 2008).

6. Teresa Okure, Jon Sobrino, and Felix Wilfred, eds., "Rethinking Martyrdom" in *Concilium* 1(2003) (London: SCM, 2003).

7. The Maluku Christian is quoted from Doug Bandow, "Letter from Indonesia," *Chronicles*, March 2001, 41. Marc Nikkel, "Death Has Come to Reveal the Faith," in Andrew Wingate, Kevin Ward, Carrie Pemberton, and Wilson Sitshebo, eds., *Anglicanism* (New York: Church, 1998), 73–78.

8. Mark Fritz, *Lost on Earth* (New York: Routledge, 2000); Jean-Pierre Ruiz, "Biblical Interpretation," in Peter Casarella and Raul Gomez, eds., *El Cuerpo de Cristo* (New York: Crossroad, 1998), 84. Daniel Patte, J. Severino Croatto, Nicole Wilkinson Duran, Teresa Okure, and Archie Chi Chung Lee, eds., *Global Bible Commentary* (Nashville, Tenn.: Abingdon Press, 2004); Tokunboh Adeyemo, ed., *Africa Bible Commentary* (Grand Rapids, Mich.: Zondervan, 2006).

9. Quoted in Ruiz, "Biblical Interpretation," 89–90.

10. Quoted in ibid., 86–87.

11. See for example, Tony Carnes, "The Silicon Valley Saints," *CT*, August 6, 2001. R. S. Sugirtharajah, *Postcolonial Criticism and Bible Interpretation* (New York: Oxford University Press, 2002); R. S. Sugirtharajah, *The Bible and Empire* (New York: Cambridge University Press, 2005).

12. I have usually seen this phrase attributed to Bismarck, but it has been credited to both Metternich and Winston Churchill.

INDEX

Weber, Max, 168
Westermann, Diedrich, 151
White Fathers, 46, 166
Why Christianity Must Change or Die
(Spong), 11
Williams, Charles, 238
Williams, Rowan, 253
Windsor Report, 252–53
Winners' Chapel, 86
witchcraft, xii–xiii, 64, 67, 82,
123–24, 152–55, 157, 170, 194
women
abortion, 180, 184, 247
Christianity and, xiii
fertility rates, 103–4, 106, 114,
120, 206
as missionaries, 54, 56–57
ordination of, 243, 265
Pentecostalism, 96–97
subjugation of, xiii
Woodward, Kenneth, 71, 74, 150
World Christian Database, 88
World Christian Encyclopedia, 31,
132, 209, 266

World Council of Churches, 10, 15,
170, 173, 232, 239
World Factbook (Central Intelligence
Agency), 88
World Missionary Conference, 49–50,
55, 148
World Parliament of Religions, 46–47
World War I, 32, 64
World War II, 69

Xi Liaochi, 158

Yancey, Philip, 1
Yemen, 215
Yoido Full Gospel Church, 90, 159
Yugoslavia, 223

Zambia, 65–66, 156, 181, 187–88,
261
ZCC. *See* Zion Christian Church
Zimbabwe, 56, 69, 86–87, 105, 182,
189, 234, 248, 261
Zion Christian Church (ZCC), 67–68,
86, 153, 163